WORKING-CLASS UTOPIAS

WORKING-CLASS UTOPIAS

A HISTORY OF COOPERATIVE HOUSING IN NEW YORK CITY

ROBERT M. FOGELSON

Princeton University Press

Princeton and Oxford

Princeton University Press is committed to the protection of copyright and the intellectual property our authors entrust to us. Copyright promotes the progress and integrity of knowledge. Thank you for supporting free speech and the global exchange of ideas by purchasing an authorized edition of this book. If you wish to reproduce or distribute any part of it in any form, please obtain permission.

Requests for permission to reproduce material from this work should be sent to permissions@press.princeton.edu
Published by Princeton University Press, 41 William Street, Princeton, New Jersey 08540
In the United Kingdom: Princeton University Press, 99 Banbury Road, Oxford OX2 6JX

press.princeton.edu

Front cover: Groundbreaking ceremony at Co-op City, 1966. Kheel Center for Labor-Management Documentation & Archives, Cornell University Library.

Library of Congress Cataloging-in-Publication Data

Names: Fogelson, Robert M., author.
Title: Working-class utopias : a history of cooperative housing in New York City / Robert M. Fogelson.
Description: Princeton : Princeton University Press, [2022] | Includes bibliographical references and index.
Identifiers: LCCN 2022006725 (print) | LCCN 2022006726 (ebook) | ISBN 9780691234748 (hardback ; alk. paper) | ISBN 9780691237954 (ebook)
Subjects: LCSH: Co-op City (New York, N.Y.)—History—20th century. | Housing, Cooperative—New York (State)—New York—History—20th century. | Housing policy—New York (State)—New York—History—20th century. | BISAC: ARCHITECTURE / Urban & Land Use Planning | HISTORY / United States / 20th Century
Classification: LCC HD7287.72.U62 N536 2022 (print) | LCC HD7287.72.U62 (ebook) | DDC 334/.109747275—dc23/eng/20211110
LC record available at https://lccn.loc.gov/2022006725
LC ebook record available at https://lccn.loc.gov/2022006726

British Library Cataloging-in-Publication Data is available

Design and composition by Julie Allred, BW&A Books
This book has been composed in Macklin
Printed on acid-free paper. ∞
Printed in the United States of America
10 9 8 7 6 5 4 3 2 1

To Aurora Sosa Alvarez and Miguel Sosa Alvarez
and
the memory of Fannie Fogelson and Bessie Richman

CONTENTS

PROLOGUE

On November 24, 1968, several thousand New Yorkers assembled in a remote section of the northeast Bronx known as Baychester to celebrate the dedication of the world's largest housing cooperative. A joint effort of organized labor, New York State, and New York City, it was called Co-op City. And it was being built on 300 acres near the intersection of the Hutchinson River Parkway and the New England Thruway. A huge green-and-white-striped tent—"as big," wrote one observer, "as a football field"—was rented to accommodate the crowd, many of whose members had already bought apartments in what Governor Nelson A. Rockefeller described as "a whole new city within a City." After they filed in, Monsignor Joseph T. V. Snee, administrator of the Catholic Center of Co-op City, gave the invocation. The governor and a handful of other dignitaries made speeches. The Cardinal Spellman High School Band played the national anthem (and other familiar pieces). Six families were presented with symbolic keys to the community. And Rabbi Solomon I. Berl, spiritual leader of Young Israel of Co-op City, offered the benediction. As everyone who attended the festivities knew, Co-op City was far from finished. Only one of the high-rise apartment houses was ready for occupancy. And the first eighteen families would not move in for another two weeks. Indeed, it would be more than three years before its 35 towers, ranging from 24 to 33 stories, and 236 three-story townhouses were fully occupied. But there was still much to celebrate, not the least of which was how much progress had been made in the three years and nine months since Rockefeller unveiled the plans for Co-op City.[1]

Presiding over the dedication of Co-op City was Jacob S. Potofsky. A towering figure in the labor movement, Potofsky was president of the Amalgamated Clothing Workers of America, a post he had held since 1946, when he

succeeded Sidney Hillman, who had formed the union in 1914. He took great
pride in the Amalgamated's construction of one of the oldest (and most successful) housing cooperatives in New York City in the late 1920s. Located in
the Bronx, not far from Van Cortlandt Park, and known as the Amalgamated
Houses, it consisted of six apartment buildings that cost over $1.8 million
and provided housing for about 300 working-class families. Also representing organized labor was Thomas Van Arsdale, who sent greetings from his father, Harry Van Arsdale Jr., who was unable to attend. The older Van Arsdale
was the head of Local 3 of the International Brotherhood of Electrical Workers as well as president of the New York City Central Labor Council, a federation of about 500 trade unions affiliated with the AFL-CIO. It was under
Van Arsdale's stewardship that the IBEW built a huge housing cooperative
known as Electchester a few years after World War II. Located in Queens on
a 60-acre site that formerly housed the Pomonok Country Club, it contained
38 apartment buildings that cost $20 million and provided housing for more
than 2,100 working-class families. Also on hand at the festivities was Peter
J. Brennan, president of the Building and Construction Trades Council of
Greater New York, a federation of trade unions, many of whose members saw
Co-op City as a godsend, a source of much-needed jobs now that there was no
more work to be done at the New York City World's Fair of 1964.[2]

As well as head of the Amalgamated Clothing Workers, Potofsky was
president of the United Housing Foundation, which was the developer (or, as
it was referred to at the time, the sponsor) of Co-op City. A nonprofit federation of sixty-two trade unions, civic groups, and housing cooperatives, the
UHF had been formed in 1951 to promote cooperative housing in New York
and other cities. It was run by Abraham E. Kazan, the driving force behind
the Amalgamated Houses and widely regarded as the father of cooperative
housing in the United States. By the mid-1960s, however, Kazan was well
into his seventies and in poor health. Although he was well enough to attend
the groundbreaking ceremonies at Co-op City, which were held on May 14,
1966, he had taken a leave of absence from the UHF in January 1966 (and
would retire a year later). To replace him as president, the board, most of
whose members were well-known New York labor leaders, selected Potofsky, who was also in his seventies. And to run the foundation it picked Harold Ostroff, who was appointed executive vice president. Ostroff, who had
grown up in the Amalgamated Houses, went to work for the UHF in his late
twenties and in time became Kazan's right-hand man. Speaking on behalf
of the UHF, he told the crowd, "We take great satisfaction in providing the

people, who have become partners in this enterprise by investing their hard earned savings in Co-op City, with the best possible housing at the best possible price." He also stressed the foundation's debt to Kazan, whose "vision and practical realism and leadership" had paved the way for Co-op City and many of New York's other housing cooperatives.[3]

Representing New York State was Governor Rockefeller. The second son of John D. Rockefeller Jr. and heir to one of the world's largest fortunes, the young Rockefeller had worked in the family business before going into politics in his late forties. He was elected governor in 1958, defeating the Democratic incumbent, W. Averell Harriman, in a stunning upset. He was re-elected in 1962, 1966, and 1970 (and served until late 1973, when he resigned to become vice president in the Ford administration). Although a Republican, Rockefeller was a strong supporter of the state's Limited-Profit Housing Companies Law, also known as the Mitchell-Lama act, after its sponsors, Senator MacNeil Mitchell and Assemblyman Alfred A. Lama. Enacted in 1955, it was designed to spur the construction of middle-income housing in New York and other cities. To implement the law, Rockefeller prevailed on the legislature in 1960 to create a public authority known as the New York State Housing Finance Agency and empowered it to grant long-term, low-interest mortgages to middle-income housing projects, both rental and cooperative. It was the SHFA—whose executive director, Paul Belica, attended the dedication, presumably standing in for his boss, James W. Gaynor, chairman of the SHFA—that loaned the UHF $261 million to build Co-op City, enough, it was believed, to cover 90 percent of the cost of construction. Speaking on behalf of the state, Rockefeller told the crowd that this loan "is the finest investment we've ever made." Calling Co-op City "a noble monument to the social conscience of the labor movement," he praised Kazan and the other leaders of the UHF and, with a nod to Potofsky, declared, "We're ready to bank them again."[4]

New York City was also represented at the festivities, though not by anyone of (or even close to) the stature of Rockefeller. Among the most eminent of the New Yorkers who did not attend was Robert F. Wagner Jr., the son of the former US senator of the same name, Wagner had served as mayor of New York from 1954 through 1965 and, after leaving office, was named US ambassador to Spain. It was during Wagner's third term that the city approved the UHF's plans for Co-op City, began work on its streets and sewers, and granted the development a partial abatement on its property taxes, a measure that was designed to keep the monthly carrying charges within the reach of middle-income families. Also absent was Wagner's successor, John V. Lindsay, a former congressman from Manhattan's Upper East Side who had run for mayor with the support of the Republican and Liberal parties but did not take office until after the UHF started clearing the site. Among the few high-ranking city officials on hand was Herman Badillo, a leader of New York's large and rapidly growing Puerto Rican community who had been elected borough president of the Bronx in 1965. Addressing the crowd, Badillo stressed his strong support for Co-op City, but criticized the city government for failing to provide the services and facilities that would be needed by its tens of thousands of residents. Saying that he had already helped smooth the way for the construction of Co-op City, he pledged to do his utmost to get additional personnel and equipment for the nearby Forty-Seventh Police Precinct and to push for a subway linking Co-op City with the Bronx and Manhattan.[5]

Also on hand at the dedication of Co-op City was Robert Moses, who had almost single-handedly transformed greater New York in the mid-twentieth century. In recent years he had stepped down (or been forced out) as City Construction Coordinator, a member of the City Planning Commission, chairman of the Slum Clearance Committee, and, what was by far the most powerful of his many posts, chairman of the Triborough Bridge and Tunnel Authority. Now eighty years old, he was no longer a force to be reckoned with. But Moses had long admired Kazan—who had defended Moses against his critics on more than one occasion. Moses had also supported the UHF in most of its efforts to build housing cooperatives in Manhattan and the outer boroughs. Indeed, Harold Ostroff told the crowd, it was Moses who had set in motion the events that led to the development of Co-op City. In May 1964, he pointed out, Moses had informed the UHF that William Zeckendorf, New York's most flamboyant real estate developer, was eager to sell a large site in the Bronx—half of which had been leased to a now-defunct amusement park known as Freedomland—that was suitable for a large-scale housing project. And it was on this site that the UHF was building Co-op City. Addressing the audience, Moses praised the foundation's leaders, "who wrought this miracle when others [meaning planners, academics, and naysayers in general] chattered piously about salvation" and built nothing. If the UHF and other like-minded organizations would build housing cooperatives like Co-op City for the residents of Bedford-Stuyvesant and New York's other run-down neighborhoods, Moses went on, it would not be long before there were no slums left in the city.[6]

A good many housing cooperatives had been built for working-class families in New York before Co-op City. Among the first were twenty-five small apartment houses that were erected in Sunset Park, Brooklyn, in the late 1910s and early 1920s by a group of Finnish-Americans who had migrated to the United States in the late nineteenth century. A handful of labor unions and Jewish mutual aid organizations soon followed the lead of the Finnish Home Building Association—but in the Bronx, not Brooklyn. As well as the Amalgamated Houses, they built the Shalom Aleichem Houses, a socialist co-op; the Farband Houses, a Zionist co-op; and a group of houses known simply as "the Coops," many of whose residents worked in the garment industry and leaned toward the Communist Party. The cooperative housing movement came to a standstill during the Great Depression. But spurred by organized labor, it picked up after World War II. In the forefront was the IBEW; the Amalgamated Clothing Workers, which built Hillman Houses on the Lower East Side in the late 1940s; Local 6 of the International Typographical Union, which erected the Big Six Towers in Queens a decade later; and, among others, the Amalgamated Meat Cutters and Butcher Workmen of North America, which constructed Concourse Village over the New York Central's rail yards in the Bronx in the early 1960s. Most of these unions were also affiliated with the UHF, which sponsored several housing cooperatives of its own in the 1950s and 1960s, the largest of which was Rochdale Village. Built on 120 acres in Queens, the former site of the Jamaica Racetrack, it cost more than $95 million, housed 5,860 families, and was finished a year before ground was broken for Co-op City.[7]

But New York's other housing cooperatives were dwarfed by Co-op City, which was enormous—or, in the words of the *Cooperator*, a UHF publication, "colossal." When finished, it would provide apartments for 15,372 families, nearly three times as many as Rochdale Village, more than five times as many as Penn South—which was sponsored by the UHF, underwritten by the International Ladies' Garment Workers' Union (ILGWU), and built in Manhattan, a few blocks north of the Garment District, in the late 1950s and early 1960s— and almost as many as all the other UHF housing cooperatives combined. As well as the world's largest housing cooperative, Co-op City was the country's largest apartment house complex. It had nearly 3,000 more apartments than Parkchester, which the Metropolitan Life Insurance Company had built in the Bronx in the early 1940s, and almost 7,000 more than Stuyvesant Town, which the giant insurance company had erected in Manhattan a few years later. What with 35 residential towers and 236 townhouses, six public schools, which would have space for 10,000 students, three shopping centers, eight garages, which would provide parking for nearly 11,000 autos, a few houses of worship, and a community center, fire station, post office, and public library, Co-op City would indeed be a city within a city. And it would be a good-sized city too. When fully occupied, it would be home to between 55,000 and 60,000 people. If Co-op City were not part of New York City, wrote the *Washington Post* in 1971, it would be the thirteenth-largest city in New York State. It would have more residents than White Plains, almost as many as Binghamton, and about half as many as Albany.[8]

By virtue of its size, Co-op City was, in the words of Governor Rockefeller, "the crowning achievement thus far of the cooperative housing movement." It was also, said Harold Ostroff, a "lasting symbol" of the "monumental work" of Abraham Kazan. Recognizing that Co-op City was probably Kazan's swan song, the UHF held a luncheon in his honor following the groundbreaking ceremonies in May 1966. After a round of speeches, Robert Szold, a former president of the UHF, presented him with an engraved shovel. But as far as Ostroff and his colleagues were concerned, the UHF was just getting started. "As spectacular as Co-op City is," he said at its dedication, he was hopeful that similar developments would one day be "rather commonplace." If possible, the UHF would like "to build 40 [housing cooperatives like Co-op City]." Indeed, he went on, "we are anxious to rebuild Harlem, the South Bronx, Bedford-Stuyvesant, and Jamaica." Like Kazan—who conceded that even though several housing cooperatives had been built on the Lower East Side, many New Yorkers still lived in buildings that were "not fit to live in"—Ostroff was not satisfied with the cooperative housing movement's progress. But he was confident that housing cooperatives like Co-op City "would go a long way towards rehousing the two million New Yorkers now living in sub-standard slums." Not only should more Co-op cities be built, said Robert Moses, but they could be built. "All that is needed is to induce men like Jacob Potofsky, David Dubinsky [president of the ILGWU], and Harry Van Arsdale to lead and Abraham Kazan to be their executive." What they had done in New York others could do in cities all over the country, Ostroff pointed out.[9]

After the dedication of Co-op City was over, many of the prospective residents—or, as Ostroff preferred to call them, the "cooperators"—took advantage of the opportunity to inspect the sample apartments on the fifteenth floor of the one building that was just about finished, a 24-story structure with 410 units. Although, wrote the *New York Times*, its lobby was still "littered with ganglia of wires and cables and its concrete floors [were] still bare"—and although Co-op City was still a construction site, full of debris, dust, and partially completed structures—the visitors were favorably impressed. The apartments, which ranged from three and a half to six and a half rooms, were spacious, at least by New York standards. They had hardwood floors, an eat-in kitchen, ample closet space, and central air-conditioning, a great amenity at a time when most middle- and even upper-middle-class families in New York did not even have room air conditioners. The apartments were sun drenched and well ventilated too. Many had sweeping views of the Hutchinson River and Midtown Manhattan, and some of the larger ones had balconies. The apartments were also relatively inexpensive. They cost $450 a room, a onetime payment that was returned when the owner sold his shares in the cooperative. And the carrying charges, which were supposed to cover Co-op City's fixed costs and operating expenses, came to $25 per room per month, utilities included. Little wonder, Ostroff said at the dedication, that 10,000 New Yorkers had already applied for an apartment at Co-op City. And, added George Schechter, vice president of the UHF, more than 6,000 had already selected their apartment and paid for it.[10]

For Ostroff and his colleagues, the flood of applications was extremely gratifying. It revealed that many New Yorkers—among them Joseph A. Gosik, a forty-six-year-old police officer (with a wife and three children) who was the 10,000th applicant—were not put off by Co-op City's critics, who took strong exception to the remoteness of the site, the sterility of the plan, and the banality of the architecture. None of the critics had ever built housing, let alone housing with central air-conditioning, for $25 a room, Ostroff pointed out. Indeed, New York's private developers were hard pressed to construct rental housing for less than $45 a room. The flood of applications also indicated that many New Yorkers were aware, in Ostroff's words, that "the size, type and amenities of our apartments stand well ahead of much of the housing built in the country today." Moreover, he wrote a few months later, Co-op City would not cost the taxpayers anything. Even with the partial abatement, it would soon generate $7 million a year in property taxes, more than fifteen times as much as the prior owner had been paying. By providing more than 15,300 spacious and sanitary apartments and by increasing the supply of cooperative housing by 55 percent, Co-op City would go a long way toward alleviating New York's chronic housing shortage, which, said Rockefeller at the groundbreaking ceremony, was especially acute for low- and middle-income families. "There are plenty of $100-a-room apartments in New York City," he pointed out, "but few indeed that provide good living under $25 a room." Co-op City, he stressed, was a "heartening sign that the massive job for rebuilding the cities of America can be done," especially if organized labor and state and local authorities worked together.[11]

Besides giving tens of thousands of New Yorkers a chance to own their own homes, Ostroff said, Co-op City would also give them the option of staying in the city and thereby help stem "white flight." The exodus of middle-class whites from the cities to the suburbs, wrote two journalists, "had begun after World War II and threatened the viability of central cities all over the country." At the dedication of Seward Park, which had been built by the UHF on the Lower East Side in the late 1950s, Moses went so far as to say that cooperative housing would even encourage some New Yorkers who had moved to the suburbs to return to the city. Like Ostroff, Moses stressed that by providing apartments for the residents of Bedford-Stuyvesant and other run-down neighborhoods, housing cooperatives like Co-op City would also help get rid of New York's slums. "The breeding places of disorder, crime, violence, and desperation," the slums, said Moses, were a "malignancy that will yield only to uncompromising surgery." They must be demolished, he said in a speech at Rochdale Village, until "not a vestige of them [is] left to remind us of their infamy."[12] For Potofsky and the other elder statesmen of the labor movement, Co-op City also confirmed what Kazan had been saying for decades. The solution to the housing problem—a problem that had plagued New York and other cities for a century—was not tenement-house reform. Nor was it model tenements or public housing. Rather it was cooperative housing. Spacious and sanitary apartments could be built for working-class families, but only by adhering to the principle of self-help that had been adopted first at the Amalgamated Houses and later at Co-op City and the UHF's other housing projects.

CHAPTER 1

THE ORIGINS OF COOPERATIVE HOUSING

Toward the end of his career, Abraham E. Kazan received many honors besides the engraved shovel that former UHF president Robert Szold handed him at Co-op City's groundbreaking. A few years earlier Mayor Robert F. Wagner Jr. presented him with a certificate of appreciation for the "pioneering efforts" that "have given thousands of families homes to enjoy and places of human dignity in our city." In May 1964 the Citizens Housing and Planning Council gave him its Annual Public Service Award. And in October 1965 Kazan was honored at a huge block party on the Lower East Side. It was followed by a dinner at the Cooperative Auditorium on Grand Street at which he was praised by Governor Nelson A. Rockefeller, Senator Jacob K. Javits, and Robert Moses, who said that Kazan had contributed more to New York "than all the thousands of noisy reformers and pundits together." The Amalgamated Dwellings and three other Lower East Side housing cooperatives that made up what was commonly referred to as Cooperative Village used the occasion to announce the establishment of a scholarship in his name for Cooper Union students who were studying the architecture of low-income housing. And three years later the New York City Council renamed the part of Columbia Street that ran through Cooperative Village from Grand to Delancey Abraham E. Kazan Street. Following his death in December 1971, nearly a thousand New Yorkers gathered at the Cooperative Auditorium to pay tribute, in Rockefeller's words, to "a child of the Lower East Side," "a quiet man" who "believed in *doing*—more than talking," a man who became the "father of Cooperative Housing in the United States" and a "dreamer of a world without slums." A decade and a half later Kazan was one of the first sixteen New Yorkers to be inducted into a hall of fame that was sponsored by the Real Estate Board to honor the men who had built the city.[1]

Born in 1889, Kazan spent his childhood not, as Rockefeller said, on the Lower East Side, but on a large estate about thirty miles from Kiev, Russia. Owned by a retired Russian general, the estate was managed by Kazan's father, a Russian Jew. Kazan finished the equivalent of two years of high school in a nearby town. But realizing that a quota system that limited the number of Jewish students prevented him from continuing his studies in Russia, he decided to migrate to the United States. His older brother, who was afraid that he was about to be drafted into the Russian army, joined him. Leaving Russia in 1904, they traveled together as far as Rotterdam. While his brother went to Philadelphia, Kazan sailed to New York. For a year he lived with relatives on the Lower East Side and worked in the garment industry. But when his father, whose position on the estate became untenable after the general died, decided to move the rest of the family to the United States, he and his brother joined them on a Jewish agricultural settlement in Carmel, New Jersey, one of almost a hundred such settlements formed in the United States in the late nineteenth and early twentieth centuries. It was in Carmel that Kazan learned English and acquired a rudimentary knowledge of socialism. And it was there that he developed a deep-seated sympathy for working people and labor unions, a sympathy that was reflected in his decision to join a rally that was led by an ILGWU organizer against a Philadelphia garment manufacturer who was trying to break a strike by subcontracting work to a Carmel factory owner. Kazan was arrested and charged with inciting a riot. But after a three-day trial, he was acquitted, perhaps, he later recalled, because a few members of the glass workers union were on the jury.[2]

At loose ends in Carmel—and at odds with his father, who was worried that his son might be deported if he continued to support the ILGWU local—Kazan, then about nineteen, decided that it was time to return to New York City. Moving back in with his relatives on the Lower East Side, he worked for a year in a factory as a timekeeper and bookkeeper. He also joined Local 35 of the ILGWU. Through the contacts he had made in Carmel, he then got a job as an errand boy at ILGWU headquarters. He worked for the ILGWU for nine years and, by dint of hard work and great ability, ended up as secretary (or head) of Local 35. Kazan also took classes at night and for a while attended Brooklyn Polytechnic Institute. In the meantime he fell under the influence of a Scot named Tom Bell, whom he met at a private library in

Yorkville, a working-class neighborhood on Manhattan's Upper East Side. "An anarchist with a literary bent," writes historian Peter Eisenstadt, Bell persuaded Kazan that in order to improve their lot America's workingmen should not replace capitalism with socialism, which would still leave the managerial class in charge of the means of production, but rather should set up their own businesses and manage them themselves. As Kazan later wrote, cooperative enterprises of all kinds could be established, ranging from groceries, bakeries, florists, drugstores, and barber shops to factories, hospitals, hotels, movie theaters, and insurance companies. Once told by Governor Rockefeller that with his know-how he could have gone into business and "made a fortune"—which, coming from a Rockefeller, was high praise indeed—Kazan replied that he had never been interested in making a fortune, "only in building the cooperative commonwealth."[3]

At Bell's suggestion, Kazan joined the Cooperative League of the USA, a fledgling organization whose fifteen or twenty members met at a settlement house on the Lower East Side to spread the principles of self-help and mutual aid to the working class. The group also opened a hat store on Delancey Street and a restaurant on Second Avenue—which was known, says Eisenstadt, for "good talk and poor food"—but neither lasted very long. Kazan had more success after the outbreak of World War I. With New York (and other cities) facing a severe shortage of sugar, shopkeepers were not only raising prices but also refusing to sell sugar to customers unless they also bought other products that they did not want. Seeing an opportunity to put his principles into practice, Kazan met with Benjamin Schlesinger, president of the ILGWU, which was committed not only to increasing wages and improving working conditions but also to enhancing the lives of its members outside the sweatshops. Kazan asked Schlesinger to support his plan to buy sugar in bulk and sell it at cost to the union's 7,000 members. Schlesinger gave his blessing. Kazan approached the American Sugar Refining Company, which rebuffed him, saying that his scheme would interfere with its business. But with the help of Jonathan C. Day, the city's food commissioner, and a $500 loan from Dr. George M. Price, a strong supporter of organized labor, he acquired 50,000 pounds of surplus sugar from the US Army. To store and sell it, he rented space from Local 35. This venture went so well that in the aftermath of the war, a time when the price of food was soaring, Kazan came up with the idea of buying matzohs in bulk and selling them at, or slightly above, cost to union members. The demand for matzohs was so great at Passover that by the time the holiday was over he had sold 100,000 pounds.[4]

Buoyed by the success of the sugar and matzoh business, Kazan and a few associates at the ILGWU launched a more ambitious enterprise. They opened a cooperative grocery store on the Lower East Side. From the start, the store did poorly. And it soon went out of business—though not before generating a good deal of ill feeling between Kazan and his associates. Believing that the union was losing interest in his cooperative activities and treating him more like a clerk than the secretary of a local, Kazan left the ILGWU in late 1918 and went to work for its rival, the Amalgamated Clothing Workers of America, where he was put in charge of the records department. Under the leadership of Sidney Hillman, the Amalgamated was even more committed than the ILGWU to improving the quality of life of its members outside the sweatshops. Although Hillman and Jacob S. Potofsky, the assistant secretary, supported cooperatives, they saw them, in Eisenstadt's words, as "part of a broader political program of workers' advancement" and "a temporary substitute for a comprehensive social democracy," and not, as Kazan did, as "an end in itself." Despite these differences, Hillman and Potofsky soon gave Kazan an opportunity to prove himself. The Amalgamated, Potofsky told him, was about to surrender the charter of a credit union that had been mismanaged by one of its locals and now had too many bad loans on its books. Kazan, who viewed the credit union as "a poor man's savings bank," urged Potofsky to hold off and let him try to put the business on a sound financial footing. Potofsky was amenable, provided that Kazan worked at the credit union as a volunteer. It took time, but Kazan eventually turned the business around, an accomplishment that helped bolster his position at the Amalgamated.[5]

Although Kazan had more than enough to do at the Amalgamated, he kept looking for ways to further his personal agenda. And before long he found one. Shortly after World War I he noticed that many members of the credit union were having trouble finding a decent apartment at a reasonable rent. The reason, Kazan knew, was that there was a serious housing shortage in New York City. Residential construction had slowed down after the war broke out in Europe. And after the United States went to war, it came to a standstill. With too many tenants and two few apartments, vacancy rates plummeted to unheard-of levels, from 2 percent in March 1919 to less than one-third of 1 percent in April 1920. In an attempt to capitalize on the tight housing market, most landlords raised the rents, sometimes several times a year. In response, some tenants moved to less expensive (and usually less desirable) apartments. Others appealed to their landlords to rescind (or at least reduce) the rent hikes. And to make ends meet, others cut back on food, clothing, and other household expenses. Still others went on rent strikes. When faced with eviction, they fought the landlords in court and even resisted the efforts of the marshals to oust them. The situation grew so grave that in 1920 the state legislature imposed rent control in New York (and a few other big cities), a measure that did much to reduce the rent hikes but little to increase the housing stock. For Kazan, the housing shortage was a golden opportunity. If one person could save or borrow the money to become the landlord of fifty families, Kazan reasoned, why couldn't fifty families pool their resources and then build (or buy) and manage their own apartment house? And if enough New Yorkers came to realize the advantages of becoming their own landlord, it would go a long way toward solving the housing problem and building a cooperative commonwealth.[6]

OOO

The origins of New York's housing problem went back to the mid-nineteenth century, more than half a century before Abraham E. Kazan arrived at Ellis Island. As early as 1834 Gerrett Forbes, the city's chief health officer, decried "the crowded and filthy state in which a great portion of our population live." The victims of the many greedy landlords whose sole objective was to cram "the greatest number of human beings in[to] the smallest space," they were stowed "like cattle, in pens," added John H. Griscom, a prominent New York physician, a decade later. These concerns were shared by the Association for Improving the Condition of the Poor, which was established in 1843 by a group of well-to-do merchants and other businessmen, most of whom resided in spacious single-family houses in fashionable neighborhoods far from the Lower East Side slums that were home to most workingmen and their families, many of them recent immigrants from Germany and Ireland. Combined with what historian Roy Lubove calls "the rapidly deteriorating housing conditions," the AICP's crusade against the slums eventually prompted the authorities to act. In 1856 the New York State Assembly appointed a select committee to look into working-class housing in New York and Brooklyn, which was at the time an independent city and the third-largest in the country. It found that conditions were abysmal, a result of private avarice and public lethargy and "the offspring," in its words, "of municipal neglect." Too many tenants lived in "hideous squalor." The "dim, undrained courts [were] oozing with pollution"; the "dark, narrow staircases [were] decayed with age, reeking with filth, overrun with vermin"; the floors were "rotted"; the ceilings were "begrimed, and often too low to permit [a person] to stand upright"; and the windows were "stuffed with rags."[7]

New York's housing problem grew even worse in the second half of the nineteenth century. Fueled by massive immigration from southern and eastern Europe, the city's population soared from under one million in 1870 to over three million in 1900, two years after the consolidation of New York and Brooklyn. Most of the newcomers, many of them Italians and Russian Jews, settled on the Lower East Side, where, like other immigrants before them, they rented apartments in single-family homes that had been converted into three- and four-family tenement houses; in newly built tenements, "squat three- and four-story [and later five- and six-story] boxes of wood and brick," in Lubove's words; or even, in some cases, in "dark, damp cellars or renovated stables and warehouses." Concern about the housing conditions of the working class also grew steadily after the Civil War, especially among the city's elites, and reached a peak at the turn of the century, shortly after the publication in 1890 of *How the Other Half Lives*, a vivid account of life and labor on the Lower East Side written by Jacob A. Riis, a Danish immigrant who was working as a police reporter for the *New York Evening Sun*. In response to the growing concern, the authorities set up several bodies to look into the housing problem of the working class. The most notable were the Tenement House Committee of 1894—whose report, writes Lubove, was "the most thorough study ever made of tenement house life in New York"—and the Tenement House Commission of 1900, most of whose findings were published in a two-volume opus edited by Lawrence Veiller, the most influential tenement-house reformer of the time, and Robert W. De Forest, a prominent New York lawyer and the city's first tenement-house commissioner.[8]

According to Veiller and other tenement-house reformers, the crux of New York's housing problem was twofold. The tenements, they pointed out, were extremely overcrowded. Three and four families lived in run-down houses that had been built for one family. And as many as twelve to sixteen families rented 200- or 300-square-foot apartments in flimsily constructed railroad flats. On the Lower East Side, and especially in the Italian and Jewish neighborhoods, it was not uncommon for a family, even a family with several children and perhaps one or more grandparents, to take in lodgers and boarders. Nor was it unheard of for two families to share one apartment. It was in these tiny apartments that the workingmen and their families cooked and ate, socialized with friends and relatives, and slept, sometimes in bedrooms as small as six by six feet and occasionally more than one to a bed. As Jacob Riis wrote of the Jewish immigrants on the Lower East Side, their apartments were also their workshops. "You are made fully aware of it before you have traveled the length of a single block in any of these East Side streets, by the whir of a thousand sewing-machines worked at high pressure from the earliest dawn till mind and muscle give out together. Every member of the family, from the youngest to the oldest, bears a hand." Besides sewing clothing, the immigrants rolled cigars, made artificial flowers, and washed the laundry of the well-to-do. ("Monday was laundry day," wrote historian Elizabeth Ewen, "and the entire household was turned upside down; the clothes were washed in big tubs filled with water boiled on the stove, then put out to dry on the famous clotheslines of the Lower East Side.")[9]

If New York's tenement houses were extremely overcrowded, so were the working-class neighborhoods in which they stood. With the houses built cheek by jowl, on narrow 20-by-100-foot (or 25-by-100-foot) lots, and with fewer than 65 acres of parks south of Fourteenth Street, or only one acre for every 11,000 residents, Lower Manhattan was one of the most densely populated neighborhoods not only in the United States but in the world. By the mid-1890s, when New York's population was approaching two million, it had 76 persons per acre, which was high, if not quite as high as Paris, Berlin, and a handful of other European cities. But the density of Manhattan, which was home to more than nine of every ten New Yorkers, was nearly twice as high. And in some of Lower Manhattan's most congested wards, the density ranged from nearly 370 to more than 700 persons per acre. Indeed, in one part of the eleventh ward, which was located on the Lower East Side, there were almost 1,000 persons per acre, which was even higher than in the most crowded parts of Bombay, one of the world's most congested cities. Whether measured by the number of people per room or the number of persons per acre, overcrowding was the "greatest evil" of the tenements, wrote E.R.L. Gould. Another prominent tenement-house reformer, Gould was born, raised, and educated in Canada, went to graduate school at Johns Hopkins University, and, after receiving his PhD in 1886, became one of the leading authorities on working-class housing in Europe and America (and head of the City and Suburban Homes Company, the largest builder of model tenements in New York, about which more later).[10]

As well as extremely overcrowded, Gould and others pointed out, the tenements were highly unsanitary. According to another state legislative committee, which was set up in the mid-1860s, the tenement houses were built so close to one another, side by side and sometimes even back to back, that little or no sunlight (and not much in the way of fresh air) penetrated into many of the rooms, and especially not into the tiny, often windowless, interior bedrooms. The apartments were not only dark but often dank. In some low-lying neighborhoods, a group of public health experts found in the mid-1860s, the basement and cellar rooms—whose squalor, writes Lubove, "defied imagination"—were subject to periodic flooding at high tide, at times to "a depth of six inches to a foot." The water was sometimes so high that the children had to stay in bed until ebb tide. Very few working-class New Yorkers had hot running water. And according to the Tenement House Committee of 1894, whose staff investigated the living conditions of more than a quarter of a million tenement-house dwellers, only about 300 families had access to a bathtub in their homes, a situation that the committee described as "a disgrace to the city and to the civilization of the nineteenth century." Hardly any working-class New Yorkers had private toilets either. As the Tenement House Commission of 1900 pointed out, one block on the Lower East Side, which was bounded by Chrystie, Forsyth, Canal, and Bayard Streets, had 39 tenements and nearly 2,800 tenants, but only 264 water closets, most of which were located in the halls or the basements. Many other tenement houses had no water closets at all, but only a privy vault, a type of outhouse that was usually located in the rear yard.[11]

If the sanitary conditions left much to be desired inside the tenement houses, they left even more to be desired outside. More often than not, the streets were strewn with garbage, sometimes because the trash cans, many of which were crammed beyond capacity, were not emptied as often as necessary and other times because the residents simply tossed their garbage out of the windows. The rotting garbage made a fertile breeding ground for all sorts of insects and rodents, which moved easily between the streets and the houses. And the privy vaults often overflowed, reported the Council of Hygiene, whose objective was to improve housing and sanitary conditions in New York. (Formed a year after the Draft Riots of 1863, the council was an offshoot of the Citizens' Association, which was organized by Peter Cooper, John Jacob Astor Jr., and other wealthy New Yorkers to combat corruption and inefficiency in municipal government.) Indeed, it was not until 1867 that the local authorities enacted an ordinance that required landlords to connect privy vaults (and, for that matter, water closets) to the sewers. Making matters worse, New York's working-class neighborhood houses were full of stables, distilleries, junkyards, slaughterhouses, and a wide range of other noxious businesses, which contributed much to the filth, not to mention the stench, of everyday life. By virtue of the extreme overcrowding and highly unsanitary conditions, the tenement houses and their surroundings were "totally unfit to be the shelter for [even] the lower animals," wrote B. O. Flower, a muckraking journalist and editor of *The Arena*, which was published in New York and Boston, in the mid-1890s.[12]

Gould, De Forest, and other upper-middle- and upper-class New Yorkers were genuinely concerned about the plight of the tenement-house dwellers, many of whom led hard lives and often died at an early age. But they were also afraid that the abysmal housing conditions that degraded the working class would endanger the well-to-do. As I have written elsewhere, this fear grew out of a widespread belief in environmental determinism—the belief that people were profoundly influenced by their physical surroundings. "Strong-willed, intelligent people may create or modify environment," wrote Gould; "[but] the weaker-willed, the poor, and careless and the unreflective become subject to it." Into which category the tenement-house dwellers fit, he had no doubt. "Populous masses, crowded together one thousand to the acre, as they are in some parts of New York, are absolutely unable to resist the influences by which they are surrounded." From this perspective, the residents of the slums were not so much wicked as weak. What they are, said the Association for Improving the Condition of the Poor in the mid-1850s, is a result of "circumstances over which they have but little control; and vain will be the effort to elevate their character, without first improving their physical condition." It was this belief in environmental determinism that prompted the *New York Times* to write in 1880 that "the condition of our tenement-house population is the source of the worst evils, physical and moral, in this City." Gould agreed. "As they now exist," he wrote two decades later, "the tenements are standing menaces to the family, to morality, to the public health, [to the public safety], and to civic integrity." And, he went on, "it is to be hoped that it will not require some public calamity to arouse the people to their danger or their duty."[13]

Gould and other tenement-house reformers hammered away at this point in articles, lectures, and books. Demoralized by the extreme overcrowding and inadequate sanitation, deprived of the independence and privacy vital to its well-being, the working-class family disintegrated. Fathers, their prospects poor and hopes fading, fled their dreary apartments and headed for the nearby saloons, where they found temporary solace in alcohol, which they could ill afford, and the companionship of other drinkers. Mothers, worn out by the strain of running a household in so hostile an environment, gave up. Instead of delighting in their children, Gould wrote, they were "soured into ill-feeling and brutalized into a state of callous indifference." Just as the adult "goes to the saloon," wrote William Howe Tolman, secretary of the City Vigilance League, a reform group that was set up in the mid-1890s, so the child "goes to the street," where, in the absence of parks and playgrounds, "boys, while yet of tender age, are introduced to viciousness and petty crime," Gould pointed out. And "young girls, from their earliest teens, engage in an almost hopeless struggle for moral preservation." The tenement house blocks the "development of true domestic life," Gould insisted, "[and] every member of the family from earliest childhood becomes prey to those forces which drag down, a stranger to those which uplift." The *Times* felt much the same way. "What," it asked, "can be hoped from the influence of schools, churches, civilization, and religion in laborers' families, who live twenty to a room, of all ages and both sexes, and thus pass a great part of their lives?"[14]

The tenement house also fostered immorality, its critics charged. It is "the most fruitful breeding ground for vice," wrote Gould—"the cradle, nursery, kindergarten, school, [and] university ... of the dependents, defectives, and delinquents," added Tolman. The crux of the problem, said the *New York Times*, was that the tenement house "saps self-respect, weakens the resistance to temptation, aggravates the evil passions, and breeds the habit of unmanly and unwomanly conduct." Or as the AICP put it, "Physical evils produce moral evils. Degrade men to the conditions of brutes, and they will have brutal propensities and passions." If "it be hard for a dyspeptic millionaire, surrounded by the delights of affluence, to be a good Christian," Gould stressed, "how much more difficult for a poor man, living in squalor and filth." And how much more difficult for a poor woman, who had to share her cramped quarters with one or more male lodgers and boarders. Of particular concern to the critics was the plight of the girls and young women. "If a female child be born and brought up in a room of one of these tenement-houses," wrote Charles Loring Brace, founder of the Children's Aid Society and author of *The Dangerous Classes of New York*, which was published in 1880, "she loses very early the modesty which is the great shield of purity. Personal delicacy becomes almost unknown to her. Living, sleeping, and doing her work in the same apartment with men and boys of various ages, it is well-nigh impossible for her to retain any feminine reserve, and she passes almost unconsciously the line of purity at a very early age."[15]

The tenement house endangered public health too, its critics claimed. Inspired by what Lubove calls the "bacteriological revolution" of the late nineteenth century—the discovery that "specific organisms were responsible for specific diseases"—they charged that the dark, dank, poorly ventilated, and highly unsanitary tenements provided fertile grounds for the germs that carried typhoid, diphtheria, and other infectious diseases, including tuberculosis, or "the white plague," which, said the Tenement House Commission of 1900, "[had] become practically epidemic" in New York's working-class neighborhoods. "No one will deny that sickness bears a close relation to bad housing," argued Gould, or that the high incidence of mortality in the tenements was a result of their physical conditions. Nor was the danger confined to working-class neighborhoods, Gould and others pointed out. Many of the tenement houses stood "perilously close" to middle- and upper-middle-class neighborhoods. Their residents rode on streetcars, worked in stores, and went to schools. How could anyone be confident that they were not inadvertently infecting other people? Moreover, the tenement-house dwellers sewed clothing, rolled cigars, and made artificial flowers that were sold to other New Yorkers. If ill men and women, a sickly child, or an ailing grandparent worked on these goods, how could anyone be confident that they were not contaminated? Small wonder that Jacob Riis described the tenement houses as "the hot-beds of the epidemics that carry death to rich and poor alike."[16]

The tenement house threatened public safety as well, its critics contended. Unless conditions improved in the congested working-class neighborhoods, the AICP warned in the mid-1850s, the poor would soon "overrun the city as thieves and beggars, endanger public peace and the security of property, and tax the community for their support." Jacob Riis shared the AICP's concern. Writing a few decades later, he stressed that the tenements were "the nurseries of pauperism and crime." Every year they spewed out tens of thousands—even hundreds of thousands—of beggars, tramps, and criminals, many of whom ended up in the city's asylums, workhouses, and jails. Instead of staying home, boys hung out in saloons, where they learned contempt for law and order and joined gangs, which initiated them into a life of delinquency and criminality. The tenement house was also a serious fire hazard, its critics pointed out. Often made of wood—and even if made of brick, full of inflammable material—most of them were highly combustible. As the Tenement House Committee of 1894 reported, less than one-third of New York's dwellings were tenement houses, but they were the site of more than one-half of the city's fires. And once the fires started in the working-class neighborhoods, it was very hard to prevent them from spreading to the middle- and upper-middle-class enclaves. This was a grave source of concern in the late nineteenth and early twentieth centuries, a time when major conflagrations devastated Boston, Chicago, Baltimore, and several other American cities.[17]

Not the least of the many objectionable features of the tenement house, in the mind of Gould and other reformers, was that it undermined civic life. It was "a menace to a republic form of government," wrote William Tolman. Or as Henry Morgenthau, a New York lawyer and one of the city's most prominent real estate men, put it, the tenement house was "an evil which is gnawing at the vitals of the country"; unless it was wiped out, "our great body politic will be [grievously] weakened." According to the reformers, the first- and second-generation immigrants were rendered so passive by the physical conditions of the working-class neighborhoods that come election day they were unable to do anything but the bidding of the ward bosses, the leaders of Tammany Hall, the Democratic political machine that was widely blamed for the rampant corruption (and widespread incompetence) of city government. The same conditions also rendered the newcomers highly susceptible to radical movements, the reformers claimed. As Gould wrote at the turn of the century, "The genesis of 'isms [by which he meant socialism, communism, and anarchism] most often takes place in the miserable tenements of a great modern city." Gould's remark struck a responsive chord in a society that had been racked by fears of class warfare since the late 1870s—a society that had "enough dynamite [in it] to overturn any government in Europe," as Chauncey M. Depew, a prominent lawyer and businessman, the president of the New York Central Railroad, and later a US senator, told New York's Charity Organization Society.[18]

OOO

New York's housing problem was serious, Gould and other reformers believed, but it could be solved. (Or, as Riis put it, "The poor we shall have always with us, but the slums we need not have.") Hence they mounted a vigorous campaign to upgrade working-class housing, a campaign that got underway in the mid-nineteenth century and picked up momentum in the late nineteenth and early twentieth centuries. At its core were three distinct, but more or less complementary, objectives. By far the most important was to prevent builders from erecting new tenement houses that were as bad as the old ones. To this end the reformers urged the state legislature to impose a wide range of regulations for new tenements, most of which were designed to reduce overcrowding and improve sanitary conditions. Despite strong opposition from real estate interests, the legislature enacted a series of tenement-house laws, the earliest of which was the Tenement House Law of 1867, a half-hearted, largely symbolic act, writes historian Lawrence M. Friedman, that did little "to check the growth of the slums." The legislature passed another tenement-house law in 1879 that was only slightly more stringent than the 1867 law. But twenty-two years later it finally enacted a law with some teeth. Known as the Tenement House Act of 1901, it was drafted by Lawrence Veiller and his associates on the Tenement House Commission of 1900, supported by Governor Theodore Roosevelt, and signed by his successor, Benjamin B. Odell Jr. The most sweeping tenement-house law yet enacted in the United States, it applied not only to New York but also to Buffalo, the state's second-largest city, and served as a model for tenement-house reform in New Jersey, Connecticut, Indiana, and other states.[19]

The Tenement House Act of 1901 did much to improve housing conditions in New York's working-class neighborhoods. Among other things, it reduced congestion. It prevented builders from erecting tenements that covered the entire lot. It also imposed a height limit of five stories on nonfireproof buildings (unless they were 40 feet wide or more) and six stories on fireproof buildings. It also prohibited the construction of rear tenements except on lots at least 50 feet wide. The act increased light and ventilation and banned the narrow air shafts that were common in the many so-called dumbbell tenements built in the late nineteenth century. And it required that builders install windows in interior rooms and provide every room with at least 400 cubic feet of air for each adult and 200 cubic feet for each child under twelve. The act improved sanitary conditions too. It required that every apartment contain not only a sink but also a water closet, "of durable non-absorbable materials," which could be entered "without passing through any bedroom." And it outlawed the notorious privy vault. The act reduced the risk of fire as well. It mandated that builders construct the stairways, halls, and air shafts of fireproof materials and install metal rather than wooden fire escapes, consisting, in Lubove's words, of "open iron platforms connected by stairs on the outside of each apartment." To enforce these and the dozens of other regulations, which had hitherto been placed in the less than capable hands of the building and health departments, the act created an independent Tenement House Department, which, according to Lubove, was headed by Commissioner De Forest but run by Veiller, the deputy commissioner.[20]

But conditions in New York's working-class neighborhoods still left much to be desired after the passage of the Tenement House Act of 1901. As even Veiller conceded twenty years later, the slums had continued to grow. Part of the problem was that the Tenement House Department was hard pressed to enforce the law. It had too few inspectors—fewer than one for every 500 tenement houses in 1916. Overworked and underpaid, they were often willing to overlook minor violations (and, for a price, even major ones). When they issued citations, it sometimes took the courts a year or more to process them. And when a building was condemned, it was very hard for the tenants to find another place to live. Given the acute housing shortage after World War I, Tenement House Commissioner Frank Mann said that he often had no choice but to "close one eye, and sometimes both." The enforcement of the tenement-house regulations had so broken down, wrote the New York State Board of Housing in 1930, that it was more serious to deface a public park "than to maintain a tenement house in such conditions as to continually menace the health and safety of its occupants." Another part of the problem was that most of the provisions of the act applied only to the new tenements—the "new-law" tenements, as they were commonly referred to. As a result, millions of New Yorkers still lived in the old-law tenements, which, wrote one observer, were "without heat, without baths, and affording little more accommodation than shelter from rain and snow." Moreover, the act did nothing to increase the postwar housing stock, which was still in extremely short supply. As Edith Elmer Wood, a leading member of a new generation of housing experts, wrote in 1919, "The best restrictive legislation is only negative. It will prevent the bad. It will not produce the good, especially it will not produce it at a [reasonable] rental."[21]

Another objective of the tenement-house reformers was to demonstrate that it was possible to build good apartments, charge a reasonable rent, and still make a modest profit—or, in Gould's words, to show that "the proper housing of the great masses of working people can be furnished on a satisfactory commercial basis." Out of this belief emerged the model tenement movement, a movement that spread from England to America in the second half of the nineteenth century. In the vanguard was a small group of wealthy New Yorkers (and Bostonians) who held that "investment philanthropy" (or "philanthropy and 5 per cent")—an approach, said Gould, that occupied "a middle ground between pure philanthropy and pure business"—offered a solution to the housing problem of the working class. Underlying this approach was the assumption that the wealthy—or, in Gould's phrase, "the large-hearted rich"—would be willing to underwrite the construction of model tenements that yielded a modest rate of return. Operating on this assumption, the reformers set up several model tenement companies, of which Brooklyn's Improved Dwellings Company, formed in the late 1870s by Alfred T. White—"the undisputed evangelist of [the] model tenement gospel," in Lubove's words—was the best and Manhattan's City and Suburban Homes Company, set up in the mid-1890s by a group of affluent New Yorkers and headed by Gould from 1896 until his death in 1915, was the largest. These companies built tenements with more space and better sanitation than most ordinary tenements. Although Veiller was skeptical, White, Gould, and others had high hopes that the model tenements would not only provide good housing for some workingmen and their families but also inspire commercial builders to provide good housing for many others.[22]

For a while it seemed that these hopes might be realized. White's first model tenement, the "Home Buildings," was, in Lubove's words, "an immediate, influential success" that showed that it was possible to build spacious and sanitary apartments for working people and still earn a modest return on the investment. Besides erecting two other model tenements in Brooklyn, White inspired a few New Yorkers to follow his lead. But when it came to model tenements, the *Times* complained in the late 1870s, New York lagged far behind Brooklyn, not to mention London. And so in 1896 a group of prominent New Yorkers organized the City and Suburban Homes Company, a "praiseworthy" enterprise, wrote the *Tribune*, that was the most auspicious sign thus far that New York might soon solve its housing problem. With Gould at the helm, City and Suburban raised several million dollars from New York's wealthiest residents, among them J. P. Morgan, Jacob H. Schiff, and Mrs. Alfred Corning Clark, the widow of the only son of one of the founders of what became the Singer Manufacturing Company, the world's leading maker of sewing machines. With this money, the company erected several model tenements, the first of which was the Alfred Corning Clark Buildings on the Upper West Side and the largest of which were the First Avenue Estate and the York Avenue Estate on the Upper East Side. (The company also built the Tuskegee and Hampton estates on the Upper West Side, which provided housing for 174 "colored" families, and Homewood, a community of just over 100 single-family homes in Brooklyn.) By 1916, a year after Gould died in an accident while vacationing in Glacier National Park, City and Suburban had erected 41 tenement houses, which contained nearly 3,000 apartments and provided shelter for about 11,000 working-class New Yorkers.[23]

But even before Gould's untimely death, the City and Suburban Homes Company was on the wane. So was the model tenement movement. At the same time that City and Suburban built 41 model tenements, commercial builders erected more than 27,000 ordinary tenements. For every model tenement built between 1902 and 1916 by semi-philanthropic companies, more than 300 were erected by commercial builders. Of the 2.9 million New Yorkers who lived in tenements in 1917 and paid $25 a month or less in rent, City and Suburban housed only one-third of 1 percent, and all the semi-philanthropic housing companies only two-thirds of 1 percent. More-over, the model tenement movement lost what little momentum it had after World War I. With the price of labor and materials soaring, City and Subur-ban found it very hard to build new housing. As Allan Robinson, Gould's suc-cessor, said in 1922, "The cost of building is so great that tenements cannot now be put up to rent for people of moderate means." Indeed, after finishing the First Avenue Estate in 1915, the company did not build another tenement house in Manhattan, and it erected only two small housing complexes else-where in the city, one in Brooklyn and the other in Queens. City and Subur-ban also found it very hard to persuade "the large-hearted rich" to invest in model tenements. Some were reluctant to settle for a modest return on their capital. Others were put off by the stigma attached to the tenement-house business. Still others thought that it was impractical and even immoral to resort to philanthropy to solve the housing problem. City and Suburban sur-vived, but only as a management company. And though it provided some "wholesome places to live," writes Friedman, the model tenement movement did little to house working people, even less to inspire commercial builders, and virtually nothing to abolish the slums.[24]

Yet another objective of the tenement-house reformers was to expedite the movement of the working class from tenement houses in the center of the city to single-family homes on the periphery. This movement, it was widely assumed, would in time drain the slums. New-law tenements were better than old-law tenements, the reformers believed, and model tenements were better still. But no matter how well built, a tenement was inferior to a single-family home and a tenant inferior to a homeowner. How much could be expected from a workingman, said Veiller, whose "home is but three or four rooms in some huge building in which dwell from twenty to thirty other families [and] whose home is his only from month to month." Democracy, he added, "was not predicated on a country made up of tenement dwellers, nor can it so survive." Gould agreed. The model tenement was not the "acme of achievement," he conceded. At best it was a way station between the "promiscuous and common life of the ordinary tenement and the dignified, well-ordered life of the detached home." And speaking of homeownership, he declared, "Every man undertaking it is helped to a far greater degree than he could be in the best class of model tenements. He becomes reflective, careful, prudent, wedded to order and rational conservatism, and usually turns a deaf ear to specious 'isms." To encourage workingmen and their families to leave the tenements, Gould and other reformers campaigned for cheap and convenient rapid transit. Following the conventional wisdom, they assumed that by providing service to undeveloped, hitherto inaccessible, and relatively inexpensive land on the periphery, rapid transit would enable working people to move from the city to the suburbs and live there in modest versions of middle- and upper-middle-class "bourgeois utopias."[25]

The campaign to drain the slums made some headway. Between 1902 and 1914, more than 5,000 old-law tenements, with nearly 3,700 units, were demolished. The pace of demolition slowed during World War I, but picked up in the mid and late 1920s. More than 90 percent of these tenements were in Manhattan, and most of them were on the Lower East Side. Some were condemned by the Board of Health and the Tenement House Department. But many more were torn down to make way for schools, parks, playgrounds, streets, and other public improvements. No fewer than 200 tenements were demolished for the approaches to the Williamsburg Bridge at the turn of the century and even more for the approaches to the Manhattan Bridge a decade later. Other tenements were knocked down to make way for commercial and industrial enterprises, prompting Jacob Riis to say, "Business has done more than all other agencies together to wipe out the worst tenements. It has been New York's real Napoleon III," the French emperor who presided over the reconstruction of Paris in the 1860s. As a result, hundreds of thousands of residents were displaced—more than 13,300 for a few small parks in the notorious Mulberry Bend neighborhood of the Lower East Side and more than 16,000 for the construction of the huge new Pennsylvania Railroad Station on the West Side. And as the reformers hoped, some of these residents moved to Williamsburg, Brownsville, and other neighborhoods in nearby Brooklyn. Taking advantage of the construction of the Interborough Rapid Transit (IRT) subway, others left their old neighborhoods and rented more spacious and sanitary apartments (or, in some cases, bought small single-family homes) in Upper Manhattan and the Bronx.[26]

But as Veiller and other reformers acknowledged, the campaign to drain the slums was hardly an unqualified success. Although some working people moved from the center to the periphery, many others did not. Some stayed in the slums because they had no choice. Holding menial and often highly insecure and poorly paid jobs, they could not afford to rent an apartment in a new-law tenement, much less buy a home of their own, especially if it was not in walking distance of their workplace. Others stayed put even though they could have left. Indeed, Tenement House Commissioner De Forest said, with regret, that most tenement-house dwellers, even many who worked outside the city, were reluctant to move away from the Lower East Side. Some placed a much lower value on the importance of housing than the reformers did. A close family, loving and hardworking parents, and happy and well-behaved children counted for more than a spacious and sanitary apartment. As Sam Levenson, a Jewish comedian who grew up in a squalid tenement house in East Harlem, wrote, "My environment was miserable; I was not." Others wanted to spend as little as possible on rent, especially if the money saved might be enough for a newcomer to bring a wife, parent, or sibling from Europe to America, to open his own business, or to allow his children to stay in school (and perhaps take advantage of opportunities closed to their parents). Still others preferred to live close to relatives and friends who spoke the same language, worshiped at the same churches and temples, and supported the institutions that kept their culture alive. For many first- and second-generation immigrants it made little or no sense to move to better housing on the periphery if it forced them to sever the ties that gave meaning to their lives.[27]

By the early 1920s, if not earlier, some New Yorkers were skeptical that stringent regulations, model tenements, and rapid transit could solve the housing problem. Indeed, wrote the Housing Committee of the New York State Reconstruction Commission, a blue-ribbon body that had been appointed by Governor Alfred E. Smith after World War I, it had long been "economically impossible" to provide working people with decent homes at reasonable rents. If private enterprise was not up to the task, these New Yorkers concluded, "what else is there left to do except for the state or municipality to step in," namely, to build good housing for working people and rent it to them at cost. In the vanguard of the campaign for what became known as "public housing" were the socialists, among them Judge Jacob Panken, who declared that it was the only way to solve the housing problem. Other New Yorkers came to the same conclusion. As Belle Moskowitz, an aide to Governor Smith, put it, "If [New York] cannot get housing in any other way, if it cannot get it through the speculative builder, if it cannot get it through co-operative associations or any other fashion, the city will have to build it." Smith came out in favor of public housing too, as did Fiorello H. La Guardia, president of the New York City Board of Aldermen, and Henry H. Curran, borough president of Manhattan. Even Stewart Browne, a prominent real estate man (and something of a maverick in real estate circles), who opposed public housing in principle, saw no alternative. *The Nation*, a Progressive periodical, agreed. Pointing out that private enterprise offered no hope for relief, that capital "must have its interest," and that landlords "will exact the utmost farthing," it wrote in 1920 that only the government "can give homes to the people who need them and provide the homes that will be needed in the immediate future."[28]

From the start the calls for public housing aroused a storm of opposition, especially from the real estate interests and tenement-house reformers, two groups that were usually at odds with one another. Public housing was un-American, its opponents charged. And it was socialistic. The state should no more house the people than it should feed them, said a Bronx real estate man; nor should it provide them with clothing, motorcars, and theater tickets, added Veiller. Public housing was also paternalistic, a form of "charitable relief, however disguised," that would demoralize the tenants, said another critic. And given the sordid history of machine politics in New York, a prominent lawyer warned, "it would in all likelihood result in a veritable orgy of political favoritism and corruption." Public housing was objectionable on practical as well as ideological grounds, argued its opponents. Public officials could not put up housing "any cheaper, better or quicker" than private builders, said the New York Real Estate Board. The city did not have the money to build working-class housing, argued an insurance company executive, and if it tried, it would drive private enterprise out of the business and thereby exacerbate the housing shortage. Why would anyone build an apartment house, he asked, "if the city stands over him with power, whenever it please[s], to go into the business of producing space for less than it is worth and destroying the value of his property." Gould spoke for many New Yorkers when he wrote, "There is nothing in foreign experience with municipal housing of working people to render its repetition with us either desirable or attractive." To tax one class for the benefit of another "is bad principle and worse policy," he went on. "Municipal regulation, not municipal ownership, is the best watchword for American policy."[29]

These objections were groundless, said the supporters of public housing. They responded to the charge that it was un-American by noting that New York and other big cities had already built public waterworks, schools, and markets and established public hospitals, clinics, and dispensaries. Countering the charge that public housing was socialistic, they argued that, if anything, public housing would prevent radicalism from taking hold among the working class. (Indeed, remarked a self-styled "intensely conservative" New York City architect, if providing houses, schools, and other facilities for workingmen and their families is socialism, "then up to this point I am ready to be called a Socialist.") And to the charge that public housing was paternalistic, one New Yorker pointed out that the city already operated municipal ferries without, he added, demoralizing the riders. Nor was public housing impractical, its supporters stressed. It was widely accepted in "every other civilized country in the world," claimed Dr. Royal S. Copeland, the city's health commissioner. To the charge that it would exacerbate the housing shortage by driving private enterprise out of the business, its backers responded that "the field is large enough for everybody." Moreover, wrote *The New Republic*, another Progressive periodical, "building [working-class housing] for profit has never worked, works abominably now and will certainly never work tolerably well in the future."[30] In the aftermath of World War II, the advocates of public housing put forward several proposals to authorize New York to go into the housing business, including one to empower the city to build working-class housing on land it already owned in the Bronx. But in the face of strong ideological, political, financial, and possibly even constitutional constraints, none of these proposals went anywhere.

OOO

Like many New Yorkers, Abraham E. Kazan doubted that private enterprise was capable of providing spacious and sanitary housing for working-class families. As he was well aware, there had been a great surge in residential construction in New York in the 1920s, a surge that was "without precedent," wrote the New York State Commission of Housing and Regional Planning. Between 1923 and 1928 commercial builders erected more than 20,000 apartment houses with more than a third of a million units—or enough to house over 1.5 million people. But as Kazan also knew, virtually all of the new housing was much too expensive for working people. As a result, said

Clarence S. Stein, an architect, planner, and chairman of the Commission of Housing and Regional Planning, many New Yorkers still lived in substandard apartments that were "a menace to the health and welfare of the community as a whole" and remained stuck in slums that were "the worst in the world" and "a disgrace to civilization." But unlike La Guardia, Curran, and other New Yorkers, Kazan had strong reservations about public housing. If the government went into the housing business, he conceded, it might well succeed as a builder (and provide housing for "one part of the population at the expense of another"). But the results might "become more harmful than beneficial," he argued. "Instead of developing the idea of self-help, it will destroy it"—and thereby eliminate "the possibility of mutually building a better and finer community to the advantage of those who live there." If neither private enterprise nor public authority was up to the task, Kazan reasoned, it was time to give cooperative housing a chance—to apply the principles of self-help and mutual aid that had first emerged in Western Europe in the mid-nineteenth century and spread to the United States not long after.[31]

The cooperative movement made much less progress in the United States than in Western Europe because "cooperation thrives where wages are low and the struggle for existence is keen," wrote Louis H. Pink, a New Yorker who would later serve as the United Housing Foundation's first president. The United States, "with our great natural resources," was "too individualistic." What was true for cooperative enterprise in general was true for cooperative housing in particular. According to the US Bureau of Labor Statistics, there were only about 40 housing cooperatives in the United States in 1925, all but two of which were in New York City. Of the 32 about which the bureau had data, one was in Milwaukee, whose mayor, Daniel W. Hoan, a well-known socialist, was a strong supporter of cooperative housing. It consisted of 105 single-family homes. Twenty-two of the other housing cooperatives were in Brooklyn, among them several tenement houses that were built in the Sunset Park neighborhood in the late 1910s by a group of Finnish-Americans. Their success prompted Clarence Stein to ask, "Why is it that the Finns can put up houses on the cooperative plan and we cannot?" Another nine housing cooperatives were in Manhattan. Some were built by Jewish benevolent organizations. And one, which went up in East Harlem in the early 1920s and consisted of five tenement houses, was sponsored by the People's Tabernacle, an evangelical church, many of whose parishioners had recently moved out of the neighborhood. "My dream is to turn New York from a city of slums into a city of homes," said its pastor, Rev. H. M. Tyndall.

If each of New York's 1,000 churches followed the People's Tabernacle's lead, 50,000 working-class families would soon own their own homes. "What a transformation that would be!" he said. "And what a wonderful way to keep a parish together!"[32]

Although these Brooklyn and Manhattan cooperatives housed fewer than 2,000 families—or fewer than two of every 1,000 New Yorkers—there were signs that cooperative housing was gaining momentum. The number of housing cooperatives rose steadily, if not sharply, after World War I. And all but a handful of them went up in the early and mid-1920s. What is more, a few labor unions were showing a growing interest in cooperative housing. In the forefront were the Amalgamated Clothing Workers, the ILGWU, and a few other needle trades unions, many of whose members had been hard hit by the postwar housing shortage, which had driven vacancy rates down to record levels and sent apartment rents skyrocketing. During the early 1920s the Amalgamated, the ILGWU, and a group consisting of tenants' leagues, religious organizations, and an insurance company came to the conclusion that the housing problem of the working class could only be solved by applying the principle of "collective self-help" and thereby eliminating the landlords and their excessive profits. At its annual convention in 1924 the Amalgamated passed a resolution in favor of building a housing cooperative. And a year later the Amalgamated Clothing Workers Corporation, which had been formed by Abraham Kazan and other members of the Amalgamated's credit union, acquired thirteen acres in the North Bronx, at the edge of Van Cortlandt Park, for what would become the Amalgamated Houses. At the same time the ILGWU joined forces with a few other needle trades unions to sponsor a $2 million housing cooperative in the South Bronx, which would be designed by Andrew J. Thomas and constructed by the Labor Home Building Corporation. Known as the Thomas Garden Apartments, it would provide homes on the Grand Concourse for roughly 170 working-class families.[33]

Besides the support of some influential New Yorkers like Clarence Stein, the needle trades unions had a couple of other things going for them. During the 1920s the United States was in the midst of a nationwide "Own Your Own Home" campaign. Led by the US Department of Labor and the National Association of Real Estate Boards, the campaign was based on the deep-seated (and long-standing) view that homeowners were better, happier, more productive, and more responsible than tenants. As Secretary of Commerce Robert Lamont said in 1931, "It is doubtful whether democracy is possible where tenants overwhelmingly outnumber home owners." The Own Your Own Home campaign was focused on the residents (or prospective residents) of single-family homes. But many New Yorkers were convinced that the benefits of homeownership applied to apartment-house dwellers as well. Starting in the late nineteenth century, a few New Yorkers had built cooperative apartment houses for the well-to-do, mainly on the Upper East Side and other posh Manhattan neighborhoods. Several others followed suit after World War I. And in an effort to circumvent the Emergency Rent Laws, which imposed rent control in New York and Buffalo in 1920, still others converted rentals into cooperatives. A few housing cooperatives were also erected for the middle class, the most notable of which was Jackson Heights, a group of garden apartments in Queens built by Edward A. MacDougall after World War I. Although some Americans believed that it was better for workingmen to rent than to own—indeed one public official told a group of city planners, "There is no more hazardous investment than city property"—many others were convinced that what was good for the well-to-do and the middle class was good for working people too.[34]

At the outset both the Thomas Garden Apartments and the Amalgamated Houses ran into serious financial trouble. Not long after it broke ground for the Thomas Garden Apartments, the Labor Home Building Corporation found that it had underestimated the cost of construction. In an attempt to salvage the project, it sold the site to John D. Rockefeller Jr., the oldest son of the founder of Standard Oil and a staunch conservative who favored cooperative housing as a way to head off public housing. The apartment house, a five-story walk-up, was finished in 1927. Rockefeller also financed the erection of three other housing cooperatives for working people, the largest and best known of which was the Paul Laurence Dunbar Apartments in Harlem. Also designed by Andrew Thomas, it was one of the only housing cooperatives in New York for African Americans. When completed in 1927, it provided homes for more than 500 families. The Amalgamated Houses also languished for a while, mainly because Kazan and his associates were unable to raise the capital. But things changed after 1926, when, in an attempt to spur low-income housing and promote slum clearance, the state legislature passed the Limited-Dividend Housing Companies Act. Under this act, which was administered by the newly created New York State Board of Housing, cities were allowed to exempt new residential construction from property taxes for up to twenty years—provided the housing company raised one-third of the capital from shareholders; limited its dividends to 6 percent;

and charged no more than $12.50 per room per month in Manhattan, $11 in Brooklyn and the Bronx, and $10 in Queens and Richmond. If certified by the Board of Housing, the company would be exempt from state taxes and fees and, in some cases, could be granted the power of eminent domain.[35]

More than a year after the state legislature passed the 1926 housing act, the municipal authorities adopted an ordinance that empowered the city to grant a tax abatement for up to twenty years to any limited-dividend company that built a new apartment house before January 1, 1937. In the meantime, Kazan met with Darwin James, chairman of the State Board of Housing. Shortly afterwards the board designated the newly formed Amalgamated Housing Corporation as the state's first limited-dividend housing company. Sidney Hillman then prevailed on the Metropolitan Life Insurance Company to give the corporation a twenty-year first mortgage of $1.2 million, which was enough to cover two-thirds of the cost of the Amalgamated Houses. (Metropolitan Life was one of the few major New York corporations that had made an effort to solve the city's housing problem. Under a 1922 state law that allowed insurance companies to invest up to 10 percent of their assets in low- and moderate-income housing, it had underwritten the construction of 2,000 apartments in Long Island City that rented for $9 a room.) Under the 1926 law, the shareholders had to provide the other one-third of the capital, or about $625,000, which came to $500 per room. But many prospective shareholders did not have the money. Kazan therefore appealed to the Amalgamated Bank, which agreed to lend them one-half of the $500. And to attract New Yorkers who could not afford even $250 a room, he persuaded the *Daily Forward*, the city's leading Yiddish-language newspaper, to set up a $150,000 line of credit at the Amalgamated Bank, whose president, Adolf Held, was also president of the *Forward*. Prospective shareholders who could come up with half the money could then borrow the other half from the bank, using their equity as collateral. The *Daily Forward* also made the Amalgamated Housing Corporation a short-term loan of $125,000 when construction costs exceeded the original estimate.[36]

To design the Amalgamated Houses, Kazan hired Springsteen & Goldhammer, a firm that had been formed in 1919 by two former Cooper Union students, George W. Springsteen and Albert Goldhammer, who built a thriving practice in the 1920s, specializing in apartment houses mainly in the Bronx. Ground was broken on Thanksgiving Day 1926, and the formal opening took place on Christmas Day, by which time all but one of the buildings were finished. The event attracted hundreds of New Yorkers, many of whom had already bought one of the 303 apartments and some of whom attended a dinner in the evening at which Fiorello H. La Guardia, Belle Moskowitz, Jacob Panken, the city's first socialist judge, and other dignitaries praised the Amalgamated's housing cooperative. What the new residents, their guests, and other visitors saw was a group of six five-story walk-up brick buildings designed in mock-Tudor style. Occupying only half the site, they were erected around a large rectangular courtyard (with a fountain in the middle). This "interior park of exceptional beauty," wrote Edith Elmer Wood, provided ample space for lawns, trees, and even birds. As Abe Miller, one of the many garment workers who moved into the Amalgamated Houses, said in 1928, "Where we used to live in New York there was never a blade of grass to be seen and nothing grew but rent." Now "the grass is at my door-way," he remarked, and "when I wake up in the morning the birds sing for me." By New York standards, the apartments, which had from two to six rooms, were spacious. They had central heating, electric lighting, gas stoves, hardwood floors, and well-equipped bathrooms. And all the rooms had windows that provided the residents with plenty of fresh air and natural light as well as views of the courtyard, Van Cortlandt Park, and the Jerome Park Reservoir.[37]

For New York's working-class families, the Amalgamated Houses was "quite a big bargain," Kazan later recalled. Besides putting down a modest $500 a room, they paid only $11 per room per month in maintenance fees (or carrying charges), which was substantially less than what most tenants paid to rent comparable apartments in the city. For this fee, which was enough to cover the fixed costs and operating expenses, the residents got more than just spacious and sanitary apartments, but also a wide range of services and amenities that were designed, in Kazan's words, to make the Amalgamated Houses "a community rather than just an apartment house." Among these services were a cooperative grocery store, a cooperative laundry, tearooms, gymnasiums, reception rooms, soundproof music rooms, a nursery, a kinder-garten, and even an auditorium. The Amalgamated Houses favorably im-pressed many Americans. La Guardia called it "the greatest step forward in housing improvements ever made in this city." The *Times* agreed, noting that it was "the finest and largest development of low-rent housing in the entire city." Edith Elmer Wood wrote that it was without doubt "the best and most successful cooperative housing thus far seen in the United States." And Louis Pink, a member of the State Board of Housing, went so far as to say that it was "perhaps the finest tenements yet erected by anybody." Even more important to Kazan and his associates, the Amalgamated Houses was so attractive to many New Yorkers that all the apartments were occupied almost as soon as the buildings were completed—one-third by members of the Amalgamated, one-sixth by members of other needle trades unions, and the remaining one-half by other workers, professionals, and small tradesmen.[38]

As Peter Eisenstadt has written, 1927 was a banner year for the fledgling cooperative housing movement in New York. Besides the Amalgamated Housing Corporation, three Jewish fraternal organizations completed large housing cooperatives in the Bronx that year. The United Workers Association, many of whose members were Communists, built a group of five-story apartment buildings on Allerton Avenue that housed 339 working-class families. A year later it erected another group of buildings with 365 units. A Jewish nationalist group formed the Yiddische Cooperative Heim Association, which put up the Shalom Aleichem Houses on a site overlooking the Jerome Park Reservoir, not far from the Amalgamated Houses. It provided housing for 220 families. And the Jewish Workers' Cooperative Homes Association, which had roots in the socialist-Zionist movement, built a housing cooperative with 125 apartments on Williamsbridge Road. It erected another in early 1928 and then yet another, sponsored by the Farband Cooperative Housing Corporation, later in the year. At about the same time Kazan, who was the manager (and a resident) of the Amalgamated Houses as well as president of the Amalgamated Housing Corporation, found that he had hundreds of applications for apartments in his office, but no vacancies. So at his behest, the corporation decided to construct two other housing cooperatives adjacent to the Amalgamated Houses, one on a site it owned and the other on land it bought. Metropolitan Life provided most of the money, and the rest came from the New York Trust Company. The Amalgamated made loans to prospective residents who could not afford the $500 per room. When completed, one in the late 1920s and the other in the early 1930s, the new buildings added more than 300 apartments to the Amalgamated Houses.[39]

By virtue of these and other more modest efforts, New York was in the forefront of the fledgling cooperative housing movement, well ahead of Chicago, Philadelphia, Detroit, and other cities. Indeed, by 1930 one-half of the cooperative housing in the United States—the value of which exceeded $500 million—was in New York. But virtually all of New York's housing cooperatives were in Brooklyn and the Bronx, not in Manhattan and especially not on the Lower East Side. As the *Times* wrote in 1902, of all the city's neighborhoods the Lower East Side was the one "that stands most immediately in need of reform." It was there "that the metropolitan population is densest and that the various evils, moral and sanitary, constituting our great tenement problem are specially aggravated and pervasive." Although a strong supporter of the model tenement movement, the *Times* had taken the City and Suburban Homes Company to task for erecting its tenement houses on the Upper East and West Sides. But Gould and his successor, Allan Robinson, were reluctant to build on the Lower East Side. So were Kazan and his associates. For one thing, the neighborhood was so congested that there was virtually no vacant land. And what little land was on the market consisted mainly of small and prohibitively expensive parcels. For another thing, it seemed extremely risky to put up an apartment house that, in Kazan's words, would be "surrounded by a sea of slums." Even more skeptical was Alexander M. Bing, president of the City Housing Corporation, which constructed many posh apartment houses in Manhattan (and also developed Sunnyside Gardens in Queens and Radburn in New Jersey). To erect an apartment house on the Lower East Side, he said, would be "like planting a rose in an ashcan of garbage."[40]

Things changed not long after Franklin D. Roosevelt succeeded Al Smith as governor in January 1929. Following in Smith's footsteps, Roosevelt began to look for ways to spur the rebuilding of the Lower East Side. He invited Aaron Rabinowitz, a prominent real estate man and member of the State Board of Housing (and its representative on the board of the Amalgamated Housing Corporation), to meet with him, Lieutenant Governor Herbert H. Lehman, and others in Albany. At the meeting Rabinowitz said that it was possible to build spacious and sanitary apartments on the Lower East Side— and not as a philanthropic enterprise, but as a sound business proposition. Lehman, a former partner at Lehman Brothers, an investment bank that had been founded by his father and two of his uncles, and a onetime trustee of the Henry Street Settlement, was intrigued. He asked Rabinowitz if it was possible to build a housing cooperative on the Lower East Side for no more than $12.50 per room per month, the maximum allowed for a limited-dividend company under the 1926 housing act. Rabinowitz assured him that it was. Shortly afterwards the two men joined forces and soon came up with $800,000, part of which they used to buy a square block on the Lower East Side bounded by Grand, Columbia, Broome, and Delancey Streets. They also agreed to finance construction until all the apartments were sold and to set up a fund from which prospective purchasers could borrow part of the initial $500-a-room payment. Since neither Rabinowitz nor Lehman, both of whom were very impressed by the Amalgamated Houses, had ever built a housing cooperative, they decided that rather than develop the site themselves they would ask Kazan and his associates to take over the project and construct and manage the buildings.[41]

Kazan was leery about building on the Lower East Side, afraid that a failure there would deal a serious setback to the cooperative housing movement. But he deferred to Hillman, who believed that the Amalgamated had much to gain and—since Rabinowitz and Lehman were putting up the money—nothing to lose. Shortly afterwards the union formed the Amalgamated Dwellings Corporation, a limited-dividend company, with Hillman as president, Kazan as vice president (and de facto general manager), and Rabinowitz as treasurer. Kazan retained Springsteen & Goldhammer to design the project and persuaded the Bowery Savings Bank, which had a large financial stake in the Lower East Side, to lend the company $960,000. Demolition began in late 1929, and construction ended a year later. What was known as the Amalgamated Dwellings consisted of a group of six- and seven-story elevator buildings at the center of which was a 24,000-square-foot courtyard. (The design so impressed the American Institute of Architects that it awarded the Amalgamated Dwellings a medal for the best example of a six-story apartment house erected in 1930.) The 236 apartments, 50 percent with one bedroom, 40 percent with two bedrooms, and 10 percent with three bedrooms, were large, bright, well ventilated, and well equipped. Like the Amalgamated Houses, the Amalgamated Dwellings included a handful of cooperative enterprises and a host of services and amenities, among them a playground on the roof of one of the buildings. By the time the Amalgamated Dwellings received a certificate of occupancy, only half of the apartments had been sold, partly because of the reputation of the Lower East Side and partly because of the downturn in the American economy. But by late 1931 all but five of them were occupied.[42]

oOo

Neither Hillman nor Kazan was inclined to rest on his laurels. At the banquet that followed the formal opening of the Amalgamated Houses, Hillman said that the union was already planning to build another housing cooperative with as many as 1,000 apartments elsewhere in New York, possibly somewhere on the Lower East Side. Kazan also wanted to press ahead, not only to provide quality housing for working-class New Yorkers but to set an example for wage earners everywhere in the country as well. "It was my hope," he later recalled, "that [cooperative housing] would not be limited to the city of New York, but would extend to other cities, and [in the process would eventually] solve the housing problem." If things went as planned, both Kazan and Hillman believed that before long garment workers and other Americans of "moderate means" would be "housed in dwellings of a very different character from that they have been compelled to live in for the last generation." But things did not go as planned. Even before they finished the Amalgamated Dwellings, the United States was caught up in the Great Depression, by far the worst economic crisis in its history. The stock market plummeted, banks collapsed, businesses foundered, and unemployment skyrocketed. With builders reluctant to build and investors hesitant to invest, residential construction of every kind—rental and cooperative, single-family and multifamily—came to a standstill. During 1933 and 1934, when the depression was at its worst, 115 apartment houses were constructed in New York, only 2 percent as many as in 1923 and 1924.[43]

As Kazan observed in mid-1932, the Great Depression was "the acid test" for cooperative enterprise, and especially cooperative housing. At issue now was not whether additional housing cooperatives would be built, but whether the existing ones would survive. The Amalgamated Houses was hit very hard. Many residents lost their jobs, and many others had to take pay cuts. Before long some were hard pressed to pay their monthly carrying charges, without which the Amalgamated Housing Corporation could not make its mortgage payments and meet its operating expenses. Indeed, so many residents fell behind that by 1936 the corporation had more than $150,000 in unpaid carrying charges. To make ends meet other residents decided that they had no choice but to move out, sell their shares in the cooperative, and ask management to return their equity. Although management had a moral obligation to give them back the money they had invested, it had not set up a reserve fund to repurchase the shares. So long as there was a strong demand for the apartments (and a long waiting list of prospective purchasers), Kazan had not seen a need for such a fund. But during the depression the demand weakened and the waiting list dwindled. Many working-class New Yorkers could no longer afford to invest $1,500 to $2,500 in an apartment. And in view of the economic downturn, many others thought it was too risky. With vacancy rates rising and housing prices falling, many New Yorkers now thought that it made more sense to rent an apartment than to buy one. For Kazan this was a serious problem. A failure to honor its commitment to repurchase the shares would not only discourage New Yorkers from moving into the Amalgamated Houses but also make cooperative housing much less appealing.[44]

As the economy went from bad to worse, Kazan took a number of steps to ease Amalgamated Houses' fiscal plight. Following his cooperative principles, he set up a relief fund, to which each resident was asked to contribute a minimum of $1 a month. (The money would be returned, without interest, when the crisis was over.) Needy residents could borrow up to $400, without interest, but with a flat fee of 2 percent to cover handling costs. Although the fund was voluntary, many residents who still had jobs made generous contributions. To help the Amalgamated Housing Corporation repurchase the shares of residents who moved out, Kazan also diverted funds from the project's cooperative shops and services. At one point what was known as the A.H. Consumers Society held $275,000 worth of the corporation's stock. Although it ran counter to his beliefs, Kazan even rented some of the vacant apartments. Under a complicated arrangement, the tenant put down $100 a room and then signed a two-and-a-half-year lease at a fixed rent that was slightly higher than the monthly carrying charges. At the end of the lease, he could move out and get back his initial payment. Or he could buy the apartment for $500 a room, which a good many did. Kazan was not sure that this arrangement was legal. Nor did he ask the State Board of Housing to approve it, which he probably should have done. But as he pointed out, "We were too preoccupied to save the organization to [worry about] whether it was legal or not." So long as the board was convinced that a resident was making a genuine attempt to pay his maintenance fees, management would take no action against him. But it was prepared to oust anyone who could afford to make his payments but refused to do so.[45]

By virtue of these steps, the Amalgamated Houses was able to cover its fixed costs, pay its operating expenses, and honor its obligations to the shareholders. So was the Amalgamated Dwellings, which was not hit as hard by the depression as the Amalgamated Houses. Most of its residents, many of whom were professionals and small shopkeepers, still had jobs. And thanks to Rabinowitz and Lehman, who authorized a loan up to the par value of the stock, the Amalgamated Bank was able to provide the Amalgamated Dwellings Corporation with the money to buy back the shares of the residents who moved out of their apartments. The Finnish-American housing cooperatives in Brooklyn also weathered the storm. But as Andrew S. Dolkart has pointed out, most of New York's other housing cooperatives failed. Among the most notable failures were the Thomas Garden Apartments and the Allerton Avenue Apartments, which were commonly referred to as the "coops." At the Thomas Garden Apartments, which had been started by a consortium of needle trades unions and then taken over by John D. Rockefeller Jr., so many of the residents lost their jobs that by 1934 only 24 of its 166 apartments were still cooperatives. At the Allerton Avenue Apartments, the ownership of which had been transferred from the United Workers Association to a mortgage company in 1928, management initially refused to evict the unemployed residents who could not pay their maintenance fees (and even let in other unemployed workers who had lost their homes). But in 1933 the mortgage company went bankrupt; the new owner treated the "coops" as a rental property and sold it to a private landlord a decade later.[46]

Writing in the mid-1930s, Kazan acknowledged that the cooperative housing movement had not made much progress in the United States. It was very hard, he pointed out, to persuade lending institutions to provide the necessary funds and to convince prospective purchasers to invest their life savings in what they viewed as a highly speculative venture. But Kazan was not discouraged. In a relatively short time he had accomplished what few people thought possible: the construction of high-quality, low-cost housing in New York City. Taken together, his three projects—the Amalgamated Houses, the Amalgamated Dwellings, and another housing cooperative with 115 apartments that went up in the Bronx in the late 1920s—housed more than 850 working-class families. The Amalgamated Houses impressed not only housing experts like Edith Elmer Wood and Louis H. Pink but also private developers like Alexander Bing. After visiting the Amalgamated Houses, he told his staff, "Here are a bunch of tailors who know nothing about construction, and nothing about selling real estate, and [yet] they succeeded in creating a large development and making it work." The residents, who took great pride in owning their own homes, were delighted. And as Rabinowitz observed, "Their whole lives changed. Overnight these people took on new standards. After a while 300 families, formerly unknown to each other, lived in peace and tranquility and with a sense of consideration for each other that was beautiful." Even more remarkable to Kazan was the Amalgamated Dwellings, which he called "an oasis in the desert," a beacon of hope in a neighborhood "surrounded by dilapidated buildings, old rickety tenement houses where filth and disease are plentiful."[47]

Although the Great Depression took a heavy toll on cooperative housing, Kazan remained steadfast in his belief that it was the only solution to the housing problem. Unlike private enterprise, which he held responsible for

the sorry state of housing in America's cities, cooperative housing was designed to build homes for people rather than to generate profits for investors.
And unlike public housing, which some Americans now favored as a way to
revive the moribund construction industry, it was designed to strengthen
the idea of self-help rather than to weaken it. Besides creating "a close bond"
among the residents, cooperative housing would turn each shareholder into
a "self-respecting citizen who has solved the housing problem through his
own initiative," thereby encouraging self-reliance as opposed to "helpless dependence." Not least of all, cooperative housing was a way to develop "the
idea of self-government."[48] Kazan remained optimistic that cooperative
housing would surge once the depression was over. And given his experience in building and managing the Amalgamated Houses and Amalgamated
Dwellings, he was as well prepared as anyone to lead the surge. He knew
that it might be a few years before the depression was over. But what he did
not know—what he could not have known—was that shortly after the nation
started to recover from the depression it would go to war against Germany,
Japan, and Italy. For the duration there would be little money, material, or
labor to build cooperative housing or anything else that was not needed to
win the war.

CHAPTER 2

COOPERATIVE HOUSING AFTER WORLD WAR II

Late in 1945, a few months after the end of World War II, *Life* magazine warned that the nation was facing "an acute housing shortage." The shortage, which was estimated at 3.5 million dwellings, left many Americans "shocked and bewildered," wrote *Life*. "Everywhere people desperately sought places to live. In San Francisco a family of four moved into a renovated mortuary and called it home. In Omaha a newspaper advertisement read, 'Big icebox 7 by 17 feet. Could be fixed up to live in.'" Elsewhere homeless veterans were demanding that barracks and war plants be converted into houses and even threatening to march on Washington. A million families were already doubling up, said *Life*, living with in-laws, relatives, and friends. And given that only 460,000 new homes would be built in 1946, there would be three times as many families in the same bind the next year. The situation was especially dire in New York City, which had a shortage of 430,000 dwellings. To make matters worse, many New Yorkers lived in substandard apartments, more than 100,000 of which lacked private toilets and nearly 250,000 of which had no central heating. With the vacancy rate below 1 percent, the lowest since the late 1910s and early 1920s, tens of thousands of New Yorkers were forced to double up or live in Quonset huts and other temporary structures. As Walter Mansfield, a former captain in the Marine Corps, told a reporter in 1945, it was "far easier to locate a sniper in the jungles of China than to find an apartment in New York City." Several years later Ira S. Robbins, executive vice president of the Citizens Housing and Planning Council, a civic group whose members included some of the city's largest real estate developers, said, "Decent housing at a moderate price is scarcer [in New York] than deer on Central Park lawns."[1]

The origins of the postwar housing shortage went back to the late 1920s and early 1930s, when the nearly decade-long boom petered out. Residential construction, which had come to a virtual standstill during and immediately after World War I but picked up in the mid-1920s, began to decline in 1929 and 1930. In New York City fewer than 2,000 apartment houses were built in 1929 and fewer than 1,000 in 1930, down from under 4,000 in 1926 and nearly 5,000 in 1927. Things went from bad to worse in the city during the Great Depression, which reached its nadir in the mid-1930s: builders erected only 52 apartment houses in 1933 and only 63 in 1934, far fewer than in any year since the turn of the century. All told, they put up fewer than 3,000 apartment houses in the 1930s, down from almost 25,000 in the 1920s. Moreover, for every apartment house that was built in New York between 1931 and 1940, nearly three were demolished. Residential construction started to revive slowly in 1939 and 1940. But it declined sharply again after the nation entered World War II. Hamstrung by the wartime ban on non-essential construction, New York City's builders erected only eleven apartment houses in 1943, twenty in 1944, and five in 1945. Indeed, fewer apartment houses were added to the city's housing stock in the 1940s than in any other decade in the twentieth century. Small wonder that so many veterans like Captain Mansfield were hard pressed to find housing in New York and other big cities when they came home.[2]

According to many public officials and other experts, no group was hit harder by the postwar housing shortage than the millions of American families that earned between $2,000 and $4,000 a year. Making up about one-third of the population, they were what New York State Housing Commissioner Herman T. Stichman called "the 'forgotten famil[ies].'" They made too little to afford private housing, especially private housing in New York and other big cities, and even to take advantage of the Housing Act of 1934, a New Deal measure that was designed to stimulate the construction industry and thereby reduce unemployment in the building trades. Under this act the Federal Housing Administration (FHA) encouraged builders to build and lenders to lend by insuring residential mortgages, most of which were written for single-family homes in suburban communities. These "forgotten famil[ies]" also made too much to qualify for public housing. As I pointed out earlier, the campaign for public housing got underway shortly after World

War I, when many Americans lost faith that private enterprise could provide decent housing for working-class families. But it made little headway until the mid-1930s, when the Roosevelt administration gave its support to a bill, sponsored by Senator Robert F. Wagner of New York, that would become the Housing Act of 1937. Under what was known as the Wagner-Steagall Act, the United States Housing Authority was empowered to make grants to local public housing authorities, which would build apartment houses and lease the units to families whose income did not exceed five (or, in some cases, six) times the rent. The many working-class families that earned too little for private housing and too much for public housing were in a "no-man's land," said Robbins in 1949. For them, "the outlook is particularly bleak."[3]

In the eyes of Robbins and other New Yorkers, the outlook was bleak not only for these working-class families—many of whom, wrote a *Times* reporter in 1952, still "live in old tenements that are in violation of building laws, share inadequate quarters with other families, or skimp on food and other necessaries to pay out a disproportionate share of their wages to landlords"—but also for the nation's cities. Unable to find apartments in the cities, many working- and middle-class residents moved to the suburbs. This exodus, which was facilitated by federal mortgage insurance (and later by federal highway programs), did serious damage to both the cities and the suburbs, wrote a New York State task force on housing. It deprived the cities of the "hard working, conscientious, and responsible citizens ... without whom neither business nor government can function." It also reduced the cities' retail trade, depressed their tax base, and accelerated the spread of blight in many of their older residential neighborhoods. At the same time it forced the suburbs, which were inundated by a huge wave of newcomers, to build schools, streets, sewers, and other facilities that imposed a heavy burden on their taxpayers. Unless much more housing was built for middle-income families, wrote a *Times* reporter, most experts believed that New York would soon become "an urban core inhabited mainly by those wealthy enough to afford luxury apartments or poor enough to remain in slums or qualify for public housing. And it will be surrounded by a metropolitan area of small homes peopled by the middle class who abandoned the city voluntarily or were forced out by high rents." The consequences would be dire, said Robert W. Dowling, the president of City Investing Company, a major New York real estate firm. "Both the one-class middle-income suburb and the two-class city made up of the highest and lowest income groups are uneconomic, antisocial, un-American and undemocratic," he declared.[4]

There were a few ways to alleviate the postwar housing shortage in New York and other cities, some experts believed. One was to encourage private builders to take advantage of the state's limited-dividend housing program, which was designed to reduce the cost of housing (and thus the rent of apartments) by providing tax abatements for new residential construction. Another way was to persuade the municipal authorities to put up more public housing, the demand for which so far exceeded the supply that there was a waiting list of more than 300,000 families in New York City in the early 1950s. Yet another was to promote the construction of nonprofit housing cooperatives in which low-income families could buy an apartment for a down payment of $250 a room and carrying charges of $14.50 per room per month. Cooperative housing could go a long way to alleviating the housing shortage, said Stichman. Abraham E. Kazan agreed. "If capably managed," he said in 1947, cooperative housing "offers one of the few opportunities for the moderate-income family to obtain new housing at this time." Other prominent New Yorkers also thought that cooperative housing was extremely promising. Among them were Robert Moses and Louis H. Pink, a former chairman of the New York State Board of Housing and a member of the New York City Housing Authority. Even some of New York's leading real estate men were in favor of cooperative housing. Dowling was one. Another was David Tishman, president of Tishman Realty and Construction Company, who endorsed cooperative housing in 1947 after returning from a tour of Scandinavia. He was especially impressed by what he saw in Sweden, where cooperatives provided housing for low-income families in 120 of the country's 125 towns.[5]

Tishman urged the United States to follow Sweden's lead and make nonprofit cooperative housing an integral part of national housing policy. Thus far the federal government had been reluctant to do so. The issue had come up more than a decade earlier, when Rexford G. Tugwell, head of the Resettlement Administration, and a few other members of Franklin D. Roosevelt's administration came out in favor of federal aid for housing cooperatives for low- and middle-income families. Tugwell's position was shared by several housing experts, among them Edith Elmer Wood, Clarence S. Stein, and Catherine K. Bauer, all of whom believed, as Bauer told a congressional committee in 1935, that private enterprise was "totally unable to provide adequate new housing at a rental or sale which families in the middle and lower income group can pay." Also in favor of cooperative housing was Herbert U. Nelson, executive vice president of the National Association of Real Estate Boards, the industry's leading trade group. Nelson saw cooperative housing as a bulwark against public housing, which he viewed as "European socialism in its most insidious form." But while Congress was willing to provide mortgage insurance for middle-class Americans and public housing for working-class Americans, it was unwilling to provide support for cooperative housing in the 1930s, perhaps in part because of what historian Matthew Gordon Lasner calls the widespread belief that such housing "was fine for the rich, but not for the middle class, let alone the working class."[6] Whether Congress would be more receptive to cooperative housing after World War II—whether it would see it as a partial solution to the postwar housing problem—remained to be seen.

OOO

The issue came to a head shortly after President Harry S. Truman delivered the annual State of the Union Address in early January 1950, a little over a year after he stunned the nation by defeating the Republican candidate, New York State governor Thomas E. Dewey. In line with his pledge to ensure a "Fair Deal" for the American people, Truman called on Congress to "enact new legislation authorizing a vigorous program to help cooperatives and other nonprofit groups build housing which [lower-middle-income] families] can afford." ("Lower-middle-income families" was how Truman and other Americans referred to working-class families after World War II.) There was "no reason why decent homes should not be within the reach of all," he said, adding, "We have laid the groundwork for relieving the plight of [low- and middle-income] families in the Housing Act of 1949," which he had signed in mid-July. This act, also known as the Taft-Ellender-Wagner Act, was the first comprehensive housing act since the Wagner-Steagall Act. To help low-income families, it empowered the United States Housing Authority to make grants and loans to local housing authorities to build 810,000 new low-rent public housing units. And to help middle-income families, it increased by $500 million the amount the FHA was authorized to provide in mortgage insurance for private housing. (The act also provided $1 billion in loans and grants to enable cities to redevelop slums and blighted areas, about which more later.) But despite the passage of the Taft-Ellender-Wagner Act, Truman pointed out, there was still "an acute shortage of housing" for lower-middle-income families. Now it was time for Congress to turn its attention to this group, which, in the words of Charles Abrams, a New York lawyer and longtime advocate of housing reform, had thus far been "almost completely ignored."[7]

Although the Democrats regained control of both the Senate and the House in November 1948, it was far from clear how Congress would respond to Truman's call for federal aid for cooperative housing. Several months earlier Senator John Sparkman, a Democrat from Alabama, had introduced a bill to amend the Housing Act of 1949. At about the same time Representative Brent Spence, a Democrat from Kentucky, filed a similar bill. Included in both bills was a provision, known as Title III, which established a Cooperative Housing Administration (CHA), a separate and, like the FHA, largely autonomous agency within the Housing and Home Finance Agency (HHFA). Authorized to spend up to $500 million (and, with the approval of the president, up to $1 billion), the CHA was empowered to make direct government loans to help housing cooperatives and other nonprofit groups build homes for lower-middle-income families. The interest rate would be 3 percent, and the amortization period would be sixty years. To raise funds for these loans, the CHA would issue bonds and sell them to the Treasury Department. By virtue of the low interest rate, the long amortization period, the elimination of speculative profits, and the economies of cooperative enterprise, it was estimated that the price of a two-bedroom apartment would be reduced to about $62 a month. This was one-third less than the price of a similar apartment insured by the FHA and, said the Senate Committee on Banking and Currency, well within the reach of the millions of "hard-working citizens" who earned between $2,500 and $4,000 a year and made up "the backbone of this country." It was estimated that at least 60,000 dwellings (and, if the president approved the appropriation of an additional $500 million, as many as 120,000) would be built under this program.[8]

The Sparkman bill (S. 2246) was referred to the Senate Committee on Banking and Currency, whose Subcommittee on Housing and Rents, chaired by Sparkman, held hearings in late July. The Spence bill (H.R. 5631) was sent to the House Committee on Banking and Currency. Chaired by Spence, it held hearings in late July and early August. Both hearings, which went on for several days, were extremely contentious, especially when it came to federal aid for cooperative housing. Title III was supported by representatives of labor unions, veterans groups, religious organizations, and consumer groups, all of which argued that federal aid for cooperative housing was the only way to provide decent homes for lower-middle-class families. It was opposed by spokesmen for financial institutions, real estate interests, and other business groups, all of which insisted that direct loans to housing cooperatives would do irreparable harm to market housing in particular and to private enterprise in general. Despite this opposition, a sharply divided Senate Committee on Banking and Currency reported the Sparkman bill out in early August, though it reduced the amortization period from sixty to fifty years. But the bill languished in the Senate, in part because of a lack of support from the Truman administration, whose chief spokesman, Raymond M. Foley, administrator of the HHFA, had serious reservations about Title III. As he saw it, the proposal to provide direct loans to housing cooperatives and other nonprofit groups marked such a "substantial departure" from existing federal policies that it required more "careful study." Things went no better in the House, which passed the Spence bill in late August, but only after deleting the provision to provide $1 billion for direct loans to housing cooperatives and other nonprofit groups.[9]

The campaign for federal aid for cooperative housing picked up a few days after Truman delivered his State of the Union Address. Leading the campaign was Senator Burnet R. Maybank, a former mayor of Charleston and governor of South Carolina who was chairman of the Senate Committee on Banking and Currency. Maybank had recently returned from Europe, where he had been favorably impressed by the housing cooperatives there. Convinced that they were sorely needed in the United States, he set out to deal with the objections to federal aid for cooperative housing that had been voiced at the Senate hearings a few months earlier. And with Sparkman's blessing, he introduced several amendments to S. 2246. Instead of the Cooperative Housing Administration, the amended bill established the National Mortgage Corporation for Housing Cooperatives (NMCHC) as a division of the HHFA rather than as a separate, largely autonomous agency within it. The NMCHC was empowered to make long-term, low-interest loans to housing cooperatives, but its bonds would be sold not to the Treasury Department but on the open market—that is, to banks, insurance companies, savings and loan associations, and other private lending institutions. The loans would be insured by the federal government and capped at $2 billion. The amended bill had the strong support of the Truman administration, which viewed it as a big improvement over the original bill. While it was not a "final and complete answer to all of the [country's] housing problems," said Foley, it was a "much needed and desirable addition to the present housing programs of the Federal Government." And so was a similar bill, H.R. 6618, which had been introduced in the House by Representatives by Spence.[10]

The second round of hearings, which were held in late January and early February, were even more contentious than the first round. In favor of the amended bills—though not of the provision that moved the program from a separate, largely autonomous agency of the HHFA to a division within it—were the same groups that had supported the original bills. As William Green, president of the American Federation of Labor (AFL), argued, private builders were not capable of meeting the nation's "minimum housing needs." They had put up only slightly more homes in 1949 than in 1925, when the United States had 35 million fewer people. And most of the new homes were too expensive for lower-middle-class families. Given that cooperative housing could be built for less than conventional housing, Green urged Congress to pass the amended bills as soon as possible. Robert F. Wagner Jr., borough president of Manhattan and spokesman for Americans for Democratic Action, agreed. So did Rev. John O'Grady, secretary of the National Conference of Catholic Charities, who pointed out that cooperative housing would provide much-needed housing for lower-middle-class families, many of which were being displaced to make way for highways and other public improvements. It would also provide much-needed housing for many hard-strapped World War II veterans, said Robert S. Dinger, a spokesman for the American Legion. Cooperative housing worked well in Europe, argued Jerry Voorhis, executive secretary of the Cooperative League of the USA. Citing the success of other cooperative enterprises in the United States, he saw no reason why it would not work well here. Under the amended bills, all the federal government was being asked to do was to make long-term, low-interest loans to housing cooperatives with money provided by private lenders.[11]

These claims were groundless, the opponents of the amended bills told the congressmen. Speaking for the same groups that had opposed the original bills, they pointed out that residential construction was booming. Since the end of the war, said Rodney M. Lockwood, president of the National Association of Home Builders, private builders had constructed 3.5 million new homes, enough to house 13 million families. In 1949 alone they built one million homes, which was, he pointed out, "an all-time record." Many of these homes were well within the reach of the lower-middle class, added John C. Thompson, president of the National Association of Real Estate Boards, most of whose members did not share Herbert U. Nelson's belief that cooperative housing could serve as a bulwark against public housing, especially not after the passage of the Housing Act of 1949. Private enterprise was fully capable of solving the housing problem without the intervention of the federal government, insisted William A. Reckman, a spokesman for the American Bankers Association. It had already made great progress. And now, he went on, "is the time for a respite from further legislation to give private enter-prise an opportunity to finish the job." Nor was there any evidence that co-operative housing could be built for less than conventional housing, argued Oscar R. Kreutz, a spokesman for the National Savings and Loan League. Cooperative housing might reduce costs, but only because of the extremely generous loans that were authorized by the amended bills. Since it would not be subject to what he called the "hard-boiled management" of real estate de-velopers, it might even raise costs. And pointing to the dismal record of co-operative housing in New York during the Great Depression, Kreutz warned that it was a very risky venture.[12]

The amended bills were a form of "class legislation," declared Thomp-son. They provided long-term, low-interest loans for some Americans, but not for others. As well as unfair, they were inflationary, Kreutz argued. By funneling $2 billion into the housing market, they would drive up the cost of labor and materials and thereby raise the price of conventional housing. The amended bills would also undermine the government's existing housing pro-grams. Both the Federal Housing Administration and the Veterans Admin-istration were authorized to insure residential mortgages, but only for much shorter terms and at much higher rates. If the amended bills were passed, said Thompson, "what inducement would there be for the so-called middle-income family, veterans or nonveterans, to use FHA or VA loans?" And how, asked Horace Russell, a spokesman for the National Savings and Loan League, could the savings banks, life insurance companies, and other lend-ing institutions compete with an agency like the NMCHC that was autho-rized to issue such "uneconomic and unrealistic" loans? In time the federal government would come to dominate the residential mortgage business, to the detriment not only of the private lenders but also of their depositors and policyholders. "Now is the time to stop it," Lockwood argued. The amended bills were no less objectionable than the original bills, he pointed out. The long-term, low-interest loans were nothing but "a thinly disguised form of direct lending." To say that they would promote private enterprise was gob-bledygook. Indeed, said Russell, the amended bills were "pure socialism," a view that was shared by Richard M. Hurd Jr., vice president of Teachers In-surance and Annuity Association and son of the late Richard M. Hurd, one of the country's foremost real estate economists.[13]

The supporters of the amended bills vigorously denied these charges. The federal government was already doing a good deal to provide housing for the lower and middle classes. There was no reason why it should not do as much for the lower-middle class. Far from discouraging builders from building and lenders from lending, the new program would promote the stability of the construction industry and create new opportunities for private investment. And, said O'Grady, it would also foster homeownership, which was widely regarded as one of the strongest bulwarks against socialism and communism in the postwar period. Housing cooperatives were no more socialistic and communistic than agricultural cooperatives and consumer cooperatives, insisted Voorhis. Cooperative enterprise had deep roots in American society, Walter P. Reuther, president of the United Auto Workers and chairman of the national housing committee of the Congress of Industrial Organizations (CIO), told the Senate Committee on Banking and Currency. It was not something that was "brought over in a black bag from Moscow." Pointing to John D. Rockefeller Jr., Howard C. Shepard (president of National City Bank), Beardsley Ruml (chairman of the board of R. H. Macy's), Gerard Swope (former president of General Electric), and other prominent businessmen and corporate executives who were in favor of cooperative housing, he said, "Anybody who attempts to say that these fellows are advocating isms in America is either insane or downright dishonest." By charging that cooperative housing was a step toward socialism and communism, the opponents of the amended bills were waging "an ideological battle just to throw up smoke screens and confuse the issue [in an attempt] to block [the construction of] decent housing [for lower-middle-class families]."[14]

After concluding its hearings, the Subcommittee on Housing and Rents approved S. 2246 on February 7 by a vote of six to one—and on a motion by Paul Douglas, an Illinois Democrat, it also turned the NMCHC back into a separate, largely autonomous agency. Two days later, however, the Committee on Banking and Currency voted seven to six to defer action for two weeks, pending a study of the bill's impact on the national economy. Although Thomas B. McCabe, the chairman of the Federal Reserve Bank, spoke out against the bill, Maybank, Sparkman, and their Democratic colleagues pressed ahead. They rejected an amendment sponsored by two Republicans—Irving M. Ives of New York and Charles W. Tobey of New Hampshire—that would have eliminated the NMCHC and in place of it authorized the FHA to insure individual mortgages for housing cooperatives. After reducing the government's commitment from $2 billion to $1 billion, putting the NMCHC back under the HHFA, and making other concessions, the committee approved S. 2246 by a vote of nine to four. The bill, which reached the floor of the Senate in mid-March, provoked a heated debate over cooperative housing. Leading the opposition was John W. Bricker, a Republican from Ohio and the only member of the Subcommittee on Housing and Rents to vote against the bill, and Harry P. Cain, a Republican from Washington. Both senators argued that the cooperative housing provision was unnecessary and that its long-term, low-interest loans were discriminatory, inflationary, and, worst of all, socialistic. On March 15 Bricker offered an amendment to strike the provision from S. 2246. Although Maybank and Sparkman strongly opposed the amendment, enough southern Democrats joined forces with conservative Republicans that it was adopted by a vote of forty-three to thirty-eight. With that issue resolved, the bill was passed by a voice vote.[15]

The cooperative housing measure ran into stiff resistance in the House as well. At the outset its prospects seemed bright. On February 22 the Committee on Banking and Currency reported out H.R. 6618 by a vote of eleven to four, and two weeks later the Rules Committee voted by a narrow margin to send the bill to the floor of the House. But before it reached the floor, the Senate adopted the Bricker amendment. And the House Republican Policy Committee, a group of twenty-five prominent congressmen, announced that it would oppose the cooperative housing measure. The debate began on March 22. Leading the opposition was Jesse P. Wolcott of Michigan, the ranking Republican on the Committee on Banking and Currency, who said of the measure, "It's inflationary, it's discriminatory, [and] it's socialistic." Siding with Wolcott was Charles W. Vursell, a Republican from Illinois, who denounced the measure as "a wild-eyed spending scheme" that follows "the Moscow party line." Although several congressmen from both parties, among them Eugene J. McCarthy, a Democrat from Minnesota, and Jacob K. Javits, a Republican from New York, defended the measure, its supporters realized that they did not have the votes. In a last-ditch attempt to save it, Wright Patman, a Texas Democrat, offered two amendments, one that reduced the funding for the NMCHC from $2 billion to $500 million and another that raised the interest rate on its loans from 3 to 4 percent. Although supported by Spence, chairman of the Committee on Banking and Currency, both were defeated. Wolcott then moved to strike the cooperative housing measure from the bill. With 81 Democrats joining 137 Republicans, the House approved the motion by a vote of 218 to 155. By a lopsided margin, it then passed the bill, which was now known as H.R. 7402.[16]

Two weeks later Senate and House conference committees met to iron out the differences between S. 2246 and H.R. 7402. The result of nearly twelve hours of almost continuous negotiations was a bill that provided additional funds for the FHA and generous loans for World War II veterans, but virtually nothing for cooperative housing. What became the National Housing Act of 1950 was then approved by both houses and sent to the president. Although Truman, who had lobbied hard for federal aid for cooperative housing, was sorely disappointed, he signed the act on April 21. The defeat of the cooperative housing measure was due in large part to the opposition of the many conservative Republicans who voted in favor of the Bricker amendment and the Wolcott motion. Also decisive was the opposition of the many southern Democrats who broke ranks with the congressional leadership and the Truman administration. It did not help that the measure was opposed not only by the chairman of the Federal Reserve Bank but also by the United States Chamber of Commerce, a highly influential business group that shared the Fed's concern about inflation. Nor did it help that Tighe E. Woods, a high-level official at the HHFA, said at a press conference in late February that the long-term, low-interest loans for cooperative housing "[didn't] make sense." And not least of all, it did not help that the debate over federal aid for cooperative housing coincided with the second great Red Scare in American history. Indeed, it broke out shortly before the Senate adopted the Bricker amendment, when Senator Joseph R. McCarthy of Wisconsin declared in a speech to the Republican Women's Club of Wheeling, West Virginia, that he had a list of 205 members of the Communist Party who were working in the State Department.[17]

Speaking to the Mortgage Bankers Association of America shortly after the National Housing Act of 1950 was passed, Senator Sparkman insisted that federal aid for middle-income cooperative housing was not a "dead issue." Vowing to continue his campaign, he predicted that Congress would enact the necessary legislation "sooner or later." But as he later found out, the campaign had lost much of its momentum. Most congressmen, Democrats as well as Republicans, were reluctant to authorize the federal government to make long-term, low-interest loans for cooperative housing. All they were willing to do was to approve an amendment to Section 213 of the National Housing Act of 1950 that empowered the FHA to insure mortgages for middle-income housing cooperatives. The mortgages could cover up to 90 percent of the replacement costs—and up to 95 percent if World War II veterans made up at least half of the prospective purchasers—but in no case more than $8,100 a dwelling and $1,800 a room. Under this amendment, moreover, cooperative housing had no advantages over conventional housing. In both cases the amortization period was no longer than forty years and the interest rate was no lower than 4 percent. At the outset it was not clear whether many housing cooperatives would take advantage of Section 213. Nor was it clear whether they would be developed by nonprofit cooperatives or by commercial builders. What was clear was that whether cooperative housing was going to help the many lower-middle-income families that could not afford private housing and did not qualify for public housing depended not so much on what was done in the nation's capital as on what was done in its other cities.[18]

ooo

In no American city were the prospects of nonprofit cooperative housing brighter than in New York. No other city had wrestled longer and harder with the housing problem of the working class. Indeed, for decades New York had led the way in the campaigns for tenement-house reform, model tenements, and public housing. And it now stood, wrote one observer in *Architectural Forum* in the late 1950s, as "the unrivaled 'co-op' capital in the nation, both in the luxury type and in the lower-middle-income type." It was also the home of Abraham E. Kazan, who was widely regarded as the father of nonprofit cooperative housing in the United States, and the site of his two greatest achievements, the Amalgamated Houses and the Amalgamated Dwellings, both of which had survived the Great Depression and now provided high-quality housing for thousands of middle-income families. Writing in *Survey Graphic* about the Amalgamated Houses in the late 1940s, Evelyn Seeley remarked, "The twenty-year record of this country's pioneering cooperative housing project points a way to decent homes for everyone." In the words of Jacob S. Potofsky, president of the Amalgamated Clothing Workers of America, it had dispelled "once and for all the fiction that decent living is only for the privileged." As for the Amalgamated Dwellings, Seeley went on, this "modern and bright and airy" development was "a shining example ... of what cooperative effort can do [even] in the midst of dilapidation." Writing in the *Ladies' Home Journal* a decade later, Margaret Hickey observed that the Amalgamated Dwellings provided "*HOMES*, NOT JUST HOUSING." And through its cooperative governance and cooperative activities, it also fostered a strong sense of community.[19]

New York was also home to a great many nonprofit groups, among the most important of which were its labor unions. In 1947 the city had more than 1,100 private-sector union locals, whose roughly one million members

made up one-quarter to one-third of the workforce. Among them were small
ones, like the Wholesale Paint Salesmen's Union, and large ones, like the
Transport Workers Union Local 100, whose 35,000 members ran New
York's mass transit system. Also among them were industrial unions, such
as the Industrial Union of Marine and Shipbuilding Workers of America, and
craft unions, such as the Ironworkers Local 40, whose members assembled
the steel frames for the city's skyscrapers. Especially powerful were the needle trades and building trades unions as well as the unions that represented
workers in communications and entertainment. Thanks to the growth of the
city's economy, the support of the Roosevelt administration, and above all
the passage of the National Labor Relations Act of 1935, which gave workers the right to organize and engage in collective bargaining, many of New
York's unions were larger and stronger than ever in the late 1940s and
early 1950s. A case in point was the International Ladies' Garment Workers' Union, the city's largest labor organization. When David Dubinsky took
over as president in 1932, the ILGWU had fewer than 25,000 members, who
were sharply divided along ethnic, religious, and ideological lines. It was also
broke. By 1950 its membership had grown to 150,000. Committed to improving the lives of its members outside the sweatshops, it operated sixteen medical clinics, four radio stations, and a resort in the Poconos. When Dubinsky
stepped down as president in 1966, the ILGWU had 450,000 members and
half a billion dollars in pension funds, welfare funds, and reserves.[20]

Few labor unions and nonprofit groups had the wherewithal of the
ILGWU. And even fewer were able and willing to undertake large-scale cooperative housing on their own. Indeed, the Amalgamated Clothing Workers
would probably not have built the Amalgamated Houses if the state legislature had not passed the Limited-Dividend Housing Companies Act of 1926,
which empowered New York and other cities to grant a tax abatement to
new residential construction for up to twenty years. And the Amalgamated
would probably not have erected the Amalgamated Dwellings if Aaron Rabinowitz and Herbert H. Lehman had not provided the capital to acquire the
site and underwrite the construction.[21] Things were much the same after
World War II. On their own New York's labor unions and other nonprofit
groups would have been hard pressed to build cooperative housing that
was within the means of lower-middle- and middle-income families. They
would also have been hard pressed to acquire the sites for large-scale housing cooperatives and to raise the capital to cover the costs of construction.
They therefore needed help from both the state and the city. And they got

it, thanks in large part to the support of such powerful officials as Nelson A. Rockefeller, governor of New York State from 1959 to 1973; Robert F. Wagner Jr., borough president of Manhattan from 1950 to 1953 and mayor of New York City from 1954 to 1965; and Robert Moses, the longtime chairman of the Triborough Bridge and Tunnel Authority who was also the New York City Construction Coordinator, a member of the New York City Planning Commission, and chairman of the New York City Slum Clearance Committee (SCC) in the late 1940s and 1950s.

In their efforts to build cooperative housing after World War II, New York's labor unions and other nonprofit groups had a few things going for them, chief among them a handful of state, local, and federal programs that were meant to stimulate residential construction and promote slum clearance. The oldest of these programs was adopted in 1920, when the state legislature enacted more than a dozen laws that imposed rent control in New York and other big cities. Most of what were known as the Emergency Rent Laws were designed to prevent rapacious landlords from taking advantage of hard-strapped tenants. But one, chapter 949, was designed to alleviate the acute postwar housing shortage. Enacted over the objections of many owners of prewar apartment houses, chapter 949 empowered the state's cities and towns to exempt new residential structures from property taxes until January 1, 1932, provided that construction was completed after April 1, 1920, or commenced before April 1, 1922, and completed within two years (or, if already under construction, by September 17, 1922). As an enabling act, chapter 949 had to be approved by New York City's Board of Aldermen, where it triggered a long, drawn-out battle. Its supporters argued that the law would stimulate residential construction and thereby alleviate the housing shortage. Its opponents countered that the law was a "sop" to real estate interests and would cost the city tens of millions of dollars that could be better spent on building homes for working people. The issue was resolved in February 1921, when the Board of Aldermen voted to adopt chapter 949, though only after limiting the tax abatement to $5,000 for each house and up to $1,000 for each room and no more than $5,000 for each apartment. Although Fiorello H. La Guardia, president of the Board of Aldermen, called the measure "a monumental blunder," the Board of Estimate gave its approval a month later.[22]

Even after chapter 949 went into effect, it remained highly controversial. Its supporters credited the law for the tremendous surge in residential construction in New York City in the early and mid-1920s—a surge, they stressed, that had done much to alleviate the postwar housing shortage. Its opponents responded that the surge was a result not so much of the tax abatement law as of the pent-up demand. They also pointed out that the rents in virtually all the new apartment houses, and especially the new Manhattan apartment houses, were well beyond the means of New York's lower- and middle-class families. (Chapter 949 was also challenged in the courts. Early in 1923 John M. Tierney, a Bronx municipal court judge who had been elected to the State Supreme Court in 1916, held that the law was unconstitutional. But shortly thereafter the First Department of the Appellate Division overruled him.) Chapter 949, which was set to expire in 1922, was extended to 1923 and then to 1924. And in 1924, after a round of hearings by the New York State Commission of Housing and Regional Planning, the state legislature passed a bill that would have extended it for another year, a bill that was signed by Governor Alfred E. Smith. But after another long, drawn-out battle, in which the opposition contended that chapter 949 was a boon for builders, not for tenants, and that it was a way to raise profits, not to lower rents, the Board of Aldermen refused to give its approval. In the absence of strong backing from New York City, the state legislature allowed chapter 949 to lapse in April 1925, after only five years, but not before it had set a precedent that New York was prepared to exempt new housing from property taxes as a way to stimulate residential construction.[23]

Although Governor Smith had signed the Emergency Rent Laws in his first term, he never wavered in his belief that the best way to protect New York's hard-strapped tenants from rapacious landlords was not to impose rent control but to encourage residential construction. In his third term, after losing to Republican Nathan L. Miller in 1920 and defeating him two years later, he prevailed upon the state legislature to pass the Limited-Dividend Housing Companies Act of 1926, which was designed to spur private builders to erect housing for working-class families under the supervision of a new State Board of Housing. To hold down costs, the act included a tax abatement for new residential construction for up to twenty years. (The rule of thumb, Robert Moses later said, was that a full [or 100 percent] abatement would reduce rents by $12 per room per month and a partial [or 50 percent] abatement by $6 per room per month, which were not trivial amounts for most lower- and middle-class families.) To deal with the objections that tax abatements were a boon for builders but not for tenants—that they did nothing but encourage the construction of upper-middle- and upper-class apartment houses in Manhattan and single-family homes in the outer boroughs—the act provided that in order to qualify for an abatement a company would have to agree to limit its dividends to 6 percent and to charge no more than $12.50 a room in Manhattan, $11 a room in Brooklyn and the Bronx, and $10 a room in Queens and Richmond. A year later the Board of Aldermen and the Board of Estimate approved the act. Not long after the State Board of Housing designated the Amalgamated Housing Corporation as New York's first limited-dividend housing company, thereby paving the way for the construction of the Amalgamated Houses.[24]

Also included in the Limited-Dividend Housing Companies Act of 1926 was another more controversial provision, one that would in time have far-reaching implications for the nonprofit cooperative housing movement. The provision, which was designed as much to promote slum clearance as to stimulate residential construction, employed the power of eminent domain in a novel way. At the request of a limited-dividend housing company, and with the approval of the State Board of Housing, the city would condemn the land on which the company intended to build, paying no more than fair market value. Whether the housing was rental or cooperative did not matter. The city would then transfer the property to the company, which would reimburse the city for its expenses.[25] The provision was designed to solve a problem with which the governor, who had grown up on the Lower East Side, was familiar. A great many people owned real estate not only on the Lower East Side but also in the Gas House District, a run-down neighborhood in the East Twenties, and in other purported slums and blighted areas. Although most of the buildings there were old and dilapidated, they were highly profitable and thus extremely valuable. Hence many of the property owners were unwilling to sell except at highly inflated prices—and perhaps not even then. It was therefore very hard, if not impossible, for most developers to assemble enough land at a reasonable price to build one or more large apartment houses for lower- and middle-income families in these neighborhoods. Although Rabinowitz and Lehman would soon acquire the land for what became the Amalgamated Dwellings without taking advantage of eminent domain, other developers would later see it as the only way to solve a very knotty problem.

The Limited-Dividend Housing Companies Act did much less than expected to stimulate residential construction and promote slum clearance. Taking effect two years before the onset of the Great Depression, its timing left much to be desired. Most existing housing cooperatives went under in the 1930s. And not even Abraham E. Kazan, who was working day and night

to keep the Amalgamated Houses and Amalgamated Dwellings afloat, was
inclined to undertake new ones. Nor did the 1926 act spur private builders to erect middle-income housing in the slums and blighted areas. Thus in
an attempt to induce savings banks and insurance companies to invest in
these neighborhoods, Robert Moses and a few other influential New Yorkers prevailed upon the state legislature to enact the Redevelopment Companies Law of 1942 and then to amend it a year later. As amended, the law
allowed these institutions to invest in limited-dividend housing companies
and construct middle-income housing. It also empowered the city to condemn property in slums and blighted areas and sell it to designated redevelopment companies. The law also gave the companies a tax abatement
for up to twenty-five years. It contained limits on dividends and rents, but
allowed the companies to circumvent these limits by repaying the accrued
exempt taxes. It was under this law that the Metropolitan Life Insurance
Company, which had built a large middle-income housing project in Queens
in the 1920s and a much larger one in the Bronx in the late 1930s and early
1940s, erected Stuyvesant Town and Peter Cooper Village in the Gas House
District shortly after World War II. And it was after this law was enacted
that Kazan started thinking about building a large housing cooperative on
the Lower East Side adjacent to the Amalgamated Dwellings.[26]

Given that the fair market value of real estate in the slums and blighted
areas was very high, there were limits as to how much property could be
condemned under the Redevelopment Companies Law. But these limits
were largely removed when Congress passed Title I of the Housing Act of
1949. Under Title I, which was a radical and even unprecedented measure,
the cities could take property in slums and blighted areas, clear it, and then
sell the vacant land to developers at a reduced price, a price that was low
enough to assure them a reasonable return. Strongly supported by downtown businessmen, big-city mayors, and city planners, most of whom were
trying hard to find ways to curb decentralization, Title I was not designed
to provide decent housing and pleasant neighborhoods for the low-income
residents of the slums and blighted areas. Rather it was designed to induce
the well-to-do to move back from the periphery to the center and thereby
shore up the central business districts and ease the cities' fiscal plight. Although the developers were supposed to build "predominantly residential"
structures, they could erect not only high-priced apartment houses but also
office buildings, convention centers, and other commercial facilities. Moreover, a year before Congress passed the Housing Act of 1949, Mayor William

O'Dwyer appointed Robert Moses, who was already City Construction Co-ordinator, chairman of the Slum Clearance Committee. As a result, no city was better prepared to take advantage of Title I than New York. And though Moses "generally hated unions and held workers in contempt," historian Joshua B. Freeman writes, he was more than willing to work with Kazan and his supporters in the labor movement.[27]

Eminent domain and tax abatements were powerful inducements for prospective developers of middle-income housing. But before they could build, they had to come up with the capital. And with only a few exceptions—the most conspicuous of which was Metropolitan Life, one of the country's wealthiest companies—they had to borrow it. Most savings banks and in-surance companies were reluctant to invest in what they regarded as highly risky ventures. Governor Smith had tried to resolve this problem in the mid-1920s, when he urged the state legislature to include in what became the Limited-Dividend Housing Companies Act of 1926 a provision that would have created a state housing bank and empowered it to provide funds to cover two-thirds of the projects' costs. But in the face of stiff opposition from Republican legislators, the proposal was shelved. And that was where things stood until 1955, a year after W. Averell Harriman was elected gov-ernor, when the state legislature passed the Limited-Profit Housing Compa-nies Act—also known as the Mitchell-Lama act, after its sponsors Senator MacNeil Mitchell, a Manhattan Republican, and Assemblyman Alfred A. Lama, a Brooklyn Democrat. Under this act the state was authorized to pro-vide long-term, low-interest loans to private companies for up to 90 percent of the cost of new middle-income housing projects. To finance the loans, the state would issue general obligation bonds. The Mitchell-Lama act also gave the housing companies tax abatements of 40 to 100 percent for thirty years. For their part, the companies were obliged to cap their return on equity at 6 percent. And to ensure that the new apartment houses were occupied by middle-income families, the law restricted access to families whose income was no more than six (or, in some cases, seven) times the rent or, in the case of cooperatives, the carrying charges.[28]

The Mitchell-Lama act was a major breakthrough, but it had a serious drawback. Under the New York State Constitution, the state could issue general obligation bonds only if they were approved in a statewide refer-endum. Before the passage of the Mitchell-Lama act, the voters tended to support bond issues for housing. But afterwards, Hilary Botein points out, their support ebbed, especially in upstate New York. A $100 million bond

issue was defeated in 1956. And though another $100 million bond issue
was narrowly approved two years later, it was clear to Nelson A. Rockefeller, who was elected governor in 1958, that the state had to do more to stimulate private investment in middle-income housing. Hence he appointed a
blue-ribbon task force to look into the issue in early 1959. Chaired by Otto L.
Nelson Jr., vice president in charge of housing for the New York Life Insurance Company, it was made up of a dozen bankers, businessmen, civic leaders, and government officials. The task force submitted an interim report in
March and a final report in May, in which it warned that the acute housing
shortage was responsible for the exodus of middle-class families to the suburbs and the spread of blight in New York and other big cities. Out of the task
force reports came a host of recommendations to stimulate the construction
of middle-income housing, by far the most important of which called for the
creation of the New York State Housing Finance Agency. At the urging of
Rockefeller, who argued that the SHFA would help solve the state's housing
problem by encouraging private capital to invest in low- and middle-income
housing—which, he said, was "the American way of doing things"—the legislature passed a law creating the nation's first state housing finance agency
in March 1960. The governor signed it a month later.[29]

One of many quasi-public authorities that proliferated during Rockefeller's fifteen years as governor, the SHFA was designed to increase the flow
of private capital into middle-income housing and, in the words of Senator
MacNeil Mitchell, break "the housing log jam." It was extremely successful,
at least in the short run. The SHFA owed its success in large part to what
Rockefeller called a "rather imaginative, somewhat ingenious" scheme that
was supposedly the brainchild of John N. Mitchell, a Wall Street lawyer (who
would later serve as Richard M. Nixon's attorney general and afterwards
would be convicted and imprisoned for his role in the Watergate scandal).
Under this scheme, the SHFA would issue "moral" obligation bonds, as opposed to "general" obligation bonds. These bonds were backed, not by the
full faith and credit of the state, but only by the promise that the state would
help out if the agency ran into financial problems. Hence they did not require
the approval of the state's voters. Nor were they subject to the state's constitutional debt limit. Given that moral obligation bonds were tax-exempt,
highly rated by Standard and Poor's, and deemed appropriate investments
for commercial banks by the US Comptroller of the Currency, the SHFA had
no trouble selling them—and selling them at relatively low interest rates. And
the lower the interest rates, the lower the construction costs and the rents

or carrying charges. Originally authorized to borrow up to $525 million, the agency sold so many bonds in the 1960s that by the early 1970s it had an outstanding debt of $3.8 billion. Before long the SHFA revived the Mitchell-Lama program, which had languished for a lack of funds, and thereby spurred the construction of middle-income housing, both rental and cooperative.[30]

OOO

Organized labor had built a good many housing cooperatives in New York City even before the state legislature passed the Mitchell-Lama act and created the State Housing Finance Agency. In the lead was the Amalgamated Clothing Workers of America, whose efforts were headed by Abraham E. Kazan, president of the Amalgamated Housing Corporation. Given that private housing could not be built to rent for less than $30 per room per month, which was far more than most working-class families could afford, Kazan believed that cooperative housing was the only way to solve the postwar housing problem. Even before the war he had wanted to construct another housing cooperative on the Lower East Side. And after the war he grew concerned that the Amalgamated Dwellings might soon be "engulfed by the surrounding slum buildings," a concern that was shared by the Bowery Savings Bank, which held the mortgage on the Amalgamated Dwellings and other Lower East Side properties. With the blessing of Jacob Potofsky, Kazan came up with a proposal to demolish sixteen blocks adjacent to the Amalgamated Dwellings and replace the old tenement houses with new housing cooperatives. He submitted the proposal, which would be carried out under the amended Redevelopment Companies Law, to the City Planning Commission, which referred it to Robert Moses, one of its most influential members. Moses rejected the proposal, saying it had no merit whatsoever. After recovering from what he called "a stunning blow," Kazan met with Moses, who by then was having second thoughts. In what was the beginning of a long and for the most part mutually beneficial relationship, Kazan and Moses hammered out an agreement under which the East River Housing Corporation (ERHC), which was headed by Kazan, would demolish four blocks of tenement houses adjacent to the Amalgamated Dwellings and build 800 cooperative apartments on the site.[31]

At the outset things went smoothly, at least by New York standards. The state housing commissioner designated the East River Housing Corporation a redevelopment company, and the City Planning Commission and the Board of Estimate approved the project, which was called the East River

Cooperative Apartments. Under prodding from Robert Moses, the city condemned the sixty-five tenement houses on the site and the ERHC took title in June 1946. At the request of Mayor O'Dwyer, the city granted the corporation a partial tax abatement. When it came to financing, however, Kazan ran into trouble. He had assumed that the Bowery and a handful of other savings banks would provide the mortgage, but the banks would not make the loan for less than 4 percent, a rate that Kazan believed would make the carrying charges too high for prospective residents. Kazan's close associate Louis H. Pink, a former New York State superintendent of insurance, suggested that he try the Mutual Life Insurance Company of New York. At the behest of Moses, Mutual Life agreed to lend the East River Housing Corporation $7 million at 3¼ percent. As a condition of the loan, however, Mutual Life insisted that East River obtain a completion bond, which the fledgling company was in no position to do. The problem was solved by Robert Szold, another close associate of Kazan's and a partner in the law firm that represented the Amalgamated Clothing Workers of America. Szold prevailed on the Edward A. Filene Good Will Fund, a Boston philanthropic foundation on whose board he sat, to provide a de facto completion bond by depositing $250,000 in the Amalgamated Bank. Construction started in July 1947. And three years later work was finished on the last of the three twelve-story apartment houses of what had by then been renamed the Hillman Houses, in honor of the founder and first president of the ACWA, who died in 1946.[32]

At about the same time that Kazan was working on a proposal to build the Hillman Houses in Manhattan, he was also drawing up a plan to enlarge the Amalgamated Houses in the Bronx. Under the plan, which was made public in March 1947, the Amalgamated Housing Corporation would construct five new buildings with 750 apartments, half of which would be reserved for veterans, on a site adjoining the Amalgamated Houses. The cost was $6.5 million. Since the Amalgamated Housing Corporation already owned the land, most of which was vacant, the project was relatively straightforward. But it still needed help from the state and the city. With State Housing Commissioner Herman T. Stichman and City Construction Coordinator Robert Moses in favor of the project, Kazan soon got what he needed. The state legislature lifted the ceiling on rents and carrying charges in limited-dividend projects outside of Manhattan from $13 to $15 per room per month. And at the behest of Mayor O'Dwyer, the Board of Estimate provided a partial tax abatement for thirty years. Once the state and the city approved the project, financing was no problem. The first of the new buildings, a twelve-story structure, was finished in March 1951, and the others, two of twelve stories and two of six stories, were completed not long after. At the end of the year the Amalgamated Clothing Workers of America held a dinner at Manhattan's Commodore Hotel to celebrate the completion of the last unit in its 25-year, $20 million program of low-cost cooperative housing. All told, it had built nearly 2,500 apartments that housed more than 9,000 people for only $12 to $15 per room per month, which was well within the means of most working-class families.[33]

Among the many labor unions that followed the ACWA's lead was Local 3 of the International Brotherhood of Electrical Workers (IBEW), one of the strongest of New York's building trades unions. Its president was Harry Van Arsdale Jr., who saw cooperative housing as a way to ease the housing shortage in the city and reduce unemployment in the building trades. In conjunction with the Joint Industry Board, which represented many of New York's electrical contractors, the IBEW came up with a plan that was unveiled by Commissioner Stichman in May 1949. Under the plan the IBEW and the Joint Industry Board would cosponsor a $20 million cooperative that would provide homes for more than 2,000 working-class families. Known as Electchester, a name suggested by an electrical worker in a contest sponsored by the IBEW, the project would be erected under the state's Limited-Dividend Housing Companies Act of 1926. Electchester would be located in Flushing, a neighborhood in Queens, the second-least developed of the five boroughs, on part of the site of the Pomonok Country Club, which was on the verge of disbanding. Although Robert Moses was miffed that the state was taking all the credit for a project that would need substantial help from the city, he supported it. So did Mayor O'Dwyer, Governor Dewey, and President Truman. Electchester was "an example that bears watching and emulation by other union-employer groups," wrote the *New York Times*. And, said Stichman, "it would serve notice to builders that if they don't get down to business and build houses people can afford, other groups [such as the IBEW] will join in other cooperative movements to build houses [such as those at Electchester]."[34]

As expected, the New York State Division of Housing and Community Renewal, which was headed by Stichman, approved the project. But when its sponsors applied to the Board of Estimate for a tax abatement, they ran into stiff resistance. "Veterans are paying taxes," said the president of the Taxpayers Union, "and I don't see why these groups should not also pay taxes." Electchester was not entitled to a tax abatement, added the president of the United Civic Council of Queens. It was not designed to clear the slums. Nor was it designed to provide homes for families that could not afford them. These objections notwithstanding, the outcome was never in doubt. After a spokesman for organized labor testified that both the AFL and the CIO had endorsed the project, the board granted the application. With substantial investments by union members and electrical contractors, the IBEW and the Joint Industry Board raised the necessary capital. Construction of the first of five phases of Electchester began in late 1950. Designed by Benjamin Braunstein, a Queens architect, and constructed by the Paul Tishman Company, a New York contractor, it was finished about a year later—and cited for excellence by the Queens Chamber of Commerce. The second phase got underway shortly afterwards. When the final phase was completed in the mid-1960s, Electchester consisted of 38 six- and three-story red brick buildings that cost nearly $30 million and housed more than 2,400 working-class families, most of whom were affiliated with the IBEW or the electrical industry. By charging less than comparable rental housing in Queens, offering prospective purchasers low-interest mortgages and interest-free loans, and providing a school, a shopping center, and a wide range of community facilities, the sponsors had no trouble selling the apartments, in some cases even before the buildings were finished.[35]

Another labor union that followed the ACWA's lead was the New York Typographical Union 6, which was commonly referred to as the "Big Six." Part of the International Typographical Union, which was founded in 1852, it had about 12,000 members, most of whom worked for the city's newspapers or in commercial printing plants. Although the printers would be hard hit by automation in the 1960s, their union was still a force to be reckoned with in 1958, when its president, Francis G. Barrett, announced that the Big Six intended to build 700 cooperative apartments in Queens. The project would be undertaken under the Mitchell-Lama act, which allowed the city to provide long-term, low-interest loans to nonprofit housing companies. It would be erected in Woodside, just off Queens Boulevard, on twelve acres, most of which were vacant. And it was expected to cost $12 million. The project, which would be made up of eight buildings of varying heights that covered only one-tenth of the site, would be designed by Frederick G. Frost Jr. and constructed by Ira S. Robbins, a prominent builder (and president of the City Club). In planning the project, Barrett had consulted with James Felt, chairman of the City Planning Commission, and James J. Crisona, borough president of Queens. Both strongly supported it. So did Mayor Wagner and Comptroller Lawrence E. Gerosa. As for why the Big Six was building its first housing cooperative, Barrett pointed out that its members earned on average about $7,000 a year, which left them in "that middle-income group which cannot afford conventional housing and is not eligible for subsidized housing." Only a project like the Big Six Towers, in which the down payment would be $500 a room and the carrying charges $22 per room per month, could provide them with decent housing at a reasonable price.[36]

Comptroller Gerosa approved the Big Six Towers in February 1959, and the Board of Estimate followed suit three months later. The board also gave the project a 40 percent tax abatement and a $14 million mortgage at 3½ percent for fifty years. Things went smoothly until late 1959, when David Minkins, who owned a five-acre parcel on the site, refused to sell it to the city, which, he claimed, was offering less than fair market value. (A Big Six spokesman responded that Minkins had asked $5 per square foot for land whose assessed value was 19 cents per square foot.) When the city moved to take the parcel by eminent domain, Minkins filed suit in state court, challenging the constitutionality of the Mitchell-Lama act and arguing that the city had no right to condemn property that was not needed for slum clearance or low-income housing. But a few months later Judge Arthur Markewich upheld the law and ruled that the city had the right to take Minkins's five acres. With that issue resolved, construction started, prompting a jubilant Mayor Wagner to say at the groundbreaking ceremony, which took place in December 1960, that the Big Six Towers was "another step toward our goal—the provision of housing for our many, valued middle-class families." Work went more slowly than expected, which Robbins blamed on the incompetence of the city's Housing and Redevelopment Board. "We met resistance of every possible kind," he said, "and on at least four occasions were able to get the program going again only by direct appeals to the Mayor." But the project was eventually finished, though with seven rather than eight buildings, all of which were from fourteen to seventeen stories tall. The first family, a printer, his wife, and their two daughters, moved into the Big Six Towers in August 1963, and the project was fully occupied by April 1964.[37]

Yet another labor union that followed the ACWA's lead was the Amalgamated Meat Cutters and Butcher Workmen of North America, which was founded in 1897 and represented retail butchers and packinghouse workers in New York and other cities. As early as 1949 the Amalgamated Meat Cutters came up with a plan to build a small housing cooperative for its members in Brooklyn's Crown Heights. Only the third housing cooperative to be sponsored by a labor union in New York City, it consisted of a group of six-story buildings that would cost just under $3 million and provide nearly 300 apartments for lower-middle-income families. Known as the Harry Silver Apartments, in honor of a union member who was killed while on a picket line in 1930, the project would be constructed under the Limited-Dividend Housing Companies Act of 1926. It was approved by the state in November 1949 and by the city in May 1950. By the time ground was broken in July 1951, all the apartments had been sold. About six years later the Amalgamated Meat Cutters drew up a plan for another small housing cooperative. Known as the Dennis Lane Apartments, it would be built in the Bronx at 181st Street and Belmont Avenue, a couple of miles south of the Amalgamated Houses, on land that had been condemned nearly sixteen years earlier as the site for a vocational school, which was erected elsewhere. The first privately constructed middle-income project to be financed by the city under the Mitchell-Lama act, it consisted of two fourteen-story buildings that would cost just over $4 million and contain just under 300 apartments. The project was soon approved by the state and the city, which not only sold the land to the union but also gave it a mortgage that covered 90 percent of the cost and a 40 percent tax abatement for thirty years.[38]

A few years later the Amalgamated Meat Cutters unveiled a far more ambitious plan, a plan for what would have been New York City's largest housing cooperative. Under the plan the union would build more than 5,000 apartments on forty acres of air rights over the New York Central Railroad's Mott Haven Yards in the South Bronx, a block east of the Grand Concourse. A Mitchell-Lama project, it would cost nearly $100 million. In October 1960 the City Planning Commission approved the first phase of what would be called Concourse Village, which would have almost 1,700 apartments and cost about $31 million, and hailed it "for creating needed middle-income housing without the displacement of families or business establishments." Two years later the State Housing Finance Agency gave the Concourse Village Housing Company a $30 million loan, the largest single loan yet made for middle-income cooperative housing. The SHFA also set up a $40 million fund that the city was authorized to draw on to make loans of up to $300 to prospective purchasers who could not afford to pay $550 per room. The general contractor was the Cauldwell-Wingate Company, which had to install more than 1,000 concrete columns to support the platform on which the six 25-story white brick buildings were erected. The first building was finished in 1965, the last one two years later. Altogether Concourse Village's six buildings contained 1,875 apartments. At first sales were slow, in part because many of the prospective purchasers, most of whom were white, changed their minds when they realized that they would be living alongside blacks. And though sales picked up after a while, the Amalgamated Meat Cutters shelved plans to build the second, third, and fourth sections, leaving the rest of the site in limbo for two decades.[39]

Many other labor unions made plans to build cooperative housing in New York City after World War II. Among them were the building trades unions, whose leaders viewed cooperative housing as a source of well-paying jobs as well as much-needed housing. At the urging of Robert Moses—and with the support of George Meany, president of the recently merged AFL-CIO—the lathers, steamfitters, plumbers, and operating engineers unions joined forces in the mid-1950s to sponsor a housing cooperative in the East Bronx that would contain 2,400 apartments and cost $35 million. Also among them were several unions whose members had no direct stake in residential construction. The Uniformed Sanitationmen's Association, a union in all but name that represented the city's garbagemen and was affiliated with the International Brotherhood of Teamsters, announced in 1959 that it intended to build a $6 million housing cooperative with 360 units in Queens on a long-abandoned city dump that had been the site of the World's Fair of 1939–1940. ("When people go by and see our project," said President John J. DeLury, "they'll say, 'See what the sanitation workers can do for themselves.'") A few years later the joint board of the Fur, Leather, and Machine Workers Union unveiled a plan to build a $3 million housing cooperative in Brooklyn as part of the Coney Island West urban renewal project. Named the Sam Burt Houses, in honor of the union's late president, it would provide housing for 144 middle-income families. Not long afterwards Local 1199 of the Hospital Workers Union, most of whose members were women, many of them African Americans and Puerto Ricans, announced that it was going to build a housing cooperative on 9.5 acres in East Harlem that would cost $80 million and provide apartments for 1,590 low- and moderate-income families.[40]

Of organized labor's many plans for cooperative housing in New York, not all made it off the drawing board. Perhaps the most spectacular failure was Litho City, which was sponsored by Local 1 of the Amalgamated Lithographers of America. Under the plan for Litho City, which was unveiled by its president, Edward Swayduck, in August 1961, the union proposed to build six 47-story buildings and three 41-story buildings above the New York Central Railroad's yards on the Upper West Side, from Sixtieth to Seventieth

Streets just east of the Hudson River. The project would provide middle-income housing for 25,000 New Yorkers and cost a whopping $250 million. At the request of Mayor Wagner, the union agreed to reserve 200 apartments with a northern exposure for artists who had been displaced from their studios elsewhere in the city. It also offered to construct a $15 million international student center. The plan aroused a good deal of opposition from nearby residents, public officials, and real estate men who were sorely concerned that Litho City would aggravate the traffic congestion in the neighborhood and block the river views from Lincoln House, a small housing cooperative, and Lincoln Towers, a huge rental complex that was being built by Webb & Knapp. But under strong pressure from Wagner—and with the conditional approval of Traffic Commissioner Henry A. Barnes—the City Planning Commission voted in October 1962 to certify the project as suitable for urban renewal and therefore eligible for federal funds under Section 221D3 of the National Housing Act of 1950. But it did so only after the Amalgamated Lithographers reduced the size of Litho City, which would now cost $200 million and provide housing for 12,500 people in fifteen 23- to 33-story buildings.[41]

Although the project still needed the approval of the City Planning Commission and the Board of Estimate, Swayduck was optimistic. Saying that Litho City has "got to be an architectural triumph, or I won't touch it," he asked a group of prominent architects, planners, and academics to help him choose a famous architect to join the design team, which was headed by Kelly & Gruzen, a well-respected New York firm. Among the group's recommendations were Philip Johnson and Paul Rudolph. Swayduck even thought of inviting President John F. Kennedy to attend a ceremony to mark the start of the project. (Ironically, a nine-foot model of Litho City was placed on display in Grand Central Terminal a day or two before Kennedy was assassinated on November 22, 1963.) But as a spokesman for the New York Central said, the project was "postponed and postponed." And in November 1965 the lease for the air rights expired. Swayduck blamed the railroad, saying that it had placed so many roadblocks in the way that "it [was] impossible to build." A spokesman for the railroad responded that the union was at fault because it had failed to deliver a performance bond. But as a *New York Times* reporter pointed out, Litho City's finances, "always something of a mystery, were at the heart of the project's collapse." Litho City was a private venture, not a Mitchell-Lama project, and so was not entitled to state funds. Since it was suitable for urban renewal, it was eligible for federal funds. But as a regional FHA director explained, the agency could not provide funds under Section 221D3 unless the city gave Litho City a 100 percent tax abatement. But at $38 per room per month, Litho City was not middle-income housing and did not qualify for a tax abatement. Swayduck said he was negotiating for another site in Manhattan, but nothing came of it.[42]

ooo

Many organizations other than labor unions also built cooperative housing in New York City after World War II. Among the first was a consortium of veterans' groups that formed the United Veterans Mutual Housing Corporation (UVMHC) in 1947. A nonprofit corporation that was backed by Commissioner Stichman and headed by James J. Munro, it was one of many organizations set up to solve the housing problem of returning servicemen and their families. To do so the UVMHC bought forty acres in Bayside, a quiet residential neighborhood in Queens, on which it proposed to erect more than a dozen two-story garden apartments to house 800 veterans and their families. Named Bell Park Gardens, the project was expected to cost $8.2 million. In March 1948 the Bowery Savings Bank provided the UVMHC with a $7.2 million mortgage for thirty-four years at 3.5 percent, and shortly afterwards the city gave the project a partial tax abatement. Ground was broken in November, by which time all but fifty apartments had been sold. The down payment was $240 a room, and the carrying charges were $14 per room per month. Speaking at the groundbreaking ceremony, Robert Moses praised the project, saying that it "fills the gap" between low-cost public housing and high-cost private housing. Commissioner Stichman added, "We cannot fill the need for housing with cooperatives alone, but I dare say we can build from 5 to 10 percent of it." The first residents moved in less than a year later. Bell Park Gardens was "the most exciting housing project I have ever seen," said Governor Thomas E. Dewey. It showed how a "free people" could solve the housing problem with private financing—and without the federal government. Not long after, the UVMHC built two other housing cooperatives that were near one another and not far from Bell Park Gardens—Bell Park Manor, with 550 apartments, and Bell Park Terrace, with 300.[43]

At the same time that James J. Munro was working on Bell Park Gardens, Louis H. Pink was setting up a nonprofit corporation to build a housing cooperative in Long Island City, a run-down Queens neighborhood that Robert Moses had slated for urban redevelopment. Known as the Joint Queensview Housing Enterprise, the corporation was headed by Pink, chaired by Gerard

Swope, the former president of General Electric, and supported by several of the nation's wealthiest and most influential businessmen, among them Bernard F. Gimbel, chairman of the board of Gimbels, and David Sarnoff, president of RCA. In late 1948 the corporation reached a tentative agreement with the city to purchase a largely vacant ten-acre site on which it planned to erect housing for 728 middle-income families. (To make sure that Queensview would be home to middle-income families, Pink and his associates imposed income limits on residents. They also welcomed African Americans and gave veterans a preference, though for only thirty days.) At Pink's request, the Mutual Life Insurance Company of New York provided Queensview with a $4.6 million mortgage for twenty-five years at 4 percent. The Board of Estimate not only approved the project but also granted it a tax abatement. Construction of the twelve 13- and 14-story buildings, which cost $5.8 million, got underway in the fall of 1949. After they were finished, Pink and his associates erected Queensview West, also in Long Island City. They also made plans to build a housing cooperative in Brooklyn called Kingsview, which was part of the Fort Greene slum clearance effort. Work began on the 290-unit project in 1955, shortly after Pink died and was succeeded by James Felt, a prominent real estate developer and former chairman of the City Planning Commission. It was completed a year later.[44]

Some organizations even built cooperative housing in Manhattan, which was no mean feat. One of them was the Morningside Committee on Cooperative Housing. It was set up by Morningside Heights Incorporated (MHI), a consortium of educational, religious, and medical institutions, chief among them Columbia University, that was formed in 1947 to stem the decline in the run-down Upper Manhattan neighborhood in which they were located. Headed by David Rockefeller, who had close ties to some of the Morningside Heights institutions, MHI worked with Robert Moses, who had designated Morningside Heights (and nearby Manhattanville) for slum clearance, to come up with a plan to redevelop the neighborhood under Title I. Included in the plan was a housing cooperative known as Morningside Gardens that would be erected under the Redevelopment Companies Law. Set on a nine-acre site just north of the Columbia campus, it consisted of six 20-story middle-income apartment houses. The plan, which was approved by the City Planning Commission in October 1951, provoked a long and bitter struggle, which has been well described by historian Joel Schwartz. Under enormous pressure from the many residents who were about to be displaced by Morningside Gardens, the Board of Estimate postponed action for over a year. The issue was resolved in early 1953 when the Truman administration approved a write-down for the project and the Board of Estimate gave the go-ahead. With the tenants ousted and their houses demolished, ground was broken in September 1955 for a project that cost $12.5 million, most of which was supplied by a syndicate of savings banks. Designed by Harrison & Abramovitz, the architects of the United Nations headquarters, it provided homes for almost 1,000 families, the first of whom moved in about two years later.[45]

Another organization that built cooperative housing in Manhattan was the New York City Municipal Credit Union (MCU), whose 44,000 members worked for the city government (or for the state and federal governments in the city). Together with the New York State Credit Union League, an association of 450 metropolitan-area credit unions, the MCU developed a plan to erect a $7.7 million (later $8.7 million) housing cooperative on a 4.5-acre site near City Hall and the Municipal Building that would house 400 (later 420) middle-class families. Made public in January 1956, what was called Chatham Green was a Title I project that would be constructed under the Redevelopment Companies Law. It was underwritten by the New York State Teachers' Retirement System, which provided a $7.3 million mortgage for twenty years at 5.25 percent. Much less controversial than Morningside Gardens, Chatham Green was approved without much fuss by the Board of Estimate in January 1958. It was also granted a tax abatement. At the groundbreaking ceremony, which took place in September 1959, Mayor Wagner noted that Chatham Green was New York's first housing cooperative to be sponsored by a credit union. "Let's hope," he said, "that the credit unions in other cities and states will take a leaf out of the local organization's book." A long and narrow 21-story building designed by Kelly & Gruzen, the architect of Concourse Village, Chatham Green was finished in March 1962. Even before then the Municipal Credit Union announced that it intended to erect another housing cooperative opposite Chatham Green, on the northern edge of Chinatown. Also a Title I project, it was named Chatham Towers. The project, which consisted of two 25-story buildings that cost $6.8 million and housed 270 middle-class families, was completed in 1966.[46]

Several other nonprofit organizations erected cooperative housing in New York after World War II. Among them were New York University and five other institutions of higher education that sponsored Village View in what is now the East Village; the Slovak Gymnastic Union, a group of Czech-Americans devoted to physical fitness, that sponsored the Masaryk Towers on the Lower East Side; and the Goddard-Riverside Community Center, a civic group that sponsored Goddard Towers on the Upper West Side. A good many private builders erected cooperative housing too. Among them was Stanley J. Harte, the son and grandson of prominent New York real estate developers and the sponsor of Lindsay Park. A Title I project for which the federal government earmarked $7.1 million, it was built on sixteen blocks in a run-down section of Williamsburg. Lindsay Park was designed to upgrade "the entire surrounding community," said J. Clarence Davies, the former head of the Housing and Redevelopment Board, the city agency that was supervising its construction. Estimated to cost $47.3 million, Lindsay Park consisted of seven 22-story buildings with 2,700 apartments, 70 percent of them cooperatives and the rest rentals. It also included two shopping centers, three swimming pools, glass-enclosed solariums on the roofs, and fallout shelters in the basements. The down payment was $530 a room, and the carrying charges $22.60 per room per month. As Lindsay Park was erected under the Mitchell-Lama act, the Board of Estimate gave it a fifty-year, low-interest mortgage of $41.3 million and a 40 percent tax abatement. The project, which involved the demolition of 189 run-down buildings and the relocation of 1,300 families and 300 businesses, was constructed in phases, the first of which got underway in March 1962 and the second not long after.[47]

Even the New York City Housing Authority, the nation's largest developer of public housing, considered cooperative housing an idea whose time had come. In 1955 it began to explore the idea of selling some of its projects for conversion into middle-income cooperatives. Owing to a lack of interest among prospective purchasers—and a concern that the change would raise housing costs by 80 percent—the authority shelved the idea three years later. But in 1960 Mayor Wagner announced that the authority planned to convert eight public housing projects that were under construction or in the pipeline into cooperatives. The objectives, Wagner explained, were to raise revenue for the city and reduce costs for the residents. Four of the projects were in Manhattan, and four in the outer boroughs. The authority then persuaded the state legislature to change the law to allow it to go ahead. It invited bids for the eight projects, the value of which ranged from under $4 million to over $31 million. It also looked for labor unions and other nonprofit groups to act as sponsors. Several labor unions, educational institutions, and private investors expressed interest. By late 1961 the authority had sold four of the projects, all of which were converted into middle-income cooperatives. The apartments, it turned out, were hard to sell. Some prospective purchasers objected to the design and location of the projects. Others were put off by the income limits imposed on the residents. Still others did not want to live alongside African Americans. Despite these drawbacks, the authority reached an agreement to sell three of the four other projects for conversion into cooperatives. In the words of the Cooperative League's Jerry Voorhis, the New York City Housing Authority's policy "opened a huge new door for cooperative housing."[48]

CHAPTER 3

THE UNITED HOUSING FOUNDATION

Probably no one was more gratified by the resurgence of cooperative housing in New York after World War II than Abraham E. Kazan. It was the cause to which he had devoted his life. With the backing of Sidney Hillman, president of the Amalgamated Clothing Workers of America, he had built the Amalgamated Houses and the Amalgamated Dwellings after World War I. Perhaps even more impressive, he had kept them afloat during the Great Depression. And after World War II he erected the Hillman Houses. But Kazan was not inclined to rest on his laurels. Although he was an extremely capable manager, he was not content just to run the Amalgamated Houses, the Amalgamated Dwellings, and the Hillman Houses. And though he was more knowledgeable about cooperative housing than anyone else, he was not content just to give advice to others, such as Louis H. Pink, the driving force behind Queensview and Kingsview, and Harry Van Arsdale Jr., the president of Local 3 of the International Brotherhood of Electrical Workers, the union that built Electchester. (After coming up with the idea for Electchester, Van Arsdale asked Jacob S. Potofsky, who had succeeded the late Sidney Hillman as president of the ACWA, about the Amalgamated's housing cooperatives. "I said," Potofsky later recalled, "'you go over and spend the day with Kazan. He'll tell you all about it.'"[1] What Kazan wanted to do was to build more housing cooperatives—and to encourage others to follow his lead. With the passage of the New York State Redevelopment Companies Law of 1942 and the Housing Act of 1949, he had reason to believe that the prospects for cooperative housing were brighter than ever.

But Kazan also had reason to be concerned that the Amalgamated, on which he depended so heavily, would continue to support his efforts. This concern spilled over in 1937, when Kazan wrote a letter to Hillman offering his resignation as head of the Amalgamated Housing Corporation. Kazan wanted the union to build a housing cooperative on land it already owned, almost certainly in the Bronx, but Hillman, for whom cooperative housing had never been a priority, refused to go along, perhaps out of fear that if the project failed it would tarnish the union's reputation. Although disappointed, Kazan did not resign. A decade later he ran into resistance from Potofsky too. After the Amalgamated sponsored the Hillman Houses, Kazan urged Potofsky to build another housing cooperative on the Lower East Side, one that would have run from Grand Street to the East River. Potofsky, who greatly admired Kazan, was extremely reluctant. "Kazan," he said, "what do you want—to build over the whole city?" Pointing out that the Amalgamated's board felt that enough was enough, he told Kazan, "We don't have to do everything. Interest other people." Asked a decade and a half later why the Amalgamated had not built much cooperative housing after the Hillman Houses, Potofsky replied that the Amalgamated was a labor union, not a housing company and that "we have our hands full." It was never the Amalgamated's objective to clean up the whole city, he pointed out. The union had demonstrated that it was possible to build cooperative housing for New York City's working-class families. Now it was up to other labor unions (and nonprofit groups) to continue what the Amalgamated had started.[2]

After World War II Kazan began to look for a way not only to reduce his dependence on the Amalgamated but also to build more housing cooperatives and spread his vision of cooperative living. He concluded that the best way would be to create an independent organization whose sole mission would be to promote cooperative housing. At first he tried to forge an alliance with the Finnish-Americans who had erected several housing cooperatives in Brooklyn after World War I (and kept them solvent during the Great Depression). But the Finnish-Americans were not interested. Kazan then joined forces with Shirley F. Boden, a strong supporter of cooperative housing, and James McFadden, a labor leader and later New York City's chief labor negotiator, who were attempting to form an organization of their own. Together they came up with the idea of creating not one but two new organizations. One was the United Housing Foundation. Incorporated in 1951, it would mobilize political and financial support for cooperative housing and educate the public about the benefits of cooperative enterprise. At Kazan's request, Pink agreed to serve as president. Besides Kazan, the board consisted of Boden; Robert Szold, attorney for the Amalgamated, its bank and its housing cooperatives; Percy S. Brown, treasurer of the Edward A. Filene Good Will Fund; and, among others, Frederick F. Umhey, executive secretary of the ILGWU and a close associate of its president, David Dubinsky. The other organization was the Community Services and Management Corporation, which was soon renamed Community Services, Inc. Although incorporated a year before the United Housing Foundation, it was always envisioned as a subsidiary of the UHF. CSI would be the general contractor of all the UHF-sponsored housing cooperatives. Kazan was its president, and besides Pink, Boden, and Szold, the board included Clarence S. Stein, the former chairman of the New York State Commission of Housing and Regional Planning.[3]

As Kenneth G. Wray has pointed out, the UHF got off to a rough start. Kazan strongly believed that the organization should focus its efforts on New York City. He also felt that it should adhere strictly to cooperative principles, even if it meant forgoing opportunities to build cooperative housing. Sharing his views were Pink, Szold, and Carl Stern, the former counsel to the New York State Board of Housing. But Boden believed just as strongly that the UHF should erect cooperative housing even in cases where it might have to sacrifice its cooperative principles. He also thought that the foundation should not confine its activities to New York City. Sharing his position was Roger Wilcox, a graduate of both Harvard and MIT who would later serve as president of the National Association of Housing Cooperatives. The two sides differed sharply over whether the UHF should take advantage of Section 213 of the National Housing Act of 1950, which encouraged the FHA to insure mortgages for middle-income housing cooperatives and thereby reduce interest rates and bring down construction costs. Boden had no reservations about participating in Section 213. But Kazan held that Section 213, which defined cooperatives so loosely that private builders were able to use it to build for-profit housing, was doing a great disservice to genuine cooperatives. And he would have nothing to do with it.[4] Since Kazan had recruited the other members of the board, Boden and Wilcox had little choice but to resign. Boden went on to set up the Middle Income Housing Corporation, later renamed the Association for Middle Income Housing, which was the general contractor for Morningside Gardens, Lindsay Park, and other housing cooperatives. Wilcox joined with Winslow Carlton and others to establish the Foundation for Cooperative Housing, which helped organize a good many housing cooperatives, most of them outside New York City.

After a while things settled down. Although Kazan did not become president of the UHF until 1957—when Szold, who had succeeded Pink in 1955, stepped down—he was in charge of the organization from the start. (He remained in charge until ill health forced him to take a leave in 1966 and retire a year later.) Before long Kazan took steps to strengthen the UHF. Drawing on his contacts in organized labor, cooperative housing, and the nonprofit sector, he recruited dozens of members. Among them were the ACWA, the IBEW, and a host of other private-sector unions as well as a couple of public-sector unions, among them Local 2 of the American Federation of Teachers and District Council 37 of the American Federation of State, County, and Municipal Employees. Kazan also brought into the fold dozens of housing cooperatives—not only the Amalgamated Houses and the Amalgamated Dwellings but also Bell Park Gardens, Morningside Gardens, and a few others sponsored by groups with which he was not affiliated—and some neighborhood associations and philanthropic organizations, including the Hudson Guild and the Workmen's Circle. Kazan also came up with a plan to finance the UHF, which had initially relied on membership dues of $50 a year and a loan of $500 a month from the Edward A. Filene Good Will Fund. Under this plan the CSI would charge a developer's fee of 1 percent on each of its projects, which it would turn over to the UHF. Since these projects cost millions, tens of million, and, in one case, hundreds of millions of dollars, the fees generated enough revenue to support the foundation's wide range of activities as well as to allow Kazan to give up his jobs at the Amalgamated Houses, Amalgamated Dwellings, and Hillman Houses and devote himself full-time to the UHF and CSI. As Wray has observed, this arrangement also enabled Kazan, as president of CSI, to control the purse strings of the UHF.[5]

As head of the UHF, Kazan had to decide which housing cooperatives to sponsor. Once a decision was made, he had to gain the approval of the City Planning Commission and the Board of Estimate, for which he needed the support of the mayor and other public officials, by far the most important of whom was Robert Moses. He also had to ask the city for a tax abatement, which was sometimes opposed by Comptroller Lawrence E. Gerosa. Moreover, Kazan had to secure long-term, low-interest loans from a savings bank or other financial institution, though after the State Housing Finance Agency was established raising capital was the least of the UHF's problems.

He also had to help find housing for the many tenants who would be displaced by his projects. As head of CSI, Kazan had to deal with the contractors and subcontractors to ensure that the apartments would not be too expensive for working-class families. And he had to deal with the building trades and other labor unions, which had the power to slow down construction and even bring it to a standstill. In these efforts, Kazan could count on the support of many of New York's labor leaders, among them Harry Van Arsdale Jr., head of the IBEW and, after 1958, president of the New York City Central Labor Council. Kazan could rely too on Herman J. Jessor, an architect who had worked with Springsteen & Goldhammer on the Amalgamated Houses and with George W. Springsteen on the Hillman Houses and later designed all the UHF's housing cooperatives. ("Probably no architect of equivalent obscurity has had as much impact on the visual landscape of New York," writes Joshua B. Freeman.)[6] Also of great help to Kazan was Harold Ostroff. The son of Polish immigrants who came to America in 1914, Ostroff was born in 1923 and grew up in the Amalgamated Houses. In the early 1950s he was hired as Kazan's assistant, a position he held until 1966, when Potofsky succeeded Kazan as president of the UHF and Ostroff was appointed executive vice president.

OOO

During the 1950s the UHF sponsored two small, uncomplicated, and noncontroversial housing cooperatives in the North Bronx. One was the Mutual Houses. A joint effort of the UHF and the Van Cortlandt Chapter of the American Veterans Committee, it was designed to provide housing for veterans with moderate incomes. In 1953 the sponsor, which was called the Mutual Housing Association, Inc. (MHA), and headed by Ostroff, purchased about three-quarters of an acre on Sedgwick Avenue at Stevenson Place, just south of Van Cortlandt Park and overlooking the Jerome Park Reservoir. At the outset the MHA planned to build two 13-story structures that would cost $3 million and house nearly 300 middle-income families. But in the end it erected only one 14-story building with 123 apartments, for which the down payment was $700 a room and the carrying charges were just under $23 per room per month. The building was expected to cost $1.35 million. With the help of the Filene Good Will Fund, the MHA secured a short-term loan from the Irving Trust Company. And it later obtained a long-term mortgage from the Farm Bureau Mutual Life Insurance Company of Columbus, Ohio. Designed by Jessor, it was constructed by CSI for over $1.5 million.

Even before construction started in 1954, most of the apartments, many of which had three or four rooms and a view of the Jerome Park Reservoir, were under contract. Completed in 1955, Mutual Houses was built without the help of the city, the state, or the federal government.[7]

Located on 1.7 acres across the street from the Mutual Houses was what Kazan called "its twin brother," the Park Reservoir Houses, a housing cooperative sponsored by the Park Reservoir Housing Company, which was a subsidiary of the UHF and headed by Kazan. It was built under the Mitchell-Lama act because Kazan had trouble obtaining the necessary $3.5 million from private sources. In October 1956 ground was broken for Park Reservoir's three 12-story buildings, which would end up costing $3.75 million. Among the many luminaries who spoke at the ceremony was Governor W. Averell Harriman, the son of the railroad baron E. H. Harriman and a former US ambassador to the Soviet Union. Harriman praised Park Reservoir as the first housing cooperative to be built under the Mitchell-Lama program, stressed that it would not cost the taxpayers "a single cent," and used the opportunity to urge the voters to approve Proposition 2, which would make available an additional $100 million in state credit for middle-income housing. Kazan also spoke, as did James J. Lyons, borough president of the Bronx; New York State Commissioner of Housing Joseph P. McMurray; Jacob Potofsky, who told the audience that "plenty of apartments are available at $100 a room [in New York], but very few at $17 to $20 a room"; and Comptroller Gerosa, who said that the ceremony was "a great occasion" for the Bronx as well as "a tribute to the forgotten middle class." Putting somewhat of a damper on the festivities was Robert Moses, who said that while "some progress" had been made in New York, it was "not enough." At the present rate, he warned, it would take fifty years to clear the city's slums. Designed by Jessor, built by CSI, and completed in 1958, the Park Reservoir Houses provided 273 apartments for middle-income families for $625 a room and $19 per room per month.[8]

During the 1950s the UHF also sponsored two much larger, more complicated, and more controversial housing cooperatives on the Lower East Side. The first was the East River Houses, located on Grand Street adjacent to the Hillman Houses and bordered by FDR Drive and Lewis, Cherry, and Delancey Streets. It was built on thirteen acres in a run-down neighborhood known as Corlears Hook, the site of one of several so-called blighted areas that the New York City Slum Clearance Committee, chaired by Robert Moses, had designated for redevelopment under Title I. As Moses knew better than anyone else, it was one thing to clear the slums and quite another to rebuild them. In what was for him a rare instance of understatement, he told Mayor William O'Dwyer in 1950 that efforts to induce private capital to invest in slum clearance "have not been as fruitful as we hoped." The banks, insurance companies, and real estate developers, he explained, were reluctant to enter a "new, untried and experimental field" whose procedures were "cumbersome" and whose risks were "considerable." So without abandoning his efforts to attract private capital, Moses urged organized labor to invest in slum clearance. As Joshua Freeman points out, the building trades unions, for which Moses's huge public works projects were a valuable source of well-paying jobs, were his "natural allies." And the needle trades unions could provide "a liberal façade" for his more controversial projects. Some of the unions also had substantial health, welfare, and pension funds that could be tapped for housing. Not least of all, the Amalgamated Clothing Workers, sponsor of the Hillman Houses, had shown that with Kazan at the helm it was fully capable of building a high-quality and reasonably priced housing project in a blighted area.[9]

The relationship between Moses and Kazan is especially interesting. At first glance, it would seem that Kazan had nothing in common with Moses, who had grown up in New Haven, the son of a prosperous department store owner; moved to New York as a youngster; studied at Yale, Oxford, and Columbia, where he received a PhD in political science; headed a dozen or so public and quasi-public agencies; lived in a posh enclave on the Upper East Side; and hobnobbed with the city's political and financial elite. Moreover, Moses had no interest in creating a cooperative commonwealth. But he found in Kazan a kindred spirit. Both were appalled by the slums of New York, which they regarded as the source of most of the city's social problems. And both believed that the slums could only be wiped out by large-scale demolition, not by piecemeal improvement. Like Moses, Kazan was not swayed by the argument that the slum clearance program was displacing thousands of poor people, most of whom could not afford to live elsewhere, and hundreds of small businesses, most of which would find it hard to start anew in another location. Nor was he moved by the claim that some of the buildings that would be demolished were of architectural or historical significance. To Moses, moreover, Kazan was a "doer," someone who got things done and had "survived discouragements which would have floored a weaker man" (which was pretty much how Moses saw himself). To clear the slums, Moses said, all that was needed was for men like Kazan, Potofsky, and

Van Arsdale to get involved. For his part, Kazan greatly admired Moses. In Ostroff's words, Kazan believed that, "if you got Moses to be on your side … you didn't need anything more than a handshake to know that [he] would be with you through thick and thin." When Moses (and the Slum Clearance Committee) came under attack in the late 1950s, Kazan rushed to his defense. In a letter to the editor of the *New York Times* he wrote, "Time will show that the reversal of the trend toward blight in the City of New York is primarily due to the untiring efforts of Robert Moses."[10]

As soon as Congress passed Title I of the Housing Act of 1949, Moses asked the Amalgamated whether it would be interested in building a middle-income housing cooperative on the Corlears Hook site. Given that the Hillman Houses was fully occupied—and that it had been forced to turn away prospective purchasers—Kazan was in favor of taking on the project. But for reasons that I spelled out earlier, Potofsky was unwilling to back him. Hence, Kazan decided that the newly formed United Housing Foundation would sponsor what became known as the East River Houses. Despite the success of the Hillman Houses, he had a good deal of trouble raising money. The Nationwide Insurance Company, whose president, Murray D. Lincoln, was also president of the Cooperative League of the USA, turned him down. The Bowery Savings Bank, which had underwritten Bell Park Gardens, offered to provide $6.5 million at 3⅞ percent, which was enough to cover half the cost, but only if the FHA insured the mortgage. David Dubinsky, the head of the ILGWU, was also willing to put up $6.5 million, but again not without mortgage insurance. Unfortunately for Kazan, the FHA had reservations about the project, especially about its skip-stop elevator system, under which one elevator would stop at even-numbered floors and another at odd-numbered floors. Hence the project was held up for about a year, during which time interest rates went up, prompting the Bowery Savings Bank to bow out. Kazan was still looking for funds when the FHA informed him that it would not insure the mortgage unless the UHF posted a $4 million completion bond. This "was practically a death sentence" for the project, Kazan later recalled.[11]

At wit's end, Kazan turned to Dubinsky, who had once lived in the Amalgamated Houses for a couple of years. As Kazan later recalled, he may have been hoping to capitalize on the long-standing rivalry between the ILGWU and the Amalgamated, the two dominant needle trades unions in New York City. In a departure from the union's practice of investing its funds in government bonds, Dubinsky was prepared to recommend to the ILGWU general executive board that the union give the East River Housing Corporation, the subsidiary of the UHF that was in charge of the project, a $15 million mortgage. (The mortgage was not contingent upon FHA insurance, which, Kazan told a group of visiting congressmen, saved the ERHC $4 million.) Although Frederick F. Umhey thought it was unwise to invest so much money in a long-term mortgage, the general executive board followed Dubinsky's recommendation. Of the $15 million, $11.5 million came from the union's health, welfare, and retirement funds and the rest from its general funds. (The interest rate was 4.5 percent: 3.5 percent for the mortgage itself and an additional 1 percent for private insurance, which served in lieu of FHA insurance or a completion bond.) Although $15 million was a great deal of money, especially for a labor union, the ILGWU was very wealthy. Seven years after Kazan, on behalf of the ERHC, and Dubinsky, on behalf of the ILGWU, signed the mortgage agreement at Comptroller Gerosa's office, the ILGWU informed its members that, in the words of a *Times* reporter, "it was rich and getting richer." It had $77 million in cash and other liquid assets and another $348 million in assorted health, welfare, severance, retirement, and death-benefit funds.[12]

At the same time that Kazan was looking for funds for the East River Houses, he was also seeking the city's approval of the project. Although the project had the support of a host of civic, housing, and real estate associations, it ran into strong resistance, which was fueled by the plight of the nearly 900 residents, most of whom were recent immigrants from Puerto Rico, who would be displaced by the East River Houses. Among the opponents was George H. Hallett, executive secretary of the Citizens Union. At a hearing in April 1951 he urged the Board of Estimate to defer action on a proposal to authorize the Slum Clearance Committee to begin negotiations with the Housing and Home Finance Agency for a Title I grant until the City Planning Commission came up with a master plan for tenant relocation. After Robert Moses, a member of the commission, responded that the SCC was relocating tenants every day "and getting along splendidly without the Citizens Union," the board endorsed the proposal. Less than a year later the City Planning Commission approved the plans for the East River Houses and three other Title I projects, thereby giving the city "a two-edged weapon for the clearing of substandard areas," said the commission's chairman, John J. Bennett. In May 1952 the Board of Estimate held another hearing, at which the spokesmen for the residents of Corlears Hook argued that the displaced tenants would not be able to find suitable housing at reasonable prices. But assured by William M. Ellard, chief of the city's Bureau of Real Estate, and

Harry Taylor, assistant director of Moses's Triborough Bridge and Tunnel Authority, that all the tenants would be relocated before construction got underway, the board gave its approval—and also granted the East River Houses, which was being built under the Redevelopment Companies Law, a partial tax abatement for twenty-five years.[13]

In January 1953, by which time the HHFA had signed off on a $3.7 million Title I grant for the Corlears Hook project—New York's first project to qualify for Title I funding—the East River Housing Corporation filed plans for two 20-story and two 21-story buildings. Designed by Herman Jessor and George W. Springsteen and constructed by CSI, they would cost $17.8 million and house 1,600 middle-class families. Ground was broken ten months later. Robert Szold, a director of the UHF and the Filene Good Will Fund, presided over the ceremonies, which were attended by 500 former and current residents of Corlears Hook. Kazan, Moses, and Dubinsky wielded the shovels. Moses, wrote a *Times* reporter, "had some harsh words for critics of slum clearance." "Critics build nothing," he said. "They live on mud-throwing and false, garbled statistics. If we could ostracize our critics for five or six years, half of our troubles would be over." And Dubinsky took the occasion to criticize Congress for its "heartless and inhuman disregard for America's housing needs." In what was the most moving moment of the ceremonies, he went on to say that he and many others there were returning to "the scenes of our childhood," the neighborhood in which they had grown up and in which the ILGWU was organized in the 1920s to wage "war against the sweatshop," a war that has gone on "for more than two generations." Now, half a century later, having "wiped out the sweatshop," we "return to wipe out the slum."[14]

Construction went more slowly than expected, in large part because of a dispute between carpenters and ironworkers over who would install the aluminum window frames, a dispute that started in December 1952 and dragged on for almost four months. By October 1955, however, the work was done. On hand when the East River Houses was dedicated were Mayor Robert F. Wagner Jr., Robert Moses, US senators Herbert H. Lehman and Irving M. Ives, Manhattan Borough President Hulan Jack, AFL president George Meany, and Albert M. Cole, head of the HHFA. The East River Houses was a rousing success, said Kazan. "If there was any doubt that moderate income families were in desperate need for housing, it was dispelled by the evidence of the lines of people stretching for blocks, waiting to fill out applications for apartments." In all, he added, "we had more than 5,000 applications for

1,672 apartments," the price of which was $625 a room and $17 per room per month. The *New York Times* was effusive in its praise for the East River Houses and the ILGWU. A day after the first residents moved in, it commended the union for "a notable contribution to the city of New York." The four new buildings not only replaced "an ugly blight of dilapidated tenements" but also provided "up-to-date homes for [union members and other New Yorkers] at a relatively modest cost." They also symbolized "the sensational changes" that have taken place in the ILGWU. "Here," the *Times*, said, "is a project comparable with the largest developments of commercial builders: one that will house more than 1,600 families at a cost of $19,500,000," of which "$15,000,000 has been advanced on a low-rate mortgage loan by a union that fifty years ago was a little band of garment workers who toiled long hours in dismal sweatshops for close to starvation wages."[15]

Not far from the East River Houses were 12.5 acres of run-down tenement houses that struck Kazan as a suitable site for another large housing cooperative. Located near Seward Park, the site was bordered by Grand Street on the north, East Broadway on the south, Ahearn Street on the east, and Essex Street on the west. At Kazan's behest, the Slum Clearance Committee designated what was called the Seward Park site a Title I project. Shortly before the East River Houses was completed the HHFA gave the city a $200,000 grant to begin the planning process for Seward Park. It later provided another $6.3 million to cover two-thirds of the difference between the value of the property, which was more than $9.7 million, and the price for which it was sold at public auction, which was less than $1.5 million. The buyer—indeed the only bidder—was the Seward Park Housing Corporation (SPHC), a subsidiary of the UHF that was headed by Kazan and incorporated under the Redevelopment Companies Law. Although the Seward Park Houses was expected to cost about $26 million—or roughly $6 million more than the East River Houses—Kazan had relatively little trouble raising the money. The Bowery Savings Bank provided $7.5 million and the Dry Dock Savings Bank $2.5 million. The Workmen's Circle loaned the SPHC $1.5 million. The rest of the money came from organized labor, chiefly District 9 of the Brotherhood of Painters, Decorators, and Paperhangers of America, Local 3 of the IBEW, and the United Hatters, Cap, and Millinery Workers Union.[16]

The Seward Park Houses ran into opposition from Comptroller Gerosa, New York's chief financial officer, who held that the tax exemptions given to the UHF and other sponsors of Title I projects were depriving the city of much-needed revenue. On this point he was at odds with Robert Moses, who insisted that it would be hard, if not impossible, for private developers to rebuild the slums without the benefit of a tax exemption. This "cat and dog fight," in Kazan's words, was resolved when Kazan and Gerosa reached a compromise under which the Seward Park Houses would get a full tax abatement for the first five years, a partial (and steadily decreasing) tax abatement for the next fifteen years, and no abatement at all for the last five years. The project also ran into opposition from Harris L. Present, a lawyer and chairman of the New York City Council on Housing Relocation Practices, a civic group that spoke for the many tenants who were at risk of being displaced by slum clearance and other public works. He charged that the Slum Clearance Committee was uprooting thousands of impoverished families without providing them with alternative housing at a price they could afford. Present also accused Moses of "causing unnecessary panic" by trying to pressure the residents of Seward Park into moving even before the HHFA and the city approved the project. After a daylong hearing in mid-July 1957 at which Present and more than two dozen other witnesses voiced their objections, the City Planning Commission deferred action on the SPHC's proposal for four 20-story buildings that would provide housing for 1,728 middle-income families. But at the urging of organized labor, liberal groups, and the Wagner administration, the commission approved the project in mid-August. A week later so did the Board of Estimate.[17]

The groundbreaking took place on October 11, 1958, by which time the Seward Park Houses had far more applicants than apartments. At the ceremony, which was attended by 1,000 people, Moses praised Kazan and the other "indefatigable cooperators" of the United Housing Foundation. Their apartment houses "are tops in my book," he said. "They are built cheaply and well by devoted, I might say almost fanatical, idealists, not for profit but for substantial, reliable people who have a real stake in the City." With the help of the UHF and other like-minded groups, "we shall continue to expand [the slum clearance] program and rebuild the City for those who want to stay and for those who, in increasing numbers, want to come back to town from the suburbs." By then the relocations of more than 1,400 families was well underway. Most of them, Kazan said, "have been moved with a minimum of discomfort," though very few could afford apartments in the Seward Park Houses, which cost $650 a room and $21 per room per month. "In all cases," he went on, "their living conditions are at least equal to, and in most cases, better than, those in the old dwellings." Slum clearance could be carried out without "major hardship," he claimed, so long as the sponsor was willing to help the displaced residents find other homes, a claim to which Present and other New Yorkers took strong exception. Despite a strike by the plumbers, the work went smoothly. And by 1961 the four buildings, which were designed by Jessor, constructed by CSI, and ended up costing $24 million, were finished. The apartments sold quickly—though Kazan was disappointed that many people moved into the Seward Park Houses not to build "a cooperative commonwealth" but just to improve their living conditions.[18]

ooo

During the late 1950s and early 1960s the UHF also sponsored two housing projects that were much larger than the East River Houses and the Seward Park Houses. The first, which was built on twenty acres in Chelsea, a neighborhood on Manhattan's West Side, a few blocks south of the Pennsylvania Railroad Station, was called Penn Station South (and later Penn South), though early on it was also known as the ILGWU Cooperative Houses and the Mutual Redevelopment Houses. The project had a curious history. Not long before the Seward Park Houses was completed, Moses asked Kazan if the UHF would be willing to sponsor a housing cooperative that would be located between Twenty-Third and Twenty-Seventh Streets and Lexington and Third Avenues, north of the Lower East Side and not far from Stuyvesant Town and Peter Cooper Village. Kazan brought Moses's proposal to the UHF board, one of whose members was Sasha Zimmerman, a member of the general executive board of the ILGWU. Zimmerman said that the ILGWU might be willing to cosponsor another housing cooperative with the UHF, but preferably one located in the west twenties, a few blocks from the Garment District, where many of the union's members worked. Kazan endorsed this "walk to work" project. So did Dubinsky, who persuaded the general executive board to provide up to $20 million for the project, which ran from Twenty-Third to Twenty-Ninth Streets and from Eighth to Ninth Avenues. Moses went along with the change. He viewed this run-down neighborhood of factories, lofts, warehouses, parking lots, and old brownstones, many of which had been converted into rooming houses, as a suitable site for a Title I project. And in the summer of 1956 the City Planning Commission and the Board of Estimate authorized the Slum Clearance Committee to seek federal funds for Penn Station South.[19]

The UHF submitted a plan to the Slum Clearance Committee in May 1957, and a few months later the committee approved it. According to the plan, Penn Station South would consist of nine 20- and 21-story buildings as well as a shopping center, a few gardens and playgrounds, and off-street parking for 500 cars. The project would cost $34 million and provide more than 2,500 apartments for low- and middle-income families. The price of the apartments would be $650 a room and, if the city gave Penn Station South a partial tax abatement, $23 per room per month. The plan also called for the demolition of 354 residences and 183 stores and the relocation of nearly 1,900 tenants. Two of the four churches on the site, St. Peter's Episcopal Church (Protestant) and St. Columba Church (Roman Catholic), were spared, as was the Cornish Arms Hotel. (Accused of religious discrimination, threatened with a lawsuit, and, according to Kazan, under intense pressure from religious groups, Moses later revised the plan and allowed the other two churches, St. Eleftherios Greek Orthodox Church and the Manor Community Church, an independent Protestant congregation, to remain on the site.) The plan was approved by the HHFA, which granted $12.5 million for land acquisition and $500,000 for tenant relocation. To help pay the cost of construction, which came to more than $20 million, the New York State Teachers' Retirement System offered to put up $12.5 million, though only after the project was finished. To cover the temporary shortfall, the sponsors borrowed $7 million from the Chemical Bank and $3 million from the Dry Dock Savings Bank.[20]

Not long after the plans for Penn Station South were made public, a small group of landlords, tenants, and shopkeepers formed Chelsea for Chelsea, an organization that started a campaign to block the project. Before long the campaign was taken over by the Chelsea Community Council, an organization that had been formed by about seventy neighborhood groups in 1957 and was led by Rev. Robert T. Dunn, assistant pastor of St. Columba's Church, and H. Daniel Carpenter, executive director of the Hudson Guild, a settlement house, and, ironically, a member of UHF. The council's leaders charged that the Slum Clearance Committee seriously underestimated the number of residents who would be displaced by Penn Station South and that the UHF greatly exaggerated what it was doing to help the displaced tenants. To make matters worse, there were very few cheap apartments for rent in Chelsea, and there were very few residents who could afford to buy an apartment in Penn Station South. When the City Planning Commission held hearings on Penn Station South, busloads of Chelsea residents converged on City Hall to voice their opposition to the project. Although they slowed it down, they did not stop it. The commission approved Penn Station South in

January 1959, and the Board of Estimate signed off on it five months later. The board also gave Penn Station South a partial tax abatement, though a less generous one than Kazan had asked for. In late June a group of tenants asked Judge Henry Epstein to issue a stay to prevent the city from condemning the property on the grounds that it had not taken adequate steps to relocate the 2,500 families who were about to be displaced. Epstein issued the stay, but a day later Judge Vincent A. Lupiano lifted it and denied the tenants' petition for a temporary injunction. The city promptly condemned the site and sold it for more than $3.7 million to ILGWU Houses, Inc., which had been set up by the ILGWU and the UHF to manage the project under the Redevelopment Companies Law of 1942.[21]

For many residents of Chelsea the struggle was far from over. Rebuffed in the courts, they turned to the streets. Under the leadership of the Chelsea Community Council, they launched a series of protests that were unlike any that the UHF had ever seen. Starting in late August, fifty children paraded along Twenty-Fifth Street chanting "Save our homes." And more than 400 residents jammed the auditorium of the St. Columba's school, denouncing the Penn Station South project and even hanging David Dubinsky in effigy from a lamppost. A day later a group of women pushing baby carriages picketed the UHF's relocation office on Twenty-Sixth Street, carrying placards that read THEY CAN'T PUT US OUT and CHELSEA PEOPLE UNITE TO FIGHT. Shortly afterwards thirty tenants filed affidavits with Manhattan Borough President Hulan E. Jack, spelling out the hardships caused by Penn Station South. In the meantime block parties were held to inform residents of their rights and mobilize support for the protests. After Dunn sent Jack what he called a "harrowing" report about the UHF's relocation practices, the two sides met at City Hall to resolve the outstanding issues, especially whether some of the displaced residents were tenants, who were entitled to relocation payments, or "rooming-house lodgers," who were not. But nothing much came of it. In early September more than 500 angry residents filled the auditorium of PS 33 on Twenty-Seventh Street. Speaking in English and Spanish, one resident after another attacked Penn Station South and demanded that it be put on hold until enough low-cost housing was built in Chelsea to accommodate the displaced tenants. They also decided to seek another injunction as well as to withhold their rent from ILGWU Houses, Inc., which was their landlord, and turn it over to the Chelsea Community Council, which would hold it in trust until the legal battle was over. The council's campaign annoyed Robert Moses so much that a few weeks later he asked Cardinal Francis Spellman, the archbishop of New York, to rein in Father Dunn.[22]

The Chelsea Community Council continued its campaign against Penn Station South in the fall. But it was severely weakened by a rift between a militant group led by Dunn and a moderate group led by Carpenter. The rift was so severe that in February 1960 the council shut down. By then many of its members had dropped out and the outcome was no longer in doubt. Many residents had already moved out, some on their own and others with the help of the UHF's relocation office, which had been opened in July 1959. And many others were getting ready to move. By August 1960 all the apartments were vacant. CSI then began to demolish the old buildings and erect the new ones, which were designed by Herman Jessor. Two strikes—one by Local 282 of the International Brotherhood of Teamsters and the other by Local 455 of the International Association of Bridge, Structural, and Ornamental Iron Workers—halted work for a few weeks in July 1961. And the job was not finished until May 1962, a few months behind schedule. Consisting of ten 22-story buildings, Penn Station South cost $42 million and provided housing for 2,820 families, making it the largest housing cooperative in the city and the second-largest in the country. (The largest was Leisure World, a retirement community in southern California, which was completed in 1962 and housed 6,750 families.) Even before the project was finished, more than 5,000 families applied for an apartment, for which they paid $650 a room and $24 per room per month. Penn Station South, whose "ten towering apartment buildings" had replaced "twenty acres of squalid West Side rookeries," was a manifestation of "enlightened unionism," wrote the *New York Times*.[23]

Penn Station South was dedicated on May 19, 1962. Among the 15,000 people who attended the festivities, which were presided over by David Dubinsky, were Eleanor Roosevelt, HHFA head Robert Weaver, City Council President Paul R. Screvane, Comptroller Abraham D. Beame, and Manhattan Borough President Edward R. Dudley. The speakers were Governor Rockefeller, Mayor Wagner, George Meany, Robert Moses, and Abraham Kazan. Moses praised Kazan, saying Penn Station South owed its existence to him, a man "small in stature, deceptively shrinking and mild at first glance, but a giant in accomplishment." "Look about you here and elsewhere in this City," Moses went on, "and you see his monuments." When his turn came, Kazan gave credit to the ILGWU, without whose help Penn Station South would probably not have been built. He also called attention to the "invaluable assistance" of Commissioner Moses and the many organizations, public and private, that had backed the project. The highlight of the ceremony was a speech by President John F. Kennedy. The first American president to attend the dedication of a housing cooperative, Kennedy had defeated Richard M. Nixon in part because of the strong support of organized labor. On an unseasonably hot day, with the temperature in the high nineties, Kennedy chided Dubinsky "for the sweatshop conditions under which we're working today." In a more serious vein, he then said that the ILGWU "deserves the heartiest commendations" for sponsoring Penn Station South, and he urged other labor unions to follow its lead. Kennedy concluded his remarks by telling the story of a French marshal who asked a gardener to plant a tree on his estate. When the gardener told him that "the tree won't come to flower for 100 years," the marshal responded, "in that case, plant it this afternoon." "That's the way I feel about all the tasks left undone in this country which will not be finished in our time," Kennedy told the crowd.[24]

Even before the UHF agreed to sponsor Penn Station South, Moses urged it to consider building a much larger housing cooperative in Queens. At a meeting in early October 1956 he told Kazan and his associates that the Greater New York Association (GNYA) was planning to shut down the Jamaica Racetrack, one of the three thoroughbred racetracks in the city. Although the Jamaica Racetrack was very popular with New Yorkers, the GNYA viewed it as expendable. The racetrack was more than fifty years old. And it had no direct subway connection and no room for expansion because it was hemmed in on all sides by private homes. The GNYA wanted to close Jamaica, keep Belmont, its most prestigious track, and, at a cost of more than $30 million, turn Aqueduct into a "dream track." To Moses, the Jamaica Racetrack site was extremely well suited for a large-scale housing development, one that would provide apartments for thousands of middle-income families. And it was located on about 170 acres in the geographical center of New York City. Since the GNYA (which was renamed the New York Racing Association two years later) wanted to sell the track, the city would not have to condemn it. And thus it would not have to apply to the federal government for funds under Title I. For Moses, who was fed up with the HHFA's "tremendous red tape and delay," this was a great advantage. An even greater advantage to Moses was that the site was vacant. As he told Governor Rockefeller, the project "does not involve moving people and relocating tenants." For Moses, the relocation issue was "the bugbear of Slum Clearance." And as

Kazan recalled, the efforts to clear the site on the Upper West Side for the Lincoln Center for the Performing Arts, which ran into strenuous opposition from nearby residents and businessmen, "were still fresh in his [Moses's] mind" when he met with the UHF.[25]

In his speech to the UHF, which was reported in the *New York Times* a day later, Moses spelled out his plan for turning the Jamaica Racetrack into the nation's, if not the world's, largest housing cooperative. At a cost of $52 million, the project would provide homes (as well as schools, parks, playgrounds, and other public facilities) for 4,600 middle-income families. Moses's remarks were more than a little premature. Although the GNYA had decided to close the track at the end of the 1958 racing season, it had not yet put the property on the market. And though Moses believed that the track could be bought for $3.5 million or $4 million, a spokesman for the association said that the property was worth more like $5 million. Moreover, the UHF board was ambivalent about Moses's plan. Some members, among them Harry Van Arsdale Jr., felt that the project, which was located in South Jamaica, the third-largest African-American community in New York City, was too risky. They were afraid that most whites would be reluctant to move into a black neighborhood and that most blacks could not afford to buy an apartment in the new buildings. But Kazan was "very enthusiastic" about developing such a large site for cooperative housing—and extremely pleased that Moses had so much faith in the UHF. But as he well knew, the UHF did not have the $3.5 million to $4 million to acquire the site, much less the tens of millions of dollars to erect the buildings. At the start, he later recalled, it seemed like a "hopeless task."[26]

According to Kazan, Moses was under the impression that New York's labor unions would underwrite the project. He was mistaken. Although the Amalgamated Clothing Workers of America had sponsored three housing cooperatives, it had been unwilling to invest its own money in them. And though the ILGWU had invested more than $30 million in the East River Houses and Penn Station South, it was reluctant to put more money into cooperative housing. Moreover, Van Arsdale was "not at all enthusiastic about the project," and the other members of the board did not have the resources. Hence Kazan "played for time, hoping against hope that something would come up to make this dream possible." He then came up with the idea of trying to borrow enough money to make a partial payment on the site, hoping that the New York Racing Association would take a note for the remainder. In the meantime he would look for a long-term, low-interest mortgage. To help out Moses arranged for him to meet with David Rockefeller, president of Chase Manhattan Bank, and John J. McCloy, chairman of the bank's board. Although Moses assured Rockefeller and McCloy that the United Housing Foundation had an unimpeachable record and that Kazan was a top-notch man, they were not willing to lend the UHF the money, especially not at an interest rate that was acceptable to Kazan. "McCloy said that I was dreaming," Kazan recalled. Kazan also considered applying to the Ford Foundation, but McCloy, who was its president, dissuaded him. Kazan did approach Chemical Bank (or, as it was then called, Chemical New York Trust Company), which had helped finance Penn Station South. But it was not interested. James W. Gaynor, the state housing commissioner, was willing to give the UHF a mortgage, but he had only $20 million at his disposal. Meanwhile, the New York Racing Association was becoming restive. It had to sell Jamaica to help pay for upgrading Aqueduct, and several other parties were ready to buy the old track for the asking price, which was now $6.5 million.[27]

With the NYRA running out of patience and Kazan running out of options, Moses made a last-ditch effort to salvage the project. He arranged for Kazan to meet with Governor Rockefeller at his New York City office in late 1959. Although Rockefeller's father had built a few housing cooperatives in the 1920s, among them the Thomas Garden Apartments, which was for whites, and the Paul Laurence Dunbar Apartments, which was for blacks, the governor had never had much interest in cooperative housing. But he was far more receptive to Kazan than his brother David had been. When Kazan said that he "needed someone to roll up his sleeves and go to work," Rockefeller responded that "not only was he willing to roll up his sleeves, but to take off his shirt and see that the job was done." Whether to ease the shortage of middle-income housing in New York or to curry favor with the city's building trades unions, Rockefeller was as good as his word. It took several months to work out the details, during which time Rockefeller was under constant pressure from Moses. But in February 1960 the governor announced that the New York State Teachers' Retirement System, which had previously refused to give Kazan money for the project, would put up $28.5 million at 5.5 percent. And the New York State Employees' Retirement System would provide another $28.5 million, also at 5.5 percent. Commissioner Gaynor would come up with an additional $19 million at 3.75 percent. And the down payment on the apartments was expected to yield $10 million. (Although Kazan now had enough money for the project, he felt that the 5.5 percent demanded by the two retirement systems was too high. And later he persuaded the State Housing Finance Agency to lend him the entire $57 million at a lower interest rate.)[28]

Shortly thereafter Rochdale Village, Inc., the UHF subsidiary in charge of the project, reached a verbal agreement with the NYRA to buy the racetrack for $6.5 million. It submitted the $86.5 million project to the City Planning Commission, which approved it without much fuss in early April. The project then went to the Board of Estimate, where it ran into a good deal of opposition. Rochdale Village, Inc., which was a limited-profit housing company, had applied for a 50 percent tax abatement for thirty years, but Comptroller Gerosa objected to giving a tax abatement on the twenty-seven acres that were set aside for commercial purposes. Queens Borough President John T. Clancy also opposed a provision that the surrounding neighborhood bear part of the cost of the streets, sewers, and other public improvements, which came to about $3.2 million. Two days later the board held another hearing, at which John J. Reynolds, a prominent real estate man and longtime adviser to the Archdiocese of New York, said that he had offered to buy the Jamaica Racetrack from the NYRA but had been "frozen out," presumably by Moses and Kazan, and was now willing to develop the site without a tax abatement, which he denounced as "a giveaway." But the board was not impressed, especially when, in response to a question from Mayor Wagner, Reynolds said that he intended to rent his apartments for $38 per room per month, which was almost twice as much as Rochdale Village, Inc., was planning to charge. "That," Wagner told a reporter, "doesn't sound like middle-income [housing]." Two weeks later, by which time Clancy had persuaded his colleagues to relieve the surrounding neighborhood of any part of the cost of the improvements, the board approved the project and granted Rochdale Village, Inc., a 50 percent tax abatement on the 146 acres that were devoted to residential use.[29]

Rochdale Village, Inc., bought the Jamaica Racetrack in July 1960, and under the supervision of CSI, the subcontractors began demolishing the grandstand shortly afterwards. By late September, wrote a *Times* reporter, "the hoofbeats of thoroughbreds" had been replaced by "the roar of bulldozers." Construction of the twenty 14-story apartment houses, which were designed by Herman Jessor and arranged in five clusters of four buildings apiece, went smoothly until July 1963, when the Congress of Racial Equality, the NACCP, and another civil rights organization launched a citywide campaign against discrimination in the building trades. In an effort to force contractors to hire more African Americans and Puerto Ricans, they organized picket lines at Rochdale Village and several other large projects. The objective was to block the delivery of building materials and thereby slow down or even stop construction. Thousands joined the protest. Hundreds were arrested and charged with disorderly conduct. And in a show of support, twenty-three African-American plasterers walked off the job. But the demonstrations waned in late August. And at the end of the year—by which time nearly all of the apartments, which cost $400 a room and $21 per room per month, had been sold—the first residents moved in. Completed in 1965, Rochdale Village was by far the largest housing cooperative in New York City. It had 5,860 apartments, all with central air-conditioning and almost half with balconies. A "small town," in Kazan's words, it also had parking for 3,700 cars, a power plant, a fire station, a police station, three schools, a theater, a community center, and two shopping centers, both of which were designed by the well-known architect Victor Gruen. And it ended up costing $96 million, more than twice as much as Penn Station South.[30]

ooo

Not all of the UHF's ventures were as successful as Penn Station South and Rochdale Village. A case in point is Seward Park Extension. Even before Seward Park Houses was finished, Kazan began to think about building another large housing cooperative on the Lower East Side. Before long he picked a site across the street from Seward Park Houses that was bounded by Delancey, Willett, Grand, and Essex Streets and consisted mainly of run-down tenement houses. In 1958 he filed an application with the Slum Clearance Committee to build a housing cooperative on about half of the twenty-six-acre site. The project, Kazan told Moses, would "eliminate a pocket of slums" on the Lower East Side. (Of great importance to Kazan, it would also stabilize the neighborhood surrounding the Seward Park Houses in the same way that the East River Houses stabilized the neighborhood surrounding the Hillman Houses.) The Slum Clearance Committee quickly gave its approval. In January 1959 the Housing and Home Finance Agency set aside $7 million for the acquisition of the site, which was expected to cost $12 million, and gave the city $244,000 to help with the planning. Not long after, the UHF submitted to the City Planning Commission a proposal to demolish more than 700 buildings, over 90 percent of which were deemed substandard, and replace them with four huge apartment houses that would accommodate 1,800 middle-income families. It was estimated that the project would cost $34.4 million.[31]

To Kazan's dismay, the proposal went nowhere. The City Planning Commission did not even hold hearings. Neither did the Board of Estimate. Although the project was designed to allow the venerable Henry Street Settlement Houses and a Jewish synagogue to remain standing, it called for the demolition of another old synagogue and St. Mary's Roman Catholic Church. Even though, said Kazan, the church and the synagogue should "have been condemned a long time ago as unsafe or as fire traps," both strongly opposed Seward Park Extension. Kazan offered the church a much larger site, but it rejected the offer. The synagogue was willing to move, but only if the UHF gave it enough money to erect a new building, which, Kazan pointed out, "we could not do." Kazan was annoyed because the synagogue had very few members, most of whom were not neighborhood residents but local shopkeepers who resided elsewhere and spent an hour in prayer after they came to work. Kazan was also incensed because the president of the synagogue lived at the Hillman Houses and the rabbi at Seward Park. "Being comfortably housed," he recalled, "they repaid us with their objections to have their synagogue moved to another section of the development." Kazan, who ran into a similar problem at Penn Station South, believed that the clergymen should have been more interested in providing housing than in preserving buildings. But there was not much he could do about it. "We couldn't get the city to act to condemn these properties," he told a *Times* reporter, "because city political leaders are afraid to tackle any religious institutions, whether Jewish, Roman Catholic, Protestant or any other."[32]

In an attempt to salvage Seward Park Extension, Kazan appealed to the Housing and Redevelopment Board, an agency that was established in 1960 to take over slum clearance, urban renewal, and other housing programs that had long been controlled by Robert Moses. But the three-member board, which was chaired by J. Clarence Davies, New York City's former commissioner of real estate, was not receptive to Kazan's appeal. Set up by Mayor Wagner in large part to reduce Moses's influence over housing policy, the board did not deal with problems in the same way as the Slum Clearance Committee. It was less enthusiastic about the wholesale demolition of run-down neighborhoods and more sympathetic to the plight of displaced residents and businesses. The board also had strong reservations about the aesthetics of the UHF's housing cooperatives. Designed by Herman Jessor, the buildings were all the same height and shape. In the absence of ornamentation, they conveyed a sense of what critics called a "deadly project monotony." Seward Park Extension, the board held, should have sixteen buildings of various heights and shapes, not just four huge buildings, and it should include townhouses as well as apartment houses. But as Kazan saw it, the board's proposal would drive the carrying charges up from $21 to $22 per room per month to $28 to $29 per room per month. He rejected the view that "the exterior design of a building is worth the difference of $7.00 a room per month." And it was unfair to make New York's low- and middle-income families pay $25 per room per month or more "to make the city supposedly more attractive architecturally." Unable to win the backing of the City Planning Commission and the Housing and Redevelopment Board, the UHF abandoned Seward Park Extension in the early 1960s.[33]

The UHF abandoned another large housing project on the Lower East Side at about the same time. It was called the Robert Owen Houses, in honor of a British manufacturer who was one of the pioneers of the cooperative movement. The origins of the Robert Owen Houses went back to the late 1950s, when Robert Moses designated twelve blocks on the Bowery, the home of New York's skid row, for slum clearance. The site of one of Moses's most ambitious urban renewal projects, it was located near Cooper Square and bounded by Second and Third Avenues and Ninth and Delancey Streets. Assuming that the AFL would be interested in building low-cost housing for wage earners, Moses tried to persuade George Meany to sponsor the project. When Meany showed no interest, Moses turned to Kazan and the UHF. In the meantime Abe Stark, a Brooklyn businessman who had gone into politics and was now president of the City Council, insisted that part of the site be set aside for light industry, which, he believed, would generate much-needed employment for New York's working people. Since Stark sat on the Board of Estimate, his support was essential. Hence Moses divided the site into two sections: one, from Delancey Street to Houston Street, would be for light industry and the other, from Houston Street to Ninth Street, would be for cooperative housing. With the approval of the City Planning Commission, the Slum Clearance Committee applied for federal funds under Title I. On behalf of the UHF, Community Services, Inc., submitted a proposal to erect a housing cooperative for 1,700 families, each of whom would pay $600 to $650 per room for an apartment and about $20 per room per month in carrying charges.[34]

The UHF proposal infuriated many residents and businessmen. In an attempt to block the project, they formed the Cooper Square Community Development Committee, which was led by Thelma J. Burdick, a settlement house worker. Burdick and her associates hammered away at the point that the Robert Owen Houses would be much too expensive for the current residents, most of whom were very poor and many of whom were recent immigrants from Puerto Rico. They recommended that at least part of the site should be reserved for low-cost public housing and publicly aided low-cost private housing. Burdick and her associates also protested that the UHF proposal made no provision for relocating the displaced tenants, especially the thousands who rented rooms in the Bowery's many flophouses and would "simply move out to down-grade the surrounding area." The residents of Cooper Square, said their spokeswomen, were being treated as "expendable pawns in the housing experiments of the intelligentsia." The Cooper Square Community Development Committee held rallies, distributed flyers, and took other steps to mobilize the community. And it voiced opposition to wholesale clearance at a hearing in Manhattan Borough President Hulan Jack's office. The committee also hired a city planner named Walter Thabit to come up with an alternative to the UHF proposal. Based on his report, which recommended that only six blocks be razed, the Cooper Square Community Development Committee proposed that demolition be put on hold until low-cost housing was erected on the neighborhood's vacant lots and that construction be done in phases, starting on sites where buildings were empty, and not all at once. Kazan rejected these proposals, insisting that such piecemeal construction was impractical and stressing that it would raise construction costs and carrying charges.[35]

In its attempt to block the Robert Owen Houses, the Cooper Square Community Development Committee had a few advantages. James Felt, the chairman of the City Planning Commission, was on its side. So was the Metropolitan Council on Housing, a recently formed citywide organization that championed tenants' rights. And the Slum Clearance Committee, under whose auspices the project was launched, was in disarray. It was under attack not only for its indifference to displaced tenants but also for its favoritism in selecting sponsors for the projects and its failure to properly supervise the sponsors, some of whom were involved in all sorts of financial skullduggery. The Citizens Union, which had long been critical of Moses, insisted that it was time for him to go. And even the *New York Times*, a longtime supporter of Moses and the Slum Clearance Committee, began to have second thoughts. By July 1959 Moses acknowledged that Title I was "a dead duck" in New York City, and several months later the Slum Clearance Committee was disbanded. As a result the Robert Owen Houses remained in limbo. The City Planning Commission did not hold hearings on the UHF's proposal, and

the Housing and Redevelopment Board shelved the Cooper Square urban renewal project, saying that it needed further study. Kazan was, in his words,
"disheartened" by the city's response to the Robert Owen Houses. In many
cases, he complained, the "red tape" was so bad that it often took the UHF
"twice as long to get a project approved as it [did] to build it." In this case, he
said, the red tape was "unsurmountable." Hence Kazan gave up on the Robert Owen Houses in 1960, leaving the UHF with the unenviable task of re-
funding $1.5 million to the 3,000 families that had applied for an apartment
in the project and put down a $500 deposit.[36]

Even more disheartening to Kazan was the city's response to the proposed James Peter Warbasse Houses. Named after the founder and first president of the Cooperative League of the USA, this huge housing cooperative
would have been located in Coney Island, the southernmost part of Brooklyn
and once home to Steeplechase, Luna Park, and Dreamland, the country's
most famous amusement parks in the early twentieth century. The Warbasse
Houses had its origins in the mid to late 1950s, when a former member of the
City Planning Commission called Kazan's attention to about sixty acres in
a run-down section of Coney Island that consisted mainly of one- and two-
family homes and summer bungalows and might be suitable for large-scale
cooperative housing. Although Kazan had been focusing his efforts on Manhattan, he was intrigued by the prospect. At first he thought of developing
the site under Title I. But he changed his mind when he learned that the
property was assessed at only $1.85 per square foot, which was extremely
low by New York standards, and realized that the UHF could afford to purchase the site without a grant from the federal government. To be safe, he
discussed the matter with Robert Moses, who said that he had no objections
if Kazan wanted to bypass the Slum Clearance Committee. But he hinted
that the UHF might run into political obstacles along the way. The UHF soon
came up with a plan to build thirteen to fifteen 21-story buildings under the
state's Redevelopment Companies Law. They would provide homes for more
than 1,000 middle-income families, who would pay about $20 per room per
month. The UHF then submitted a proposal for what would have been the
nation's largest housing cooperative to the City Planning Commission, which
scheduled a hearing for August 14, 1957.[37]

Two days before the hearing, and without prior notice, Fred C. Trump, a
second-generation German immigrant who was Brooklyn's biggest builder,
filed a formal objection with the commission. As Trump later acknowledged,
he was concerned that the erection of the Warbasse Houses would lead to an

exodus from his nearby Beach Haven Apartments, an 1,800-unit complex whose rents were $29 per room per month. At the hearing he focused his objections not so much on the UHF's proposal as on its request for a tax abatement, which he denounced as an "outright giveaway" that would allow "a favorite few" to avoid paying their full share of taxes. Several other Brooklyn property owners and real estate developers opposed the Warbasse Houses on the same grounds. And though spokesmen for organized labor and other groups supported the UHF proposal, the City Planning Commission put off a decision. Kazan was "dumbfounded," writes Gwenda Blair, the biographer of the Trump family. "What should have been a routine event was a fiasco." The controversy dragged on for a year—"an unusually long time," observed a *Times* reporter. The commission held a second hearing in February 1959 and a third five months later. Under pressure from the more than 3,000 New Yorkers who had applied for apartments in the Warbasse Houses—and in spite of the opposition of Brooklyn Borough President John Cashmore—the commission eventually approved the project. In July 1959 it authorized the UHF to erect twelve 20-story buildings that would house 5,184 middle-income families. It was estimated that the Warbasse Houses would cost $70 million. Provided that the city granted the project a tax abatement, the residents would pay $600 a room for their apartments and about $20 per room per month in carrying charges.[38]

But as Moses warned Kazan, the issue was far from settled. No sooner did the City Planning Commission approve the Warbasse Houses than the two sides made a determined effort to sway the Board of Estimate, which had the final say over both the project and the tax abatement. The result was a fierce debate not so much over whether the site should be redeveloped as over whether the city should grant the UHF a tax abatement. And since Kazan held that the carrying charges would be too high for working-class families without a tax abatement, the debate was also about who would redevelop the site. In defense of the Warbasse Houses, Kazan stressed that the project would not only eliminate a blighted area but also keep thousands of middle-income families from moving out of the city. He also pointed out that at present the site generated very little revenue for the city and that after twenty years the Warbasse Houses would pay its full share of property taxes. John B. Swift, president of the Brooklyn Real Estate Board (BREB), opposed the tax abatement on the grounds that families that could afford to buy apartments in the Warbasse Houses were not "entitled to be partially supported by the small home owners of Brooklyn." And Frank A. Barrera,

counsel to the BREB, insisted that New York City was in such dire financial straits that it could not afford to grant tax abatements even for so com-
mendable a project as the Warbasse Houses. He also claimed that many
private builders were ready to erect middle-income housing without a tax
abatement, a point seconded by Sidney Young, one of Trump's many lawyers and counsel to the City Taxpayers League, a civic group based in Brooklyn. Young denounced the UHF proposal as "a well-camouflaged gimmick to
plunder the city's depleted treasury."[39]

The UHF was still waiting for the Board of Estimate to hold hearings
on its proposal when Trump announced in December 1958 that he was prepared to take over the $70 million project. He claimed that his development
would generate $23 million more in property taxes than the UHF's—a claim,
said Roger Starr, executive director of the Citizens Housing and Planning
Council, that "merely proves that higher taxes can be paid if higher rentals
are charged." Although the City Planning Commission had already approved
the UHF's proposal, it felt obliged to consider two proposals from Trump. It
found one for 6,285 units unsuitable, but it viewed the other, which called
for 5,184 units, the same number as the Warbasse Houses, as "appropriate."
Under pressure to resolve the issue from the *New York Times* and the Citizens Housing and Planning Council, both of which favored the UHF plan,
the Board of Estimate asked City Construction Coordinator Robert Moses
to make a recommendation. Moses reported that while both sponsors were
reputable and both proposals well conceived, the Trump proposal was pref-
erable because it would provide both rental and cooperative housing and
generate more in property taxes. He recommended that the board approve
Trump as the sponsor of the Coney Island project (and at the same time designate the UHF as the sponsor of the Jamaica Racetrack project). Kazan was
shocked, especially because Moses had been supportive of the Warbasse
Houses from the outset. Pointing out that Trump was going to charge the
residents more than the UHF, he wrote Moses that he was "at a loss" to make
sense of his longtime ally's position. By June Kazan was so fed up that he
threatened to withdraw from the project unless the Board of Estimate approved the UHF proposal by the end of July, a threat that prompted Trump
to say that he was ready "to start immediate construction."[40]

The Board of Estimate held a hearing on the Warbasse Houses on August
20, 1959. About 500 people, most of whom supported the UHF proposal,
jammed City Hall, while members of the United Taxpayers Party, which

opposed both the UHF and Trump proposals, picketed outside dressed in sackcloth. Although the *New York Times* strongly endorsed the UHF's proposal, its prospects were not good. As a rule the board deferred to the president in whose borough the project was located. And Borough President Cashmore was opposed to the UHF proposal. Trump was his constituent, and a well-heeled and well-connected constituent at that, and Kazan was an interloper from Manhattan. Kazan had previously met with Cashmore and asked for his support. Although Cashmore told him that he was a good friend of the Jews and a supporter of the State of Israel, which seemed beside the point, he refused to back the Warbasse Houses. Jacob Potofsky had also gone to see Cashmore. "He was very friendly," Potofsky recalled, noting that Cashmore said, "'I'll be glad to help and do whatever I can.'" But instead of helping, Cashmore exercised his prerogative as borough president to block consideration of the UHF's request for a tax abatement twelve times. To complicate matters, the other members of the Board of Estimate were divided. Hence the board put a decision off to September 17. On September 6, however, Moses informed Cashmore that Trump might be willing to split the site with the UHF. "Is it not possible to work out a compromise?" he asked, and thereby "settle what looks like a prolonged controversy." The idea appealed to Cashmore, though not to Kazan. But when he realized that the Warbasse Houses could not be built unless he agreed to split the site with Trump, he went along.[41]

The Board of Estimate informally approved the agreement to divide the site in November 1959. After the City Planning Commission signed off on the project, the board formally approved it in May 1960 and authorized the city to condemn the property. Under the terms of the agreement Trump would get the southern portion, about forty acres, on which he proposed to build Trump Village, a complex of eight 20-story apartment houses, six as co-ops and two as rentals, that would have 3,800 units and cost $80 million. The UHF would get the northern portion, about twenty-seven acres, on which it intended to erect five 24-story buildings that would house 2,484 families and cost an estimated $43 million. The project dragged on for so long that the UHF was forced to raise the purchase price from $600 to $650 a room and the carrying charges from $20 to $23. The delay had two other consequences, both of which worked out well for the UHF. It gave the foundation time to persuade the Amalgamated Clothing Workers of America, many of whose members had applied for apartments in the Warbasse

Houses, to cosponsor the project. What would henceforth be known as the Amalgamated Warbasse Houses was then turned into a Mitchell-Lama project, which enabled the UHF to obtain a long-term, low-interest loan of $36.7 million from the State Housing Finance Agency. Construction, which got underway in May 1962, went smoothly. The first apartment house was finished in 1964, the last in 1965. The product of what Kazan said was the "dirtiest" and "longest" of his many struggles, the Amalgamated Warbasse Houses had 2,585 apartments—not quite as many as Penn Station South and fewer than half as many as Rochdale Village. And though it was New York's third-largest housing cooperative, it was much smaller than the James Peter Warbasse Houses would have been if the UHF had succeeded in obtaining the city's approval eight years earlier.[42]

ooo

Late in 1964 the UHF issued a report on the twenty-three housing cooperatives affiliated with the foundation. Among them were the East River Houses, Seward Park Houses, Penn Station South, Amalgamated Warbasse, Rochdale Village, and a handful of other co-ops that had been sponsored or cosponsored by the UHF. Also among them were Bell Park Gardens, the Hillman Houses, Queensview, Electchester, Big Six Towers, and more than a dozen others that had been sponsored by labor unions and other nonprofit groups. The twenty-three housing cooperatives—which did not include Chatham Green, Morningside Gardens, and Lindsay Park (and the many that were built under Section 213)—were located in every borough except Staten Island. With the exception of the Amalgamated Houses and Amalgamated Dwellings, all were built after World War II, and almost all after the UHF was founded in 1951. Indeed, five of the largest were completed in the early 1960s. All told, the twenty-three housing cooperatives consisted of 350 apartment houses that provided homes for nearly 27,000 families—or more than 100,000 people. They cost more than $357 million, of which almost $57 million came from the residents, who bought their apartments on average for just under $490 a room, and nearly $300 million from savings banks, insurance companies, union pension funds, and the State Housing Finance Agency. The residents also paid an average of $19 per room per month in carrying charges, ranging from just over $14 per room in the older co-ops to $23 to $24 per room in the newer ones. These twenty-three housing cooperatives, the report concluded, "represent the best hope of transforming vast urban areas from places where people just exist into homes where it is possible to live a good life."[43]

Kazan took great pride in the UHF's accomplishments. In just over a decade it had built thousands of spacious and up-to-date apartments for New York's working-class families. Some even had central air-conditioning, which was far from common at the time. Some also had balconies, with views, said Robert Moses, that "have no rival on Park or Fifth Avenue." In the process the UHF transformed much of the Lower East Side. It also rebuilt blighted areas in Manhattan and Brooklyn and turned an abandoned racetrack into an integrated community in Queens. As well as building better housing, Kazan told the First National Conference on Cooperative Housing in 1958, the UHF fostered "a better way of life." It set the buildings amid parks, gardens, and playgrounds, which provided the residents with plenty of sunlight and fresh air. It also encouraged a wide range of cooperative enterprises, among them supermarkets, credit unions, nursery schools, and day camps as well as all sorts of community activities, including concerts, plays, and lectures. The UHF also created opportunities, said Kazan, for the residents to apply the principles of "self-help" and "self-reliance" and to learn to "work together for the common good." Small wonder that the UHF projects were fully occupied, that the turnover rate was extremely low, and that in the Amalgamated Houses, the oldest cooperative, three generations of families "live near one another," which "is [highly] unusual in large [American] cities." Small wonder too, Kazan said, that "many people from other parts of the country come to New York and ask [him], 'How can we do the same thing back home as you are doing here?'"[44]

Kazan was well aware that the UHF had its detractors. As he said after accepting an award from the Lower East Side Neighborhood Association in 1963, some New Yorkers and New York institutions, even the venerable *New York Times*, had criticized the foundation for destroying existing neighborhoods, uprooting vulnerable tenants, ruining small businesses, and wiping out part of the city's architectural heritage. These criticisms were groundless, Kazan insisted. Before a blighted area could be rebuilt the old buildings have to be demolished and the current residents relocated, which, Kazan pointed out, was "a difficult job." But on their own or with the help of the UHF, the displaced tenants found better housing more often than not. Moreover, many of the Lower East Side's small businessmen lived elsewhere in the city or in the suburbs and were interested "in what they can take out of the neighborhood, not in what they can do towards improving it." Indeed, they were partly responsible for the deterioration of the Lower East Side. To the charge that the UHF was wiping out part of the city's architectural heritage, Kazan responded that the Lower East Side and New York's other slums did indeed have "a unique heritage all their own—a heritage of human misery and degradation." The UHF had demolished a great many "disease-ridden rookeries" that had long lined Grand Street. But, as Kazan declared, it had not destroyed "anything worth saving either here [on the Lower East Side], in Chelsea, or in Brooklyn," a point that was also made by Jacob Potofsky, who said that when it came to buildings of historical or architectural significance, there was nothing worth preserving on the Lower East Side.[45]

What troubled Kazan was not what the UHF had done, but what it had not done. Given the tremendous need for working-class housing in New York, the foundation's accomplishments "have been relatively meager," he conceded. As he told the Lower East Side Neighborhood Association, a "stone's throw" from the East River Houses, Seward Park Houses, and the UHF's other housing cooperatives "we find the same conditions that existed thirty years ago." From the windows of the foundation's new developments, he went on, "one can see blocks of buildings not fit to live in, yet fully occupied. We cannot be satisfied when we find children and adults forced to use the kitchens as bedrooms, when they share hall toilets, when four and five people of all ages sleep in one room, and when fully occupied buildings are ventilated by narrow air shafts." As Kazan told the Citizens Housing and Planning Council, which gave him its Fourth Annual Public Service Award in 1964, he was disappointed that so many New Yorkers still lacked "a decent place to live." As a result of the acute shortage of inexpensive apartments, they were forced to remain in substandard tenements, apply for public housing for which some were not eligible, or move to the suburbs, which for many was not an option. Despite the best efforts of the UHF and other nonprofit groups, the housing problem is "unsolved and grows worse," Kazan wrote in 1960. For this he blamed not only the high cost of construction but also the many public officials who were "indifferent and callous to the needs of the people." They often tied things up in so much red tape that "the boys and girls of fourteen or fifteen will be nineteen or twenty by the time the project planned for their use can be completed."[46]

Like other advocates of cooperative housing, Kazan was disappointed that so few American cities had followed New York's lead. As he remarked at the dedication of Penn Station South in 1962, what had been done in Chelsea (and elsewhere in New York) could be done in other cities. Although some housing cooperatives were built after World War II in Jersey City, Norwalk, Connecticut, and other cities, many of them by the Foundation for Cooperative Housing, they were few and far between. Cooperative housing made little headway in Boston, Chicago, and, as Jacob Potofsky pointed out, even Detroit. Given that Detroit was the home of the United Auto Workers, which was led by Walter P. Reuther, "one of the most advanced, forward-looking persons in the labor movement," Potofsky believed that Motor City should have been highly receptive to cooperative housing. Although he blamed the state of Michigan more than the UAW for the lack of cooperative housing in Detroit, he acknowledged that, notwithstanding its many advantages, cooperative enterprise had not yet "captured the imagination of the American people." Shirley F. Boden, who had broken with Kazan, left the UHF, and formed the Association for Middle Income Housing, also pointed out that New York was home to "the major portion of all the cooperative housing in the United States of America." Until it caught on in other cities—which Boden thought was only a matter time—cooperative housing "could scarcely be considered to have come of age." Jerry Voorhis, executive secretary of the Cooperative League of the USA, was also well aware that much still needed to be done. As he told the Third National Conference on Cooperative Housing in 1960, he was asked "over and over [again] why cooperative housing has thus far been largely confined to New York City."[47]

Kazan was disappointed, but not discouraged. Although he turned seventy in 1959 and some of his associates thought it was time for him to "take it easier," he had no intention of slowing down. As Potofsky said, "Kazan never stops. He is always full of plans and ideas and new projects. He would like to clear up all the slums in New York and replace them with Co-ops." How much more Kazan and his associates could do was hard to say. There was no doubt that they knew how to build high-quality, reasonably priced cooperative apartments. Nor was there any doubt that these apartments would be sold as soon as they were built, if not sooner. But by the early 1960s the ground rules had changed. Now that the State Housing Finance Agency was up and running, it would probably be easier than ever for the UHF to obtain capital. But since the Slum Clearance Committee was out of business, it would probably be harder than ever for the foundation to acquire sites. But Kazan was confident that it could be done. So was Harold Ostroff. Testifying at a public hearing in 1967, he recommended that the city close the many cemeteries in Brooklyn and Queens and replace them with housing cooperatives. "Can we afford this $157-million tax exempt luxury for the dead when the [housing] problems of the living are so pressing?" he asked. He also suggested that the city lop off the northern portion of Central Park and use it for cooperative housing, a proposal that did not sit well with Robert Moses, who had been the parks commissioner from 1934 to 1960. But even Moses was optimistic about the UHF's prospects. As he said at the dedication of Penn Station South, he firmly believed that "a giant cooperative foundation, authorized by law, sponsored by [New York City's] labor unions and headed by the indispensable Mr. Kazan can supply all the middle income housing needed in cities like New York."[48]

CHAPTER 4

CO-OP CITY

By the mid-1960s, if not earlier, Robert Moses had come to believe that the United Housing Foundation and other like-minded groups were the key to slum clearance in New York City. If these organizations could be prevailed upon to build large housing cooperatives on vacant land, as the UHF had done at Rochdale Village, they could drain the slums—and thereby eradicate what Moses called the "palpable, obvious pestilence that walks at nights and wastes at noonday." Given the opportunity to buy high-quality, low-cost units in new apartment houses, tens and even hundreds of thousands of slum dwellers would move out of the old tenement houses in Harlem, East Harlem, Bedford-Stuyvesant, Brownsville, and the South Bronx. Once these blighted areas were vacant, they could be rebuilt. And before long, Moses said at the dedication of Co-op City, "there would be no more slums [in New York City]." Although Moses had stepped down as chairman of the Slum Clearance Committee (and as City Construction Coordinator and a member of the City Planning Commission) in 1960, he was as well informed as anyone about the real estate market in New York. In May 1964, at which time he was not only chairman of the Triborough Bridge and Tunnel Authority but also president of the New York World's Fair, Moses informed Abraham E. Kazan and his associates at the UHF that a huge site in the northeast Bronx that was suitable for a large housing cooperative might be for sale.[1]

Located in Baychester near the intersection of the Hutchinson River Parkway and the New England Thruway, the roughly 400-acre site was among the largest privately owned parcels in New York City. James Butler Jr., whose family owned the Yonkers Raceway, had bought the property in the 1950s. When his plans to build a racetrack on the site fell through, Butler swapped the 400 acres in the Bronx for one acre in Midtown Manhattan owned by Webb & Knapp, a New York real estate firm headed by William Zeckendorf and leased to Orbach's, a well-established department store. Zeckendorf was born in 1905 in Paris, Illinois, where his father owned a hardware store, but grew up on Long Island, to which the family moved when he was two, and later in Manhattan. After dropping out of New York University, Zeckendorf went to work in an uncle's real estate firm. In the late 1930s he joined Webb & Knapp, a small, staid, and little-known firm that managed other people's property. In less than two decades, he turned it into one of the largest, best-known, and most aggressive real estate companies in the United States. Under his leadership, Webb & Knapp, of which he became executive vice president in 1942 and president and sole stockholder several years later, erected office buildings, developed shopping centers, and acquired deluxe hotels not only in New York but also in Philadelphia, Denver, Montreal, Washington, DC, and a host of other cities. (At one time, Zeckendorf boasted, the firm "was the biggest hotel operator in the country.") Webb & Knapp took the lead in so many urban redevelopment projects, most of which were products of Moses's Slum Clearance Committee, that Title I was sometimes referred to as the "Zeckendorf Relief Bill." Brilliant and flamboyant, Zeckendorf was, in Moses's words, a man of "immense imagination, courage and nerve." But as it turned out, he was also a man whose judgment left a good deal to be desired.[2]

Not long after Webb & Knapp acquired the Baychester site, Zeckendorf was approached by C. V. Wood, a forty-year-old industrial engineer and, in Zeckendorf's words, a promoter "who could sell snow to Eskimos." Wood had been vice president and general manager of Disneyland, Walt Disney's large and extremely successful amusement park in Anaheim, California, which opened in 1955. Fired by Disney a year later, he came up with the idea of building an even larger amusement park on the East Coast. To be called Freedomland, it would be devoted, writes historian Paul D. Nash, to "the entire panorama of American history." When Wood asked whether Webb & Knapp was willing to lease part of its 400 acres in Baychester to Freedomland, Zeckendorf said that it was. He offered Wood a long-term lease on the southern half of the site, which consisted of just over 200 acres. Zeckendorf had no plans for that part of the site, and as he later explained, he was not being asked to put any money into Freedomland. He was also confident that the project would increase the value of the other 200 acres. "How could we lose?"

he thought. After Webb & Knapp leased the land to the International Recreation Corporation, the parent company of Freedomland, Inc., Bear Stearns, Lee Higginson, and other investment banks agreed to underwrite the project, which was expected to cost $35 million, about twice as much as Disneyland. Construction got underway in 1959. And Americans everywhere awaited the opening of what was billed as "the greatest outdoor entertainment center in the history of man," the heart of which was an 85-acre amusement park designed to look like a map of the United States and filled with exhibits, said the *Times*, that told "the story of the [country's] settlement and growth." The rest of the site was set aside for parking, services, and facilities.[3]

Freedomland opened with much fanfare on June 19, 1960, which was designated "Freedomland Day" by Mayor Robert F. Wagner Jr., who praised the new amusement park as "a great means of education for the young and old." Lured by a $750,000 advertising campaign that trumpeted the wonders of Freedomland on radio and television and in newspapers, railroad stations, and subway cars, so many New Yorkers drove to Baychester on opening day that traffic came to a crawl on the Hutchinson River Parkway and New England Thruway. Before long Freedomland's parking lot, which held 8,000 cars, was full. About 61,000 people were admitted to the park, which cost $1 for adults and from 50 to 75 cents for children, exclusive of the rides and parking. Thousands more were turned away. After singer Pat Boone cut the ceremonial ribbon, customers poured in. They visited New England fishing villages and whaling ports, walked the streets of "Little Old New York," celebrated Mardi Gras in New Orleans, toured San Francisco's Chinatown and Barbary Coast, and saw the Bay Area city crumble during the 1906 earthquake. They also spent time with fur trappers in the Northwest and miners in the Southwest, stayed at a forest rangers' outpost in the Dakotas, and watched Pony Express riders set out on their long and perilous journey. They were fired on by the Blue and the Gray in the South and attacked by Indians in the Northwest Passage, from which, they were assured, they would "escape unharmed." They even helped put out the Great Chicago Fire of 1871, which was reignited every twenty minutes. To increase the excitement, the visitors could paddle canoes, ride stagecoaches and "sternwheelers," take a "transcontinental" trip in a "steam-powered Iron Horse," and zoom around two continents "in a rocket ship in Satellite City, our nation's city of the future."[4]

Although Freedomland got off to a good start—so good that General Manager Frederich V. Schumacher predicted that it would in time become as much a part of the New York scene as Central Park and the Statue of Liberty—things began to go downhill in the months ahead. Barely a week after the park opened, a stagecoach overturned, injuring ten passengers, three of whom had to be taken to a hospital. Two months later four thieves, armed with pistols and shotguns, stole nearly $30,000 from the vault and escaped by boat. Moreover, attendance declined, and revenue fell. Since the park cost much more to build than expected, Freedomland, Inc., was hard pressed to pay its bills, prompting Turner Construction and other contractors to file liens against the company. As planned, Freedomland closed in the late fall, when it became too cold to visit an outdoor amusement park in New York. But it reopened in the spring of 1961 and again in the next two springs, during which time management tried to reverse Freedomland's fortunes. To increase revenue, it attempted to attract more customers. It spent $1 million to renovate the park, built a 5,000-seat outdoor arena at which Benny Goodman and other well-known entertainers performed, and added new exhibits and rides, many of which had nothing to do with American history. To reduce expenses, management closed the park on weekdays in the spring and fall. Despite these efforts, Freedomland continued to operate at a loss.[5]

When Freedomland fell behind on its rent, Webb & Knapp took stock in the International Recreation Corporation and provided funds to pay the amusement park's bills, a move that Zeckendorf soon came to regret. Before long the firm ended up owning the company. Zeckendorf's son, William Jr., Webb & Knapp's executive vice president, was put in charge of it. As Zeckendorf later wrote, "We got into Freedomland the way the United States got into Vietnam, back-sideways, without really intending to, and only to clear up the mess somebody else had left behind." And "to get our money out," he said, "we put more money in." Unfortunately, it was money that Webb & Knapp could ill afford. By virtue of Zeckendorf's wheeling and dealing, the firm was deeply in debt. It managed to stay afloat for a while, thanks to an infusion of capital from a group of British investors and the Aluminum Corporation of America, both of which had partnered with Webb & Knapp in the past, and a $25 million loan from the Teamsters' Central States, Southeast and Southwest Pension Fund. But things went from bad to worse. In a desperate attempt to avoid bankruptcy, Webb & Knapp began selling off many of its assets. Among these assets was Freedomland, which had drained the firm of as much as $20 million. Zeckendorf unloaded the amusement park by selling 80 percent of the National Development Corporation, the Webb & Knapp subsidiary that owned it, to Hyman Green, a Florida real estate magnate who soon closed Freedomland and put it into bankruptcy. Then in June 1964, a year before Webb & Knapp itself filed for bankruptcy, Zeckendorf asked the United Housing Foundation if it would be interested in buying his 400 acres in the Bronx.[6]

OOO

Kazan had known about the Baychester site long before Zeckendorf offered to sell it to the UHF, but he had not considered it suitable for cooperative housing. As he saw it, the site had several serious drawbacks. One was its terrain. The site was a swamp—or, in the words of Nicholas Farkas, a member of Farkas, Barron & Partners, the UHF's consulting engineers, a "tidal marsh." Except for a narrow strip of land along the New England Thruway, all the land had originally been below high tide, and except for a small section of the southern portion of the site that had been raised by a former owner, much of it still was. Outside of what was left of Freedomland, the ground was covered by matted meadow grass, known as phragmites, with "water courses meandering through it," said Farkas. Especially susceptible to flooding was the part of the site closest to the Hutchinson River. To make matters worse, the bedrock was highly irregular—as much as 155 feet below the surface in some places and as little as 10 feet below in others. The site might have been suitable for an amusement park, most of whose structures were small and relatively flimsy, but not for a housing cooperative—and certainly not for the sort of high-rise housing cooperatives that the UHF had built at Penn Station South, Rochdale Village, and Amalgamated Warbasse. To provide the foundation for what would turn out to be almost three dozen 20- and 30-story towers, the UHF would have to pour millions of cubic yards of fill into the site and then drive thousands of piles into the bedrock. It would be a complicated, expensive, and, for the UHF, unprecedented undertaking.[7]

Another drawback of the site was its location. Along with most of Staten Island (and parts of southern Brooklyn and eastern Queens), Baychester was one of the most remote neighborhoods in New York City. Indeed, it was much closer to Westchester County than to Manhattan Island, which was the workplace and shopping center for most New Yorkers. If not inaccessible, the Baychester site was extremely inconvenient. The nearest subway stations, the Dyre Avenue Station on the Seventh Avenue line and the Pelham Bay Station on the Lexington Avenue line, were about a mile away. A trip to Manhattan—first a short bus ride and then a long subway trip—would take well over an hour. And given that both the Seventh Avenue and Lexington

Avenue lines were severely overcrowded, the trip would be very unpleasant. Moreover, in light of the financial troubles of the Metropolitan Transportation Authority (MTA), it was highly unlikely that either of these lines would be extended to the Baychester site in the foreseeable future. The New York, New Haven, and Hartford Railroad, which linked Connecticut and Westchester County with Manhattan, ran through the northeast Bronx but did not stop near Baychester. The Hutchinson River Parkway and the New England Thruway also provided access to Manhattan, but only for residents who owned a car and could afford to pay for parking, which was extremely expensive there. As a member of the staff of the City Planning Commission pointed out, it was hard to see why many middle-class New Yorkers would opt to rent or buy apartments in Baychester rather than in other "better-located" neighborhoods.[8]

Yet another drawback of the site was its size. Roughly half as large as Central Park, it was more than twice the size of the site of Rochdale Village, the UHF's largest housing cooperative thus far. If the foundation developed the Baychester site along the lines of Rochdale Village, the result would be the largest housing cooperative in the country, if not the world. As historian Peter Eisenstadt has written, size had long been of paramount importance to Kazan. If a housing cooperative was too small, he believed, it might be unable to sustain itself. And if built on the Lower East Side or in other run-down neighborhoods, a small housing cooperative might soon be overwhelmed by the surrounding slums. But if too big, Kazan thought, a housing cooperative might lose sight of the virtues of self-help and mutual aid. In a housing cooperative of tens of thousands of people, most of whom had little in common with one another, how would it be possible for the residents to get to know more than a few of their fellow residents? And how would it be possible for the residents to make an intelligent choice when called on to elect the leaders of the cooperative? Making matters worse, Kazan pointed out, most New Yorkers moved into the UHF cooperatives in an effort to improve their housing conditions, not to build a cooperative commonwealth. Some UHF officials had held that Rochdale Village was too large. And according to Harold Ostroff, they had favored dividing it into five much smaller, largely independent cooperatives.[9] But as large as Rochdale Village was, it would be dwarfed by a housing cooperative built on the Baychester site.

But these drawbacks were not insurmountable. Given the existing technology, it was possible to pour fill into the swamp and raise the land above high tide. It was also possible to drive piles into the bedrock and use them to support the foundations for the high-rise apartment houses. It would cost a great deal of money. But if Zeckendorf was willing to sell the land for a relatively low price—which, in view of his financial troubles, was highly likely—the overall cost of the Baychester site would not be prohibitive. Moreover, so many of New York's low- and middle-income families were still living in substandard housing that there was a strong demand for the high-quality, low-cost apartments that the UHF had been building for almost a decade and a half. As Farkas pointed out not long after work began at Co-op City, all of the UHF's housing cooperatives were "fully occupied and operating with remarkable success." Most had long waiting lists too. Among them was the Amalgamated Warbasse Houses in Coney Island, a part of New York City that was at least as remote as Baychester. In retrospect, Ostroff said, it might have been advisable to divide the Baychester site into a handful of smaller and more manageable housing cooperatives. But at the time that was not considered an option. Kazan's reservations notwithstanding, the UHF had been building larger and larger housing cooperatives even before the Baychester site came on the market. And its efforts were "a benchmark by which to measure all other housing in the cities," Julius C. C. Edelstein, executive assistant to Mayor Wagner, told the foundation's members in April 1964.[10] It also went without saying that the larger the cooperative the bigger the dent it would make in the city's housing shortage.

The Baychester site also had one advantage that helped to offset its many drawbacks. Like the former racetrack on which Rochdale Village was built, it was vacant. Other than a defunct amusement park, there was nothing there. There were no houses and no shops and therefore no residents and businessmen to be displaced and relocated. To understand why this advantage was so important, it is helpful to bear in mind a sea change that had taken place in New York (and other American cities) after World War II. During the late nineteenth and early twentieth centuries thousands of homes and shops were demolished in New York to make way for commercial projects, among them the construction of the Pennsylvania Railroad Station, which uprooted about 16,500 people in the west thirties, and the development of the Garment District, which displaced another 4,000 in the west twenties. Thousands of homes and shops were also demolished to make way for public improvements. Under the state's Small Parks Act, the city tore down 190 tenements on the Lower East Side, replaced them with the William H. Seward, Hamilton Fish, and Columbus parks, and in the process uprooted about 13,300 people. Another 10,000 residents and shopkeepers were displaced in "Little Italy" when the city extended Sixth Avenue. And to construct the approaches to the Williamsburg Bridge, the city demolished 200 tenements on Delancey Street, which drove about 12,000 people out of their homes and left the neighborhood looking, in the words of one observer, "as though a cyclone had struck it." On the Lower East Side alone nearly 700 tenements that housed 50,000 people were torn down to make way for public improvements between 1895 and 1905.[11]

Some New Yorkers resisted the city's efforts to displace them. In 1907, for example, a group of Lower East Side residents whose homes and workplaces were about to be demolished to make way for the approach to the Manhattan Bridge held a mass meeting at which they urged the municipal authorities to delay the evictions. When their appeal was ignored, several residents stormed a tenement on Madison Street and refused to leave. As the *Times* reported, "The wreckers anticipate that they are going to have to tear down some of the houses over the heads of the people." But most New Yorkers—even the many residents of Little Italy who were so upset by the proposed extension of Sixth Avenue that they came "in tears" to Rev. Anthony Demo, pastor of the Church of Our Lady of Pompeii—did not resist. And even if they had, it probably would not have done much good. For few other New Yorkers (and few if any housing reformers) were concerned about their plight. Referring to the residents of Mulberry Bend, a part of the Lower East Side that was demolished to make way for the parks that served as "[the] lungs of the poor," Jacob A. Riis wrote that they were being driven out of tenement houses that were "not fit for Christian men and women, let alone innocent children, to live in." E.R.L. Gould agreed. There was no "satisfactory way of dealing with irremediable insanitary premises than to tear them down," he insisted. Riis, Gould, and other New Yorkers felt much the same way about the displacement of working-class immigrants as Edith Abbott, a Chicago social worker. Observing a group of desolate Italian-Americans who were being evicted from a tenement house near the Dearborn Street railroad station, she wrote, "It was strange to find people so attached to homes that were so lacking in all the attributes of comfort and decency."[12]

In the aftermath of World War II, things changed in ways that few New Yorkers had anticipated. To make way for a wide range of new projects and facilities, several public authorities and city agencies demolished buildings (and in some cases entire neighborhoods) in record number. Chief among them were the New York City Housing Authority, which ran the nation's largest public housing program, and the Slum Clearance Committee, which

oversaw its largest urban renewal program. Also involved were the Triborough Bridge and Tunnel Authority and the Port Authority of New York and
New Jersey, both of which tore down buildings to make way for approaches
to their bridges and tunnels (and for the construction of the Port Authority's
bus terminal in Midtown Manhattan). Involved too was the New York City
Department of Real Estate, which was in charge of finding sites for schools,
parks, and playgrounds. Together these organizations displaced hundreds
of thousands of residents as well as a substantial number of workers. As
Stanley M. Isaacs, one of the few Republican members of the City Council,
pointed out in 1957, "Nobody can reckon the effect on city life [of the] reck-
less destruction [of buildings on] such an extensive scale as this last decade
has witnessed." What is more, said James H. Scheuer, president of the Citizens Housing and Planning Council, the demolition hit hardest at "the bottom strata of our society," which included "the sick, the old, the disabled,
[and] the economically incompetent." Making matters worse, many of the
displaced New Yorkers—as many as half in some neighborhoods and even
more in others—were African American and Puerto Rican.[13]

The displacement of so many vulnerable tenants aroused a storm of opposition, which prompted Mayor Wagner to declare in 1959 that relocation
was New York's "No. 1 problem." Leading the opposition—and in the eyes of
Robert Moses and other influential New Yorkers, jeopardizing their efforts to
rebuild the city—were several local and citywide tenants associations, many
of whose members were about to be uprooted. Allied with them was a group
of liberal organizations, which included the Americans for Democratic Action, the National Association for the Advancement of Colored People, the
American Jewish Committee, and the New York State Commission Against
Discrimination in Housing. Their spokesmen—among them, Councilman
Isaacs, Congressman Adam Clayton Powell Jr., and Harris L. Present, chairman of the New York City Council on Housing Relocation Practices—argued
that the city officials were doing little or nothing to relocate the displaced
residents, many of whom had "nowhere else to go," said Nathan Straus Jr.,
head of the United States Housing Authority from 1937 to 1942. The city had
cleared some slums, Isaacs acknowledged, but in the process it had created
many others. To ease the burden on New York's hard-pressed tenants, Present urged Governor Nelson A. Rockefeller to ask the state legislature to impose a two-year moratorium on the demolition of middle-income housing in
New York. Straus recommended that no more homes be torn down in the city
until enough public housing was built to accommodate the displaced tenants.

"You can put a side of beef in cold storage for a year," he said on radio station WMCA in 1958. "You cannot do the same for the American family."[14]

Abraham Kazan knew that many New Yorkers would vigorously oppose the attempts to demolish their homes and shops, not to mention their churches and other institutions, to make way for housing cooperatives. He also knew that many New Yorkers and New York organizations would support the opposition. The UHF managed to build Penn Station South after a long and ferocious struggle in Chelsea, in which the opposition claimed that the residents were being "moved into slums, not out of them." But as I pointed out earlier, the foundation ran into so much resistance from neighbors that it abandoned its plans for the Seward Park Extension and Robert Owen Houses. And at about the same time it shelved a plan for another large housing cooperative on the Lower East Side. Known as Delancey North, it would have run from Houston Street to Delancey Street and required the relocation of thousands of people, which was a sticking point for William Ballard, chairman of the City Planning Commission, and Milton Mollen, head of the Housing and Redevelopment Board. Like Robert Moses—many of whose projects, chief among them the redevelopment of Lincoln Square and the construction of the Lower Manhattan Expressway, ran into a great deal of resistance—Kazan was extremely disappointed by the reluctance of city officials to stand up to pressure from irate residents and shopkeepers. To rebuild neighborhoods, he insisted, it was necessary to relocate residents, which, he believed, could "be carried out without much hardship and without too much difficulty." He also pointed out that the people who were displaced to make way for UHF housing cooperatives had little trouble finding new apartments, most of which were better than their old ones.[15]

By the mid-1960s, if not earlier, Kazan realized that the relocation problem was not going away and that if anything the opposition to wholesale displacement was stronger than ever. More than anything else, it was this problem that prompted him to reconsider his view that the Baychester site was not suitable for cooperative housing. Given the widespread opposition to displacement, it would have been very hard, if not impossible, for the city to demolish houses and stores to make way for a housing cooperative in Manhattan. And even if it had been possible, what Julius Edelstein called "[the] revolt against slum clearance" would probably have deterred the city from designating the site as a Title I project. As a result, the cost of acquiring it would likely have been prohibitive. Hence the UHF had no choice but to look for a site in the outer boroughs. It would stand a better chance of obtaining the approval of city officials if the site was vacant and no buildings would have to be demolished and no residents displaced. The Baychester site, which, said the *Times*, was believed to be the largest parcel of vacant land in the city, was therefore tailor-made for the UHF. It was possible that in time New Yorkers might change their minds about the relocation problem, but Kazan did not have time. He was now in his mid-seventies and in poor health. (And with the exception of Harold Ostroff, most of his close associates were not much younger.) Kazan had already built more cooperative housing than anyone else—and more than anyone could have expected. But he wanted to build even more. Convinced that the Baychester site was his best option, he decided to take Zeckendorf up on his offer to sell it and see if they could reach an agreement on the price.[16]

Both Zeckendorf and Kazan were seasoned negotiators. And given that millions of dollars were at stake, it was not surprising that it took a while for them to reach an agreement. At the start Zeckendorf wanted $2 per square foot—or about $87,000 per acre. Since at some point he had decided to sell only 300 of the 400 acres, hoping that one day Webb & Knapp would be able to develop the other 100 acres for commercial or industrial purposes, the price came to roughly $26 million. Concerned that if the UHF paid $2 a square foot for the site (and then spent another $1 per square foot to improve it), it would have to charge more than $23 per room per month for the apartments, which was all that most working-class families could afford, Kazan offered $1 per square foot, or about $43,000 per acre, which came to about $13 million. But Zeckendorf—who, said Kazan, "thought that by shouting and pounding the table with his fist [he] could convince the others to increase the price"—would not budge. And neither would Kazan, whose organization, Jacob S. Potofsky pointed out, "was not interested in building houses for Park Avenue people." In an effort to persuade Zeckendorf to reduce the price, Kazan enlisted the help of Robert Moses, who, he hoped, could convince Zeckendorf that "the money just wasn't there." After a luncheon at Moses's office, both sides were as far apart as ever. But time was on Kazan's side. Zeckendorf, who was under intense financial pressure, eventually reduced the price to $1.20 per square foot, which came to about $52,000 per acre. Late in 1964 Kazan agreed to buy the 300 acres for roughly $15.6 million, which, wrote one observer, was an extremely low price by New York standards even "for a swamp."[17]

At the same time Kazan was negotiating with Zeckendorf, he and his associates were seeking assurances from city and state officials that they would support the construction of a housing cooperative on the Baychester site. In order for the UHF to move forward, the city would have to do more than just grant the project a tax abatement. It would also have to rezone the site, widen the streets, build the sewers, and, among many other things, lay the water mains. The UHF would also have to consult with dozens of high-ranking officials, not all of whom were in favor of the project. Some saw it as a bailout for Zeckendorf, and others said that the city did not have the money. But Mayor Wagner strongly supported the project and, as Kazan later recalled, told the foundation's leaders that "he would see to it that the [city] cooperated and worked with us." Also, in order for the foundation to press ahead, the state would have to do more than just designate the project part of the Mitchell-Lama program. It would also have to provide the capital—first the $15.6 million to acquire the site and then the hundreds of millions to build the cooperative. The UHF therefore appealed to Governor Rockefeller, who had helped persuade the State Housing Finance Agency to underwrite Rochdale Village. Speaking on behalf of Kazan, Potofsky described the UHF's plans to Rockefeller and told him that about $280 million would be needed to carry them out. "I listened for half an hour and asked questions," the governor remarked. "At the end of that time, I said, 'Look, if you can do what you say you can do, you've got the money.'" But it had to be done fast, he warned, before inflation and red tape drove up the cost. Since Rockefeller had appointed the head of the State Housing Finance Agency, the UHF had good reason to believe that it would have little trouble raising the necessary capital.[18]

ooo

By early 1965 the UHF had laid the groundwork for the development of the Baychester site. On February 9, 1965, Governor Rockefeller and Mayor Wagner held a press conference at the Commodore Hotel in Midtown Manhattan and announced that with the help of the state and city the foundation was going to build a huge housing cooperative on 300 acres in the northeast Bronx. Part of the Mitchell-Lama program, it would be called Co-op City, they told the audience, which included James W. Gaynor, head of the New York State Division of Housing and Community Renewal; Milton Mollen, head of the New York City Housing and Redevelopment Board; Peter J. Brennan, president of the Building and Construction Trades Council of Greater New York; and standing in for Abraham E. Kazan, who was in California recuperating from an illness, Jacob S. Potofsky. (Conspicuously absent were William Zeckendorf, Webb & Knapp's other officers, and the firm's many creditors.) Co-op City, Rockefeller and Wagner said, would house 15,500 middle-income families, almost three times as many as Rochdale Village and nearly 400 more than the UHF's seven other housing coopera-tives combined. When fully occupied, it would have 55,000 to 60,000 resi-dents, making it not only the world's largest housing cooperative but also the world's largest apartment development—larger than Parkchester, the Metro-politan Life Insurance Company's giant complex in the East Bronx, which had 12,280 units, and even larger, wrote the *Times*, than "any[thing] built in the Soviet Union since World War II." The project would cost an estimated $285 million, $263 million of which would be provided by the SHFA. Con-struction was expected to begin in the fall and to take about five years.[19]

Co-op City, Rockefeller and Wagner revealed, would have thirty-nine apartment houses, twenty-four, twenty-eight, and thirty-five stories tall, built of reinforced concrete and faced with brick. As usual, Herman J. Jessor would be the architect and Community Services, Inc., would be the general contractor. The apartments, all of which would have central air-conditioning and some of which would have good-sized terraces, would range from one to three bedrooms and from 900 to 1,500 square feet. By virtue of a long-term, low-interest loan from the State Housing Finance Agency and a 50 percent tax abatement from New York City, they would cost about $450 a room and roughly $22 to $23 per room per month in carrying charges, which was well within the reach of most working-class families. (Even with the tax abate-ment it was expected that Co-op City would generate about $5.5 million in property taxes, or about ten times as much as the site was currently yield-ing.) Co-op City would also have 10,500 parking spaces (8,800 of which would be located in underground garages), a shopping center, a community center, a recreation area, and its own power plant, the largest in the city except for those of Consolidated Edison. It would include four elementary schools, two junior high schools, a library, a firehouse, and a police station, all of which would be built by the city on land provided by the UHF. Plenty of land—indeed, more than 80 percent of the site—would be set aside for parks, playgrounds, and other open spaces. Co-op City, said Wagner, would enlarge New York's supply of middle-income housing, stimulate employment in the building trades, and, with the help of Peter Brennan, provide jobs for African Americans and Puerto Ricans, the lack of which had triggered the strike at Rochdale Village. If anyone asked whether lily-white unions would be used to build Co-op City, "tell them [the problem's] all taken care of," Brennan ad-vised Wagner.[20]

Not everyone was as enthusiastic about the UHF's plan as the mayor. A case in point was Joseph F. Periconi, a native New Yorker and three-term Republican state senator who had been elected borough president of the Bronx in 1961. Two days after the press conference he lashed out at Rockefeller and Wagner for failing to notify him beforehand. As a matter of "common courtesy," they should have invited him to the press conference, he insisted. Periconi also complained that the governor had given the impression that the project had already been cleared by the many public agencies whose approval was necessary. He had a point. The City Planning Commission had not held hearings on Co-op City, much less approved it. Neither had the Board of Estimate, of which Periconi was a member. Indeed, it was not until February 11, two days after the press conference, that the project was taken up by the Board of Estimate. The decision to make public the plan for the world's largest housing cooperative before submitting it to the Board of Estimate "makes whatever action the board takes now a farce," declared Periconi. A week later Periconi softened his opposition. He said that he supported the project, but insisted that the local community planning boards and the residents of the Bronx should have a say in its development. He pointed out that the Seventh Avenue and Lexington Avenue subways were already severely overcrowded, a point that was also made by Hyman Bravin, chairman of the Bronx County Liberal Party, who warned that "there will be standing room only during the morning rush hours [on these lines]." Periconi also stressed that the Forty-Seventh Police Precinct, which covered Co-op City, was seriously undermanned and that four elementary schools and two junior high schools would not be enough for the tens of thousands of new schoolchildren.[21]

Other New Yorkers objected to Co-op City on aesthetic grounds. Chief among them were the members of the Committee for Excellence in Urban Architecture, a group of professors of architecture and their students, most of whom were affiliated with Columbia University, Cooper Union, and Pratt Institute. On February 19, a week and a half after the press conference, the committee sent a letter to Rockefeller and Wagner denouncing Co-op City as "the negation of the ideals of [President Lyndon B. Johnson's] Great Society." The project had evolved "without safeguards as to the quality of design and planning," said the committee, and Herman Jessor's plan relied on "outdated design formulas which have already been proven inadequate." Especially offensive to the committee was the "extreme" height of the thirty-nine apartment houses, which, in the words of a *Times* reporter, would create "a feeling of alienation in anyone who lived in them." The project should be "subject to a review by an advisory board of qualified professional architects and planners," the committee insisted. Percival Goodman, an associate professor of architecture at Columbia, called Co-op City "a disgrace to humanity," saying that "just because it keeps the rain off doesn't make it a worthy place to live in." Michael Trencher, a spokesman for the students on the committee, held that since the state was underwriting the project there should have been a design competition. "Instead," he said, "it's just going to be thrown up." Kazan, who had little patience for anyone who criticized his housing cooperatives on aesthetic grounds, responded that none of the critics had ever built houses that working-class families could afford. He would listen to any group, provided it had "a practical plan for producing housing at $21 or $23 a room."[22]

The UHF's project aroused still other concerns, many of which were spelled out by the staff of the City Planning Commission even before Kazan agreed to buy the Baychester site. In a series of reports that were issued in late 1964, the planners reviewed the foundation's original proposal, which called for the construction of 17,150 apartments that would house about 61,000 people, or slightly more than Santa Barbara, California, and slightly less than Independence, Missouri. The project, the planners reported, would do much to increase New York's supply of middle-income housing and thereby deter many of the city's middle-class families from moving to the suburbs. But these benefits would come at a high cost—at least $75 million. Given that the Lexington Avenue and Seventh Avenue subway lines were already severely overcrowded, the city (or the MTA) would have to purchase an additional 120 subway cars, which, at $110,000 a car, would come to $13.2 million. An as yet undetermined amount would also have to be spent to lengthen the subway platforms. Another $3.5 million would be needed for buses that would run from the site to the subway stations. At least $9.8 million would have to be spent on the site's street system and the modifications of the adjacent street system, the planners reported. Nearly $2.3 million would be required for sewers and almost $1.7 million for water mains. Among other things, schools would cost about $18.7 million, health and welfare facilities roughly $5 million, and libraries, playgrounds, and other recreational facilities an estimated $4.5 million. These expenditures might well force the city to cut back what it would otherwise spend on community renewal and other programs, the planners pointed out.[23]

The planners also had several concerns other than what the UHF project would cost the city. They believed that it was too dense. Despite the foundation's claims, they held that it was not necessary to build 17,150 apartments (or about 76 per acre) to keep the carrying charges down to $21 to $22 per room per month. The foundation could reduce the size of the project substantially without raising the carrying charges by more than 40 cents a room. The planners were also concerned that the project consisted exclusively of high-rise apartment houses. "As families move through the growth cycle," they stressed, "their housing needs shift. Established and valued members of a community are forced to leave when they are unable to find quarters in the immediate vicinity which are appropriate to changing family needs." Hence the UHF would be well advised to include garden apartments and single-family homes in the project. The planners also contended that the project did not provide enough parking spaces and that given the remoteness of the site and the size of the development the UHF did not set aside enough space for private and semiprivate cultural and community facilities. The planners pointed out that the UHF's project might depress the market for other Mitchell-Lama developments, some of which were already finding it hard to attract tenants. Noting that New York had other better-located neighborhoods, some of which offered housing at similar prices and with similar amenities, the planners even cautioned that if the UHF developed the Baychester site along the lines of the current proposal, its appeal would be "so limited as to make the entire venture economically unsound."[24]

The staff passed its concerns on to the City Planning Commission. And on the commission's recommendation, the UHF reduced the project's density, cutting the number of apartments from 17,150 to 15,500. It also hired a well-regarded firm of landscape architects to work on the site plan. In the meantime the commission consulted with the various municipal agencies that were responsible for developing and operating Co-op City's public facilities. On April 28, 1965, two and a half months after Rockefeller and Wagner broke the news, the City Planning Commission held hearings on the UHF's revised proposal. Opposed to the project were spokesmen for Community Planning Board No. 12, which represented the neighborhood adjacent to Co-op City. They pointed out that the project would overwhelm the existing transit lines and other public facilities. In the event that it was built, they recommended that the Lexington Avenue and Seventh Avenue subways be extended to Co-op City. Also opposed was the Municipal Art Society, whose spokesman criticized the project for a lack of "physical or social variety" and argued that it would create an "economic ghetto," an argument that was made as well by the Metropolitan Committee on Planning and the Architects' Renewal Committee of Harlem. The American Institute of Architects (AIA) sharply criticized the project too. Its spokesmen contended that "the spirit of the tenants" would be "dampened and deadened by the paucity of their environment." They urged the City Planning Commission to undertake a thorough investigation of how best to build housing for the next generation of New Yorkers before it approved Co-op City.[25]

In favor of the project was the UHF, whose representatives claimed that Co-op City would provide decent housing for middle-income families at a reasonable price. They also stressed that the foundation had built other housing cooperatives whose residents took an active part "in the affairs of the community." And they insisted that Co-op City would be as racially and economically diverse as Rochdale Village, where 20 percent of the residents were African American and average household incomes ranged from $3,000 to $11,000 a year. The Citizens Housing and Planning Council also supported the project. Co-op City was not an "ideal community," its spokesman acknowledged, but neither was it an "inhuman environment inhumanly scaled." He also pointed out that the residents of the foundation's other housing cooperatives, many of whom had been living in them "successfully and happily" for years, "included people of widely varying backgrounds, education, occupations, and ways of thinking." (Although in favor of Co-op City, the council's spokesman expressed concern about the lack of rapid transit at Co-op City. He also recommended that the city provide low-rent housing in the adjacent area and that the foundation set aside adequate space for religious institutions.) Bronx Borough President Periconi, who had apparently gotten over being snubbed by Rockefeller and Wagner, was also in favor of Co-op City. But he insisted that the city ensure that rapid transit was provided for the project, that the public facilities were developed in a timely fashion, that part of the site was set aside for industrial use, and that adequate community facilities were available not only for future residents of Co-op City but also for current residents of the northeast Bronx.[26]

Even before the City Planning Commission held hearings on Co-op City, most of the more than a dozen members had already made up their minds. Following a site visit on April 21, only one said that he was opposed to the project. The city would be better off spending the money on its many run-down neighborhoods, he argued. A few other commissioners had reservations. One was concerned that the UHF had not provided enough details about the site plan. Another was worried that the shops, schools, and other community facilities would not be ready when the residents moved in. Two others were troubled that the UHF's plan did not include a high school. And one commissioner, who stressed that the city was losing manufacturing jobs, wondered whether the site could not be better used for light industry, though he also made the point that "things have gone so far that the project will not be stopped." But these commissioners still supported Co-op City, as, of course, did the others who had no reservations. Hence it came as no surprise that on May 12 the City Planning Commission approved Co-op City. As for Community Planning Board No. 12's claim that the project would overwhelm the Lexington Avenue and Seventh Avenue subways, it said that rapid transit was a problem not so much for Co-op City as for the entire northeast Bronx. In response to the AIA's proposal that the project be shelved until a thorough study was made of the city's housing needs, it pointed out that many such studies had been made in the past and many more would be made in the future. "But in the meantime, we must try to build housing accommodations as best we know how, to meet the urgent needs of our citizens."[27]

The City Planning Commission also made a series of recommendations, most of which were designed to improve Co-op City and assuage its critics. It ordered the UHF to revise the site plan, especially as it related to public facilities. The UHF would also have to get the commission's approval for the design of the garages, all of which would have to be "completely enclosed." Less burdensome to the UHF were the recommendations that it work with the various municipal agencies on the development of the street system and other public facilities and with the MTA on the provision of adequate bus service. The UHF was also urged to consult with religious and social groups that wanted space in Co-op City, a matter of great importance to the Rev. Harry J. Byrne, a member of the City Planning Commission as well as the executive secretary of the Committee on Housing and Urban Renewal of the Archdiocese of New York. In response to the concerns that Co-op City would become an "economic ghetto," the commission urged the UHF to set aside "an appreciable number" of apartments that would cost between $18 and $20 per room per month, which was $3 to $5 less than the projected carrying charges. Going even further, it also recommended that the UHF explore with the New York City Housing Authority and the New York State Division of Housing and Community Renewal the possibility of making some apartments available at "low-rent public housing levels," which the foundation was highly unlikely to do. In an attempt to generate employment near Co-op City, which was a high priority for Periconi, the commission also called on the city's Department of Commerce and Industry to try to induce light industry to set up shop in the area north of Co-op City.[28]

On May 20, a little over a month after the City Planning Commission approved Co-op City, the Board of Estimate began to review the project. By then it had received reports not only from the City Planning Commission but also from the Bureau of the Budget and the Housing and Redevelopment Board, to which the UHF's plan had been referred on February 11, two days after the Rockefeller-Wagner press conference. (For some reason the Board of Estimate had not yet heard from the comptroller, corporation counsel, commissioner of real estate, and Bronx borough president, to all of whom the plan had also been referred.) In mid-June the Board of Estimate held hearings on Co-op City. Speaking against the project were the Chester Civic Improvement Association, whose representative argued that Co-op City would overwhelm the existing community resources in the neighborhood, and the Bronx Taxpayers Council, whose spokesman contended that it was inappropriate for the state and the city to give so much money to a private organization. Also opposed was the New York chapter of the American Institute of Architects, which had recently criticized Co-op City's plan as "distressingly naïve, monotonous and lacking in understanding of human activity." But given that the project had the support of Governor Rockefeller, Mayor Wagner, Bronx Borough President Periconi, and, not least of all, New York City's powerful building trades unions, the outcome was never in doubt. As soon as the hearings were over the Board of Estimate approved Co-op City and granted it a 50 percent tax abatement for thirty years. On the advice of Budget Director William F. Shea, it also required that 90 of the 300 acres be given to the city for streets and other public improvements.[29]

Once the Board of Estimate gave its approval, only one obstacle remained. It was removed in mid-July when the State Housing Finance Agency, which was headed by James W. Gaynor, gave the Riverbay Corporation, the housing company the UHF had set up to build and manage Co-op City, a long-term, low-interest loan of $250.9 million. The culmination of six months of negotiations, the loan was supposed to cover 90 percent of the cost of Co-op City, which was estimated to be $283.7 million. The other 10 percent would come from Co-op City's 15,000-plus families, each of which would pay $450 a room for its apartment. The loan was by far the largest ever made by the SHFA, and almost half as much as all the loans that the agency had made since it was established in 1960. It exceeded the assessed value of all the buildings in Rockefeller Center, and it "would be enough," wrote the *Cooperator*, a publication of the UHF, "to purchase the Empire State Building many times over." No other agency in the country would even have considered such a loan, Rockefeller remarked at the press conference. The result, said Gaynor after the contract was signed at the Wall Street offices of the Morgan Guaranty Trust Company, would be "an extraordinary example of how the public and private sectors of our society can cooperate to develop facilities neither could produce alone." Shortly thereafter the SHFA sold $50 million in short-term notes to private investors and then advanced the Riverbay Corporation $14.9 million, with which it completed the purchase of the Baychester site.[30]

ooo

By the early fall work was well underway at Co-op City. Farkas, Barron & Partners, the consulting engineers who had worked for the UHF on the East River Houses, Penn Station South, and most of its other housing cooperatives, was trying to figure out how to fill the site, drive the piles, and lay the foundations for the buildings. At the same time Zion & Breen Associates, the landscape architects, were attempting to revise the site plan in ways that would deal with the concerns of the City Planning Commission. Herman J. Jessor, the UHF's architect, was putting the finishing touches on the design of the apartment houses, parking garages, and other buildings. And Community Services, Inc., the general contractor, was beginning to negotiate with the subcontractors that would prepare the site and erect the buildings. Although the first apartment houses would probably not be ready for occupancy for at least two years, CSI, the sales agent for Co-op City, opened an office on West Twenty-Third Street at which prospective residents could apply for an apartment and put down a deposit. The UHF was also holding seminars—on Mondays and Wednesdays in the Bronx and Tuesdays and Thursdays on the Lower East Side—at which applicants could meet their future neighbors, find out about the progress of Co-op City, and learn the principles of the cooperative movement. In charge of all the work except the UHF seminars was the Riverbay Corporation, whose president was Abraham Kazan and whose board included Jacob Potofsky, Robert Szold, Harold Ostroff, and other UHF leaders. As a Mitchell-Lama project, Co-op City was supervised by the New York State Division of Housing and Community Renewal.[31]

Of CSI's many tasks, by far the easiest and least expensive was demolishing Freedomland's buildings and their concrete foundations. All it took were laborers, bulldozers, and sticks of dynamite. Much harder and more expensive was filling the swamp and raising the site. (Unless the site was raised by at least twelve feet, wrote the *Times*, "the project's basements would become extensions of Eastchester Bay at high tide.") As Nicholas Farkas pointed out, the problems were twofold. The first was that roughly five million cubic yards of hydraulic fill, a mixture of sand and water, was needed for the job. But not enough sand was readily available, not even from the bottom of the Hutchinson River or the Long Island Sound. It was, however, plentiful in Gravesend Bay, off Coney Island, which was about twenty-five miles from Co-op City. To bring the sand to the site, CSI hired the Construction Aggregates Corporation, a Chicago firm, which outfitted a dredger named the *Ezra Sensibar*, in honor of the company's president. It was manned by two crews of forty, each of which worked twelve hours at a stretch. Starting in early September 1965, twice a day and seven days a week, the crew sucked 4,500 cubic yards of sand from Gravesend Bay. The ship then steamed up the East River, passed under the Hell Gate Bridge, which connected Manhattan with the Bronx, entered the Long Island Sound, and about three and a half hours later anchored off Orchard Beach. (The *Ezra Sensibar* could not go all the way to Co-op City because it drew twenty-seven feet when fully loaded, which was too deep for the Hutchinson River.) After the ship docked, employees of the State Division of Housing inspected the fill to make sure that it consisted mainly of fine grain sand that would undergo minimal settling.[32]

The second problem was that the fill had to be delivered to Co-op City, which was three miles away. On Farkas, Barron & Partners' recommendation, the crew poured water into the ship's hoppers to produce a slurry of 90 percent water and 10 percent sand. The slurry was then pumped into a pipe twenty-six inches in diameter. As the *Times* reported, the pipe came ashore alongside Orchard Beach and passed through picnic groves before it dropped into Orchard Beach Lagoon, which was often used "as a racing course for water crews." It then crossed a swamp, went under Shore Road, surfaced, ran beneath the New Haven Railroad tracks, surfaced again, dove under the Hutchinson River Parkway, crossed another swamp, and finally passed below the Hutchinson River to Co-op City. Next the slurry was pumped into smaller pipes and spread over the site, first over the north and higher section of Co-op City, which covered about 230 acres and contained four of the five housing clusters, and then to the south and lower section, which covered about 70 acres and contained the fifth housing cluster. The operation was done, wrote the *Times*, under the watchful eyes of thousands of "happy seagulls," for whom it was "a gigantic free lunch counter." The work was finished in May 1968, a little over two and a half years after it was started. And it cost $7.2 million—which came to $1.90 per square foot and $25,000 an acre. To put it another way, said Farkas, the price of the improved land was $1,500 per apartment, which was very low for property in New York City. The project was "an excellent example of how marginal land can be utilized for large-scale housing development."[33]

From the beginning, wrote Farkas, it was clear that Co-op City's buildings "would have to be supported on piles and that such piles in most cases would bear on rock." And for "the sake of economy," he pointed out, the buildings would "be sited away from locations that would require long piles and kept clear of steeply sloping rock surfaces." To gather information about the depth and contour of the bedrock, International Resources and Geotechnics, Inc., conducted seismic surveys, a process that uses small charges of dynamite to measure ground waves as they rebound from rock strata. Based on these surveys, Farkas, Barron & Partners decided where to locate the buildings. But since the surveys were not "sufficiently detailed," the firm arranged for Reliable Drilling Company and Raymond Concrete Pile Company to make "exploratory borings"—one or more for each 2,500 square feet of the foundation. All told, 1,900 borings were made, which came to 48,000 linear feet, or about nine miles. Joseph S. Ward & Associates, soil consultants, then analyzed samples taken from the borings. It submitted a report to Farkas, Barron & Partners spelling out for each building the type, size, and bearing capacity of the proposed piles. Based on this report, the consulting engineers prepared the plans for the foundations and the specifications for the subcontractors. All told, Farkas wrote, 56,000 piles were driven, which came to 1.68 million linear feet and cost $10.5 million. The piles varied greatly from building to building: some were as shallow as 10 feet and others were as deep as 100 feet. (As expected, all but two of the buildings and all but two of the garages were built on piles.) The cost per apartment also varied, ranging from $333 in some buildings to $485 in others.[34]

As the swamp was filled and the piles were driven, several changes took place that had an impact on Co-op City, though how much of an impact is hard to say. As I pointed out earlier, Abraham Kazan, who had been suffering from serious health problems, was forced to take a leave of absence as president of the United Housing Foundation in January 1966. Succeeded by Jacob

Potofsky, Kazan retired a year later. Although Kazan stayed on as president of the Riverbay Corporation and CSI for about a year, most of the day-to-day work was done by Harold Ostroff, Kazan's longtime right-hand man, who was promoted from assistant secretary to vice president of Riverbay in 1966 and named president of CSI a year later. For nearly a decade he served as Co-op City's chief executive and chief spokesman. As a result of concerns raised by the City Planning Commission and the State Division of Housing and Community Renewal, the Riverbay Corporation revised its original plan in a handful of ways. Instead of thirty-nine apartment houses, all of which would have been twenty-four stories and of uniform design, Co-op City would now consist of thirty-five buildings, with some of twenty-four stories, others of twenty-six, and still others of thirty-three. The buildings would also come in three styles, which were referred to as Tri-Core, Chevron, and Tower. To avoid monotony, Herman Jessor covered the facades of the buildings in bricks of many colors, including red, pink, and chocolate. And under pressure, the Riverbay Corporation included in the revised plan 236 townhouses, each with two apartments. When completed, Co-op City would house 15,372, not 15,500, middle-income families.[35]

Ground was broken for Co-op City on May 14, 1966. Although work had already begun on the power plant, the ceremony marked what the *Cooperator* called "the official beginning of construction of the world's largest cooperative undertaking." To preside over the festivities the UHF picked its president, Jacob Potofsky. And to deliver the speeches it invited Governor Rockefeller, Abraham Kazan, Robert Moses, Herman Badillo, the recently elected borough president of the Bronx, and George Meany, president of the AFL-CIO. All accepted, though Meany, who was recovering from surgery, was unable to attend. Instead he sent congratulations, as did President Lyndon B. Johnson, who praised the UHF for its "farsighted endeavor to provide so many people with a better place in which to live." Also unable to attend was James W. Gaynor, commissioner of the State Division of Housing and Community Renewal and chairman of the State Housing Finance Agency. Conspicuously absent from the ceremonies were former mayor Robert F. Wagner Jr., a strong supporter of Co-op City who had stepped down in 1965 after three terms in office, and his successor, former congressman John V. Lindsay. Following the groundbreaking ceremony, the UHF held a luncheon for 300 people, which was hosted by Harry Van Arsdale Jr., Francis Bloustein, vice chairman of the City Planning Commission, Paul Belica, executive director of the State Housing Finance Agency, and Jerry Voorhis, executive secretary of the Cooperative League of the USA, were the speakers. And as I noted earlier, Kazan was presented with an engraved shovel.[36]

About 2,000 people, many of whom had already applied for apartments in Co-op City, attended the groundbreaking ceremonies. There, on a cool, cloudy day, they watched as Rockefeller, Potofsky, Kazan, Moses, Badillo, Ostroff, Robert Szold, and Peter Brennan dug the first symbolic holes at Co-op City. (Standing next to them were six youngsters, two of whom were children of prospective Co-op City residents and two of whom were daughters of Commissioner Gaynor.) Many of the dignitaries also addressed the crowd. Rockefeller praised the UHF for providing "better living for 55,000 of our fellow New Yorkers" and doing much to solve the city's acute housing problem. "There are plenty of $100-a-room apartments in New York City," he said, "but few indeed that provide good living [for] under $25 a room." Potofsky lauded Co-op City as an example of "grass roots democracy at work." It was a place whose residents "will come from all walks of life and will represent all races, colors and creeds [and] will use the same schools, the same stores, the same churches." Kazan told the crowd that he hoped Co-op City's residents would "learn to live together through the method of self-help." Badillo said it was his hope that Co-op City would become an integral part of the Bronx rather than an isolated and self-contained community. And Moses praised Kazan, Potofsky, and Van Arsdale for leading New Yorkers "out of the wilderness of ancient rookeries" and pointing the way to "a promised land." "The hope of slum clearance is in the cooperatives," he declared, not "the dead hand of government ownership." "The Needle Trades [unions] have shown the way," he said. "They have furnished the models and the inspiration. Give them the tools and with the aid of other unions and other realists they can finish the work."[37]

Once the groundbreaking ceremonies were over, construction began in earnest. Given that Co-op City would be home to as many people as there were in Bangor, Maine, Daytona Beach, Florida, and Bloomington, Indiana, it was a huge undertaking, among the largest ever in New York City. Involved were not only dozens of subcontractors (and the host of municipal agencies with which they had to deal) but also hundreds of iron and steel workers, steamfitters, welders, carpenters, electricians, plumbers, painters, plasterers, and other craftsmen, not to mention a good many teamsters, laborers, and elevator operators. The project was not only very large but also extremely complicated. And everything had to be orchestrated with great care. For example, the windows had to be installed before the bricklayers and carpenters went to work. Otherwise the apartments would be exposed to the elements and work would have to be stopped for much of the winter. The electricians would have to stay ahead of the bricklayers too. It was also very hard to know how long it would take to build the high-rise apartment houses. Some were taller than others. And some would be built on bedrock near the surface, others on bedrock well below the surface. How soon the buildings could be completed also depended on organizations over which CSI had little or no control. Among them were the utility companies and the City of New York, which was in charge of paving the streets, building the sewers, and laying the water mains. And as Harold Ostroff told the Riverbay Corporation Board of Directors shortly before the work was finished, "the completion dates projected by New York City were seldom, if ever, adhered to."[38]

CSI made "steady progress" in 1967, Ostroff reported. It laid the foundations for many of the apartment houses, erected the steel frames for several others, and poured the concrete and laid the bricks in still others. One garage was almost finished, and two others were well underway. Work had also begun on Shopping Center One. Things also went well in 1968. By the end of the year most of the apartment houses were under construction, the power plant was nearly finished, and excavation had started on the townhouses. Late in 1968, by which time the first apartment house was ready for occupancy, the UHF decided that it was time to celebrate the opening of Co-op City. The dedication, which I described earlier, was held on November 24 and carried out with much fanfare. Early in December the first residents, some of whom had been given symbolic keys at the dedication, moved into their new homes. The plan, said George Schechter, vice president of CSI, was for sixteen families to move in every day. "That's all the four elevators can handle," he explained. If all went well, one apartment house would be filled every month and all the buildings would be completed within three years. The first residents were "in a sense pioneers," wrote the *Times*, which noted that for the time being they would be living in a community that was "without schools, markets, easy access to the subway and paved roads." Moreover, said the *Cooperator*, it was the first residents and the more than 15,000 other middle-income families who follow in their footsteps who would "bring to fruition the promise of Co-op City" and the cooperative housing movement of which Co-op City was, in Governor Rockefeller's words, "the crowning achievement."[39]

Things went much less smoothly at Co-op City in 1969 and 1970. A severe shortage of plasterers slowed down construction, especially in the townhouses, which required more painstaking work than the apartment houses. The problem was eventually resolved by bringing in plasterers from Canada. But in the meantime, Ostroff said, it took "an inordinate amount of overtime and Saturday work to keep the construction going." The rapid pace of construction, at the peak of which about 500 apartments were being completed each month, also put a tremendous strain on the manufacturers of flooring, kitchen cabinets, closet doors, and other fixtures. Moreover, during the summer of 1969, when most of the contracts between the employers and the unions expired, several labor disputes racked Co-op City, most of which were more disruptive than the struggle between the carpenters and iron workers over who would install the aluminum window frames at the East River Houses. One dispute started in late July, when Local 282 of the International Brotherhood of Teamsters went on strike at Co-op City as well as at the World Trade Center, the Port Authority of New York's two 110-story office buildings that were then under construction in Lower Manhattan. The strike was begun by a group of truckers who hauled ready-made concrete to the site. It quickly escalated when the truckers who transported lumber, plumbing supplies, and other building materials refused to cross the picket line. As the strike dragged on, many craftsmen, even some who had no qualms about crossing the picket line, "had to knock off," said a CSI clerk, because they had no materials to work with.[40]

Even more disruptive was the strike by Local 1 of the International Union of Elevator Constructors (IUEC), whose members operated the elevators that carried the carpenters, plumbers, and other craftsmen to the upper floors of Co-op City's thirty-five high-rise apartment houses. (A different union represented the workers who operated the elevators that carried the building materials.) After their contract expired on July 1, the union's 2,500 members walked off the job, not only in Co-op City but also in other large-scale private and public projects in New York. The strike hit Co-op City especially hard, keeping many craftsmen from working on the apartment houses that were still under construction and preventing many residents from moving into the ones that were already finished. After a while the employers, who were represented by the National Elevator Association, offered the IUEC a new contract that would have raised wages and fringe benefits by more than 40 percent. But against the advice of their leaders, the rank and file rejected it in late August. Things went from bad to worse in September. At the request of Fire Commissioner Robert O. Lowery, who feared that without elevators his department would be unable to fight fires in high-rise buildings under construction, Buildings Commissioner John T. O'Neill banned work on all structures of more than fifteen stories, bringing construction to a halt on many of Co-op City's unfinished apartment houses. The elevator operators' strike was a calamity, said George Schechter in early October. What with the higher construction costs and lower carrying charges, "there's no way to calculate what we're losing."[41]

With the help of federal mediator Matthew Miller, the union and the association reached a tentative agreement on a new three-year contract on October 10. A week and a half later the rank and file ratified it and thereby brought the three-and-a-half-month strike to an end. Construction then resumed at a normal pace. By August 1970, Ostroff reported, the concrete work had been completed on all the high-rise buildings, townhouses, and garages. And the brickwork was well underway. Shopping Center One was finished, Shopping Center Two was under construction, and Shopping Center Three was in the planning stage. Four garages were open, and the others were nearly finished. By the end of the year, he predicted, twenty-one of the thirty-five high-rise apartment houses would be "more or less fully occupied." Six months later Schechter announced more good news. All the buildings would be fully occupied by the end of 1971, he said. Four of the five schools would be open by then, and a high school would be ready for students in January 1973. Schechter was not far off the mark. The last family, Hector and Sheila Pastrana and their five children, moved into Co-op City in March 1972, slightly more than three years after the first families had moved in. By then all the garages were open. So were two schools, one elementary school and one intermediate school. And two more schools would open in the fall. About seven years after the UHF bought the Baychester site and roughly six years after it held the groundbreaking festivities, construction was more or less over at Co-op City. Speaking at the ceremony at which the Pastranas were given the keys to their three-bedroom apartment in one of the townhouses, Ostroff said that if Co-op City "were built anywhere else but in New York City it would be one of the wonders of the world."[42]

ooo

Speaking at the dedication of Co-op City, Harold Ostroff said that there was much to celebrate, not the least of which was that "some 50,000 people have voluntarily chosen to stay in New York in a community which they will collectively own and operate." But as large as Co-op City was, he went on, it "does not begin to meet the needs which exist in the city [for low- and middle-income housing]." What was needed for "the two million New York-ers now living in horrible sub-standard slums" was not one Co-op City but forty Co-op cities. And the UHF, he declared, "stand[s] ready" to build them—and thereby transform Harlem, Bedford-Stuyvesant, South Jamaica, and the South Bronx—"just as fast as the city and state are committed to such programs." Governor Rockefeller said that he was "delighted" by Ostroff's remarks that the UHF was ready to build Co-op cities all over New York. Claiming that the United States was "on the threshold of a new era in coping with our great urban problems," he declared that Co-op City showed what could be done not only in New York but all over the country, a point that was also made by Ostroff a few years later. Among the other New Yorkers who believed that Co-op City and other large-scale cooperatives would go a long way to solving the city's housing problem and getting rid of its slums and ghettos was Robert Moses, who was one of the other speakers at the dedication. Indeed a few years after work began at Co-op City he came up with what he called a "workable, uncompromising plan" to raze the central Brooklyn slums, move some 160,000 residents into a huge housing coop-erative at Breezy Point and Fort Tilden in Queens, which would be known as Atlantic Village, and then rebuild Bedford-Stuyvesant, Brownsville, and East New York.[43]

Despite what Ostroff said, it was highly unlikely, if not inconceivable, that the UHF (or other nonprofit organizations) would build forty Co-op cities in New York to house more than two million people—or about one of every four New Yorkers. But during the late 1960s and early 1970s there were signs that the foundation might well undertake at least two large hous-ing cooperatives, one in Brooklyn and the other in Jersey City. Early in 1967 Governor Rockefeller and Commissioner Gaynor asked UHF president Jacob Potofsky if the foundation would be willing to sponsor a housing cooper-ative on 150 vacant acres in Canarsie. The site had been assembled a few years earlier by a developer who planned to build rental housing on 110 acres and a shopping center on the other 40 acres, but subsequently abandoned the project. Although Potofsky was well aware of the "tremendous need" for middle-income housing in New York, he was not sure that the foundation could take on another large project at the same time that it was working on Co-op City. But when he was advised by the UHF staff that the preliminary work on Co-op City was "substantially completed," he recommended that the board accede to the request of the governor and the commissioner, pro-vided that the state and the city met several conditions. Among them were

that the state advance funds for the purchase of the land, that the city provide valuable tax breaks, and that the price of the apartments be no more
than $450 a room and no more than $25 to $26 in carrying charges. The
board went along with Potofsky's recommendation, and the state and city
accepted his conditions. In late June Rockefeller made public the UHF's plan
for a large housing cooperative that would be called Twin Pines Village.[44]

According to the plan, which was strongly supported by the governor,
the UHF would build forty-three apartment houses, ranging from sixteen to
twenty-one stories, that would accommodate 6,000 middle-income families
and, as usual, would be designed by Herman Jessor. It would also provide
parking for 5,000 automobiles in several three- to six-story covered garages. A Mitchell-Lama project, Twin Pines Village was expected to cost just
under $137 million, 90 percent of which would be underwritten by a long-
term, low-interest loan from the State Housing Finance Agency. Thanks in
part to a tax abatement from the city, the price of the apartments would
be $450 a room and $22 to $23 per room per month in carrying charges,
though for 20 percent of the units the carrying charges would be only $18
to $19 per room. Mayor John V. Lindsay also backed the project, though he
had reservations about what he called its "unimaginative" design. But Clarence D. Funnye, a member of the board of the National Committee Against
Discrimination in Housing, vigorously opposed Twin Pines Village. He argued that the construction of this "mammoth self-contained community"
would undermine the ongoing efforts to stabilize Canarsie, a neighborhood
that was "presently in a state of extreme racial and economic flux." It would
drain tenants from "existing transition areas," spurring "the rapid ghettoization" of the very districts that public authorities and private citizens were
"trying to save." Funnye also stressed that Twin Pines Village, which was
only three miles from Kennedy International Airport, would be "racked with
almost constant noise of nerve-shattering level." For this reason the Federal
Aviation Administration also opposed the project. This opposition notwithstanding, Twin Pine Village's prospects looked extremely promising at the
end of 1967.[45]

Another opportunity for the UHF arose in March 1972, when Mayor
Paul T. Jordan of Jersey City, who had recently visited Co-op City, invited
Harold Ostroff to meet with him and Abraham L. Wallach, the city's director of planning. Jordan told Ostroff that Jersey City was planning to redevelop its run-down waterfront, roughly 3,000 acres that overlooked Lower
Manhattan, Ellis Island, and Liberty Park, the home of the Statue of Liberty.

The site, much of which was owned by Jersey City, the Penn Central Railroad, and the federal government, would be used for residential as well as industrial purposes. "We want the middle class to come back to Jersey City," Jordan said. Would the UHF be interested in taking part in the project and building a housing cooperative on the site? he asked. Ostroff replied that it would. At the heart of what the city and the foundation envisioned was, in Ostroff's words, "a new town within a town," and not just, as Jordan put it, "another bedroom community for lower Manhattan." Called Liberty Harbor, it would be even larger than Co-op City. Located on a 700-acre site, it would contain 20,000 middle-income apartments, which would accommodate about 60,000 people (and increase the population of Jersey City by almost 25 percent). It would consist of high-rise and low-rise apartment houses as well as schools, shopping plazas, and perhaps a station on the Port Authority's commuter line. As a first step, Ostroff recommended that Jersey City commission the UHF to undertake a series of economic, engineering, and financial studies, which, he hoped, would be paid for by the city, state, and federal governments.[46]

Six months later Jersey City, the UHF, and National Kinney Corporation, whose president was Paul Milstein, a New York real estate mogul, signed a contract that authorized the foundation to prepare a master plan for Liberty Harbor. National Kinney would pay for it. In return, the company would have an option to purchase and develop the site. The plan for what Jordan called the "largest residential and industrial development proposed for any metropolitan area in the United States" was made public in September. It called for an industrial park that would create 12,000 new jobs, a waterfront park that would be a "showcase" for the state's bicentennial celebration, said Governor William T. Cahill, and a 20,000-unit housing cooperative that would consist of garden apartments, townhouses, and apartment towers. The UHF, which, said Jordan, had "the kind of experience and social commitment that we need if we are to get adequate housing [in Jersey City]," had an option to build the co-op. Liberty Harbor, which was expected to cost about $2 billion, was a milestone for both the UHF and Jersey City, wrote the *Cooperator*. It was the first time that the foundation planned to build a housing cooperative outside of New York City. And it was "the realization of a dream of city officials to transform a blighted area into a 'new town' overlooking New York harbor." Liberty Harbor "might rightfully be called an offspring of Co-op City," the *Cooperator* went on. "It was the inspiration of the cooperative community in the northeast Bronx that lead [sic] officials of Jersey City to dream about what could be done to revitalize their own city." Among the many supporters of Liberty Harbor was Robert Moses. After visiting the site and joining Jordan for lunch, a get-together that was arranged by Ostroff, Moses said that he was "delighted" by the project. "This is the kind of thing I was fighting for back in the thirties and forties for New York City."[47]

Although both Twin Pines Village and Liberty Harbor got off to a good start, it was not clear that they could overcome the many obstacles in their path. Nor was it clear that the UHF would build other Co-op cities, much less, as the *Lawyers Title News* wrote, that Co-op City would "serve as a model for the rebuilding of American cities." What was clear was that the UHF would have to move ahead without Abraham E. Kazan, who, after taking a leave of absence in 1966, retired in 1967 and died four years later, a few months before the last families moved into Co-op City. The foundation could count on the support of Nelson A. Rockefeller, to whom, Ostroff said, "we will be endlessly [in] debt," until late 1973, when he resigned as governor and succeeded Gerald R. Ford as vice president. But it could not expect help from Robert F. Wagner Jr., who stepped down as mayor at the end of 1965, or from Robert Moses, who was no longer a force to be reckoned with after he was forced out as chairman of the Triborough Bridge and Tunnel Authority in 1968. Still, the UHF had a sterling reputation. It had the backing of organized labor. And in Harold Ostroff it had a worthy successor to Kazan. Moreover, the Mitchell-Lama act was still on the books, and the State Housing Finance Agency still had plenty of money to lend. As Ostroff pointed out at the dedication of Co-op City, the UHF was committed to building "the best possible housing for the lowest possible cost for low and middle income [New Yorkers]."[48] But whether it would be able to live up to its commitment depended on a great many things, not the least of which was how well Co-op City (and its other housing cooperatives) fared in the years ahead.

CHAPTER 5

A MORE OR LESS AUSPICIOUS START

Once construction got underway at Co-op City and the first of the residential towers began to rise—seemingly, wrote Eden Ross Lipson, a young city planner, "from nothing in the middle of nowhere"—Ostroff and his associates hoped that the project's critics would come around. But their hopes were dashed. Instead of subsiding, the criticism intensified. In the forefront were spokesmen for the Municipal Art Society and the New York City chapter of the American Institute of Architects. Other critics included Walter McQuade, who wrote about architecture for *The Nation, Life, Fortune*, and *Architectural Forum* and also sat on the City Planning Commission; Peter Blake, an architect, author, and editor-in-chief of *Architectural Forum*; Roger Starr, executive director of the Citizens Housing and Planning Council; Elinor C. Guggenheimer, a onetime member of the City Planning Commission and later a candidate for president of the City Council; Harry Schwartz, chairman of the New York City chapter of Planners for Equal Opportunity; and Clarence D. Funnye, chairman of the Harlem chapter of the Congress of Racial Equality and a member of the board of the National Committee Against Discrimination in Housing. Co-op City was also criticized by *Time*, by *Newsweek*, and, in an otherwise mostly favorable editorial, by the *New York Times* as well as by several journalists, including Roberta Brandes Gratz, who wrote a series of articles about it for the *New York Post* in 1968, and Jack Newfield and Paul Du Brul, who described Co-op City as an "urban Stonehenge."[1]

Much of the criticism of Co-op City was aimed at its architecture. After praising Co-op City for providing high-quality, low-cost housing for middle-income families, Peter Blake declared that its residential towers were "fairly hideous," especially from the outside. And "most of the view from the inside is going to be of somebody else's outside." Ada Louise Huxtable, who wrote about architecture for the *Times*, objected to its "standard cookie-cutter" design. Roberta Brandes Gratz called Co-op City "the most banal housing development I have ever seen." *Time* was, if anything, even more critical. Co-op City's huge buildings, which "can be seen from miles away," were "glum and graceless structures," it wrote. Pointing out that its 15,372 apartments had hardwood floors, ample closets, and central air-conditioning, *Time* acknowledged that, "at $450 per room down and $25 per room in monthly maintenance charges, Co-op City is an unbeatable bargain." But "it is relentlessly ugly; its buildings are overbearing bullies of concrete and brick. Its layout is dreary and unimaginative." *Newsweek* agreed. "Viewed from the roaring six-lane expressways that snake their way around its 300-acre expanse," it said, "the towers of New York's Co-op City rise bleak and spectrally through the smog, a prospect so remote and cheerless that affluent commuters often shudder when they pass it." Its more than thirty apartment houses are "just great slabs of monotonous, non-ziggurat design, totally devoid of any humanizing aesthetic scale." In the eyes of its many critics, wrote *Times* reporter Joseph P. Fried, Co-op City was nothing less than an "esthetic disaster."[2]

According to some critics, not only was Co-op City unsightly, a blot on the landscape of the northeast Bronx, but as Walter McQuade said, it was also "sterile." Its huge residential towers produced "a sense of alienation" among the occupants. The United Housing Foundation, *Time* wrote, made "little effort to create neighborhoods at Co-op City, or a feeling of community. Instead, residents are treated like clean socks, rolled up and tucked into gigantic bureau drawers." The result, it went on, is that Co-op City is "shaping up as an eminently depressing place to live." *Newsweek* made much the same point. Quoting the American Institute of Architects, it warned that "the spirits of the tenants would be dampened by the paucity of their environment," which, even one UHF official conceded, would have nothing in the way of the small candy stores and other shops that enlivened many of New York's neighborhoods. One of the most outspoken critics of the "tower-in-the-park" approach adopted by the UHF at Co-op City and most of its other projects was Lawrence Halprin, a native New Yorker who had studied landscape architecture at the Harvard Graduate School of Design and later went on to head his own firm in San Francisco. On the recommendation of Mayor John V. Lindsay's Task Force on Urban Design, Halprin made a study of several residential developments that had recently been built in New York. He found that these projects, most of which were made up of tall towers surrounded by open spaces, were "sterile and uninviting" and thus "disastrous for the city." They isolated the residents and left them feeling alienated. Even in nonprofit cooperatives like Penn Station South, which was located in the bustling Chelsea neighborhood, "architectural and planning alienation is followed by personal alienation."[3]

The critics charged that Co-op City was poorly planned too. As Elinor C. Guggenheimer pointed out, "You don't design cities of 55,000 as though you are designing a housing project." But that, wrote the *Times*, was exactly what the UHF did at Co-op City. Its philosophy, said Fred Williams, executive director of the Municipal Art Society, "is to get up the housing and hope the city will follow them into a new area with services." Or as Ada Louise Huxtable put it, "Beyond the provision of some basic shopping facilities and the space allotment for necessary public services that the city must follow along and provide, everything else is expected to fall into place." Co-op City's environmental and social planning was "minimal," she said, an example of "planning fence-mending" and "posterior planning by negotiation" and an indication of how "the greatest city in the world stumbles on." The result, wrote the *Times*, is that Co-op City's first residents "are going to be plagued by a shortage of schools, streets and utilities," as well as by "poor transportation." Indeed, said *Time*, they will "have to bus their kids to nearby schools and shop in a make-do supermarket on the bottom floor of a garage" and hope that one day a new subway line "will connect the project directly with New York City." This "deplorable situation," said the *Times*, "shows the folly of large-scale housing developments without coordinated planning for the public services that [they] will require." For this the critics blamed not only the UHF but also the municipal agencies that, as the *Times* put it, "took their usual leisurely time" in providing the necessary services and facilities for Co-op City.[4]

Co-op City was also criticized, wrote the *Times*, on the grounds that it "has 'siphoned' off middle-class white families from Central Bronx areas where they feel threatened by an influx of Negroes and Puerto Ricans." This criticism was fueled by "white flight," which spread through New York and other big cities after World War II. "Such an exodus," the *Times* pointed out, "is said to leave [many old] neighborhoods unstable and ripe for speculation" and even blockbusting. A case in point was the once-fashionable Grand Concourse, which had been 98 percent white in 1950 and was expected to be less than 50 percent white by 1975. Co-op City would not only destabilize these old neighborhoods, the critics argued, but would also spur the creation of new ghettos, most of whose residents would be African Americans and Puerto Ricans. Moreover, the critics insisted, Co-op City and other UHF cooperatives were doing nothing to meet the housing needs of New York's low-income families. While the UHF was doing more to attract African Americans to Co-op City than to its other cooperatives, these efforts were "minimal," said Betty Hoeber, director of the open-housing program of the New York City Urban League. To remedy this situation, Jerome Liblit of the New School for Social Research and Clara Fox of the United Neighborhood Houses urged the city to purchase apartments for low-income families in Co-op City, a proposal that Harold Ostroff strongly objected to on the grounds that it would split the community into two distinct groups, only one of which would have much of a stake in the community.[5]

Co-op City even came under attack on environmental grounds. In a letter to the *Times* published in November 1969, a year before the US Environmental Protection Agency was established, Gregory Battcock, an associate professor of art history at Paterson State College, declared that "the Bronx may have lost its last chance for a natural wildlife preserve when the City approved the construction of Co-op City" on a "huge, almost empty site containing lakes and streams." Ignoring the fact that much of the Baychester site had been turned into an amusement park several years before William Zeckendorf sold it to the United Housing Foundation, Battcock claimed that it "was much more valuable to the city empty than it now is containing $296 million in housing." He then went on to say, "This badly designed project not only abuses the natural amenities of its own site—it ignores the natural advantages that older, partly occupied sites had to offer." The municipal authorities would have been better advised spending their money on razing tacky houses in run-down neighborhoods and renovating community institutions elsewhere in the city than on squandering it "upon this ill conceived, ecologically destructive scheme." Co-op City, Battcock concluded, "is, in fact, an old fashioned conception that is little more than capitalist exploitation." The decision to approve its construction "is perhaps the biggest blunder committed in New York City in the name of progress."[6]

ooo

As expected, the UHF leaders defended Co-op City against its critics. George Schechter, the foundation's vice president, said that Co-op City was "aesthetically pleasing." While it may not be a great example of contemporary design, "it stands up well. It will probably not get an award [for its] architecture but it's nothing that New Yorkers should be ashamed of." Responding to criticism that Co-op City's residential towers lacked the "lavishly decorated lobbies frequently found in new apartment buildings," Harold Ostroff pointed out that Co-op City's lobbies and corridors were meant to be "functional and attractive," not "'showplace' public areas." Why spend money on lobbies, he said, "when people don't live in lobbies." Far better, added Schechter, to spend it on hardwood floors, air-conditioning, modern kitchen appliances, and other things that middle-income families needed. Herman Jessor, who not only designed most of the UHF's cooperatives but also devoted many years to Co-op City, weighed in as well. The project's residential towers "are pleasant in proportion and color values," he wrote, and the open colonnades on the ground floor provide residents with unobstructed views of Co-op City's parks and playgrounds. Speaking at the UHF's annual meeting in 1973, at which Ostroff presented him with an award for "his outstanding vision, talent, ability, and competency," Jessor took issue with the critics who complained about Co-op City's "cookie-cutter" design. "When they built the Taj Mahal and the pyramids," he said, "they didn't have to think about money and people," which were the constraints under which he and the UHF labored in building Co-op City.[7]

In their defense of Co-op City, the UHF leaders received welcome if unexpected support from Robert Venturi and Denise Scott Brown, both of whom were extremely influential, if somewhat iconoclastic, architects. The principals of Venturi, Scott Brown & Associates, a successful firm based in Philadelphia, and the authors of "Learning from Las Vegas," a highly controversial article published in *Architectural Forum* in March 1968, Venturi and Scott Brown wrote an essay in *Progressive Architecture* in February 1970 entitled "Co-op City: Learning to Like It." In it they took issue with the critics (and, less so, with the defenders) of Co-op City. Co-op City, they said, was not "hideous" or "sterile." Rather it was "conventional" and "ordinary." And these "are good or potentially good qualities." Indeed, they went on to say, "we should rejoice in [its] ordinariness." Co-op City "is not all right," Venturi and Scott Brown wrote, but "it is *almost* all right." It could have been better designed, though at a high cost that might perhaps be justified "for buildings of unique civic importance," but not for "everyday structures of the private city." Its site planning also left something to be desired. So did the UHF's decision to build Co-op City all at once and at a relatively high density. But, wrote Venturi and Scott Brown, these reservations "should not permit us, as we tend now to do, to castigate Co-op City as something we grew out of in the 1930s." If Co-op City has "an air of New-Deal idealism," they concluded, it should force us to reconsider "our aesthetics and philosophies, because Co-op City is more successful than some newer ideas."[8]

Venturi and Scott Brown also had doubts about the charge that Co-op City and other similar high-rise developments would isolate the residents from one another and leave them feeling alienated. This claim, they wrote, "is not proven. There exists no body of evidence linking social pathology with bleak or beautiful architecture and some evidence that people carry their social patterns, as well as their social ills, with them from housing type to housing type." Harold Ostroff was even more skeptical. "We do not subscribe to the theory that people become frustrated, alienated or dehumanized by the size and shape of buildings," he wrote in the *American Federationist*, a publication of the AFL-CIO. George Schechter agreed. "We don't believe height creates alienation," he told a *Times* reporter in 1968. "Everybody loves Co-op City except the critics," he said a year later. Most of them do not understand "that it isn't buildings that dehumanize people—the problem is whether the people have a sense of community." And there was a strong sense of community in Co-op City, one resident wrote in 1971. The so-called experts who made "those dire predictions of 'alienation' and 'hostility'" failed to take into account the "tremendous sense of community" that would be "engendered [in Co-op City] by the cooperative spirit," he pointed out. Three years after the first residents moved in Co-op City had one community center, which was used by 7,000 people each week. Two more were "nearing completion," and 150 religious, social, and community groups had already been organized. "And more are coming."[9]

The UHF leaders also denied the charge that Co-op City was poorly planned, that it had been treated as just another housing project rather than a city of more than 50,000 people. Ostroff acknowledged that many of the necessary facilities and services, including the streets, sewers, and schools, were not ready by the time the first residents moved in—and in some cases not even by the time the last residents joined them. But, he insisted, the fault lay not with the foundation but with the city, whose work was "slow and inadequate." As a result, said Schechter, the construction of Co-op City had far outpaced the provision of the necessary facilities and services. Probably no one was more critical of the city's efforts than Herman Badillo. Despite repeated warnings, he said, the Lindsay administration—which had taken office in 1966, a year after he was elected borough president of the Bronx—"has completely failed Co-op City. Private enterprise has done its share, but the city is 100% behind schedule." The nub of the problem, he added, was that about thirty different agencies, chief among them the Department of Public Works, the City Planning Commission, and the Board of Education, were involved in Co-op City. And each had its own leader, agenda, and budgetary constraints. What was needed, Badillo argued, was a coordinator who had direct access to Mayor Lindsay and could bring pressure on the various city agencies to pick up the pace. (Before long Lindsay appointed Byron T. Conrad of the Department of Public Works to be the coordinator for Co-op City, a decision that was hailed by the UHF's leaders.)[10]

The UHF's leaders also dismissed as groundless the charge that Co-op City was siphoning off middle-class white families from the Grand Concourse and other Bronx neighborhoods that were experiencing an influx of African Americans and Puerto Ricans. They pointed out that "white flight" had been well underway before Co-op City was conceived, a point that many city officials conceded. Moreover, argued Schechter, many middle-class white families would have moved from the Bronx to Queens or the suburbs even if Co-op City had never been built. Indeed, said the UHF's leaders, of the first 6,800 families that selected an apartment at Co-op City, only about 10 percent came from the Grand Concourse. Ostroff also stressed that the UHF was strongly committed to integrated housing. As evidence, he pointed to Rochdale Village, where 4,000 white families lived happily in the middle of an otherwise "all Negro community." And what had been done in Rochdale Village was being done at Co-op City, he pointed out. In an attempt to integrate Co-op City, the UHF took out ads in African-American and Hispanic newspapers and distributed promotional literature through Open City, a division of the Urban League that helped African Americans and Puerto Ricans find homes outside the ghettos. Supporting Ostroff's claim that the UHF was in the forefront of the effort to create diversified communities, a British visitor wrote in early 1973 that "a wide mix of race, ethnicity and age" distinguished Co-op City from Columbia, Maryland, Reston, Virginia, and most other recent developments in suburban America.[11]

Also groundless was the charge that Co-op City was an environmental disaster, wrote George Trinin, a New York architect who had worked for the State Division of Housing and Community Renewal in the 1950s, and who, so far as I can tell, had no connection to the United Housing Foundation. In a letter to the *Times* published in December 1969, Trinin wrote that far from an idyllic wildlife setting, as Professor Battcock claimed, the Baychester site had been "a vast swamp covered with short brush and few trees"—and the remains of Freedomland. It had only one lake, "a man-made hole created for drainage." The UHF's surveyors, Trinin added, "had to fight off the huge mosquitoes which had taken over the area, and were beset by scurrying rats every foot of the way as they took their measurements." To Battcock's charge that Co-op City was "little more than capitalist exploitation," Trinin responded that the UHF was "one of the truly dedicated cooperatives groups in the housing picture today" and had built Co-op City and its other large-scale housing cooperatives "without any profit." With its low down payments and modest carrying charges, Co-op City was "a far cry from capitalist exploitation." Moreover, Trinin argued, Battcock's charge that the approval of Co-op City was the "biggest blunder" ever committed in New York in the name of progress was "debatable to say the least." Given the "crying need for housing in the city," Trinin concluded, "the creation of modern centrally air-conditioned apartments for 60,000 people is just as much of a boon as preserving neglected swampland for mosquitoes and rats."[12]

As the debate over Co-op City dragged on, one contemporary wrote that the huge housing cooperative "was reminiscent of a Broadway theatrical spectacular [that is] lambasted by critics and loved by droves of ticket buyers." His comment was on the mark. By April 1966, a month before the groundbreaking ceremonies were held, roughly 4,500 New Yorkers had applied for apartments in Co-op City. Each of them put down a deposit of $500, which was held in escrow by the Amalgamated Bank. To accommodate the growing number of applicants, Community Services, Inc., moved the applications office from Grand Street on the Lower East Side to Twenty-Third Street and Eighth Avenue, a much more central location. (The office's staff of ten was headed by Ida Vozick, who had been in charge of the application offices at Penn South, Amalgamated Warbasse, and other UHF projects.) CSI also held pre-occupancy informational meetings for the prospective residents at the Amalgamated Houses Community Center in the Bronx and the United Housing Foundation Conference Hall in Manhattan. As the pace of construction picked up at Co-op City—and as the UHF sang the praises of Co-op City in the *New York Times* and other newspapers—the applications poured in, even in the slow summer months. By late 1967 Co-op City was receiving about twenty to twenty-five applications a day. And by late

September 1968, two months before Co-op City was dedicated and the first residents moved in, 7,500 families had bought apartments and another 1,500 had put down deposits.[13]

A good many families—ultimately as many as 10,000 and perhaps even more—withdrew their applications. And as promised, CSI refunded their deposits. But for every family that withdrew its application, several others submitted applications of their own. By early 1969 the number of applications passed 14,000. And Vozick and her staff stopped taking deposits for one-bedroom apartments and put applicants for these units on a waiting list. By late 1970, *Newsweek* reported, all of Co-op City's one- and two-bedroom apartments had been sold, "although many of them haven't even been built yet." Several months later Harold Ostroff predicted that by the end of 1971 all the apartments, even the three-bedroom apartments, would be allocated. By mid-1971 Co-op City had nearly 16,000 applicants—or slightly more applicants than it had apartments. As a result, *City News* reported, Vozick and her staff were telling the many New Yorkers who came to the office to file an application that "Co-op City is completely filled up. [All we can do is] put you on a ten-year waiting list"—on which there were already more than 5,000 other families. By then CSI had reduced the staff of the applications office, which later moved from West Twenty-Third Street to Co-op City. Julius Palmer, a member of the Riverbay Corporation Board of Directors, even suggested that the applications office should be closed, a step, he said, that would save Co-op City a good deal of money. But this suggestion was rejected on the grounds that CSI, not the Riverbay Corporation, was paying for the applications office, which, Schechter pointed out, "isn't costing Co-op City a cent."[14]

According to the State Division of Housing and Community Renewal, which made a survey of Co-op City in mid-1968, roughly 75 percent of the first 6,000 applicants came from the Bronx, though contrary to the conventional wisdom, not all of them from the Grand Concourse, noted the real estate economist Frank S. Kristof. Another 23 percent came from Manhattan, Brooklyn, and Queens, and only 2 percent from outside the city (and Staten Island). Of the slightly more than 12,000 people who lived in Co-op City in 1970, the US Census Bureau reported that about 80 percent were white, the large majority of whom were first- and second-generation Jewish immigrants. Among them was my maternal grandmother, Bessie Richman, who was born in Russia, migrated to the United States as a teenager, worked as a seamstress on the Lower East Side, married a grocer with whom she had four children, and after his death moved from Manhattan to the East Bronx, then to the West Bronx, and then, in her eighties, to Co-op City. She was joined there by her son Grant, a New York City taxi driver who had been living with his wife and four children in a public housing project in the North Bronx. Thanks in part to a concerted effort by the UHF, Co-op City was more integrated than most of New York's other housing cooperatives. About 13 percent of the residents were African Americans, one of whom, a New York City police officer, said that Co-op City gave him "a chance to get in on the ground floor, instead of settling for some place that the white man had used and left." Another 7 percent were Hispanics, most of them Puerto Ricans.[15]

Whatever their race and ethnicity, most of Co-op City's residents were members of the lower-middle and middle classes, the groups for which the Mitchell-Lama program was designed. The large majority worked in the private sector. Among them, wrote a *Los Angeles Times* reporter in late 1972, by which time Co-op City was fully occupied, were accountants, actors, beauticians, bus drivers, butchers, buyers, and, at the other end of the alphabet, upholsterers, waiters, welders, and window washers. To this list one observer added druggists, grocers, hotel workers, shop clerks, and steamfitters. A small but significant minority, which included many African Americans, were employed in the public sector as firemen, policemen, sanitation men, corrections officers, and transit workers. The typical household earned $7,000 to $8,000 a year in 1970. Few families that earned less than $5,000 a year could afford to buy an apartment at Co-op City, which cost $450 a room and, to begin with, $23 per room per month in carrying charges. Under the Mitchell-Lama guidelines, which limited access to families that earned no more than six (and, in some cases, seven) times the carrying charges, few families whose annual income was more than $15,000 were eligible to live in Co-op City. By the mid-1970s a good many residents—perhaps as many as 29 percent, according to the New York State Comptroller's Division of Audits and Accounts—were retirees who lived on Social Security benefits and/or private pensions. For many of them, wrote Eden Ross Lipson, Co-op City offered "a perfect solution, a way of staying in New York and staying independent on [a] modest income."[16]

Many New Yorkers moved to Co-op City because they were desperate to get out of their old neighborhoods. They were troubled by the influx of African Americans and Puerto Ricans. As a former resident of the Upper West Side recalled, he and his wife were the only white people on their block. For most New Yorkers, moreover, "a good school is a white school," said a city schoolteacher. Many New Yorkers were also deeply concerned about crime and violence. As an elderly resident of Co-op City remarked, her former apartment in the Bronx had been broken into three times, and her husband had been mugged several times. "We were afraid to go out at night," she said. In her old neighborhood, recalled Supreme Court justice Sonia Sotomayor, whose family moved from a public housing project to Co-op City when she was a teenager, "gangs were carving up the territory and each other" and the area "was starting to look like a war zone." Some landlords stopped taking care of their buildings, many of which were very cold in winter, very hot in summer, and full of rats and roaches all year round. Others filled their houses with welfare recipients, sometimes more than one family to an apartment. "White flight" also hit many shopkeepers very hard, especially in the Bronx. Some closed early in the evening. Others put steel gates in front of the doors and covered the windows with plywood boards. "One more year and I've had it," the owner of a candy store told a *Times* reporter. Asked if he intended to sell the business, he replied, "Sell it! You don't sell a store around here any more. You just close it down." A kosher butcher agreed. "You couldn't buy a store on this block 10 years ago for any amount of money. Now they'd just give it to you." As Leo Akerfeld, a shoemaker who sold "Slightly Used Shoes" from his shop on 169th Street, told a reporter in 1970, the problem was that "everybody who can has moved to Freedomland," which is how some New Yorkers still referred to Co-op City.[17]

Some New Yorkers also moved to Co-op City because they wanted to own a home of their own or to live in a cooperative. But most were drawn to Co-op City because, in the words of a housewife and mother of a ten-month-old, it was "the best housing buy in the city." At a time of a severe housing shortage and near-record low vacancy rates, it was very hard for lower-middle- and middle-class New Yorkers to find an apartment that rented for less than $45 per room per month, which was about twice as much as Co-op City's carrying charges. Co-op City might have been at "the end of the earth," wrote Sotomayor, but the apartments were spacious and the rooms were "twice the size of those cubbyholes in the projects" in which she grew up. The apartments also had eat-in kitchens with modern appliances and well-crafted cabinets, hardwood floors, and, in some cases, terraces with panoramic views. They even had plenty of heat and hot water, sunlight in every room, off-street parking at a modest price, and central air-conditioning. "For the price," said an elderly man who had moved to Co-op City from Hunts Point, "you can't beat it." Remarked another resident, "If you want champagne at Coca-Cola prices, this is it." Some residents viewed the move to Co-op City as a stop-gap. "I never wanted to live there," said Charles Rosen, a typographer who worked for the *New York Post*, but he and his wife felt that they could no longer live in their run-down neighborhood on the Upper West Side. When they moved to Co-op City in 1970, the Rosens expected to stay only a couple of years, but others viewed the move to Co-op City as permanent. As Arthur Taub, who also moved to Co-op City in 1970, recalled, "We were looking for someplace we could live forever. We thought [Co-op City] was Shangri-La."[18]

OOO

But Co-op City was not Shangri-La, at least not when the Taubs and thousands of other families moved into their apartments in the late 1960s and early 1970s. Although it was supposed to be what another Co-op City "pioneer" called "the last oasis left to middle-class families [in New York City]," it was more like a "desert," Taub recalled. "Everywhere the ground was just sand that had been dredged from the bottom of Gravesend Bay and pumped in from Orchard [Beach]." Indeed, "there were still seashells, lying around." Arthur Oshins, who moved into Co-op City a year before Taub, was stunned by "the massive rubble-strewn lot." There were, he wrote, no streets, no paths, no trees, no benches, and no play areas. Although she was delighted with the spacious rooms, freshly painted walls, and well-equipped kitchen, another pioneer complained that her apartment looked out "on a bleak, windswept landscape, mounds of dirt piled haphazardly between sand and skeletons of steel rising in the gray sky." Even Arnold Merritt, Co-op City's first general manager, conceded that in late 1968, when the first families moved in, the landscape was "unesthetic, dark and uninviting." The buildings "stood like spectors [sic] in an area full of construction debris." "Swirling sand was everywhere," and "there wasn't a tree to be seen or a blade of grass." Edward Aronov, who succeeded Merritt in early 1971, defended Co-op City on the grounds that in any large-scale development much remained to be done after the first families moved in. But even so, many of Co-op City's pioneers felt like they were living in the middle of a construction site—a site that Ada Louise Huxtable described as "a desolate limbo."[19]

A year after the first residents moved in, Co-op City was not only bleak but, except for the apartment houses that had been finished or were under construction, empty. "There was basically nothing there," Arthur Taub recalled. There were no stores, only a temporary supermarket that had been set up in Garage No. 1; to get there, Taub said, his wife "had to push a shopping cart through the sand." Co-op City did not have a bank or post office either. Nor did it have a church or a temple, though the Riverbay Corporation did provide temporary space for religious groups. Meetings had to be held in basement bicycle, carriage, and storage rooms, none of which had sufficient lighting and adequate heating. Although the UHF had given the city ninety acres for public facilities, Co-op City did not have a firehouse or a police station. Nor did it have a public library. A bookmobile was supposed to come twice a week, but, remarked one irate resident, it "seldom shows up." Even more disheartening, Co-op City did not have a school. Although the local officials had agreed to build an educational park in Co-op City that would house two elementary schools, two intermediate schools, and one high school, there was no chance that they would be ready by the time the first students arrived. Hence the Board of Education set up temporary (and, in some cases, portable) classrooms in Co-op City. Children attended classes and ate lunch "in a garage!" parents complained. The Board of Education also bused some students to schools outside Co-op City, many of which were severely overcrowded, and sent others to Evander Childs, the high school closest to Co-op City.[20]

It was true, as Edward Aronov claimed, that in Co-op City and other large-scale developments much always remained to be done after the first residents moved in. And it was true, as George Schechter argued, that it was largely the fault of the municipal authorities that there were no schools, libraries, and other public facilities in Co-op City in the late 1960s and early 1970s. But it was also true that Co-op City left much to be desired when the first residents moved in. It was far from "the Promised Land" that Arthur Oshins and the other pioneers hoped to find because of a critical decision made by Harold Ostroff and his associates. As Arnold Merritt pointed out, the UHF could have left the completed buildings empty "until everything was finished." But, he pointed out, this option was not acceptable to the prospective residents, who said, "Just move us in. We can't wait." (Many of them had already been waiting several years. If forced to wait much longer, some might have decided to move elsewhere and to ask CSI to refund their down payment.) Nor was this option acceptable to the UHF. Even after construction was done, it would have been very expensive to heat and otherwise maintain empty buildings. Full of copper, wire, appliances, and electrical equipment, the buildings would also have been ripe for vandalism if no one was living in them; so would the grounds, where all sorts of tools and supplies were stored. Even in the occupied buildings vandalism was a serious problem, said Rabbi Perry Cohen, a member of the Riverbay Corporation Board of Directors, in April 1971, one that cost the residents more than $600,000 a year.[21]

There was another (and even more important) reason that Ostroff and his associates did their utmost to fill Co-op City's buildings as soon as they were finished—and sometimes even when minor work still remained to be done on the apartments. The residents did not start to pay their carrying charges, which were initially set at $23 per room per month, when they bought their apartments, only when they moved into them. As George Schechter pointed out in May 1970, these charges came to about $50,000 a month in each of the occupied buildings. If Riverbay had not allowed the residents to move into the first thirty-four apartment houses until the thirty-fifth was finished (and until the landscaping was done and the schools and other public facilities were open), it would have cost the corporation a great deal of money—$1 million a year, according to Al Smoke, a member of the Riverbay Corporation Board of Directors, or even more, according to Ostroff. Management could ill afford to lose this money, which was needed to pay Co-op City's fixed costs and operating expenses. (As I point out later, this was becoming a very serious problem because Co-op City cost more to build than anticipated, forcing the Riverbay Corporation to borrow more money from the State Housing Finance Agency at much higher interest rates.) Hence every effort was made to fill the buildings as quickly as possible. As Arnold Merritt wrote in late 1970, by which time eighteen of the apartment houses were fully occupied, "No other Housing Development has ever undertaken so large a task of moving so many families in so short a period of time."[22]

Ostroff was confident that, in the words of one of his associates, things would soon "settle down" in Co-op City. And for the most part he was right. As Ada Louise Huxtable, one of the project's many critics, wrote in late 1968, Co-op City was extremely bleak when the first residents moved in. But at a cost of $5.4 million—and under the supervision of Zion & Breen Associates, a firm that was perhaps best known for its design of Paley Park, New York City's first (and much-celebrated) "vest-pocket" park—the grounds were transformed in the next three years. It was, said Huxtable, "one of the most successful landscape jobs that ever turned a lemon into lemonade." More than half the site—the 177 acres that were not built on—was covered with grass and "embellished with masses of willows, Lombard poplars, London plane trees and Japanese black pine." A member of the Executive Committee of the International Cooperative Alliance said that he had not seen "such an expanse of grassy, tree-shaded grounds anywhere in New York, outside of Central Park." At the center of the two-story shopping center was a paved courtyard with islands of ivy and willow. And "well-selected equipment, including typees, climbing devices and simple wooden forms, are scattered through the sand gardens and across the lawns." The result, Huxtable said, "is a successful demonstration of how to humanize housing that many people thought was beyond help." Everything, she added, "has been done to soften the project's gigantism at eye level, where it counts." Many of the residents were as favorably impressed as Huxtable. "I saw this dump turned into a beautiful place, plant by plant," said Mrs. Anthony Ruggieri, whose family moved into Co-op City in December 1968.[23]

The landscape was not the only thing that had changed since the first residents moved into Co-op City, wrote Lorraine Holtz, a resident of one of the townhouses, in July 1973. In addition to residential towers and townhouses, it now had three shopping centers, one of which contained a cooperative supermarket that included a pharmacy and optical center. There were also restaurants, hairdressers, clothing stores, a movie theater, and "just about anything [else] the residents might want." Co-op City even had a public library, a postal substation, and an office of the New York Telephone Company as well as branches of the Amalgamated and Dollar Savings banks. There were "places of worship for people of all religious and ethnic backgrounds," Holtz said, and "not one but three community centers that act as the hub of community life." Moreover, what was called the North East Bronx Educational Park, "one of the finest tributes to our community," was just about finished. Under intense pressure from Co-op City residents and Bronx politicians, who were fed up with the Board of Education's temporizing, the state legislature had authorized Community Services, Inc., to build the educational park. The project cost tens of millions of dollars, part of which came from the state and the rest from the city, and took longer than expected. But the first school, PS 153, opened in September 1971 and the last one, Harry S. Truman High School, two years later. Co-op City did not have a firehouse. Although the Fire Department was ready to build one on a site that the Riverbay Corporation offered the city, construction was delayed by a dispute over its location. Nor did Co-op City have a police station. And though it had doctors' offices and medical facilities, it lacked a hospital, which, wrote Holtz, was "one of the great, and possibly one of the most immediate of our needs."[24]

During the late 1960s and early 1970s Co-op City also ran into a couple of problems that stemmed from far-reaching decisions by the UHF. In an effort to provide high-quality housing that lower- and lower-middle-class New Yorkers could afford, the foundation designed Co-op City almost entirely as a high-rise residential complex, one in which 97 percent of the families lived in twenty-four- to thirty-three-story apartment houses. Hence the great majority of the residents were completely dependent on the elevators. But as one complained in late 1970, "The elevators are out of service more often than they are in service." Many residents, including the elderly, the infirm, and mothers with baby carriages, were forced to walk up ten or more stories to get to their apartments. The elevators break down so often, said another resident, that it "almost makes you a prisoner in your own apartment." Even worse, some residents got stuck in the elevators. In one case a mother and her two young daughters were trapped in an elevator for two and a half hours, during which time she had to pry open the door for ventilation. Mechanics rescued them and made the necessary repairs. But to many residents, it seemed that no sooner were the elevators repaired in one building than they broke down in another. As Herbert Schneiderman, Co-op City's assistant manager, acknowledged in early 1971, "the elevator breakdown problem is one of the most serious facing cooperators, particularly in the newly opened buildings." And as a member of the Co-op City Advisory Council, which consisted of representatives from the apartment houses and townhouses, pointed out, it is "one of the basic problems that doesn't seem to get solved here."[25]

Co-op City's residents did not take the problem lying down. Some wrote letters to the *Co-op City Times*, the Riverbay Corporation house organ and one of Co-op City's two community newspapers, and the Westinghouse Electric Corporation, the firm that manufactured, installed, and serviced the elevators. Other residents complained to the Riverbay Corporation and its maintenance office as well as to city and state agencies. Still others spoke out at meetings of the Co-op City Advisory Council. Lawrence Sivak, chairman of the Advisory Council, told the Riverbay Corporation Board of Directors that, "almost without exception, all buildings are having constant elevator breakdowns," and not just the new ones but the old (or "settled") ones as well. The council was "flooded" with complaints about the elevators, he added. Ninety-five percent of the residents of Building 9 signed a petition protesting the failure of the Riverbay Corporation, the UHF, and the Co-op City Advisory Council to solve the problem. A resident of Building 13 called attention to Westinghouse's slogan, "You can be sure if it is Westinghouse." "Can be sure of what?" he asked. Certainly not Co-op City's elevators, which broke down every day. Another resident warned that unless the problem was solved in the near future, some families would move out of Co-op City and others who could not afford to move would be forced to live in "33 story walk-ups." A resident of Building 17 even believed that it was time for his fellow residents to file suit against Riverbay. Management pointed out that they would in effect be suing themselves, to which he responded, "Must we sacrifice a resident—have someone suffer a heart attack, a miscarriage, or some other fatality—before we [do] something?"[26]

The residents blamed Riverbay (and, to a lesser extent, Westinghouse) for the problem. Conceding that some of the breakdowns were due to "mechanical faults," management expressed its "extreme dissatisfaction" to Westinghouse, brought pressure on the firm to live up to its contractual obligations, and even threatened to withhold its payments until service improved. It also hired the Herk Elevator Company to put in place a preventive maintenance program and assured residents that Riverbay porters would inspect the elevator tracks on a regular basis. But management also held residents, movers, and other elevator riders partly responsible for the problem. They dropped cigarette stubs and other debris on the floors, which prevented the doors from opening and closing. And they used wedges and other devices to hold the doors open when moving bulky items into the apartments. (Management also claimed that children and newsboys regularly misused the elevators, but did not say how.) Residents, management stressed, should "be on the alert for acts of vandalism in the elevators and [should] report all suspicious activity to the Security Department immediately." They were also urged to be patient. As Abe Bluestein, Co-op City's business manager, pointed out in August 1970, every high-rise apartment house in New York City has problems with elevators at the beginning. "It takes one and a half to two years to clear up the bugs in the[se] complex machines." The elevators "operate smoothly and without interruption" in "older cooperatives," he pointed out. Before long they would work well in Co-op City too. And so they did.[27]

In an attempt to build the huge housing cooperative that became Co-op City without having to relocate hundreds, if not thousands, of residents and businesses, the UHF made another far-reaching decision. It bought one of the most remote sites in New York City. To many residents, *Newsweek* wrote, it seemed that their homes in the Bronx were almost as far from their offices in Manhattan "as Brasilia is from Rio de Janeiro." To get to work, they had to take a bus from Co-op City to either the Dyre Avenue or Pelham Bay subway station, both of which were about a mile away, and then ride one or more trains for at least an hour on what *City News*, Co-op City's other community newspaper, called "one of the slowest, dirtiest, hottest subway systems in the world." ("The only good thing," said a resident who took the Seventh Avenue subway from Dyre Avenue to Midtown Manhattan, "is that you always get a seat, since it is the first stop on the line.") The trip took so long, remarked a Wall Street accountant, that to get to work by 9:00 a.m. he had to leave Co-op City at 7:15 a.m. The subway was often unreliable too, said another resident. "When I really need to get somewhere, I take a cab." For some residents the commute was more than they could bear. A case in point was Helen Rosenfeld, who had worked for six years as a bookkeeper and office manager in Midtown Manhattan. Two weeks after moving to Co-op City and spending four hours a day commuting, she quit her job. "I just found it impossible to come home, shop for food and prepare dinner for a family," she told a *City News* reporter.[28]

There were, it was widely believed, several steps that the authorities could take to alleviate Co-op City's transit problem. One was to extend the Seventh Avenue and Lexington Avenue lines to Co-op City or build the Second Avenue subway to connect Midtown Manhattan with the northeast Bronx. William J. Ronan, chairman of the Metropolitan Transportation Authority, agreed that Co-op City needed rapid transit. But the authority, which was facing a $120 million deficit, did not have the funds to extend either of the existing subway lines, which would have cost $20 million, much less build the Second Avenue subway, a project that had been in the works for nearly half a century and would have cost billions of dollars. At best it would be many years or even decades before a subway reached Co-op City. Another thing the MTA could do was to lease the tracks of the New York, New Haven, and Hartford Railroad, and then run trains from Connecticut and Westchester County that would stop at Co-op City and elsewhere in the Bronx on the way to Grand Central Station, the railroad's monumental terminal in Midtown Manhattan. Although this scheme was supported by the Riverbay Corporation, it never made it off the drawing boards. Neither did another scheme that was conceived of by the North American Monorail Corporation and backed by Bronx Borough President Robert Abrams. Although NAMC claimed that a monorail could transport passengers from Co-op City to Grand Central in twenty minutes, relieve congestion on the subway, and reduce pollution in the city, it could not be built without large subsidies from the federal, state, and local governments, which were highly unlikely to be forthcoming in the foreseeable future.[29]

It soon became clear that in the short run there was only one thing that the local officials could do to ease Co-op City's transit problem. And that was to authorize a private firm to operate express buses between Co-op City and Midtown Manhattan. This scheme, which was proposed in late 1969 by Andrews & Clark, an engineering firm that was retained by the UHF, was a far from optimal solution to the problem. But it had one tremendous advantage. Since the buses would operate on the existing highways and streets, it would not cost the city (or the MTA) any money. Hence the Board of Estimate gave the New York Bus Service Company a temporary franchise in late 1970—and, over the objections of Fifth Avenue business interests, a permanent one a couple of years later. Under the terms of the franchise, the buses would leave Co-op City Monday through Friday every fifteen minutes from 6:30 a.m. until 8:00 a.m. and every thirty minutes until 3:00 p.m. They would return to Co-op City every thirty minutes from 10:30 a.m. until 4:00 p.m., every fifteen minutes until 5:30 p.m., and every thirty minutes until 7:00 p.m. They would run through the Bronx, across the East River, and down Fifth Avenue, stopping at Fifty-Seventh, Fiftieth, Forty-Second, Thirty-Fourth, and Twenty-Third Streets. On the way back they would take Madison Avenue. The one-way fare was $1, though a ten-trip ticket was available for $8.50. With Borough President Abrams and other dignitaries on hand, the first express bus left Co-op City in mid-January 1971. The riders, reported the *City News*, "had nothing but praise for the service which for the most part got them to mid-town Manhattan in 45 minutes. There was not waiting for buses to take them to subways. They are not getting off one subway and waiting in cold underground terminals for another."[30]

ooo

Although Co-op City was pretty much a self-contained community, it was still very much a part of New York City. As such, said Ed Marshall, Co-op City's director of community affairs, it ran into many of the same problems as other neighborhoods, not the least of which was crime. During the early 1970s Co-op City had several burglaries and robberies. Thieves broke into apartments, stole cash and jewelry, and, in the case of two window cleaners, took $116 from a resident's purse. In a rush to get away, they left behind their rags and window spray and "didn't even finish the job," the resident complained. Using a crowbar, thieves also pried open a coin machine in one of Co-op City's laundry rooms. Often armed with guns or knives, they attacked their victims on the streets, in the elevators, and even outside the supermarket, where they struck one employee in the head with a revolver and stole more than $3,000 in receipts. Early in 1970, wrote the *City News*, there was "an epidemic" of auto theft. Some cars were taken from the garages and others from the streets. There was also a rash of bicycle thefts in mid-1972. Several assaults occurred in Co-op City as well. And though rare, rapes and attempted rapes were not unheard of. Early in 1970 a man attempted to rape a ten-year-old girl on the way home from school. And late in 1972 two men raped a fifteen-year-old girl in a stairwell. There were even a few cases of white-collar crime in Co-op City. In one a twenty-year-old woman teller embezzled $5,000 from the Co-op City branch of the Dollar Savings Bank. She gave it to her boyfriend, she told the FBI. In another case two "Con Gals," as the *City News* referred to them, promised two other women that they would double their money "at the drop of a wallet" and then swindled one out of $3,000 and the other out of $2,000.[31]

These incidents notwithstanding, most residents felt safer in Co-op City than in their old neighborhoods, many of which were so dangerous that people were afraid to go out at night and shopkeepers were afraid to stay open in the evening. And according to the New York Police Department, they had good reason to feel safer. The Forty-Fifth Police Precinct, which Co-op City became a part of in May 1969, had a lower crime rate than all but eight of New York's seventy-six precincts—and all but five excluding Central Park, Prospect Park, and the harbor. The crime rate was even lower in Co-op City than in the rest of the Forty-Fifth Precinct. But not all the residents were reassured by these figures. Some held that crime was Co-op City's most serious problem. And others who were aware that Co-op City had a low crime rate stressed that "we would like to keep it that way." To prevent crime the residents urged the Forty-Fifth Precinct to assign more officers to Co-op City. And Riverbay called on the NYPD to open a police station in Co-op City, arguing, in vain, that "If Mt. Vernon, a community of 50,000, only five minutes away from us, has a Police Department of its own, surely we should have a Police Precinct in Co-op City." To augment the NYPD, Riverbay set up a security department whose fifty officers patrolled Co-op City seven days a week, twenty-four hours a day, most heavily between 6:00 p.m. and 2:00 a.m. The NYPD and Riverbay's security department prevented some crimes and caught some criminals, but their record was not unblemished. Late in

1970 Richard F. Ferguson, a member of the Co-op City Advisory Council, accused police officers of harassing his daughter and other Co-op City residents and declared that he and his neighbors were not prepared "to give up our rights and freedoms as citizens as the price of increased police protection." And late in 1973 detectives from the Bronx district attorney's office arrested two security guards and charged them with stealing $1,000 worth of meat from a Co-op City kosher butcher.[32]

Another problem had to do with race. As Harold Ostroff said at a roundtable discussion of Co-op City that was shown on channel 13, a New York City public television station, the UHF had done its utmost to make Co-op City "an integrated community." And its efforts had been relatively successful. Co-op City had a good many African Americans (and Puerto Ricans), many more than most other housing cooperatives. A case in point was Electchester, where virtually all the residents were white. (Indeed, in April 1965 a group of New Yorkers picketed the Midtown Manhattan office of the New York City Central Labor Council, charging that Harry Van Arsdale Jr., president of the NYCCLC and Local 3 of the International Brotherhood of Electrical Workers, had reneged on his pledge to open Electchester to African Americans and Puerto Ricans.) But as Elbert Tolson, vice president of Co-op City's Black Caucus, pointed out, the community was sharply divided along racial lines. The problem was not that whites and blacks had organizations of their own. As one resident said, if Young Israel was not integrated, neither was the Black Caucus. Nor were the two other groups, the Concerned Black Cooperators and the Co-op City branch of the National Council of Negro Women, both of which spoke for Co-op City's African Americans. Rather, said Ostroff, the problem was that many white residents brought to Co-op City "the unfortunate carry-overs of prejudice." Or as one resident put it, "When you move here, you moved your prejudices in with your furniture."[33] As a result, many African Americans (and, to a lesser degree, Puerto Ricans) felt that they were not being treated as equals in Co-op City.

The issue came to a head in April 1970, when the first election was held for the Advisory Council. "Not a single black was elected," wrote Tolson. Not a single Puerto Rican was elected either. A manifestation of "the same old racism," the election was designed "to systematically exclude blacks from participation in the decision-making process." "If this is cooperative living," Tolson said, "NO THANKS!" Indeed, he went on, Co-op City's African Americans would be better off setting up an advisory council of their own. Ostroff took strong exception to Tolson's remarks, denying that Co-op City residents were racist, insisting that cooperatives had long been in the forefront of the struggle for open housing and stressing that "it ill-behooves groups who do not choose to participate in the democratic process to complain about their failure to be represented." A heated debate ensued. At the heart of the debate, which raged in letters to the editors of the *Co-op City Times* and *City News* as well as at a town meeting sponsored by the Advisory Council and attended by more than 1,000 residents, was how to achieve minority representation on the Advisory Council. After wrestling with the issue for more than a month, the council decided to hold a special election for representatives from Buildings 1 through 6 in which only African Americans and Puerto Ricans would be eligible to vote. This temporary measure would be replaced by a permanent arrangement once the new members took office. After the election, which was won by four African Americans and two Puerto Ricans, race relations were still strained, but they were no worse in Co-op City than in many other neighborhoods and probably better than in some.[34]

Still another problem had to do with labor—or, to be more precise, organized labor. Although organized labor, notably the Amalgamated Clothing Workers and the ILGWU, was the mainstay of the United Housing Foundation, none of the trade unions whose members were employed at Co-op City or the UHF's other housing cooperatives was inclined to cut management any slack. In bargaining over wages, benefits, and working conditions, they dealt with Community Services, Inc., and the Riverbay Corporation in pretty much the same way that they dealt with other employers, among them the owners of 750,000 rental units who were represented by the Bronx Realty Advisory Board. And if these unions could not reach an agreement with management on a new contract, they would not hesitate to go on strike. During the building of Co-op City the elevator operators walked off the job, thereby preventing craftsmen from working on the high-rise buildings that were under construction and families from moving into the apartments that were ready for occupancy. The teamsters, who transported supplies to the construction site, also went on strike, bringing much of the work to a halt. So did the steamfitters, metal workers, and other craftsmen. In September 1973, by which time the construction was done and the buildings were fully occupied, Co-op City's 400 porters, maintenance men, and security guards, all of whom were members of Local 32-E of the Service Employees International Union, walked off the job when their contract expired.[35]

The strike, which went on for five days, was extremely disruptive. Residents were forced to take out their garbage. Since they could not use the incinerators and compactors, they left it on the street, where it piled up, prompting city officials to declare the mounds of garbage a public health problem and authorize the Sanitation Department to remove it. Supervisory personnel made emergency repairs, and NYPD officer worked extra tours. Making matters worse, several acts of vandalism occurred in Co-op City during the strike. (Edward Aronov blamed them on "goon squads" that were roving around the project and, he implied, acting on behalf of the union. Jacques Buitenkant, Local 32-E's general counsel, denied the charge. "If any vandalism is being committed," he said, "I suggest that the authorities look to the people who have been replacing the striking workers.") The vandals broke light bulbs and set fires in trash baskets. They also opened fire hoses, allowing water to pour into hallways, forcing children, armed with mops, to try to stop it from flowing into the apartments. Water poured down elevator shafts too, bringing elevator service to a halt in some buildings. Many residents who tried to climb the stairs were "met by ankle-deep streams of waters," wrote the *Times*. And some residents were trapped briefly in the elevators "when water filled the pits at the bottom of the shafts." The strike came to an end when, with the help of the New York State Mediation Board, Riverbay and Local 32-E agreed to a two-year contract under which the workers received a $15-a-week raise in the first year and another $15-a-week raise in the second—as well as improved overtime, holiday, and sick-leave benefits.[36]

Not long after moving in many residents realized that Co-op City left some things to be desired that they had not anticipated. To their dismay, many apartments were very noisy. In Co-op City, as in other high-rise developments, some residents had to put up with the noise of their neighbors' radios and televisions, especially if they were placed next to the adjoining walls, which, said Edward Aronov, acted as "a huge sounding board." Other residents whose apartments were located next to the incinerator shafts had to put up with what the *Co-op City Times* called "the shake, rattle and roll" of the garbage as it tumbled into the basement. To deal with this problem management asked residents to stop using the incinerators after 10:00 p.m. Worst of all, many residents lived in apartments that overlooked the New England Thruway, a busy interstate highway along which, said Pearl Bloom, chair of the Co-op City Civic Association's Anti-Noise Committee, "tractor-trailers under heavy loads and traveling 55 miles per hour" roared twenty-four hours a day every day. The noise from these trucks was a serious problem, reported New York's Bureau of Noise Abatement, a division of the city's Environmental Protection Administration. To alleviate it, Co-op City leaders joined with Westchester County officials, some of whose constituents lived near the thruway, to urge the state to plant trees and other greenery along the highway, lower the speed limit from sixty to fifty miles an hour, and, among other things, enact a law to reduce the decibel levels of the trucks. But little came of these efforts.[37]

What one Co-op City resident called the "constant and sickening" noise from the New England Thruway took a heavy toll on him and many others and made it "impossible [for them] to lead a normal life." Rabbi Perry Cohen agreed. "Family after family" spent "sleepless nights" because of noise pollution, he said. Many residents were not only unable to sleep, added Pearl Bloom, but also "unable to open windows" and "unable to use [their] terraces." Left to their own devices, the residents dealt with the noise in all sorts of ways. Some stuffed plugs into their ears or took sleeping pills at night. In an attempt to drown out the noise from the trucks, others turned up their radios, which probably did not endear them to the neighbors. And still others bought soundproof windows or moved their beds into rooms that did not overlook the thruway. Some residents even thought about moving out of Co-op City. To highlight the problem the *City News* wrote a story about Sam Sternlicht, one of the hundreds of residents of Building 1 who suffered from noise pollution. Monday through Friday Sternlicht got up at 5:00 a.m. and drove to his job in New Jersey, from which he returned after 6:00 p.m. He went to bed about 9:00 p.m., but found it impossible to sleep because of the "booming noise of tractor-trailers pounding along the New England Thruway." So he spent every weekend at his daughter's house on Long Island, where he was able to sleep and "get himself rested for the next week's work."[38]

Many apartments, most of which were on the top floor of the high-rise buildings, were also in bad shape. Although the buildings were structurally sound, the walls of these apartments had big cracks, some of which, wrote the *City News*, ran "from floor to ceiling in large jagged strips." As Jacob Feld, a consulting engineer who was retained by the State Division of Housing and the Riverbay Corporation, explained, the root of the problem was in the roofs, which expanded and contracted with changes in temperature and thereby put enormous pressure on the walls below. When the pressure became too much, the walls cracked. The problem became so serious for Irwin and Dana Wolfe, a couple who had been living in Co-op City for nearly two years, that in November 1971 they began to withhold their monthly carrying charges. Instead of sending the money to Riverbay, they deposited it in a bank account, hoping that by so doing they could force management to repair the cracks in the walls. They also hoped that other residents who suffered from the same problem would follow their lead. Two months later Riverbay started eviction proceedings against the Wolfes. In their defense, the Wolfes claimed that much of their apartment was in such bad shape that it was not livable. The case went to court, where it was postponed four times. After much haggling, the parties settled in June 1972. The Wolfes agreed to pay what they owed, less some legal expenses. And Riverbay agreed to re-pair the walls—and also to let the Wolfes live in a furnished apartment else-where in the building while the repairs were being made.[39]

To everyone at Co-op City it was clear that the cracked walls were a problem that would have to be resolved, that the roofs would have to be modified and the apartments would have to be repaired. But it was also clear that the work would cost a great deal of money, at least a few hundred thousand dollars and perhaps as much as a few million. And it was not clear where the money would come from, mainly because it was not clear who or what was responsible for the problem. Was it the architect or the subcon-tractors? Or was it CSI, the UHF or the State Division of Housing? Was the problem a result of poor design or shoddy construction, sloppy workman-ship or inferior materials? Feld analyzed the problem. Although he said that the UHF knew about the problem before construction was completed and, wrote the *City News*, "took no action in the hope that the cracking would not spread," he did not assign blame. Hence in August 1972 representatives of Riverbay, the UHF, and the State Division of Housing held a meeting to discuss the question of financial responsibility. Although they agreed that the cracked walls were not, as one participant said facetiously, "an act of God," they did not agree on much else. Even after the meeting, remarked Al Smoke, a member of the Riverbay Corporation Board of Directors, "it will not be possible for any top-ranking professional engineer to be able to deter-mine conclusively that the difficulties were due to fault of any single factor or agent in the construction of Co-op City." To resolve the issue, Riverbay hired another consulting engineer, Milton Alpern, who studied the problem for five months and then issued a report in March 1973 in which he blamed the problem on the use of the wrong construction materials, namely what he called "wet insulation." Although Alpern's report bolstered the case that the cost of repairs should be borne by the subcontractors, not the residents, the matter was far from settled.[40]

Some residents had other complaints about Co-op City, one of which was its policy about pets in general and dogs in particular. Under a provision of the occupancy agreement between the Riverbay Corporation and Co-op City's shareholders, the residents were not allowed to keep a dog on the premises. To do so was grounds for eviction. Although such a ban was not uncommon in New York City apartment houses, it was an extremely sore point for a few residents, among them Iona Flagg. When she moved into Co-op City in early 1970, she complained that she had to leave her poodle behind. "She was as much a part of our family as our children," she wrote to the editor of the *Co-op City Times*. How many of Co-op City's more than 15,000 families would have "to find new homes for their pets?" she asked. And how many would have to be "put in shelters, used for experiments, destroyed or left to wander the streets[?]" "Anyone who loves pets," she went on, "will take care of them and their property." As for the claim that pets abused property, she pointed out that in her two months at Co-op City she had seen much property defaced—by people, not by pets. She even said that some of the robberies at Co-op City would have been prevented if pets were allowed to live there. Flagg believed that the ban was unfair and that many other residents felt the same way. Although strongly held, her views did not impress the editor of the *Co-op City Times*, who responded that the people who moved into Co-op City knew beforehand that dogs were not allowed.[41]

Some residents who agreed with Flagg ignored the ban and, in violation of the occupancy agreement, brought their dogs with them. A case in point was George Klinghoffer, who moved into Building 5 on May 1, 1969. On May 2 the Riverbay Corporation notified him that he could not keep his dog, a German Shepherd named Dutchess, in his apartment. Three days later it demanded that the dog be removed. Klinghoffer refused, saying that he had bought Dutchess as a guard dog after armed robbers had held up his pharmacy on West Tremont Avenue several times. "If I give up my dog," he argued, "I give up my business, and that means I give up my livelihood." And at sixty-four he would be hard pressed to find another job. Unmoved, Riverbay filed suit in Bronx Superior Court in late May and asked for a summary judgment enjoining Klinghoffer from keeping a dog in his apartment. The judge denied the motion on the grounds that Riverbay had waived the right to enforce the ban because it had accepted the May rent while the dog was living in the apartment. Riverbay appealed. In late August the First Department of the Appellate Division reversed the trial court's decision and granted Riverbay's motion for a summary judgment enjoining Klinghoffer from keeping a dog in his apartment. In a unanimous decision, the five-judge panel held not only that Riverbay's ban on dogs was "reasonable and enforceable," but also that the acceptance of the May rent did not constitute a waiver of the right to enforce it.[42]

ooo

In late April 1972, a month after the last family moved into Co-op City, the *Co-op City Times* published an article about the UHF by George Schechter, vice president not only of the UHF but also of CSI and the Riverbay Corporation. Although he briefly mentioned Penn Station South, Rochdale Village, and the foundation's other housing cooperatives, Schechter devoted most of the article to Co-op City. Speaking for the UHF, he declared, "We are proud of what we have accomplished in Co-op City," which he called "the best housing buy in New York City." In only seven years the UHF had built housing for more than 15,300 lower-middle- and middle-income families, all of whom enjoyed spacious apartments, "10–15% larger in area than in any other middle-income development," and central air-conditioning, "previously only for the 'luxury housing' market." Along with the 35 residential towers and 236 townhouses, the UHF had also provided community centers, with auditoriums for public events and lounges for senior citizens as well as nursery schools, baseball fields, basketball courts, bicycle paths, and other amenities that were rarely found in other housing developments. It was also constructing an educational park "WITHOUT ANY BUILDER'S PROFIT." Pointing out that Co-op City was something that no other organization "would or COULD" have undertaken, Schechter declared that the UHF deserved a great deal of credit not only for building the world's largest housing cooperative but also for building it at a time "when housing production has virtually stopped in New York City, when all rents have skyrocketed [and] when families have been running from the city."[43]

Co-op City also made a favorable impression on some Americans and even a few Europeans who were in no way affiliated with the UHF, CSI or the Riverbay Corporation. Among them was a small group of reporters who were sent by *Apartment Ideas*, a magazine devoted to apartment living, to visit Co-op City in 1971 and talk with some of its residents. What they learned was that Co-op City "isn't the most charming place." Dominated by its thirty-five huge towers, it was, as critics charged, "too gray, too stark, too huge for anybody to call home." But most residents were not troubled by "the sniping from critics." Indeed, they were pleased with Co-op City, mainly because it provided them with "nice, new, livable apartments that they can afford—a prerogative people are taking for granted in steadily fewer cities around the country and a rarity in New York." Also favorably impressed by Co-op City was Mark L. Hinshaw, an English journalist who wrote an article about it in *Architectural Digest*, a British periodical, in 1973. At a time, he said, "when most Americans who are wealthy enough or white enough" are fleeing to the suburbs, Co-op City was an encouraging development. With its large apartments, which provided "almost twice the space for half the price of other comparable apartment developments," it was "a bargain." It was also a place in which "people actually enjoy living." Another Englishman, Peter Goodbody, who spent two weeks in Co-op City in 1973 as a guest of a pen pal, even found Co-op City more appealing in many ways than Basildon and Britain's other much-heralded "New Towns."[44]

Co-op City was more than a housing cooperative, Schechter pointed out. It was also a vibrant community, as vibrant a community as any in New York City. The sense of community was reflected in many ways, perhaps the most striking of which was the pace at which the first residents formed the 200 or so voluntary associations around which their social lives revolved. By the time Co-op City was fully occupied (or shortly thereafter) it had a Boy Scout troop, a Girl Scout troop, Little League teams, a Twenties Club, a Mr. and Mrs. Club, a Young Marrieds Club, and a Senior Citizens Association. Many other groups were organized along racial, ethnic, and religious lines, among them the Black Caucus, the Spanish American Club, Young Israel, Hadassah, and the Golda Meir Club. The Democratic, Republican, and Liberal parties were all represented at Co-op City, as was the League of Women Voters. Many of the other voluntary associations were an outgrowth of activities for which the residents had a passion. There was the Co-op City Orchestra, Co-op City Glee Club, Co-op City Arts Council, a parent-teacher association, and an association for the mentally handicapped. There were also clubs for amateur astronomers, bicyclists, bowlers, civil libertarians, photographers, environmentalists, weight lifters, and square, tap, and ballet dancers. Most of these groups sponsored a wide range of activities, which prompted Edward Aronov to ask, "Where else in New York City [but in Co-op City] do hundreds of people these days leave their apartments at night to go to meetings, lectures, concerts, [and] dances at Community Centers or Community Rooms?" (Indeed, in mid-June 1971 over 1,100 Co-op City residents attended a concert of the New York Philharmonic that was held in the community center. The New York City Central Labor Council sponsored the concert, and Aaron Copland conducted the orchestra, which performed Prokofiev's "Classical" Symphony, Bruch's G minor Violin Concerto, and two of Copland's own works.)[45]

The sense of community was also reflected in how the residents dealt with one another day to day. They are "genuinely friendly," wrote one observer. "They talk to each other and help one another." Indeed, said Aronov, who had spent most of his life in big cities before moving to Co-op City, "I have never experienced the sense of neighborliness, the quality of small-town familiarity in a big city that we enjoy here." Another resident who was impressed by the sociability of her neighbors was Barbara Boyd. Along with her husband, who worked in Manhattan as a men's tie cutter, and their three children, she had moved to Co-op City from Brooklyn, where they lived in an apartment directly over the boiler, which "fumed all night and made the kids cough." During the family's first week in Co-op City, "everybody on my floor stopped by to introduce themselves," she told a reporter. "Now where did you ever hear of that in this city." The sense of community was reflected too in the way the children played in the streets (where, said another observer, the residents were much less likely to be attacked by muggers than "smacked by kids on tricycles, bicycles, even unicycles"); the young couples strolled hand in hand along Co-op City's promenades; the senior citizens sat on the benches, talking with their new friends; and the residents, Protestants, Catholics, and Jews alike, worshiped in their makeshift churches and temples. The sense of community flourished in Co-op City, said Mark Hinshaw, in large part because it was a housing cooperative and the residents, all of whom held shares in the Riverbay Corporation, felt that it belonged to them.[46]

Schechter acknowledged that Co-op City had problems. He was also well aware that many residents had complaints—and not only about noise levels and cracked walls. Some residents complained that Riverbay's office workers were indifferent and even hostile, that requests for service often went unanswered, sometimes for days and even weeks, and that maintenance men were "goofing off during working hours." Other residents pointed out not only that here and there manholes were open, electrical wires were hanging loose, and refuse was piling up, but also that many apartments had broken windows and leaky faucets and many buildings had defective washers and dryers and faulty incinerator doors, some of which were almost impossible to open "without getting a full face of ash." Still other residents were infuriated by Co-op City's teenagers, who "love wanton destruction for its own sake." "They can't pass a wall or bench without scrawling stupidities on it with indelible marking pens," one resident said. "They can't pass a newly planted tree without shaking it. They can't walk through a clean hallway without littering it. They can't use a public facility without wrecking it." Other residents were fed up with the senior citizens, some of whom spent the day sitting on beach chairs in front of their buildings, forcing other residents to run "an obstacle course" when they returned home. The residents of some buildings also complained that management provided better service to other buildings. Lorraine Holtz complained that townhouse residents were treated like "Second Rate Citizens," pointing out that though they paid the highest carrying charges they received the poorest service.[47]

Other residents held that many of these complaints were groundless—or, at the very least, exaggerated. Co-op City's halls were "spotlessly clean," wrote "a very happy Co-operator" in October 1969. "In a year or two this will be the most wonderful place in the city," he predicted. "To me," said another resident in August 1970, "it is a great joy to see my neighbors sitting in front of their buildings. It gives me a feeling of security [and] shows that people can live in peace and harmony." Co-op City has a its problems, wrote yet another resident in July 1972, but for "countless thousands" it "represents hope and renewal. It is as refreshing as a dip in a cool, filtered pool on a scorching summer day." Moreover, several residents who were interviewed for a television news program in August 1969 felt that whatever its shortcomings Co-op City was "much better than the place they left." And after spending two days and three nights in Co-op City with his wife and daughter in the summer of 1970, a state housing official found that many other residents felt the same way. Seven months later the Riverbay Corporation issued a report in which it claimed that that the overwhelming majority of residents were satisfied with Co-op City. As proof it pointed out that of the 8,750 families who moved into Co-op City in its first twenty-seven months only thirty-five (or 0.04 percent) moved out. And most of these families moved out because they bought a single-family house elsewhere in the city or took a job elsewhere in the state or country. Pointing out that "only five families moved out because Co-op City wasn't what they wanted," Abe Bluestein declared, "We [the Riverbay Corporation] must be doing something right."[48]

CHAPTER 6

FISCAL TROUBLES

As Abraham E. Kazan and his associates knew, Co-op City was going to be very expensive. But just how expensive was far from clear, Harold Ostroff said. When he and Kazan prepared Co-op City's budget in 1964, "we were required to estimate the cost of construction which would not be completed for five or more years. We were required to estimate [a great many] factors which would occur over these years, many unforeseen and unforeseeable. In essence, we were required to estimate the state of the national economy, inflation, wage rates, interest rates, [and, among other things,] the progress of the Vietnam War." All this had to be done, Ostroff went on, for "a proposed development which had no precedent," a development that was not only the largest housing cooperative in the United States, with almost three times as many apartments as Rochdale Village, the second-largest, but also "the largest apartment complex" in the nation, larger even than Stuyvesant Town, the Metropolitan Life Insurance Company's huge project in Lower Manhattan. Taking these considerations into account—and drawing on the United Housing Foundation's experience with Rochdale Village and Amalgamated Warbasse—Kazan and his associates estimated that Co-op City would cost just under $283.7 million, which was about three times as much as Rochdale Village. Most of the money, roughly $258.5 million, would be spent on construction. The remainder would be allocated mainly to land acquisition, finance charges, and professional services. Close to 90 percent of the cost would be covered by the New York State Housing Finance Agency—which had agreed to give the UHF a $250.9 million mortgage, by far the largest mortgage it had ever issued—and just over 10 percent would come from the residents, whose down payments of $450 per room would bring in $32.8 million.[1]

The UHF was well aware that Co-op City could not have been built for $283.7 million. One reason was that the original estimate was based on the preliminary plan for Co-op City, which had been modified by the City Planning Commission even before ground was broken. The revisions of the site plan, street system, and other features increased the cost by almost $8.1 million. Another, and even more important, reason was that it was Kazan's practice to underestimate the cost of the UHF's housing cooperatives. As Henry Nussbaum, director of the Finance Bureau of the New York State Division of Housing and Community Renewal, pointed out in the early 1970s, Kazan felt that if he came up with more realistic estimates, "he would lose bargaining power when it came time to negotiate with subcontractors and suppliers"— and, he might have added, with the building trades unions. Kazan also underestimated the cost of Co-op City and the UHF's other housing cooperatives in an effort to keep the carrying charges as low as possible, preferably no more than $20 to $23 per room per month. By so doing, wrote Cynthia Ann Curran, he hoped to be able to offer prospective residents "a deal they could not refuse." Kazan and his associates were concerned that if the carrying charges exceeded $25 per room, the apartments would be out of the reach of the low- and middle-income families for whom the UHF was building its housing cooperatives.[2]

Commissioner James W. Gaynor and the staff at the Division of Housing. which was responsible for overseeing the development of the state's Mitchell-Lama projects, were well aware of Kazan's practice of underestimating the projected costs of the UHF's housing cooperatives. After reviewing the foundation's proposal for Co-op City, the division calculated that the construction costs would come to $272.7 million, or $14 million more than the UHF's estimate, and the total development costs close to $300 million. It was well within the Division of Housing's authority to withhold its approval of the proposal (or to ask the UHF to submit a revised budget). Without its approval, the State Housing Finance Agency would not have provided the funds for Co-op City. But as Nussbaum pointed out, the Division of Housing had by then given up trying to change Kazan's practices. As Frank S. Kristof, the real estate economist (and onetime high-ranking official in New York City's Housing and Development Administration), explained, the Division of Housing needed the UHF as much as the UHF needed the Division of Housing. If the Division of Housing ordered the UHF to base its estimates on more realistic (or less optimistic) assumptions and thus increase its construction costs, there was a good chance that the foundation would abandon the project. It might even stop building Mitchell-Lama housing. And if the UHF, which was a mainstay of the state's low- and middle-income housing program, withdrew from the program, it was unlikely that another organization would fill the void. Given that $14 million was only about 5 percent of the estimated cost of Co-op City, the Division of Housing approved the UHF's proposal. And the State Housing Finance Agency provided the funds.[3]

Underlying the UHF's estimate that Co-op City could be built for not too much more than $283.7 million were two assumptions. The first was that the project could be completed in about five years—a relatively short time for so large an enterprise. If it took longer than five years to finish Co-op City, costs would go up. The general contractor, Community Services, Inc., the UHF subsidiary that was headed by Kazan and, after he stepped down, by Ostroff, would be forced to renegotiate with its subcontractors. And every two or three years the subcontractors would be obliged to renegotiate with their employees. Among them were the carpenters, plumbers, bricklayers, electricians, and ordinary laborers as well as the teamsters who transported the building materials to the site and the elevator operators who transported the tradesmen up to the tenth, twentieth, and even thirtieth floors of Co-op City's residential towers. Virtually all these workers belonged to powerful labor unions, none of which was inclined to give CSI a break because of the UHF's affiliation with the Amalgamated Clothing Workers of America, the International Ladies' Garment Workers' Union, the International Brotherhood of Electrical Workers, and other bastions of organized labor in New York.[4] Also, if it took more than five years to finish Co-op City, revenue would go down. Although the residents had to pay $450 per room when they bought their apartments, they did not have to start paying their carrying charges until they moved in. And the longer it took the Riverbay Corporation to fill the apartments, the less money it would have to cover its fixed costs and operating expenses.

The second assumption underlying the UHF's estimate that Co-op City could be built for not much more than $283.7 million was that the cost of living in the United States—and thus the cost of construction in the northeast Bronx—would be relatively stable over the five or so years during which Co-op City would be built. Given the postwar history of the Consumer Price Index (CPI), this was by no means an unreasonable assumption. Although the CPI soared in the immediate aftermath of World War II, it fell sharply in 1948 and 1949. After rising again in 1950 and 1951, it dropped to below 1 percent in the early 1950s, went up a bit in 1956 and 1957, and remained below 2 percent from 1958 to 1965—the year in which work got underway at Co-op City. Construction costs followed much the same pattern. According to the *Engineering News-Record* index, they went up only slightly in the late 1950s, and according to another index, they rose only 2.5 percent a year between 1960 and 1965.[5] The cost of capital remained relatively low as well. During the early 1960s tax-exempt municipal bonds yielded 4 percent or less. And it was highly unlikely that the interest on New York State Housing Finance Agency bonds, the sale of which would provide the funds to build Co-op City, would be higher than 4 percent. During the UHF's first dozen years, Kazan and his associates had to deal with the relocation of displaced tenants, the machinations of private developers, the most notable of whom was Fred C. Trump, and a host of other knotty problems. But before 1965 inflation was not one of them.

With hindsight it is inconceivable that Co-op City could have been built for $283.7 million, as the United Housing Foundation estimated, or even for $300 million, as the State Division of Housing calculated. Indeed, in 1976, only four years after the last residents moved into Co-op City, the Division of Audits and Accounts, a branch of the New York State Comptroller's Office, reported that in view of the actual construction costs and initial carrying charges, the development had been heading "toward a financial crisis" even before the first residents moved in.[6] To uncover the roots of Co-op City's fiscal troubles, it is therefore necessary to explain why the assumptions underlying the UHF and SDH estimates turned out to be unfounded—why, in other words, it took CSI longer to build Co-op City than expected and why construction costs soared in the years during which Co-op City was erected.

ooo

According to Charles J. Urstadt, a lawyer and real estate man who had worked for William Zeckendorf in the late 1950s and early 1960s and who succeeded James W. Gaynor as commissioner of housing and community renewal in January 1969, there were two main reasons it took not five but seven years to build Co-op City. One reason was that the city was unable to provide the infrastructure for the project on schedule. Although the UHF had the strong support of Mayor Robert F. Wagner Jr. (and his successor John V. Lindsay)—as well as of Bronx Borough President Herman Badillo

(and his successor Robert Abrams)—CSI ran into one roadblock after another in its dealings with the municipal agencies that paved the streets, put
in the sewers, and laid the water mains. In some cases the city's failure to
adhere to its schedule blocked access to the construction sites; in others it
delayed the completion of the apartment houses and prevented the residents
from moving into their units when they were ready for occupancy. The city's
procrastination severely troubled Harold Ostroff and the UHF's other leaders. Referring to the city's delay in completing the Bushnell Avenue sewer
extension, which was preventing CSI from putting in the underground pipes
and wires that would supply heat and electricity to several buildings, Ostroff called his experience with the municipal bureaucracy "a total exercise
in futility and frustration." "I am literally at my wit's end," he wrote Merril
Eisenbud, the city's environmental protection administrator, in late 1969.[7]

The other reason it took longer to build Co-op City than expected was
that the development was racked by several industrial disputes, some of
which turned into highly disruptive strikes. By far the most disruptive of
these strikes started on July 1, 1969, a day after the contract expired between
Local 1 of the International Union of Elevator Constructors (IUEC) and the
Elevator Manufacturers Association (EMA). The IUEC, which had been organized under a slightly different name in 1901, represented the workmen who
installed, maintained, and repaired the elevators that carried the plumbers,
electricians, and other tradesmen to the upper floors of high-rise buildings
under construction. The EMA's members were firms that manufactured the
elevators, the largest of which were the Westinghouse Electric Corporation,
the Otis Elevator Company, and the Haughton Elevator Company. Relations
between the IUEC and elevator manufacturers had long been strained. As
recently as February 1967 the 14,000 members of the IUEC walked off the
job when, as a result of a dispute over wages, the workers and their employers, who were represented by the National Elevator Manufacturers Institute,
were unable to agree on a new contract. The strike, which dragged on for
more than a month, halted the construction of many high-rise buildings all
over the country. Settled in March with the help of the Federal Mediation
and Conciliation Service, it was widely regarded as a victory for the IUEC.[8]

A little over two years later Local 1, which was far and away the largest local in the IUEC, and the EMA reached an impasse in their efforts to
come to terms on a new contract. Although the union's leaders had accepted
the EMA's offer of a $3.25-an-hour wage hike, the rank and file rejected it.
And on July 1 more than 2,000 elevator constructors walked off the job.

The strike dragged on through the summer, when the rank and file again ignored the recommendation of the leadership and voted down an even more generous offer from the EMA. The strike halted the construction of an estimated $100 million worth of office buildings, apartment houses, and other high-rise buildings in projects all over the city. Perhaps no project was hit harder than Co-op City, most of whose residential towers were under construction. Although Local 1 did not set up a picket line at Co-op City, which many workers would not have crossed, the shutdown of the elevators was "calamitous," said George Schechter, vice president of CSI. Without elevators, the carpenters, bricklayers, and other tradesmen had to climb twenty and even thirty flights of stairs to get to their workplace. Many were exhausted. A few suffered heart attacks, and some just stopped working. The strike not only slowed down construction at many of Co-op City's residential towers but also prevented many of the newcomers from moving into buildings that were ready for occupancy.[9]

Things went from bad to worse in the early fall. At the urging of Fire Commissioner Robert O. Lowery, who was afraid that his force could not cope with fires in high-rise buildings that did not have working elevators, Building Commissioner John T. O'Neill ordered a halt on the construction of all buildings that were 150 feet or higher. O'Neill's order affected roughly sixty buildings, twenty-five of which were in Co-op City. As a result, 10,000 to 15,000 tradesmen were laid off, a matter of great concern not only to Peter Brennan, president of the Building and Construction Trades Council of Greater New York, but also to Mayor John V. Lindsay. In an effort to bail out the unions and the developers, Lindsay issued an order that work could resume on high-rise buildings provided, as the *Times* put it, "adequate fire protection measures were taken." Under pressure from the mayor, and with the help of Matthew Miller, a federal mediator, the IUEC and EMA resumed talks. In early October—by which time the members of Local 3 of the International Brotherhood of Electrical Workers (IBEW) had also walked off the job—the union and manufacturers reached an agreement on a three-year contract that increased wages by about $3.50 an hour. The rank and file ratified the agreement. Not long afterwards, the IBEW and the Elevator Industries Association settled their dispute.[10]

Many other unions—as many as twenty-one, according to one estimate—went on strike in the summer of 1969, though not for nearly as long as Local 1 of the International Union of Elevator Constructors. Chief among them was Local 282 of the International Brotherhood of Teamsters. The strike began

in early July when a small group of drivers who hauled ready-mixed concrete walked off the job and a much larger group of drivers who transported
lumber, plumbing supplies, and other building materials refused to cross the
picket line. Some tradesmen went to work, but many others, including the
bricklayers, who had no bricks to lay, "had to knock it off," said Joseph Qua-
ley, a Co-op City job clerk. Before long one-third of the carpenters, one-half
of the painters, and all but a few of the bricklayers were out of work. The
steamfitters, sheet-metal workers, and several other tradesmen also went on
strike when their three-year contracts with CSI's subcontractors expired at
the end of June and the unions were unable to reach a new agreement with
the New York Building Trades Employers' Association, which represented
most of the city's high-rise builders. These strikes were highly disruptive,
Ostroff observed, because many tradesmen could not start their work until
other tradesmen finished theirs. A case in point was the bricklayers, who
could not lay bricks in the winter until the steamfitters put in the pipes, the
electricians laid the wires, and the carpenters installed the windows.[11]

As Schechter acknowledged, it was very hard to calculate the full impact
of the many strikes that racked Co-op City in the summer of 1969 (or, for
that matter, the several strikes that took place there in subsequent years),
but it was, to say the least, substantial. By virtue of the elevator constructors' and teamsters' strikes, many residents were unable to move into their
apartments when the buildings were ready for occupancy, which cost Riverbay Corporation hundreds of thousands of dollars, if not more, in carrying charges. (Indeed, some of the buildings were occupied as many as five
months later than anticipated.) As a result of the strikes, most of the workers received a raise of 40 to 50 percent in wages and fringe benefits over
the next three years, which greatly increased the cost of construction of the
roughly 35 percent of Co-op City that had not yet been finished. Also, to
avoid a shutdown during the elevator constructors' strike, the Riverbay Corporation had to hire many additional watchmen and laborers. According to
Ostroff, it took fully six to eight months to recover from the effects of the
elevator constructors' strike, which greatly slowed down construction. But
even if construction slowed down (or ground to a halt), the Riverbay Corporation still had to pay its fixed costs, the bulk of which consisted of interest
payments on the State Housing Finance Agency bonds and property taxes
owed to the City of New York.[12]

Making matters worse, construction costs soared in the seven years
during which Co-op City was built. The main reason, Ostroff pointed out,

was that the project was constructed during "the worst inflationary period in the last thirty to forty years." Although Co-op City was a huge development, he said, it was not so huge that it could escape being caught "in the whirlpool of the national economy." Szold, Brandwen, Meyers & Altman, the UHF's lawyers, agreed, stressing that the inflationary spiral that began in the mid-1960s had driven the cost of living up to "historic heights." Commissioner Urstadt blamed most of Co-op City's fiscal problems on "the nation's current inflationary spiral"—which was described as "rampant" by some observers and as "runaway" by others. So did the Budget Committee of the Riverbay Corporation Board of Directors, some of whose members were at times at odds with Ostroff.[13] As I will discuss later, many Co-op City residents (and the lawyers who represented them) attributed the project's fiscal troubles not so much to inflation as to skullduggery by the UHF and CSI and to mismanagement by the Riverbay Corporation. But down through the early 1970s Ostroff and his associates never wavered in their belief that Co-op City's soaring construction costs and fiscal troubles were a result of the inflationary spiral that racked the American economy in the mid and late 1960s.

The American economy had undergone two severe bouts of inflation before the UHF acquired the site for Co-op City. The first occurred during and shortly after World War I. According to the US Bureau of Labor Statistics, the cost of living did not rise much in 1914, the year in which war broke out in Europe, or 1915. But as the war dragged on, it soared in 1916, climbing from a modest 3.3 percent in January to double digits in October. Starting in 1917, the year in which the United States joined the war, the cost of living rose at a rate "unmatched in the nation any time," wrote the Bureau of Labor Statistics (BLS) in 2014. Between December 1916 and June 1917, the Consumer Price Index (CPI) went up 18.5 percent; and the cost of most goods and services more than doubled between 1915 and 1920. Following a decade of depression, the CPI went up less than 1 percent in 1940. But as a result of World War II, it soared by 9.9 percent in 1941 and 9 percent in 1942. It fell sharply after the federal government imposed price controls in 1942, but after the controls were lifted it skyrocketed 18.1 percent in 1946 and 8.8 percent in 1947, before plummeting to 2.1 percent in 1949. During the decade before work began on Co-op City, the CPI remained very low, going up by more than 2 percent in only two years, 1956 and 1957. But it started to increase in 1966, the year in which construction got underway, and reached a peak of 6.2 percent in 1969.[14] Although inflation was not as severe in the mid and late 1960s (and early 1970s) as in the late 1910s and mid-1940s, it was severe enough that in August 1971 Richard M. Nixon imposed a ninety-day freeze on prices and wages, which was something no other American president had done in peacetime.

Nixon's freeze on prices and wages was designed to resolve a nationwide problem that affected virtually every sector of the economy (and virtually every region of the country). Housing was especially hard hit. As the UHF pointed out, inflation "play[ed] havoc" not only with the cost of maintaining old buildings but also with the cost of constructing new ones. And cooperative housing was no more "immune" to "the ravages of inflation" than conventional housing. The inflationary spiral drove up the cost of materials. Between 1966 and 1971 the price of steel, lumber, and cement—what *Engineering News-Record,* a leading trade publication, called the "Big 3"—rose about 40 percent. Copper, which was used extensively in electrical and plumbing work, increased even more. Bricks and mortar cost ten times as much in the United States in 1971 as in 1913 (and twelve times as much in New York City). The price of cranes, backhoes, tractors, welding machines, and other construction equipment also went up, though not as much as the price of supplies. Referring to the rise in the price of building materials, Julius Goldberg, vice president for construction of Community Services, Inc., remarked in late 1971: "All have gone only one way—up!" At about the same time *Engineering News-Record* observed that the recently imposed wage-price freeze "has come too late to save contractors from this year's worst materials cost inflation since 1947."[15]

The inflationary spiral drove up the cost of labor as well. Thanks in part to Abraham Kazan's skills as a negotiator, CSI's initial terms with the subcontractors (and the unions that represented their workers) were extremely favorable. But these contracts ran for only two or three years. When they expired, Ostroff warned in 1968, the labor unions would demand much higher wages (and much better fringe benefits). As a result of inflation, wages would increase much more rapidly in the future than in the past, perhaps, he observed in 1969, by as much as 41 to 51 percent over the next three years. (Making matters worse was a shortage of plasterers and other skilled workers, which forced CSI to pay what Ostroff called "an inordinate amount of overtime," both on weekdays and on Saturdays.) Ostroff's prediction was not far off the mark. Between 1966 and 1971 wages for skilled workers went up roughly 50 percent. For electricians the increase came to 51 percent, for mechanical tradesmen 55 percent, and for equipment operators a whopping 70 percent. Common laborers also received substantial raises—as much as

71 percent, according to one estimate. Maintenance men who earned $54 a week in 1965 earned $100 a week in 1969. The wages of handymen, porters, gardeners, and clerical workers went way up too.[16]

Between 1961 and 1965 construction costs in the United States rose very little. Indeed, according to the *Cooperator*, a UHF publication, they went up only 2.5 percent a year. But as a result of the sharp increase in the cost of materials and labor, they soared in the years during which work was underway at Co-op City. These costs went up 7.1 percent a year, wrote the *Cooperator*, or about 50 percent, noted the *Engineering News-Record*. According to Julius Goldberg, construction costs increased by about as much in these seven years as in the previous fifty-one. The increase was especially sharp in the late 1960s and early 1970s. In New York, which had the highest construction costs of any city in the country, they were 10 percent higher in 1969 than in 1968, 11 percent higher in 1970 than in 1969, and 17 percent higher in 1971 than in 1970. One indicator of the soaring construction costs in New York was that a typical Mitchell-Lama apartment that could be built for $50 to $60 a room in 1969 cost $85 to $100 a room to build in 1972. Another indicator was that in 1966 the Division of Housing and Community Renewal, which oversaw the Mitchell-Lama program, would not approve a project whose rents or carrying charges came to more than $30 per room per month. Five years later it was approving projects whose rents and carrying charges were as high as $80 per room per month, which, Ostroff pointed out, was "hardly housing that families with average incomes can afford."[17]

As early as September 1968 Ostroff acknowledged that the cost of the work yet to be done at Co-op City would be "considerably higher than originally estimated." He later conceded that construction costs might rise by as much as 5 to 8 percent a year (and as much as 15 percent before Co-op City was finished). But as a result of inflation, which, Ostroff pointed out, affected "all the hundreds of items that constitute development work," Co-op City's construction costs went up by much more. In June 1965 it was estimated that the construction costs would come to $258.5 million. But they rose to $267.8 million in March 1967, $268.1 million in January 1968, and $270 million in March 1968, and then soared to $310.5 million in September 1969 and $340.5 million in May 1971. (Most of the increase was spent on the residential towers and townhouses, which turned out to be much more expensive than expected; the rest was expended on the garages, commercial structures, community facilities, and, among other things, site planning.) In all, construction costs came to nearly $82 million more than anticipated—an increase of more than 30 percent. Project costs, which included land acquisition, professional fees, and, far and away the largest item, finance and carrying charges, climbed from $283.7 million in June 1965 to $422.7 million in May 1971, by which time most of the work had been done. To put it another way, Co-op City cost nearly 49 percent more than Kazan and Ostroff had estimated.[18]

ooo

As Ostroff told the Riverbay Corporation Board of Directors, Community Services, Inc., could have ordered its subcontractors to stop work on Co-op City until the rate of inflation—and thus the cost of labor and materials—returned to normal. If it did so, he pointed out, "the actual brick and mortar cost of construction would not have been significantly increased." But, he went on to say, "the total cost of development ... would have increased far beyond the change in actual construction cost." Even if the subcontractors stopped work, the Riverbay Corporation would still have had to pay the interest on the State Housing Finance Agency's bonds. It would also have had to pay property taxes to the City of New York. And it would have lost what Ostroff called the project's "pre-occupancy income."[19] Hence, he pointed out, to stop construction "would have been so prohibitively expensive as to be unthinkable," a view that his associates shared. But if CSI were to press ahead, the Riverbay Corporation would have to find additional funds. It could raise the price of the apartments, which were originally set at $450 per room. But a modest increase would place the cost of the apartments out of the reach of the lower- and middle-class New Yorkers for whom Co-op City was built. And even a substantial increase would not generate enough money to cover the soaring cost of construction.

In order for CSI (and its subcontractors) to continue work on Co-op City, Ostroff and his associates concluded, the Riverbay Corporation had no choice but to borrow more money from the State Housing Finance Agency, which had given it a $251 million mortgage in 1965. Indeed, Ostroff went so far as to say, without an infusion of additional capital from New York State, "the entire enterprise would have collapsed." Thus, starting in early 1967, Riverbay made the first of several applications to the SHFA for additional funds. Fortunately for Ostroff and his associates, the agency had plenty of money. It was also in no position to turn down Riverbay's applications. If Co-op City was not finished—if, in other words, the more than 15,000 families did not move into their apartments and begin to pay their carrying charges—Riverbay would not have been able to make the interest payments on the SHFA bonds. And as a result the agency would have been hard pressed to find a market for its bonds, which would probably have brought the Mitchell-Lama and other state housing programs to a halt. Hence in March 1967 the agency provided Riverbay with an additional $9 million, which raised Co-op City's mortgage to $260 million. As construction costs continued to rise, it gave Riverbay another $70 million in September 1969. And in May 1971 the SHFA granted the corporation an additional $60 million.[20] All told, Co-op City's mortgage went up from $251 million to $436 million, or more than 70 percent.

This huge infusion of capital solved Riverbay's short-term fiscal problem and enabled CSI to continue work on Co-op City, which, as mentioned earlier, was finished in the early 1970s. But it also created a long-term fiscal problem for the corporation, a problem that was much more serious than Ostroff and his associates anticipated. They were well aware that Riverbay would have to come up with the money not only to amortize a mortgage of $436 million, rather than $251 million, but also to pay the interest on $436 million. But they were not aware of how much interest rates would go up in the late 1960s and early 1970s. During the early 1960s tax-exempt municipal bonds, both general obligation bonds and moral obligation bonds, sold for about 3.75 percent. (Indeed, when New York City started its Mitchell-Lama program in the late 1950s, Housing and Development Administrator Albert A. Walsh pointed out, it was able to sell its bonds for 3.25 to 3.50 percent.) And in the mid-1960s, interest rates on municipal bonds averaged about 3.75 percent. Hence when the UHF began planning Co-op City Kazan and his associates estimated that interest rates would be no higher than 4 percent. Even some of New York's savvy real estate men were just as optimistic. As late as mid-1965, three and a half years before he became commissioner of housing and community renewal, Charles J. Urstadt said he was confident that the SHFA would be able to sell its bonds for 4.5 percent.[21]

During the next few years, however, the capital markets went "completely haywire," in Urstadt's words, and interest rates on municipal bonds soared to "unprecedented heights." According to the Bond Buyer Index, the rates went up to 5.80 percent in August 1968, 6.26 percent in August 1969, and 7.02 percent in May 1970—which, as William F. Meyers, the Assistant Commissioner of Housing and Community Renewal, informed Urstadt, was "the highest figure in the 75 years that the Index has been maintained." As a result, the interest rates on the State Housing Finance Agency's bonds for Co-op City were much higher than anticipated. The first $91.7 million, which were sold in May 1968, yielded 5.20 percent. Another $63 million was sold in November 1969 at 6.75 percent. And yet another, $74.3 million, which was sold in April 1970, yielded 6.60 percent. The fourth bond issue, which went on the market in January 1971 and brought in $42.5 million, went for 6.47 percent. And the fifth, which was sold eight months later and provided Riverbay with an additional $100 million, yielded 6.40 percent. (Another $1.8 million was raised through the sale of short-term bond anticipation notes, the return on which was 8 percent.) The soaring interest rates left Ostroff (and Riverbay's other officers) stunned. At a town hall meeting held at Co-op City in September 1971, he said, "If, five years ago, someone told me that non-taxable state housing finance bonds, which were then selling for three and three quarters percent, would rise to six and one half percent, I'd [have said] he was a damn fool."[22]

Forced to borrow an additional $140 million from the State Housing Finance Agency and to pay more than 6 percent on most of the SHFA's bonds, Ostroff and his associates soon realized that their original estimate for Co-op City was far off the mark. In 1965, for example, Riverbay projected that interest payments would be only about $6.2 million a year. By 1971 they came to more than $70 million. (To put it in a way that would have made more sense to Co-op City's residents, each 1 percent increase in interest rates added more than $4 per room per month to the carrying charges. By the mid-1970s, according to one estimate, the interest payments came close to $30 per room per month on each of the project's more than 15,000 apartments.) When combined with Co-op City's other fixed charges—which included New York City property taxes, State Housing Finance Agency and State Division of Housing supervisory fees, and title and recording expenses—the interest payments drove the finance charges up from $12.3 million in 1965 to more than $94.1 million in 1971. In other words, Co-op City's finance charges went up more rapidly than its construction costs, which rose from an estimated $258.5 million in 1965 to a projected $340.5 six years later. In the end the finance charges, which were originally expected to be less than one-twentieth of the construction costs, turned out to be more than one-third.[23]

Inflation had a profound impact not only on Co-op City's construction costs and finance charges but also on its operating expenses. As Edward Aronov, Co-op City's general manager, told the Riverbay Corporation Board of Directors in early 1974, "In a quarter of a century in the housing management field I cannot recall a [time in which] an uncontrollable inflation has played such havoc with an operational budget."[24] Building, in Nelson

A. Rockefeller's words, "a whole new city within a City" was a monumental undertaking. But as Aronov knew probably better than anyone other than Harold Ostroff, so was running it. Even with a workforce of more than 650 handymen, porters, gardeners, security guards, and other employees in 1972, Aronov and his staff had their work cut out for them. They had to provide heat, hot water, and air-conditioning to Co-op City's more than 15,300 apartments. They also had to make sure that the residents had gas and electricity. Co-op City's employees had to maintain more than 200 acres of roads, parks, playgrounds, lawns, and other public spaces as well as provide security to the residents and shopkeepers and, when need be, make repairs in a timely manner. It was also their job to ensure that the elevators and laundry machines were working, that the hallways were clean and well lit, and, among other things, that the garbage was collected, compacted, and put out for pickup by the New York City Sanitation Department.

At the outset, Ostroff later acknowledged, the UHF did not anticipate the profound impact that inflation would have on the cost of labor, which was one of the two main components of Co-op City's operating budget. But as the cost of living soared in the late 1960s, many of Riverbay's employees, most of whom were members of Local 32-E of the Service Employees International Union, found it very hard to make ends meet. In September 1973 Local 32-E prevailed on Riverbay to give its members a roughly 40 percent wage hike over the next three years. Under the new contract the wages of porters rose from $100 a week in 1970 to $139 a week in 1973, and the wages of handymen and other workers who were better paid than porters went up even more. Negotiations for a new contract got underway late in the summer of 1973, when the cost of living was still soaring. Much as Ostroff feared, they soon got bogged down over two issues—the length of the contract and the amount of the wage hike. Local 32-E initially asked for a two-year contract that would provide an additional $75 a week for its members, a demand that was later scaled down to $20 a week each year. Riverbay rejected the union's proposal and instead offered the workers a three-year contract that would give them an additional $12 per week in the first year, $14 per week in the second, and $16 per week in the third.[25] (The offer was based on an agreement that Local 32-E had reached with the Bronx Realty Advisory Board, which represented most of the borough's landlords other than the Riverbay Corporation.)

The old contract expired on September 15. And against the advice of Local 32-E's leaders, the rank and file promptly voted to go on strike. A day later roughly 400 workers walked off the job. To reduce the impact of the strike, the supervisory personnel made emergency repairs, the residents cleaned the buildings, the children policed the grounds, and the NYPD dispatched additional officers to Co-op City. Before long, however, conditions deteriorated—partly as a result of acts of vandalism, for which Local 32-E denied responsibility and blamed replacement workers. Garbage piled up, lights were broken, and fire hoses were opened, leaving some residents temporarily trapped in the elevators when water flooded the shafts. Making matters worse, some elevator repairmen and office workers refused to cross Local 32-E's picket lines. A few days later Riverbay management, concerned about the impact of the strike on public safety, and especially about the well-being of residents of the upper floors of the high-rise buildings, caved in. It agreed to give the workers a two-year contract, with a $15-a-week raise each year, increasing wages from $170 to $200 a week or more. It also liberalized the policies about sick leave, vacation time, and other fringe benefits. Urging the rank and file to ratify the agreement, which they promptly did, Robert Chartier, the union's leader, called it "the greatest contract in Local 32-E history." And though the new contract would cost Riverbay an additional $300,000 in the first year (and even more in the second), "it was the best we could do," said Aronov.[26]

Nor did the UHF anticipate the profound impact that inflation would have on the cost of utilities, which was the other main component of Co-op City's operating budget. The price of fuel oil went up very little in the early and mid-1960s. But it started to rise in the late 1960s and soared in late 1973 and early 1974, when the Organization of the Petroleum Exporting Countries (OPEC) imposed an embargo on Middle East oil, a move that was designed to undermine support for the state of Israel in the United States and Western Europe. From 9.6 cents a gallon in September 1973, fuel oil climbed to 32 cents a gallon in March 1974, raising Co-op City's operating budget by $3 to $4 million. "The increase in the cost of oil is robbery of the first order," said George Schechter. "Arab imperialism has reached into the pocket of every resident of Co-op City, of everyone in the whole world, to enrich the coffers of a handful of rulers, not even the general population of the Arab countries." Harold Ostroff added that it might be time to consider nationalizing the fuel oil industry. The price of electricity also soared in the early 1970s. Consolidated Edison, which relied heavily on oil to generate power, steadily raised its rates, partly by taking advantage of a fuel adjustment clause that was written into its contracts and partly by applying to the state's Public Service Commission for what Ostroff called "astronomical" rate hikes. The result was that Co-op City's electric bill more than doubled after the Arab oil embargo, climbing from about $3 per room per month to $7 per room per month. Calling Consolidated Edison's rate hikes "the straw that broke the camel's back," Ostroff warned that they would spur an exodus of middle-income families from New York City.[27]

As Lawrence Sivak, a resident of Co-op City and a member of the Riverbay Corporation Board of Directors, observed in March 1974, Co-op City was "traumatized by the unbelievable increases in electricity and fuel oil costs." To lessen the trauma Riverbay's management tried hard to hold down energy costs. Late in 1973 it joined forces with several other housing cooperatives affiliated with the UHF in an effort to negotiate a lower price for fuel oil. Together they invited a dozen suppliers to submit bids for what would have been the largest private purchase of fuel oil in greater New York. But six of the suppliers declined, and five could not provide as much fuel oil as was needed. Only Paragon Oil, a division of Texaco, was willing to make a commitment, but not at a substantially lower price. Riverbay also considered shifting from fuel oil to natural gas, which was less expensive, and even converted its furnaces so that they could burn gas as well as oil. But it was far from clear that enough natural gas would be available in wintertime. Along with the leaders of other housing cooperatives, Ostroff and his associates also repeatedly urged the Public Service Commission to deny Consolidated Edison's applications for a rate hike, stressing that Con Ed's rates were already the highest in the country and twice as high as the rates of the New York Power Authority, which served residents and businesses upstate. Riverbay management also took steps to conserve oil and electricity and prevailed on many residents to follow its lead. Although these measures reduced consumption, they did little to cut costs. For as Edward Aronov pointed out, energy costs were a function of national and international forces that were well beyond the control of a housing cooperative, even one as large as Co-op City.[28]

By 1975 Co-op City was in serious financial trouble. According to Aronov, who was responsible for preparing the budget for the fiscal year that started on April 1, the cost of fuel oil was still rising and was projected to reach $5.15 million, or $5.88 per room per month. Also rising was the cost of electricity, which was expected to come to $6.31 million, or $7.20 per room per month. (To Aronov, it was especially demoralizing that Co-op City would have to spend more than twice as much on electricity even though it consumed 8 percent less.) The total cost of utilities, which included gas and water, was expected to come to $12.82 million, or 23.94 percent of the budget and $14.66 per room per month. Wages and salaries also went up, though not nearly as much. They were projected to reach $4.20 million, or 7.88 percent of the budget and $4.80 per room per month. When combined with the cost of repairs and maintenance and other items, Co-op City's operating expenses were estimated to be $21.93 million, which was 40.93 percent of the budget and $25.08 per room per month—or slightly more than the original carrying charges, which were supposed to be enough to cover construction costs and finance charges. (The other 59.07 percent was earmarked for fixed costs, the bulk of which went for interest and amortization of Co-op City's mortgage.) Given that the project's expenses were expected to come to $53.58 million and its income to $43.82 million, Aronov estimated that Co-op City would run a deficit of roughly $10 million, which was almost twice as large as the deficit for the previous year. To make matters worse, Co-op City had already depleted its reserves. As Aronov pointed out, for the first time since Co-op City opened there were no excess construction funds to offset "a portion of the budget deficit."[29]

OOO

As Co-op City's fiscal problems grew worse, a consensus emerged that the solution required "government assistance," in the words of Lawrence Sivak. Harold Ostroff agreed. So did Al Abrams, chairman of the Co-op City Advisory Council, which represented Co-op City's roughly 60,000 residents.[30] By "government assistance" Sivak and the others meant legislative action by the state and, to a lesser degree, the city and the federal government. Leading the campaign for legislative action were the Riverbay Corporation and the Co-op city Advisory Council, especially its Inter-Community Committee. Supporting them were many of Co-op City's civic, social, and political organizations, among them the United Democratic Club of Co-op City and the Hutchinson River Republican Club. Far from being on its own, Co-op City was joined by other UHF housing cooperatives and city and state Mitchell-Lama projects, many of which were in the same dire fiscal straits as Co-op City. Speaking for them were the Coordinating Council of Cooperatives and the Mitchell-Lama Council. Support for the campaign also came from many elected officials, Republicans as well as Democrats, all of whom were well aware of the number of registered voters in Co-op City and the other middle-income housing developments. Among the most conspicuous of them were Congressmen Mario Biaggi and Jonathan Bingham, State Senators John

Calandra and Abraham Bernstein, Assemblymen Alan Hochberg and Guy Velella, Bronx Borough President Robert Abrams, and New York City Councilman Stephen B. Kaufman.

As Ostroff pointed out, the objectives of the campaign were threefold: to reduce the expenses of Co-op City and other housing cooperatives and Mitchell-Lama projects, to increase the revenues of Riverbay Corporation and the other nonprofit companies that housed low- and middle-income New Yorkers, and to ease the burden on the many hard-strapped families whose rents and carrying charges were on the rise. Only in this way could Co-op City, the cooperative housing movement, and the Mitchell-Lama program be saved. To prevail on the authorities to enact the necessary legislation, the campaign's leaders encouraged residents to write letters to elected officials and to circulate petitions in favor of bills under consideration. They also organized town hall meetings and legislative conferences and testified before State Senate and Assembly committees. They even sponsored a series of rallies and demonstrations. To give just two examples, in February 1972 more than 1,000 Co-op City senior citizens gathered in front of Governor Rockefeller's Midtown Manhattan office, where they chanted, "One, two, three, four, Rockefeller, open the door." (They made the trip from Co-op City in twelve buses, two of which were donated by Borough President Abrams.) In April 1974 roughly 2,500 Co-op City residents joined forces with more than 4,000 residents of other Mitchell-Lama developments to form a caravan of 130 buses, which converged on the state capitol in Albany. There the demonstrators buttonholed legislative leaders. A small delegation met with Governor Malcolm Wilson, the former lieutenant governor who had succeeded Rockefeller when he replaced Spiro Agnew as vice president of the United States in 1973.[31]

The Albany caravan was one of the high points of the campaign to solve Co-op City's fiscal problems. But if the caravan was, in the words of Edward Aronov, "a rousing success," the campaign was anything but. At best the results were mixed. Chief among its successes was the effort to persuade the authorities to reduce Co-op City's expenses by increasing its tax abatement. Under the Mitchell-Lama act, which was passed in 1955, Co-op City was entitled to a 50 percent abatement on its property taxes over thirty years, though only on its residential sections. These taxes were based on the development's assessed value, which was defined as the best and highest use of the property. At the outset the assessed value of Co-op City, which was nothing but the site of a defunct amusement park, was very low. But Ostroff and his associates knew that when Co-op City was built, its assessed value would soar. So would its property taxes. In an attempt to head off a huge increase in Co-op City's property taxes, the UHF urged the state legislature to allow cities to base these taxes not on the assessed value, which Ostroff and others argued was "an archaic method of taxation" that was undermining the Mitchell-Lama program, but on what was called the shelter rent tax formula. Under this formula, which was in effect in New Jersey, Massachusetts, and a few other states, property taxes were based not on a project's assessed value but on the housing company's income—the amount that was raised by the rents or carrying charges—less the cost of providing electricity, gas, and other utilities to the residents. And in 1967 the state legislature passed an enabling act that permitted New York and other cities to adopt the shelter tax formula.[32]

During the next two years the UHF and its allies made a strenuous effort to convince Mayor John V. Lindsay and other members of the Board of Estimate to grant shelter rent tax status to Co-op City and the foundation's other housing cooperatives. It was the only way to provide low- and middle-income New Yorkers with the highest-quality housing at the lowest possible price, argued Szold, Brandwen, Meyers & Altman, the UHF's law firm. As Ostroff and his associates knew, the stakes were very high. According to the New York State Legislative Commission on Expenditure Review, Co-op City would have had to pay $21.2 million in property taxes in 1969 without a tax abatement, $10.7 million with a 50 percent abatement, and only $2.8 million under the shelter rent tax formula. Per room per month, the cost would have come to $24.38 without a tax abatement, $12.18 with a 50 percent abatement, and only $3.18 under the shelter rent tax formula. After Jason R. Nathan, the city's housing and development administrator, endorsed the UHF's proposal, Lindsay, City Comptroller Mario Procaccino, and the other members of the Board of Estimate voted unanimously in 1969 to grant shelter rent tax status to Co-op City and the foundation's other housing cooperatives. What Al Smoke, the UHF's chief lobbyist, described as "one of the most important pieces of legislation we obtained for Co-op City" saved Riverbay Corporation more than $100 million in the five years after Co-op City was fully occupied. And the Office of the New York State Comptroller estimated that for Co-op City the value of this tax abatement came to about $25 per room per month in the mid-1970s.[33]

The campaign to solve Co-op City's fiscal problems also had some success in increasing the revenues of the Riverbay Corporation and the other nonprofit companies that housed low- and middle-income New Yorkers. It did so by prevailing on the authorities to redistribute the income from the surcharges paid by a small but significant minority of residents. Under the Mitchell-Lama act, a family whose annual income came to more than six times (or, if it had four or more members, seven times) its rent or carrying charges could remain in its apartment, provided that it paid a surcharge. The surcharge, which was based on a definition of family income that was revised several times (and is much too complicated to discuss here), ranged from as low as 5 percent to as high as 50 percent of the rent or carrying charges. At the outset 100 percent of the surcharges went to the city, which was supposed to use the money to help offset part of the cost of the tax abatements. But in 1969 the UHF and its allies persuaded the state legislature and the Board of Estimate to allow the housing companies to keep 50 percent of the surcharges, which, it was argued, would enable them to hold down operating expenses. In 1974 they prevailed on the authorities to let the housing companies retain 75 percent, though not the 100 percent that the Advisory Council's Inter-Community Committee wanted. According to Edward Aronov, about 800 Co-op City residents would be subject to a surcharge in 1974, the payment of which would generate roughly $400,000 to $450,000 that year. Under the revised formula, the Riverbay Corporation would receive at least $300,000.[34]

The campaign to solve Co-op City's fiscal problems even had some success in easing the burden of the many hard-strapped families whose rents and carrying charges were on the rise. The burden was especially heavy on Co-op City's senior citizens, many of whom were retired and now lived on Social Security benefits and/or private pensions. How, asked Stephen Kaufman, an attorney for the Co-op City Civic Association, were residents on a fixed income supposed to pay the increased carrying charges? "Are they supposed to steal?" They might have to go on welfare, said Harold Ostroff, who was sympathetic to the plight of the senior citizens. But one way or another they would have to pay their carrying charges. Hence he and his associates urged the authorities to grant residents of Co-op City and other Mitchell-Lama projects who were sixty-five or older and earned no more than $4,500 a year a 100 percent exemption on their property taxes, an exemption that would have reduced their carrying charges by $3 to $4 per room per month. Borough President Abrams supported the proposal, and though some upstate legislators opposed it, both the Senate and the Assembly passed enabling acts in 1971. To the dismay of the UHF and its allies, however, the Lindsay administration objected to the legislation on the grounds that the city's financial condition was so precarious that it could not afford to lose any source of revenue. Deferring to the Lindsay administration, Rockefeller refused to sign the enabling legislation, which was subsequently shelved.[35]

The issue came to a head again in 1972. In an effort to persuade the Lindsay administration to withdraw its opposition to a tax exemption for senior citizens, representatives of the Coordinating Council of Cooperatives, an offshoot of the UHF, met with city officials. Under a compromise that emerged out of these meetings, the city would not object to a tax exemption for residents of Mitchell-Lama projects who were sixty-five or older, but only if they spent one-third of their income on housing, a provision that would sharply reduce the number of senior citizens who were eligible for assistance. And the tax exemptions would be funded not by the city government but by the income surcharges. Under pressure from senior citizens in Co-op City and other UHF housing cooperatives, the Senate and Assembly promptly passed the enabling acts. And Governor Rockefeller signed what one of the law's supporters called "a major milestone in the long, frustrating struggle to help cooperators living on low fixed incomes." During the next two or three years the UHF and its allies tried hard to liberalize the program. They succeeded in persuading the authorities to reduce the age of eligibility from sixty-five to sixty-two, to increase the maximum income from $4,500 to $5,000, and, if need be, to use general funds to pay for the tax exemption. (Less successful was the attempt to convince the elected officials to grant tax exemptions not only to the elderly but also to the disabled and handicapped.) All told, the program was a boon to many of Co-op City's senior citizens, about 1,200 of whom received $700,000 in rebates a year in the mid-1970s.[36]

Not all the efforts to ease the burden on the middle-income families in Co-op City and other Mitchell-Lama projects were successful. A case in point was the campaign led by Assemblyman Alan Hochberg to amend the Mitchell-Lama act to allow families to remain in their apartments without paying a surcharge even if their annual income was eight or, in the case of families of four or more, nine times their carrying charges. The original formula, under which a family had to pay a surcharge if its income was six or, in the case of a family of four or more, seven times its charges, made "no allowance for spiraling inflation," Hochberg pointed out. "[T]he State," he insisted, "must realize that it takes more money to live on [now] than it did when the original Mitchell-Lama program was developed. In recognizing the need for greater income, the State must revise its formula so that a middle-income family may live in Co-op City without being subject to a surcharge, when, in fact, that income is only enough to live on." David L. Smith, chairman of the Coordinating Council of Cooperatives, agreed that the formula was "outdated." So did Arthur Taub, chair of one of Co-op City's many civic associations, who argued that it "is in dire need of change." And a spokesman for the Riverbay Corporation, who called the formula "archaic and unjust," warned that it was driving many families out of Co-op City. Mayor Abraham D. Beame supported a change in the Mitchell-Lama formula, though only for families whose income was less than $24,000 a year, and Lee Goodwin, who succeeded Charles J. Urstadt as commissioner of housing and community renewal in 1973, was willing to consider revising the formula.[37]

At the request of the Co-op City Advisory Council, Hochberg filed a bill to revise the Mitchell-Lama formula in January 1973. In what he called a "victory over the forces of Conservatism," the Assembly passed the bill by a wide margin, exempting from surcharges any family whose annual income was eight or in some cases nine times its carrying charges. But as the *Co-op City Times* pointed out, Hochberg's bill stood little chance in the Senate, which was controlled by the Republicans, many of whom represented upstate New York or New York City suburbs and believed that there was no reason to further subsidize Mitchell-Lama residents. The *Times* thought that the Hochberg bill might serve as a "wedge" to facilitate passage of another bill that would have exempted from surcharges any family whose income was seven or in some cases eight times its carrying charges. But the Senate would not go along with any scheme to revise the Mitchell-Lama formula. The Republican leadership sent Hochberg's bill back to committee. Hochberg and Senator Calandra made another attempt to change the formula in 1974. The Assembly gave its approval, but by then Governor Wilson had made it clear that he would not support any change. And neither would the Senate. In the end both houses passed a bill that eased the burden on Mitchell-Lama residents slightly by allowing the heads of households to exempt earnings of other family members from the family's income and to deduct medical expenses from it. But the bill, which was signed by Governor Wilson, left the Mitchell-Lama formula unchanged.[38]

Also unsuccessful were some of the efforts to reduce the expenses of Co-op City (and other housing cooperatives and Mitchell-Lama projects). Among them were a proposal to exempt Co-op City from state and city sales taxes, which would have saved the Riverbay Corporation about $500,000 a year; a measure to eliminate the supervisory fees of the state's Division of Housing and Community Renewal and the State Housing Finance Agency, which would have saved Riverbay another $330,000 a year; and by far the most important, a proposal to persuade the authorities to provide a subsidy that would have reduced the interest rates on Co-op City's mortgage from 6 percent (or more) to 4 percent. If successful, this proposal would have saved the Riverbay Corporation a whopping $9 million to $10 million a year—or enough to wipe out its projected deficit in 1975. According to its supporters, it would also have reduced Co-op City's monthly carrying charges by anywhere from $4 to $5 to $8 to $10 per room. Al Smoke said that a mortgage interest subsidy was the UHF's "top priority," and Harold Ostroff called it the "keystone" of the foundation's legislative agenda. Mortgage interest reduction was "absolutely essential to the financial stability of Co-op City and other middle-income developments," insisted Charles K. Parness, a member of the Riverbay Corporation Board of Directors. If eight of the nine major Mitchell-Lama bills that were filed in the state legislature in 1975 were passed, he declared, "the [UHF's] legislative program must be considered a failure if the mortgage interest bill is not among them."[39]

For a few years Ostroff and his associates were cautiously optimistic that the federal government would take steps to reduce the interest rates on Co-op City's mortgage with the State Housing Finance Agency. Their optimism was based on the National Housing Act of 1968, which was passed in Lyndon B. Johnson's last year as president and designed to stimulate the construction of low-income housing and encourage homeownership among low-income families. Under Section 235, the government would help these families buy homes by providing them access to mortgages at below-market interest rates. And under Section 236, it would provide a subsidy that would enable builders of low-income housing to obtain mortgages at below-market rates. But things did not work out as Ostroff expected. Even if cooperative housing was deemed a form of homeownership, which was far from clear, Congress did not appropriate the funds to implement Section 235. And like Section 236, it applied only to new construction. In August 1972 Senator Jacob Javits and Representative Jonathan Bingham urged George Romney, Secretary of Housing and Urban Development, to provide funds for Co-op City under Section 235, but they were turned down. Eugene A. Gulledge, commissioner of the Federal Housing Administration, told Javits and Bingham that Section 235 applied only to new construction. And Co-op City had been built "prior to the submission of a request."[40] Even before the Nixon administration imposed a moratorium on Sections 235 and 236 and other federal housing programs in early 1973, Ostroff and his associates realized that they would have to focus their efforts for interest-rate reduction on Albany, not on Washington.

Thus during the early and mid-1970s they asked several state legislators to file bills to reduce the interest rates on Co-op City's mortgage from 6 percent (or more) to 4 percent, which was the rate in effect when the project was conceived. Under one bill, which was favored by the Coordinating Council of Cooperatives, the state would impose a 2 percent tax on new construction and earmark the proceeds for interest-rate reduction in Mitchell-Lama projects. Under another bill, which was sponsored by Roy Goodman and Francis Boland, chairs of the Senate and Assembly housing committees, respectively, the state would make low-interest loans to help the Riverbay Corporation and other housing companies pay off high-interest mortgages. But these and other bills ran into stiff opposition, especially from upstate legislators and in the Republican-controlled Senate. Although some opponents held that New York State's "moral commitment" to the bondholders precluded any reduction in interest rates (which was probably not the case), many others feared that the bills would have a baneful impact on the state's precarious financial condition. Despite a vigorous lobbying effort by the UHF and its allies—and the strong support of Borough President Abrams, who warned that the Mitchell-Lama program had "reached the point of collapse"—the state legislators shelved one mortgage-interest-rate-reduction bill after another. And even if the legislature had passed one of these bills, Governor Wilson, who had made it clear not long after taking office that he was opposed to using subsidies to reduce interest rates, would probably not have signed it. Indeed, as early as January 1974, Al Abrams concluded that any reduction in Co-op City's interest rates was "out of the question."[41]

ooo

Besides campaigning for government assistance, the Riverbay Corporation took steps of its own to alleviate Co-op City's fiscal problems. Some were designed to reduce expenses. At the urging of Julius Palmer, a member of the Riverbay Corporation Board of Directors who argued that Co-op City had far more employees than it needed and should lay off as many as 10 percent of them, management reduced the size of the workforce. Among the workers laid off were porters, handymen, and switchboard operators. Management also signed a two-year contract with Allied Maintenance Corporation, a large building services company, to clean all the high-rise apartment houses, a move that was expected to save $80,000 to $90,000 a year as well as to improve janitorial services. (Riverbay staff continued to supervise the cleaning of the community centers, shopping centers, and garages.) Among many other things, management replaced incandescent bulbs with fluorescent bulbs in the halls and then removed some of the fluorescent bulbs. When some residents, unhappy with the lighting in the halls, replaced the bulbs, it cut off power to the fixtures from which the fluorescent bulbs had been removed. Harold Ostroff also urged residents to conserve energy. Stressing that "electricity is not free," he called on them to turn off lights when leaving rooms. "Don't heat empty rooms," he added. Ostroff also advised residents to "make sure dishwashers [are] full before using them" and to turn off the drying cycle and "allow dishes to dry themselves"—as well as to use only enough heat and air conditioning "to be comfortable" and to "turn off that TV if no one is watching."[42]

Other proposals to lower expenses were much more controversial and in time were shelved. Ostroff suggested that management consider cutting back or even eliminating air-conditioning except in July and August. It was a "drastic step," he acknowledged, but in view of the increased cost of fuel it was "absolutely necessary." It would save $13,500 a day or $40,000 a month. The proposal was too much for the Riverbay board's Operations, Budget, and Management Committee, which was well aware that central air-conditioning was one of Co-op City's principal selling points. Julius Palmer called on management to reduce or even suspend its subsidy to the *Co-op City Times*, a weekly newspaper that he denounced as a mouthpiece for the Riverbay Corporation and the United Housing Foundation. It should only be published monthly or quarterly, he said. His proposal was supported by the *City News*, part of a chain of community newspapers owned by Hagedorn Communications, which estimated that the *Co-op City Times*, its rival, cost the Riverbay Corporation $150,000 a year. But Ostroff and others opposed the proposal on the grounds that a housing cooperative as large as Co-op City needed the *Co-op City Times* as a means of communication between management and residents. Another resident proposed that management use Co-op City's power plant to generate additional electricity and sell any surplus to Consolidated Edison. Management rejected the proposal. "Thank god we didn't do it," said George Schechter. Given the shortage of oil, it would have been "catastrophic."[43]

1. Amalgamated Houses

2. Amalgamated Dwellings

Recently completed middle-income cooperative apartment development for 1,668 families in the Corlears Hook section on the lower East Side in Manhattan. At the right is the Williamsburg Bridge to Brooklyn.

3. East River Houses

4. Penn South

5. President John F. Kennedy speaking at dedication of Penn South, 1962

6. Rochdale Village

7. Amalgamated Warbasse Houses

8. Groundbreaking ceremony at Co-op City, 1966

9. Co-op City under construction, 1968

10. Co-op City

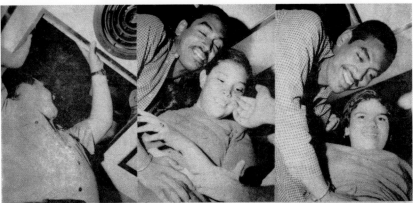

TO THE RESCUE: Police officers climb atop elevator to rescue two girls trapped in an elevator stopped on the 12th floor of 100 Darrow Place.

FREE AT LAST: Cynthia Molina, one of the two girls is lowered into elevator by police who led the girls across the top of the two cars.

SMILES: Margaret Marier, trapped in an elevator for over two hours, is all grins as her parents and friends waited anxiously for her.

11. Police rescue two girls trapped in Co-op City elevator, 1970

12. Fund-raising at Co-op City, 1971

13. Walkout at the State Division of Housing's informational meeting, 1972

Nizer, Rifkind Clash in Court

14. Louis Nizer and Simon Rifkind in front of US Court of Appeals for the Second Circuit, 1974

15. Rally at Governor Nelson A. Rockefeller's Manhattan office, 1974

16. Co-op City rent strike rally, 1975

17. Charles Rosen speaking at a rally at Co-op City, 1976

CRYING OVER HER LAUNDRY: Co-op City woman demonstrates her need for washing machines as she squeezes her laundry out in the offices of State Housing Commissioner Lee Goodwin in the World Trade Center Monday. (Photo by Robert Jones)

18. Washing laundry in Commissioner Lee Goodwin's New York office, 1976

19a. Co-op City residents transporting millions of dollars in carrying charges to the court, 1976

19b. Co-op City residents turning over to the court checks and money orders for the carrying charges, 1976

20a. Co-op City residents wheeling into court the boxes and one bag containing the checks and money orders, 1976

20b. Co-op City residents passing the boxes of checks and money orders from the truck to the courthouse, 1976

21a, b. *City News* editorial cartoons, 1974

22a, b. *City News* editorial cartoons, 1975

The Riverbay Corporation found ways not only to reduce expenses, but also to increase revenues. It raised the parking rates in Co-op City's garages, charging residents $22.50 a month (or, if they wanted an assigned space, $33.10 a month). Even after deductions for wages, utilities, and other expenses, the garages generated more than $1 million a year. Management thought about raising the rates for transient parking, which might have brought in $50,000 a year. But the Advisory Council strongly objected on the grounds that most of the transient parkers were parents, children, relatives, and friends of residents, not the general public. Management also attempted to make more money from the laundry rooms in the basements of the high-rise apartment houses, which raised almost $600,000 a year. It increased the rates for washing machines from 25 to 35 cents for a double load and from 15 to 25 cents for a single load. It raised the rate for the dryers too, though not as much. Among other things, management charged the residents of the townhouses 50 percent more for their dishwashers, freezers, washing machines, and other major appliances. It more than doubled the fee for residents who wanted to move from one apartment in Co-op City to another, a fee that was supposed to cover the cost of painting and other improvements. And with the approval of the State Division of Housing, management decided to require a nonrefundable deposit of $50 from each of the 1,000 or so families on the waiting list. At 5 percent interest, the deposits would generate $52,500.[44]

The Riverbay Corporation also considered a host of somewhat offbeat ways to raise revenue, a sign of the ingenuity and perhaps growing desperation of its leaders. Among them was a proposal to lease space in one of Co-op City's garages to a used-car dealer. Along the same line, management gave thought to renting a room or rooms, probably in one of the community centers, to New York City's Off-Track Betting Corporation, which had been established by the state legislature in 1970 and empowered to accept wagers on horse racing. Management also considered a proposal to permit a company to install vending machines for candy, soda, and cigarettes in the basements of the apartment houses. The price was a share of the proceeds. And it gave thought to negotiating with several companies that were willing to pay Riverbay for the rights to provide closed-circuit radio and television to Co-op City residents. The rights might have been worth as much as $50,000 a year. Another proposal was to lease 1,500 storage spaces in the apartment houses to residents, which, at $50 apiece, would have generated $75,000 a year. Still another proposal was to raise the fees for the use of rooms in the community centers. Management also thought about asking Co-op City's commercial tenants to agree to a voluntary rent increase as a way of absorbing part of the soaring cost of electricity. And in an effort to attract young families to Co-op City and also replenish the waiting list for two- and three-bedroom apartments, it took ads in the *New York Times* and *New York Post* and even retained a Madison Avenue public relations firm to improve Co-op City's image.[45]

By virtue of these efforts, Riverbay Corporation was able to reduce Co-op City's expenses by tens and even hundreds of thousands of dollars and to increase its revenues by tens and even hundreds of thousands of dollars more. But it would have taken millions of dollars, not hundreds of thousands, to solve Co-op City's fiscal problems. And as Larry Dolnick, chairman of the board's Operations, Budget, and Management Committee, pointed out, only a small fraction of Co-op City's budget, perhaps as small as 16 percent, was "controllable." Riverbay, he said, could not do much to reduce Co-op City operating expenses. They were a function of the soaring price of fuel and electricity, which was driven by national and even international forces that the housing company could do nothing about and by the rising cost of labor that was based largely on contractual obligations with the unions. Nor could Riverbay do much, if anything, about Co-op City's fixed costs, namely state fees, city taxes, and above all the interest and amortization of its mortgage, which came to almost $20 million, or more than one-half of Co-op City's budget, in 1974.[46] To solve Co-op City's fiscal problems—indeed to keep the huge housing cooperative solvent—would require doing something much more drastic than laying off porters, handymen, and switchboard operators, replacing incandescent bulbs with fluorescent bulbs, and charging residents more for using washers and dryers, parking in garages, and moving from one apartment to another.

That something was to raise Co-op City's carrying charges, which generated between 80 and 90 percent of Riverbay's revenue. Harold Ostroff reluctantly acknowledged as much in October 1968, a couple of months before the first residents moved into Co-op City. In a letter to prospective residents, all of whom had the option to cancel their contract with Riverbay and ask the company to refund their deposit, he pointed out that Co-op City was being built "during a period of severe inflation," which had driven construction costs, operating expenses, and finance charges well above expectations.

Although management was doing what it could to hold down costs—and at present was generating enough income to meet its obligations—he was putting the prospective residents "on notice" that at some time it would have to increase the carrying charges. By how much he did not say. Riverbay's officers and directors "will be taking all possible steps to limit the amount of the increase," he pledged, but nonetheless "an increase in carrying charges will be necessary during 1970 or 1971." To prevent "future misunderstanding," Ostroff requested that all prospective residents sign and return to Riverbay an attached statement, indicating that they "have read this memorandum and have been made aware that an increase in the carrying charges will be necessary during 1970-1971."[47]

CHAPTER 7

CARRYING CHARGES

As Harold Ostroff acknowledged on more than one occasion, it was very hard for the United Housing Foundation to estimate what it would cost to build a housing cooperative. In the case of one as large as Co-op City, which would take at least five years to complete, it was close to impossible. Still, the UHF had to come up with an estimate. It also had to figure out how much the residents would have to pay each month to cover Co-op City's construction costs, finance charges, and operating expenses. Although Ostroff and his associates did not know how much revenue would be needed for Co-op City and its other housing cooperatives, they believed that if the carrying charges were more than $25 per room per month, the apartments would be out of the reach of the lower-middle- and middle-income families for whom they were being built. Acting on this belief, the UHF charged $23 per room at Rochdale Village and $21 per room at Amalgamated Warbasse. And in May 1965 it issued an information bulletin in which it advised Co-op City's prospective residents that the carrying charges would be "approximately" $23.02 per room per month, utilities not included. The bulletin stressed that management would make every effort to keep these charges as low as possible. But since the projections were based on "presently estimated construction costs," it was possible that any increase in these costs might "increase the average monthly carrying charges somewhat above the $23.02 level."[1]

Not long after ground was broken for Co-op City in May 1966 there were signs that the Riverbay Corporation and the UHF's other housing companies might have to raise their carrying charges. In December 1966 the *Cooperator* warned that as a result of the rampant inflation, which was driving up the cost of "almost everything," many cooperatives "are going to be hard pressed to meet these costs without increased carrying charges." No one wanted higher carrying charges (or, for that matter, higher taxes), it said, but cooperatives have to pay "their fair share," and carrying charges were their primary source of revenue. One month later the *Cooperator* wrote, "Some cooperatives have been able to brave the storm to date." But many others had already raised their carrying charges, some more than once. And many others would soon find that "some increase will be absolutely necessary to keep housing corporations solvent." In some cooperatives now under construction, the *Cooperator* pointed out, the carrying charges were $30 per room per month, which was beyond the reach of most working people. Harold Ostroff was well aware of the problem. In January 1967 he told the UHF board that several of its housing cooperatives had no choice but to raise their carrying charges. And a year and a half later Robert Szold, a member of the UHF board, said that Co-op City was no exception. Most housing cooperatives were extremely reluctant to raise their carrying charges, Ostroff pointed out in August 1968, but "in an inflationary period it is almost inevitable that an increase will have to come sooner or later."[2]

The issue came to a head at Co-op City in early 1967, when the Riverbay Corporation re-examined the project's construction costs, which had initially been estimated to be $258.5 million. It found that over the past two years construction costs had increased substantially. At the insistence of the City Planning Commission and the State Division of Housing and Community Renewal, Riverbay had been compelled to come up with "a completely new site plan." It had also made costly changes to the design of the residential towers, some of which had been required by the Division of Housing. At the same time the cost of labor and materials had soared, especially in the mechanical trades. And by virtue of the procrastination of several city agencies, Community Services, Inc., had been unable to reach agreements with many of the subcontractors before it was caught up in "the general inflationary period." As a result, Riverbay estimated, it would now cost $267.8 million to build Co-op City, an increase of $9.3 million. (Given that the residential structures alone would cost an additional $15.9 million, the increase would have been much greater if Riverbay had not reduced the number of garages from nine to eight, which saved $4.2 million; dropped a plan to generate electricity at the Co-op City power plant, which saved another $3.7 million; and found several other ways to hold down expenses.) To cover the increased construction costs, Ostroff and his associates concluded, Co-op City would need approximately $10 million more from the State Housing Finance Agency.[3]

Knowing that the SHFA would not lend it additional money without the approval of James W. Gaynor, the Commissioner of Housing and Community Renewal, the Riverbay Corporation submitted an application to the Division of Housing and Community Renewal in March 1967 asking it to authorize an increase in Co-op City's mortgage from $250.9 million to $261 million. Included in the application was a schedule spelling out the increases in construction costs, finance charges, and operating expenses that left Riverbay with no choice but to apply to the state for additional capital. Under the Mitchell-Lama act, Gaynor could not approve Riverbay's application unless he was certain that the housing company could generate enough revenue to pay the interest on the additional $10.1 million and amortize the debt. It was therefore necessary for Riverbay to raise Co-op City's carrying charges. Once it did, Gaynor approved Riverbay's application to the State Housing Finance Agency. Thus in May 1967, a year and a half before the first residents moved in, the housing company issued a revised information bulletin in which it announced that the carrying charges would be "approximately" $25 per room per month. Once again it advised the prospective residents that the new charges were based on presently estimated construction costs and that if these costs increased the carrying charges might go up "somewhat" as well.[4] Given that the increase was only $2 per room (or slightly less than 8.7 percent)—and that no one would have to pay it until early 1973—the new carrying charge did not stir up much of a fuss.

Things at Co-op City went from bad to worse in 1968. Construction costs went up. So did interest rates. Indeed, when the State Housing Finance Agency sold the first $91.7 million in bonds for Co-op City in May 1968, the rate was not 4 percent but 5.2 percent, and there was no reason to think that interest rates were likely to go down in the near future. By the summer of 1968 Ostroff and his associates concluded that while it was impossible "to estimate with reasonable precision" what it would cost to complete Co-op City "the cost would be more than the $25 per room per month." At the urging of the Division of Housing's director of management, Ostroff notified prospective residents of the impending increase in carrying charges in October. George Schechter made the same point in the *Co-op City Times* less than a year later. In the aftermath of the recent settlement with the building trades unions, whose members' wages were to go up 42 percent over the next three years, he pointed out that Riverbay had anticipated an increase, "but not on the scale that the construction industry is talking about." Riverbay had also expected an increase in interest rates, "but not to the extent present rates have soared." As a result, Schechter stressed, an increase in carrying charges was inevitable. Although he did not say how much the increase would be (or when it would go into effect), he assured the residents (and prospective residents) that it would be "the least amount required" to cover Co-op City's rising costs.[5]

By August 1969 Riverbay realized that it needed an additional $69 million to complete Co-op City. Without it, Ostroff later said, "the entire enterprise would have collapsed." Hence he and his associates asked for a meeting with representatives of the Division of Housing and Community Renewal, which was now headed by Charles J. Urstadt, the agency's former deputy commissioner, who had replaced James W. Gaynor as commissioner in January 1969. To persuade Urstadt to approve an increase in Co-op City's mortgage from $261 million to $330 million, Riverbay's leaders offered to raise the carrying charges 15 percent. But after reviewing Co-op City's financials, the division's staff recommended a 16.1 percent increase. Ostroff and his associates went along, and the State Housing Finance Agency agreed to lend Riverbay an additional $69 million. By November the press reported that Riverbay intended to increase the carrying charges—by at least 15 to 16 percent, wrote the *Co-op City Times*, and perhaps by as much 20 percent, said the *City News*. Early in 1970 the Riverbay Corporation and the Division of Housing let it be known that pending Commissioner Urstadt's approval Co-op City's carrying charges would be raised from $25 to $29.39 per room on July 1. They pointed out that if the Board of Estimate had not recently granted Co-op City shelter rent tax status, the carrying charges would have gone up to $38 per room.[6]

ooo

Ostroff and his associates were extremely reluctant to raise Co-op City's carrying charges. They were well aware that an increase of 16.1 percent would work a severe hardship on many residents, and especially on the many elderly residents living on a fixed income. Ostroff and his associates were also well aware that unless Riverbay raised the carrying charges—and raised them by a considerable amount—Commissioner Urstadt would not approve the application for an additional $69 million. Without his approval, the State Housing Finance Agency would not increase Co-op City's mortgage from $261 million to $330 million. And without an infusion of additional capital, Riverbay would not be able to finish Co-op City. As Ostroff put it, "Steel structures, standing ghost like against the sky, would rust." By virtue of the nation's rampant inflation, which was driving up the costs of virtually everything, the UHF would have to abandon its most ambitious effort to provide high-quality, low-cost housing for lower-middle- and middle-income New Yorkers. The foundation had always been committed to building the best possible housing at the lowest possible cost, Ostroff pointed out. "There comes a time, however, when obligations must be met, bills must be paid, and the financial stability of this more than $326 million enterprise [must be] preserved."[7] Ostroff and his associates were confident that most of the more than 6,000 cooperators who were then living in Co-op City would understand that the time had come.

Their confidence, it turned out, was misplaced. As Urstadt pointed out, some residents objected to the increase in carrying charges on the grounds that they "were either unaware that [an increase] was pending or that they considered the amount of [the increase] exorbitant." Others stressed that a 16.1 percent increase would put a very heavy burden on Co-op City's many elderly residents. Some residents claimed that they had given up rent-controlled apartments elsewhere in New York. If they had known about the increase, said one, "they would not have moved to Co-op City." Many residents also complained that they had had no say in the decision to increase the carrying charges. Citing the poor maintenance and structural problems at Co-op City, one asked, "Why should I have to pay more when even now I'm not getting what I have paid for?" Pointing out that the elevators did not work well, that the lobbies, halls, and stairwells were filthy, that it took as long as two months to repair the ranges, refrigerators, and other appliances, and that the grounds were littered with cans, bottles, rusty nails, and broken glass, a resident of Building 11 warned that Co-op City might soon become "the world's largest cooperative-owned slum." "People who were willing to put up with certain inconveniences 'in the beginning' are finding a beginning that is endless," said another resident.[8]

One of the residents who believed that the increase in Co-op City's carrying charges was unnecessary or, at the very least, excessive was Harriet Colodney, who lived with her husband and three children in Building 5. No sooner had she moved in than Colodney emerged as one of the most vocal critics of the Riverbay Corporation and the United Housing Foundation. Early in June 1969, seven months after the first residents moved in, Riverbay turned off the air-conditioning in the middle of a heat wave.

General Manager Arnold Merritt explained that Co-op City's $2 million air-conditioning unit, the largest in the world, was brand-new and as expected was running into several problems, which the company's engineers were trying to fix. The air-conditioning would be turned on by June 16, he promised. When it was not, Colodney called a meeting, which was attended by about 100 residents. Shortly after she organized a demonstration, in which roughly 200 residents blocked access to Riverbay's administration office in Building 1. A dozen demonstrators then met with Merritt, to whom Colodney said, "The United Housing Foundation doesn't give a damn about us. We are going on a rent strike unless our demands [meaning the resumption of air-conditioning] are met." Merritt responded that "a rent strike won't help you at all." Riverbay turned the air-conditioning on a few days later. But Colodney was far from satisfied. "That's only one of our problems," she said. "We have a list of 50 things we want ironed out."[9]

Colodney felt that at the outset Co-op City had been "a very good buy" for New York's lower-middle- and middle-income families. But if the 16.1 percent increase went into effect on July 1, 1970, it would be out of the reach of these families. To prevent Co-op City from turning into an enclave for the well-to-do, Colodney believed that its residents had to join forces. And, she pointed out, since management was "treating us like tenants" rather than "like cooperators," she decided to form a tenants council. To learn how to set up this new organization, which would be called the Co-op City Tenants Council, Colodney decided to seek the advice of representatives of the Rochdale Village Tenants Council (RVTC), several of whom were invited to a meeting at the Co-op City Community Center in late January 1970. The Rochdale Village Tenants Council had been formed a little over a year earlier, said one of its members, in order to give "a voice to the people." Under the leadership of Lee Rosenson, it had recently won a majority of the seats on Rochdale Village's board of directors. One of the new board's first acts was to oust Harold Ostroff as Rochdale Village's president and replace him with Barbara Rabinowitz, a twenty-nine-year-old resident, a step that pretty much removed the UHF from the management of what had once been its largest housing cooperative. Like the Rochdale Village Tenants Council, Co-op City Tenants Council would be open to all residents, Colodney said. "We just want hard workers."[10]

The meeting, which was "highly charged," wrote the *City News*, was attended by 300 residents. Colodney, who presided over the meeting, introduced the representatives of the RVTC. Standing in for Mrs. Rabinowitz, who had just given birth and was unable to attend, was her husband, who told the audience how and why the RVTC had been created. Stan Zelman, another RVTC member, then spelled out its accomplishments. He also urged other housing cooperatives to form tenants councils of their own and to join forces "to lobby for federal, state and local subsidies for middle income housing." Also attending the meeting was George Schechter, vice president of the UHF. After thanking Colodney for inviting him, Schechter spoke out forcefully against the formation of a Co-op City tenants council. "Your responsibility is not to get yourselves a Tenants Council," he told the audience. "Your responsibility is to get yourselves a Co-op City." Although he conceded that the UHF had been too "paternalistic" at Rochdale Village, he insisted that at Co-op City and the UHF's other housing cooperatives there is no "we" or "they." The owners are "you." Rather than form a tenants council, he said, Co-op City's residents should put their trust in the Co-op City Advisory Council, which the UHF was in the process of forming to represent them. Lee Rosenson took issue with Schechter, saying that an advisory council was no substitute for a tenants council. Fearing that the Co-op City Advisory Council would turn out to be the UHF's "puppet," many in the audience agreed with her.[11]

Schechter's reservations were shared by the UHF's other leaders. Although they took pride in what the *City News* called "the extraordinary degree of community activity" at Co-op City, they believed that the attempt by Colodney and her supporters to form a tenants council was seriously misguided. As Ostroff put it, the belief that there was "an adversary position between themselves as tenants and the cooperative corporation as landlord is wholly inaccurate." Co-op City's residents and the Riverbay Corporation "are basically one and the same." Despite these reservations, Colodney and her supporters pressed ahead. They attracted a great many dues-paying members, as many as 2,000 by mid-1970. And they raised a good deal of money. The Co-op City Tenants Council's "primary purpose" was to protect the investment of Co-op City's residents, said Leonard Hanks, its vice president and, with his wife, Lorraine, a force to be reckoned with in the community. To that end it would take steps to improve the security of Co-op City, the upkeep of its buildings, and "the physical and mental well-being of our youth." Above all, it would attempt to "ascertain the actual necessity of a proposed rent increase."[12] In its effort to block the increase the Co-op City Tenants Council had the backing of several prominent elected officials, including Borough President Robert Abrams, Congressman Mario Biaggi,

State Senator John D. Calandra, Assemblyman Anthony J. Stella, and City Councilman Mario Merola.

Late in February a spokesman for the Division of Housing and Community Renewal announced that though Commissioner Urstadt had not yet decided whether to approve an increase in Co-op City's carrying charges, he had decided that Co-op City's residents were not entitled to a public hearing. On behalf of the Co-op City Tenants Council, Senator Calandra therefore wrote a letter to Urstadt in early March, asking him to reconsider his decision and to hold a hearing at which the residents could examine the financial condition of the UHF and Co-op City. To Urstadt's point that the UHF had sent the residents a letter in October 1968 advising them that the carrying charges would in time be raised, he argued that the letter did not constitute "a 'carte blanche' consent." Even conceding that the tenants had notice, he went on to say, "they certainly did not agree to any percent of increase [just to] a 'reasonable' increase," an increase that was based on the facts. And the facts, Calandra pointed out, could only be determined "by an examination of the books, records, etc., of the sponsor." Leaving aside the legal issues, Calandra pointed out, "the tenant-cooperators certainly did not envision, nor were they expected to envision, a substantial increase without first having some say in the matter." To deny them a say would be "inequitable, unjust and unfair." And to refuse to hold a public hearing would be "a travesty of justice."[13]

Urstadt knew that under the law he could approve an increase in the carrying charges without holding a public hearing on any Mitchell-Lama project that had not yet been completed. And Co-op City was still under construction. But he also knew that he could not ignore the letter from Calandra, many of whose constituents lived in Co-op City. A graduate of St. John's Law School and a former assistant US attorney, Calandra had become the leader of the Bronx County Republican Party. Elected to the State Senate in 1965, he was one of the few Republican senators from New York City. He was also a stalwart in the party that was led by Governor Nelson A. Rockefeller, who had appointed Urstadt to his post. Following up on a suggestion by Calandra, Urstadt offered to hold a meeting—though not, he stressed, a hearing—at the Division of Housing's office in Midtown Manhattan on April 16. At the meeting a dozen Co-op City residents, all of whom represented either the Tenants Council, the Advisory Council, or the Civic Association, would be given the opportunity to question Assistant Commissioner William F. Meyers about the reasons for the proposed increase. The response to Urstadt's offer was mixed. Isidor Gade, president of the Civic Association, was satisfied. So was Arthur Oshins, a member of the Advisory Council (and chairman of the Co-op City Committee for Quality Education). But Harriet Colodney, president of the Tenants Council, was disappointed. "I don't like this at all," she said. "The meeting should be open to all the people who live [in Co-op City]." Limiting it to only twelve "is not fair."[14]

Neither the Tenants Council nor the UHF lost much time in preparing for the meeting, which was put off until May and broken into two sessions. The first would be held on May 11 at Borough President Abrams's office and the second on May 14 at the Division of Housing's Manhattan office. About a week after Urstadt agreed to hold a meeting, the Tenants Council decided to hire an attorney to examine the UHF's financial records and present his findings to Assistant Commissioner Meyers. On Calandra's recommendation, the council chose Gerald P. Halpern. A graduate of Harvard Law School, he was a partner in Halpern & Rothman, a firm that he had set up with his law school classmate Jessel Rothman. And he had attracted a good deal of favorable attention when he represented the residents of Parkchester in their battle against Helmsley Spear, a major real estate firm that headed the syndicate that bought the huge apartment complex in the Bronx from Metropolitan Life in 1968 and shortly after attempted to raise the rent on about half of its more than 12,000 apartments by 5 to 15 percent. Thanks in part to Halpern's efforts, Leonard Hanks pointed out, Helmsley Spear, which had wanted an additional $750,000 a year, settled for only $300,000. The Tenants Council would pay Halpern $2,000 if the Division of Housing reduced the increase in Co-op City's carrying charges, $1,000 if it did not. Two weeks later the council held another meeting at Co-op City at which nearly 1,500 residents voted overwhelmingly in favor of retaining Halpern, who would be assisted by a group of accountants who lived at Co-op City and volunteered their services. "I think we would be very happy and satisfied if he does as well for us as he did for [the residents of] Parkchester," said Colodney.[15]

The meeting had three objectives other than to obtain an endorsement of the decision to retain Halpern. One was to increase the Tenants Council's membership and to persuade 100 members to attend the meetings with Assistant Commissioner Meyers. "I'm leaving three children [at home] and my husband is taking off a day of work so that I can go to the hearing," said Colodney. That was the least other members could do. To make it easier, the council chartered two buses to transport them from Co-op City to Borough President Abrams's office. Another objective was to give elected officials an opportunity to express their support for the council's efforts. Councilman

Merola, who declared that Co-op City's residents were entitled to a public hearing, stressed that "the more you know about what's going on, the more the fear of an unjustified rent increase will be dispelled." And Borough President Abrams, who also attended the meeting, issued a statement to the *City News* in which he declared that he opposed "any increase [in carrying charges] that will make living in Co-op City a hardship for the middle-income families it was designed to accommodate." Still another objective was to discuss strategy for the upcoming meeting with Meyers. Halpern had already announced that he would not discuss his findings before the meeting, but Colodney, who was more forthcoming, said that the Tenants Council would call attention to Riverbay's many unwarranted expenses, the elimination of which might make the increase in carrying charges unnecessary.[16]

In defense of the 16.1 percent increase in carrying charges, the *Co-op City Times* published two long articles shortly after Urstadt agreed to hold the upcoming meetings. The first, which appeared on March 7, pointed out that as a result of the nation's "rampant inflation," construction costs, finance charges, and operating expenses had soared at Co-op City. Hence the Riverbay Corporation was forced to ask the state to increase its mortgage. And to assure the state that it could pay the interest and amortization, Riverbay had no choice but to raise the carrying charges. Every effort had been made to keep these charges as low as possible, but there was nothing more that could be done. Rents were on the rise everywhere, and "Co-op City remains the best new housing buy in our city." The second article, which was published on April 4, spelled out in detail the estimates on which the new carrying charges were based. Over 65 percent of these charges were spent on interest and amortization, which, as a result of the soaring interest rates, were much higher than expected. By virtue of the UHF's success in persuading the municipal authorities to grant Co-op City shelter rent tax status, only 10 percent, which was much lower than anticipated, went for real estate taxes. A much higher than expected share, 18 percent, was spent on maintenance and operations, a result of the sharp increase in the cost of labor and materials. Despite the nation's rampant inflation, the average cost per apartment at Co-op City was only $23,380, which "is considerably less than any other [middle-income] housing [project] being built today in the City of New York," few of which had apartments as large as Co-op City's, much less hardwood floors, central air-conditioning, and a wide range of community facilities.[17]

No one defended the decision to increase the carrying charges more forcefully than Harold Ostroff. As head of both the UHF and the Riverbay

Corporation, Ostroff was so committed to cooperative housing that, in the words of Gerald Halpern, he "bridles at the use of the term 'tenants'" to refer to Co-op City's residents. At a meeting in early April that was held at the Community Center auditorium and attended by nearly 1,400 residents, Ostroff made the by-then-familiar argument that Riverbay had no alternative but to increase the carrying charges. He also insisted that it would be impossible to reduce the increase. Riverbay had done everything it could to hold down the carrying charges. And it would continue to lobby for subsidies from the state and federal governments. Unfortunately, he pointed out, housing was not one of the Nixon administration's priorities. After finishing his speech, Ostroff took questions from the audience, at which point the meeting grew more than a little testy. When Colodney asked why Riverbay management had recently decided that the Tenants Council would have to pay rent to use the auditorium, Ostroff replied that its policy was to charge any group that collected dues from its members. Before Colodney could respond, her microphone was turned off. The purpose of the meeting was to discuss the increase in carrying charges, nothing else, Ostroff explained. It was "a display of evasive goonism," Colodney said afterwards. When Congressman Biaggi, a strong supporter of the Tenants Council who was running for re-election, started to make what Ostroff thought was a campaign speech, his microphone was switched off too.[18]

ooo

Presided over by Assistant Commissioner Meyers, the meetings were held as scheduled on May 11 and May 14. But for Colodney and Halpern—as well as a handful of elected officials and dozens of Co-op City residents who assembled in Borough President Abrams's office—the first meeting got off to an inauspicious start. Commissioner Urstadt, Meyers pointed out, saw no reason to attend. He did, however, issue a statement that was read, in Gerald Halpern's words, by "one of his lack[e]ys." In it Urstadt said that he had called these informational meetings—which, he stressed, were not required by law—to provide Co-op City residents with "as full an explanation as possible" for the increase in carrying charges that was the result of the unprecedented inflationary spiral and "should come as a surprise to no one." He acknowledged that the increase would be very hard on many residents, but he insisted that the Division of Housing had no choice but to approve it. Under the Mitchell-Lama act, he could not sign off on Riverbay's request to the State Housing Finance Agency for an additional $69 million unless the housing company's projected revenue was enough to cover its construction costs, finance charges, and operating expenses. And without a 16.1 percent increase in carrying charges, it was not. "It is our hope," Urstadt concluded, "that as a result of today's session all of you come away with an awareness that the increase, difficult as it may be to absorb, is needed, is unavoidable, and is in the best interest of the ultimate success of Co-op City."[19]

The opponents of the increase made a vigorous effort to persuade Urstadt to reconsider his position. Leading the way was Halpern, who was cautiously optimistic even after hearing the commissioner's statement. He argued that the increase should be postponed until a full study was done of the United Housing Foundation books. "No one will go bankrupt if this increase is deferred," he claimed. Halpern also pointed out that the builder's fee had gone up from $2 million to $2.75 million in 1969, even though the UHF's information bulletin said that the fee was fixed and any increase was "the risk of the contractor." At the same time the architect's fee had risen from $2 million to $2.9 million. "Things like this should be explained at a hearing," he said. At the second meeting, which was held as planned at the Division of Housing's office, Halpern suggested a few things that the commissioner could do to reduce or even obviate the increase. He could defer or waive the Government Service Agency fee, which was one-quarter of 1 percent of the mortgage (or $825,000 a year). He could also disregard the current projections of extremely high interest rates, which were "based largely on guesswork." Halpern also recommended that the increase be put off until Co-op City was fully occupied. Pointing out that the 16.1 increase would yield only $865,000 in the six months after July 1, he got Harold Ostroff to concede that construction would not stop or even slow down at Co-op City if the carrying charges were not raised.[20]

Several elected officials lent their support to Halpern and the Tenants Council. Senator Calandra, who had urged Urstadt to hold a hearing, said that he was sorely disappointed. He had expected a meeting to determine whether an increase was justified, not a meeting to discuss an increase that had already been approved. "I reject these proceedings as violently as I can," he declared. Congressman Biaggi agreed. Calling the meetings "a virtual farce," he insisted that a public hearing should have been held before an increase was approved. Referring to the UHF's leaders, he said, "They knew they were being unrealistic in offering housing at such low rentals, but this was being used as a political carrot to offer the people, and the people bit!" Calling Co-op City "the people's last hope," he declared that "Riverbay

Corporation should sharpen their pencils and save every cent possible."
(Echoing Colodney, he suggested that the *Co-op City Times* be eliminated.
"This would be a savings that is certainly more than peanuts.") Borough
President Abrams also regretted that the state had approved the increase
without hearing from the residents. "The State lured you into Co-op City
under the Mitchell-Lama Law," he went on, "and it should stick by you now."
He favored changing the law to provide subsidies for residents. "After all,"
he said, "housing is no good if people can't afford to live in it." Assemblyman
Stella added that the UHF had misled the residents, who had "expected increases, but not of this nature." He called for full disclosure of the Riverbay
Corporation's financial records and insisted that no increase in Co-op City's
carrying charges be approved until that was done.[21]

A good many Co-op City residents also spoke out against the 16.1 percent
increase. They pointed out that the increase was much higher than expected.
Indeed, said Abraham Gerber, president of the Senior Citizens of Co-op City,
it was so high that "many of us [will be forced] to go [on] welfare." Betty
Rosen, who claimed that she would not have moved into Co-op City if she had
known about the increase, asked Meyers, "Where am I to go now?" "That's a
good question," he replied, "and I don't know the answer." Other residents protested that it was outrageous for Riverbay to increase the carrying charges
without doing anything to improve the quality of service. Calling the first
meeting a "farce," Jerome Glanzrock, executive secretary of the Co-op City
Civic Association, complained that the state housing authorities had created
"false hopes" among Co-op City's residents. But "we never even got our day in
court. The commissioner should reconsider his decision and hold a legitimate
hearing." Co-op City resident Louis Kleinman agreed. Pointing out that the
streets were not yet finished and the children were being bused to schools
outside the community, he asked Meyers to tell Urstadt, "You must defer the
increase for now. You must keep middle-income housing at middle-income
rates." Lorraine Hanks said that state officials "keep telling us that the people
of the world are looking at us in Co-op City to see if housing in New York will
succeed." And now they have nothing to say but that "there *might* be a subsidy" to offset the increase in carrying charges![22]

Speaking in favor of the 16.1 percent increase were William F. Meyers and
Harold Ostroff. Repeating what Urstadt said in his opening statement, Meyers declared, "The Commissioner had no choice but to approve the increase."
And responding to Halpern's suggestion that the increase be deferred, he
pointed out that if deferred it would in time be even higher. Ostroff made

the same point. "Through bitter experience," he remarked, "I have learned that delay will cost us twice as much later on." "If things change," he went on, "you have my solemn word that adjustments will be made." But he also told the audience, "This is not the last increase. There'll be more." Asked by Halpern why costs had gone up so much, Ostroff said that it had taken CSI much longer to build Co-op City than anticipated—seven years instead of five. He also pointed out that CSI had been forced to revise the preliminary site plan, which did not include the townhouses or the twenty-eight-acre educational park. Asked by Halpern what could be done to reduce the increase, Ostroff replied, "I know of nothing other than legislative relief for the high interest rates," and added, "We welcome all suggestions as to how to meet our financial obligations." The UHF's leaders were attacked at the second meeting by Harriet Colodney, who blamed them for Co-op City's fiscal problems. "You are the master builders of New York," she said, "and you goofed." Although Ostroff did not respond directly to her attack, he later told the crowd, "There was nobody around nutty enough to build Co-op City except us."[23]

The meetings left many residents disappointed and even outraged. Speaking for them was the *City News*, which published two editorials about the proceedings, one on May 14 and the other on May 21. "The people of Co-op City got a kick in the face on Monday," it said, "when a group of residents attended a so-called hearing on the proposed rent increase." Far from a hearing, "It was a farce." The increase had been decided upon a year earlier at a meeting of UHF officials and Charles J. Urstadt. Now the commissioner—referred to by the *City News* as "I Am The Law" Urstadt—has sent "his pudgy little henchman William F. Meyers," who was in charge of supervising the work of Community Services, Inc., to preside over the meetings. But Meyers, "who is openly cozy with UHF officials[,] is hardly the man to find any hanky-panky with contractors, sub-contractors, or UHF itself." Rather than give the residents of Co-op City a fair hearing, Meyers had just read Urstadt's proclamation that "an increase of 16.1 percent was stamped, sealed, approved, and would be delivered July 1." "We appreciate what the UHF is doing to build housing in New York City," the *City News* acknowledged, "and we understand how they do a job that no one else in the City seems capable of." But with the acquiescence of the Division of Housing, its leaders were operating as "benevolent despots." "This is 1970," it concluded, "not 1500. It's a time of reason, not feudalism. We live in a country of laws and men where laws are tempered with justice, not a country of lords and serfs where decisions are made by kings."[24]

No sooner was the second meeting adjourned than the opponents of the increase renewed their efforts. Halpern sent the Division of Housing a very long and well-thought-out memo spelling out the reasons why the carrying charges should not be raised on July 1. Based on a review of the documents that Riverbay submitted to the Housing Division—as well as discussions with company and state officials—he found that the increase was designed to generate enough revenue to cover a projected deficit of $7 million. But "this is a paper deficit and not a cash flow gap," Halpern pointed out. Riverbay would not have to pay all the construction costs until two or even three years after Co-op City was finished, which was expected to be in November 1972. Hence there was no urgency to raise the carrying charges in July 1970. Moreover, he wrote, there had been no previous instance in which the carrying charges on a Mitchell-Lama project had been increased before the project was finished. The fact that Co-op City was unique in many ways was no reason why "an increase has been ordered or contemplated during the course of construction" for the first time. Halpern pointed out as well that the State Housing Finance Agency had already notified the bondholders that Co-op City's carrying charges would be raised from $25 to $29.39 per room per month effective July 1, 1970. And, he held, Commissioner Urstadt was reluctant to reconsider his position out of concern that doing so might undermine the agency's "fiscal integrity."[25]

But, Halpern argued, there were several measures that could be adopted to defer, reduce, or even eliminate an increase in Co-op City's carrying charges and thereby ease Urstadt's concern and prompt him to reconsider his position. The State Housing Finance Agency could defer its annual fee, which would reduce the projected deficit by $2 million. Or it could base the fee not on the entire mortgage but only on the portion of it that had not yet been amortized. Also, Riverbay could rethink the projected interest rates, "which were compiled at a time when the money market was at its worst or highest point." If interest rates were reduced by only one-half of 1 percent, Riverbay would save $1.65 million a year. Indeed, "there has already been an easing of the bond market." And "how much better and wiser it would be to act on the basis of actual figures than on guesses." Moreover, Halpern contended, future construction costs were at best "educated estimates" and at worst "pure guesswork." It would make more sense to estimate the remaining construction costs and recalculate how much revenue would be needed when the facts were known. Another measure would be to re-estimate revenue projections, which had been reduced from $10 million in 1968 to $4.6

million in 1969 because of the strike of the building trades unions. There was good reason for "more optimistic expectations." And "it would be wise to wait for the actual figures rather than burden the tenants on the basis of 'guessestimates.'"[26]

Borough President Abrams and Assemblyman Stella attempted to block the increase by bypassing Urstadt and appealing directly to Rockefeller. In a letter written on May 15, Abrams told the governor that the Division of Housing had granted Riverbay's request without giving the residents an opportunity to challenge it. Although the Mitchell-Lama act did not mandate a public hearing, the Division of Housing had held hearings on rent increases in other developments. Before moving into Co-op City, many residents had relied on the UHF's information bulletin, which stated that the carrying charges would be $23 per room per month (or slightly higher). Under the proposed increase, the charges would be much higher. Moreover, said Abrams, "I have been advised that this in no way precludes the possibility of further increases in the very near future." The residents of Co-op City "will appreciate any relief that may be granted," he concluded. In a letter written on May 19, Stella made many of the same points. He informed Rockefeller that the Division of Housing had not only denied the residents "an open hearing" but also approved the increase over the "valid objections submitted by tenant organizations, community leaders and elected representatives." And another increase was likely in the near future. As a result, said Stella, Co-op City might well be "priced out of the pocketbooks of those for whom it was designed. Folks who had hoped to make their homes and sink roots in the Northeast Bronx [will] be forced out of our community." And the damage will be irreparable. "The co-operators at Co-op City, which will number over 55,000 when the development is completed, look to you as their last hope," Stella told Rockefeller. "Please don't fail them."[27]

Neither Abrams nor Stella was able to sway Rockefeller, who left the decision up to Urstadt. And despite Halpern's memo, Urstadt refused to reconsider his position. Hence on May 28 he wrote a letter to Riverbay, with copies to Halpern and, among others, Paul Belica, head of the State Housing Finance Agency, saying that he had approved the increase. He pointed out that under the Mitchell-Lama act he could not support Riverbay's application for an additional $69 million unless it could generate enough revenue to cover all of Co-op City's costs, which had been driven up sharply by inflation. To do so Riverbay had to increase the carrying charges, a possibility about which the residents had been notified in Ostroff's letter of October

1968. As a result, wrote Urstadt, "I had no choice but to approve the up-dated carrying charges." Although the Division of Housing was not obliged to hold a hearing, the proposed increase created so much "apparent misinformation and misunderstanding" that he agreed to hold two informational meetings and to consider suggestions from the residents and their counsel. All the information was analyzed not only by his staff but also by Meyers and William A. Conway Jr., the division's counsel, and their reports, which were enclosed, confirmed the need for an increase in Co-op City's carrying charges. Urstadt stressed that his decision "was not made lightly or arbitrarily." And he acknowledged that it would be hard on Co-op City's residents, especially the many who were living on a fixed income. But he insisted that the increase was essential to ensure "the fiscal integrity of Co-op City," to protect the investment of the cooperators, and, not least of all, to show investors that the middle-income housing program would meet its financial responsibilities.[28]

Urstadt made one concession to the residents of Co-op City. At the suggestion of Halpern and on the advice of Meyers, he arranged for the State Housing Finance Agency to defer its portion of the Government Service Agency Fee for two and a half years, a move that reduced the carrying charges by 25 cents per room per month and thereby lowered the increase from 16.1 percent to 15.1 percent. If Urstadt thought that this concession—which, the *City News* pointed out, would expire on December 31, 1972, when the increase would go back up to 16.1 percent—would placate the Tenants Council, he was sadly mistaken. "The Commissioner is treating us like dogs," said Colodney. "He has pitched us a bone and expects us to be happy about it. Since he thinks we're dogs, we want to have a little more meat on the bone." Halpern was furious as well. Speaking to 1,600 residents at the Community Center auditorium a few days after Urstadt announced his decision, he castigated the commissioner and his agency. Rather than acting as a "watchdog," whose duty was to protect Mitchell-Lama residents against "any encroachments by large housing corporations," the Division of Housing had given Riverbay everything it asked for. Halpern also warned that another increase "was in the wind and another would follow." "If you don't begin to fight them [the Riverbay Corporation and the Division of Housing] now, you will have to sometime in the future when your [*sic*] paying twice as much per room as you are now."[29]

After talking with Urstadt about his decision, Halpern made a last-ditch effort to reduce the increase. In a letter written on June 1, he informed the commissioner that as a result of the deferral of a portion of the Government

Agency Service fee, Co-op City's carrying charges would be raised $4.14 per room per month rather than $4.39. But, he went on, "as you can readily see, the impact of this relief is minimal." He suggested that the Division of Housing make available to Riverbay the full amount of the deferral, which came to $576,000, before the increase went into effect on July 1. If it did so, Riverbay would have to raise only $280,000 in 1970 to balance its budget. And it would have to increase the carrying charges by only 5.5 percent. Halpern also suggested that between July 1 and December 31, Riverbay's financial situation might improve. In the meantime, Riverbay, elected officials, and the Division of Housing should do their utmost to minimize future rent hikes. Two weeks later, however, Meyers wrote Halpern, saying, "You have not fully recognized the finality of the Commissioner's letter to Riverbay Corporation, dated May 28, 1970. Your letter merely repeats arguments which have been previously made, duly considered, and rejected." And the commissioner "has requested me to advise you that nothing further has been offered to cause him to alter, revise, amend, modify or reverse [his decision]." Now that the decision had been made, he hoped that they could all "work together toward the successful completion and operation of Co-op City."[30]

ooo

But any hope that Co-op City's residents would work together with the Riverbay Corporation and the Division of Housing had already been dashed. As soon as Urstadt approved the increase in Co-op City's carrying charges, Colodney declared, "We've just begun to fight." And the place in which to fight, said Halpern, was court. Given that the Division of Housing's actions "are in flagrant violation of elementary principles of due process," he told the residents, "I believe [you] have an excellent case to take to court and I think you should pursue an active litigation against the Riverbay Corporation [and, by implication, the Division of Housing]." He conceded that litigation would be expensive—though he could not estimate how expensive, wrote the *City News*, "because he couldn't predict how far the case would go." Following Halpern's recommendation, which was supported by Borough President Abrams, the Co-op City Tenants Council's Executive Committee voted in favor of filing suit against Riverbay in early June. A week later more than 900 dues-paying members of the Tenants Council endorsed the committee's decision to retain Halpern. To cover his $5,000 fee (and the other costs of litigation), Colodney asked each family to contribute $5. On June 26 Halpern filed suit on behalf of the Co-op City Tenants Council, asking the New York State Supreme Court to enjoin Riverbay from imposing the increase until, in the words of the *City News*, "a full and proper hearing can be conducted."[31]

On June 30, one day before the percent increase was to go into effect, Judge Thomas Dickens turned down Halpern's request for a temporary restraining order and adjourned the case for a week. Despite his ruling, the Tenants Council was on the "right track," said Leonard Hanks, who had been elected president of the council when several disgruntled members of the Executive Committee forced Colodney to step down in mid-June. "I think it is going to turn out in our favor." In the meantime he advised residents to stop paying their carrying charges until the court ruled on the council's lawsuit. If a ruling was not handed down by July 10, he suggested that they pay the old carrying charges. George Schechter called Hanks's advice irresponsible. The residents were legally obligated to pay their carrying charges, he declared. If they withhold them, "the bills don't get paid." "Do you expect us to pay the porter with an IOU?" he asked. One week later Halpern persuaded Judge Isidore Dollinger, a former assemblyman, congressman, and Bronx district attorney, to order that the increase be placed in an escrow account that Riverbay could not touch until the Tenants Council's lawsuit was adjudicated. Calling the order a "step in the right direction," Hanks pointed out that Co-op City's residents could now follow his example and withhold payment of the increase or pay the increase, "with the full knowledge that it would be held in escrow." At the request of counsel for Riverbay and Urstadt, Dollinger adjourned the case until August 4.[32]

The case, which was known as *Hanks v. Urstadt*, was tried in the Bronx County Courthouse, an imposing nine-story limestone building that stood on the Grand Concourse and 161st Street. The petitioners were Leonard and Lorraine Hanks, the Tenants Council president and treasurer, respectively. The Hankses, who were represented by Halpern, were acting for themselves as individuals and on behalf of other Co-op City residents who were opposed to the increase. The respondents were Charles J. Urstadt and the Riverbay Corporation. As commissioner of housing and community renewal, Urstadt was represented by Attorney General Louis J. Lefkowitz, a former state assemblyman and municipal court judge who succeeded Jacob K. Javits as attorney general when he was elected to the US Senate in 1957. Riverbay was represented by Szold, Brandwen, Meyers & Altman, which had long been the UHF's counsel. The case would eventually be assigned to Judge Jacob B. Grumet. A graduate of Columbia Law School, Grumet had spent much of his career as a prosecutor, first as an assistant US attorney and later as a member of Manhattan District Attorney Thomas E. Dewey's staff, and then as head of the homicide bureau under Dewey's successor, Frank S. Hogan. He was also chairman of the New York State Commission of Investigation from 1960 to 1968, when Governor Rockefeller appointed him to the State Supreme Court's First Judicial District, which covered Manhattan and the Bronx.[33]

At the core of the petitioners' complaint, which was spelled out in a statement by Halpern and an affidavit by the Hankses, was the argument that Urstadt's actions were so "arbitrary," "capricious," and "improper" that they deprived the residents of Co-op City of due process of law, which was a violation of the Fourteenth Amendment of the Constitution. Although the commissioner of housing and community renewal was not required by law to hold a public hearing before approving an increase in rents or common charges, both Urstadt and his predecessor, James W. Gaynor, had done so in the case of several limited-profit housing projects, including Rochdale Village and Amalgamated Warbasse, both of which were affiliated with the United Housing Foundation. The two informational meetings held in May 1970, the Hankses pointed out, were nothing more than "an explanation of the decision the Commissioner had already made, unilaterally and without any consultation whatsoever with the tenants." Indeed, his decision had been made in August 1969, almost a year before the informational meetings, when the Division of Housing had accepted Riverbay's estimates of its costs "without any significant review or audit" and approved its application for an increase in the carrying charges without "any change whatsoever." Indeed, said Halpern, never before had the commissioner approved an increase in the carrying charges of a Mitchell-Lama project that was still under construction.[34]

Halpern and the Hankses also contended that the increase would do "irreparable harm" to many Co-op City residents, especially the many senior citizens who lived on "rigidly limited incomes." Unable to pay $29.39 per room per month, many of them "may be forced to vacate their apartments." At least two and a half years earlier, the leaders of Riverbay and the UHF had known that the carrying charge of $25 per room was "unrealistically low and could not be maintained," said Halpern. But they nonetheless induced many middle-income New Yorkers to buy apartments in Co-op City by assuring them that the carrying charge would not be raised. "Clearly, the respondents allowed this misapprehension to continue in order to fill up the project as rapidly as possible." In their defense, Riverbay and the UHF pointed out that residents who objected to the increase were free to move out of their apartment and, if they did, would receive a full refund. But this was "a patently illusory remedy," Halpern insisted. "These tenants have no freedom to move, as a practical matter. They have given up apartments elsewhere, frequently relinquishing the benefits of rent control." They have also incurred the expenses of moving to Co-op City and decorating their apartments. "They are unable to go back [to their old neighborhoods] and have given up alternative opportunities for housing while waiting to move [into Co-op City] and while living there. They are locked-in by a grievous housing shortage."[35]

That Riverbay and the UHF were nonprofit organizations was beside the point, Halpern argued. Their primary objective "is to get this housing development built," not to keep the carrying charges as low as possible. And they "cannot be relied upon to adequately and properly protect and champion the interest of the tenants in minimizing or avoiding rent increases." That Co-op City was a housing cooperative was also beside the point. Riverbay was completely controlled by the UHF. "Not one of the directors has been selected by the tenants," Halpern went on, "and none will be for several years"—that is, not until Commissioner Urstadt issues a Certificate of Acceptability, "which is not scheduled to occur until the end of 1972 at the earliest." Not until then will the residents receive their stock in Riverbay. And "not until then will there be an election among the tenants for members of the Board." Moreover, most of Riverbay's directors "seldom, if ever, attend meetings," leaving the decisions to Ostroff, his staff, and the UHF lawyers. Given that Riverbay and the UHF are not "infallible" or "sacrosanct"—and given that the cooperative movement "has lost some of its old-time missionary zeal"—it was up to the Division of Housing to look out for the well-being of Co-op City's residents. But so far as Urstadt and his staff were concerned, the UHF, the builder of much of New York City's middle-income housing and the mainstay of New York State's middle-income housing program, "can do virtually no wrong."[36]

According to the petitioners, the remedy was straightforward. As the Hankses said, the court should issue an order restraining the respondents from imposing and collecting an increase in Co-op City's carrying charges until the Division of Housing held "a full and proper hearing" and Commissioner Urstadt made a decision based on all the evidence. Or, as Halpern put it, "The tenants are entitled to and must be given a full, meaningful pre-determination hearing." Before the hearing, Co-op City's residents should be given access to all of Riverbay's financial records, not just the "infinitesimal fraction of the whole mass" that was made available to them two days before the informational meetings. Counsel for the residents should also have the opportunity to call its own witnesses and to cross-examine the respondents' witnesses. Indeed, the Hankses went on, Riverbay should not be allowed to increase the carrying charges until Co-op City was completed and fully occupied. By then all the construction, finance, and operating costs would be known. And any application for an increase would be based on "actual fiscal requirements" rather than mere "speculative projections." Such an order would spare many Co-op City residents from severe hardship without doing any damage to Riverbay, which, the Hankses pointed out, was faced not with an "immediate ca[s]h flow deficit," but only with "a long term projection," or to Co-op City, which was in no danger of becoming insolvent without an increase in carrying charges.[37]

The respondents denied that Urstadt had deprived Co-op City's residents of due process. Far from arbitrary and capricious, his actions were in full accord with the law, the commissioner claimed. They were also "thorough" and "conscientious," said William A. Conway Jr. The allegation that Urstadt accepted Riverbay's figures "without significant review and audit and without serious question" was outrageous, Conway said. And so was the allegation that he approved the increase in Co-op City's carrying charges "without independent analysis, audit and review." After pointing out that every figure in Co-op City's construction and operating budget was thoroughly reviewed by Urstadt's staff, Ostroff went so far as to say that the petitioners' "allegation that the action of the Commissioner is arbitrary and capricious is itself arbitrary and capricious." The Division of Housing has acted in the best interests of the residents of Co-op City, Conway declared. And so has the Riverbay Corporation, Ostroff insisted. What the carrying charges should be in a housing cooperative was "a matter of judgment," he said, which was "traditionally and necessarily left to a Board of Directors." Since Co-op City's 15,500 cooperators would have 15,500 opinions, he pointed out, "someone must decide, and that someone, by necessity, law, and the Occupancy Agreement, is the [Riverbay] Board of Directors," which had always done its utmost to keep Co-op City's carrying charges as low as possible.[38]

The respondents conceded that the increase in carrying charges would be hard on the many residents who lived on a fixed income. But as Ostroff pointed out, the increase was the result of "the nationwide problem of

inflation," over which Riverbay had no control. If the residents lived elsewhere, in private houses or even in rent-controlled apartments, they would
face the same problem. Ostroff also stressed that the residents had been notified in October 1968 that the carrying charges would be raised in 1970 or
1971. And the proposed 16.1 percent increase should not have come as a surprise. Moreover, no one was living in Co-op City in October 1968. And every
prospective resident "was in a position to withdraw from the enterprise and
receive an immediate refund of his investment." Ostroff also argued that it
was "the height of irresponsibility" for the petitioners to allege that Riverbay
had induced New Yorkers to believe that the carrying charges would remain
at $25 per room per month "in order to fill up the project." Even at $29.39,
"the demand for apartments at Co-op City is legion." Given that the quality of the housing at Co-op City is world-renowned—and that the carrying
charges are lower there than in other middle-income projects that had recently been built or were under construction—it was little wonder that Riverbay is deluged by thousands of applications "which it cannot possibly hope
to fill." Conway agreed. Calling the allegation that Riverbay concealed the
increase in order to sell the apartments "illogical and factually incredible,"
he pointed out that Co-op City could have been filled "many times over at
[an even] higher price."[39]

The respondents acknowledged that the Riverbay Corporation Board of
Directors had been chosen not by the residents but by the United Housing
Foundation, which, Ostroff pointed out, had sponsored "the largest and most
successful housing developments in the City of New York." "It could not have
been otherwise," he pointed out. "Someone [had] to guide the [housing] company through the completion of construction and the occupancy of the entire project." And that "someone" had to be a board of directors. But since
there were no shareholders when Co-op City got underway, the UHF had to
designate the members of the board. "It may be argued," said Ostroff, "that
the cooperators had no choice in our selection. The fact is, however, that
they did have such choice, since they could choose either to join or not to join
the enterprise." And by joining, they gave their approval to the UHF's des-
ignees. Among the members of the board were Ostroff, who had succeeded
Abraham E. Kazan as the head of the UHF; Jacob S. Potofsky, president of
the Amalgamated Clothing Workers of America; Louis Stulberg, president
of the International Ladies' Garment Workers' Union; and Albert Shanker, president of the United Federation of Teachers. All the board members
were "singlemindedly dedicated to produce, with no profit to anyone, the

best possible housing [at] the lowest possible price." "Certainly," said Ostroff, "it would be difficult to conceive of a better group of people to protect and watch over the interests of all the cooperators."[40]

Stressing that Commissioner Urstadt had not deprived the Hankses and other residents of Co-op City of due process of law, the respondents urged the court to deny the petitioners' request that it set aside the decision to approve the 16.1 percent increase in carrying charges until the Division of Housing and Community Renewal held a public hearing. Indeed, said Conway, if the commissioner's decision was set aside long after it went into effect, "our sources of funds will evaporate, the future of such projects as Co-op City will be prejudiced and the aim of the [Mitchell-Lama act] frustrated." A hearing on a rent increase might be appropriate in private housing, Ostroff acknowledged, where "the question is whether the tenant will pay more or less rental and therefore whether the landlord will receive more or less." But it was not appropriate in cooperative housing, where the residents are owners, not tenants. "In a cooperative, the money never really leaves the payor. He takes it out of his personal bank account and puts it into the collective account," which is then used "to pay the Members' expense of home ownership." There might be an adversarial relation between landlords and tenants in private housing, Ostroff pointed out. But despite the petitioners' "self-designated appellation as 'tenants,'" this is not the case in cooperative housing, where "the payors, the Members, and the recipient, the collective Members, i.e., the corporation, are basically one and the same."[41]

Judge Grumet handed down his decision on October 14, roughly three and a half months after Halpern filed suit on behalf of the Co-op City Tenants Council. After reviewing the facts and case law, he found that Riverbay had given notice to the prospective residents in October 1968 that an increase in the carrying charges would be necessary in 1970 or 1971 and had asked them to acknowledge receipt of the notice. Grumet conceded that the Division of Housing had not held a public hearing, only informational meetings at which the residents and their counsel had the opportunity to express their views. But, he pointed out, due process "does not require [a] formal hearing." Moreover, the state legislature did not require "preoccupancy hearings." The commissioner and his staff carefully reviewed Riverbay's figures, Grumet noted, and as mandated by law, Urstadt made "a thorough and complete analysis of the costs and projected costs [of Co-op City] and based upon those made his findings [about the proposed increase in the carrying charges]." Hence, Grumet concluded, "the Commissioner fulfilled his statutory responsibility of making certain that the estimated revenues would be sufficient to pay all the [costs]." The decision to raise the carrying charges was based on "the best judgment" of the builder and the commissioner. And the court did not have the power to substitute its judgment for theirs. Ruling that the commissioner's actions were not "arbitrary, capricious, unreasonable or unlawful," Grumet denied the petitioners' motion.[42]

ooo

The reaction to Grumet's decision was mixed. As expected, Ostroff was quite pleased. "It is my hope," he said, "that now that this court action has been resolved our members will learn to work within the democratic framework of the Cooperative to resolve all future disputes." He pointed out that the Co-op City Advisory Council, whose members were chosen by the residents, was now in place and that a process was underway that would enable the residents to elect some members of the Riverbay Corporation Board of Directors. It was also his hope that in the future all internal disputes would be settled by these bodies. "Going to the courts for the resolution of internal problems can only be expensive, both as to financial costs and the maintenance of a harmonious democratic community." The *City News* was outraged by Ostroff's remarks, which it called condescending, insulting, and, in line with the prevailing attitude of Co-op City's management, paternalistic. "It is snide and presumptuous for Mr. Ostroff to insinuate that only democracy exists within the bound[a]ries of Co-op City and the Cooperative movement." Taking strong exception to his statement that "to allow the courts to mediate a dispute is undemocratic," the *City News* asked whether Ostroff would "rather have residents—who used the legal procedures to fight a rent increase—present him with a rent strike and pickets?"[43]

Unlike Ostroff, Halpern regarded Grumet's decision as "rather disappointing, to put it mildly." But it was subject to appeal, he pointed out. The Tenants Council's case, he said, was based on "new theories of law," to which appellate courts were more receptive than trial courts. And our position, he said, "would ultimately be upheld on appeal." Concerned that Grumet's ruling might serve as a precedent in future litigation, Halpern also pointed out that an appeal would act as "a brake" on future "arbitrary rent increases" by Riverbay and the Division of Housing. Leonard Hanks was sympathetic to Halpern's position. Stressing that the Tenants Council's Executive Committee strongly disagreed with Grumet, he declared, "We may have lost the first battle, but we have not lost the war." To wage the war he intended to recommend to the Executive Committee that it follow Halpern's advice and file an appeal. The Executive Committee agreed with Hanks and voted to hold a meeting at which the members would decide "whether or not to carry the fight to the [appellate court]." Although the Tenants Council had already paid Halpern $3,000 and would owe him $3,000 more if he appealed Grumet's ruling (and an additional $5,000 if he was successful), the rank and file went along with Hanks's recommendation.[44] In late November Halpern filed an appeal with the First Judicial Department of the New York State Appellate Division.

In a brief that was submitted on behalf of the Hankses "and all others similarly situated," Halpern asked the appellate court to reverse Judge Grumet's decision and order Commissioner Urstadt to grant a de novo (or new) hearing. If the court felt that a de novo hearing was not required, it should hold a plenary hearing of its own. And "in either case, Riverbay Corporation should be stayed from collecting the increased rentals" until the legal issues were resolved. Relying on both federal and state case law, Halpern argued that Urstadt's refusal to hold a public hearing deprived the residents of Co-op City of due process. His action was state action, which "vitally affects the property rights" of the appellants, and "the tenants' interests in avoiding the loss outweighs the governmental interest in summary adjudication." Pointing out that Urstadt had granted hearings on rent increases in other state-financed housing projects, Halpern argued that his action also violated the equal protection clause of the Fourteenth Amendment. Stressing that the 16.1 percent increase was "unnecessary and unjustified," he insisted that the court had the authority to grant a stay of the increase "pending final disposition of this proceeding." "To deny such relief would seriously and irreparably prejudice the tenants," Halpern concluded. "To grant it, would not cause any harm to either of the respondents [Commissioner Urstadt and the Riverbay Corporation]."[45]

Representing Urstadt was Assistant Attorney General Mortimer Sattler, who was joined by First Assistant Attorney General Samuel Hirshowitz. The commissioner's refusal to hold a public hearing did not deprive Co-op City's residents of due process, Sattler argued, much less equal protection of the law. The state legislature empowered Urstadt to make decisions without holding "a quasi-judicial hearing." To help him decide the case at hand, he relied on a qualified and experienced staff that was "in direct and constant contact with the project." "It is inconceivable," Sattler stressed, "that the Legislature intended that every rent increase for every tenant in every public housing project would require a hearing. This would impose an intolerable burden on the Commissioner." The two US Supreme Court decisions on which Halpern relied dealt with the deprivation of welfare benefits without a public hearing. But neither of these cases "by the wildest stretch of the imagination can be equated with the legislative program devised for the creation of low and middle income housing under the commonly known Mitchell-Lama Law." The relationship between Co-op City's residents and the Riverbay Corporation was not adversarial, Sattler claimed. Some of the residents might not be able to pay the increased carrying charges, but "that is a human problem, not a legal one." Given that Commissioner Urstadt's actions were neither arbitrary nor capricious, Sattler urged the court to dismiss Halpern's appeal.[46]

Riverbay's counsel, Szold, Brandwen, Meyers & Altman, made many of the same points as Sattler. The residents of Co-op City were not deprived of due process, counsel argued. Commissioner Urstadt was not required to hold a public hearing before approving an increase in Co-op City's carrying charges. The appellants' case was based on the misconception "that every governmental determination which may affect a person or group of persons gives that person or group a constitutional right to [a] hearing prior to governmental action." That "would paralyze the business of government." In the case at hand, moreover, the petitioners were informed of the grounds for the increase, provided access to Riverbay's financial records, and represented by counsel at the informational meetings. Although they were given every opportunity to review Riverbay's application and challenge the commissioner's determination, they had not submitted any evidence to cast doubt on the need for a 16.1 percent increase in carrying charges. Pointing out that Urstadt had recently approved increases in rents and carrying charges in no less than ten other housing projects without holding a formal hearing, Riverbay's counsel also argued that his action did not violate the equal protection clause. Riverbay was not oblivious to the effect of an increase on Co-op City's senior citizens. But "in any quasi-legislative action, some are hurt; some are helped." This was not a case of "a greedy landlord, seeking profit, against helpless tenants." Co-op City was a housing cooperative, the Hankses were cooperators, and if the project could not be finished, they would lose their investment. Insisting that the courts did not have the power to substitute their judgment for that of "properly designated administrative officials," Riverbay's counsel urged the justices to affirm Judge Grumet's decision.[47]

In a unanimous decision issued in early November 1971, nearly a year and a half after Halpern filed suit, the appellate court affirmed the trial court's ruling—and affirmed it without writing an opinion. (It also charged the Co-op City Tenants Council $500 for court costs.) Leonard Hanks was sorely disappointed. The Tenants Council could have taken the case to the Court of Appeals, the state's highest court, located in Albany. But as he knew, it was highly unlikely that the Court of Appeals would reverse a unanimous decision by the appellate division. Moreover, things had changed since the Tenants Council launched its campaign against the 16.1 percent increase. Early in 1971 Riverbay announced that it intended to increase the carrying charges again—and by much more than 16.1 percent. The announcement generated a storm of opposition in Co-op City. But this time the opposition was led not by the Tenants Council, but by the Advisory Council, with which Hanks promised to cooperate fully. In its effort to block the increase, the Advisory Council turned not to Gerald P. Halpern, a relatively obscure New York lawyer, but to Louis Nizer, one of the nation's best-known attorneys. As Hanks said, "Even if we have lost the first battle the war is just beginning on the second front."[48]

CHAPTER 8

THE "SECOND FRONT"

Shortly after the 15.1 percent increase in Co-op City's carrying charges went into effect, Harold Ostroff and his associates took a couple of steps to soothe what the *City News* called "the sting of resentment" that was felt by many residents. In early August Riverbay pledged to consult with the newly formed Co-op City Advisory Council before applying to the Division of Housing and Community Renewal for future increases. The response was mixed. Gerald P. Halpern, who was annoyed that Riverbay was ignoring the Tenants Council and attempting to designate the Advisory Council as the only body that represented the residents, criticized the pledge as "tokenism." "It sounds to me," he said, "that this idea of consultation is much like the meeting with Commissioner Charles J. Urstadt held after the fact on the present increase." The *City News* was less skeptical than Halpern. Calling the pledge "a heartening step," the paper wrote that it showed that the United Housing Foundation "desires to work with [the] residents [of Co-op City]." But it also pointed out that the courts had not yet ruled on the present increase and that it was far from clear that the residents would go along with another increase even if they were consulted beforehand. "Though the pledge to consult the community on future rent increases is encouraging," the *City News* wrote, "we can only think how much more it would mean for residents to elect members to the [Riverbay] board of directors."[1]

Ostroff and his associates were aware that many residents shared these reservations about the governance of Co-op City. About two weeks later the Riverbay Corporation Board of Directors voted unanimously to amend the housing company's by-laws, which provided that the board would consist of ten members, nine of whom would be appointed by the UHF and one by the commissioner of housing. (Lawrence Sivak, chairman of the Advisory Council, and Richard Ferguson, its vice chairman, attended board meetings, but as nonvoting observers.) Under the Mitchell-Lama act the residents had no say about the composition of the board until the commissioner issued a Certificate of Acceptability, which would not take place until Co-op City was completed (and perhaps not for months or even years after). Under the amendment, the Riverbay board was expanded from ten to fifteen members. The five new members, each of whom would have the same rights as the ten old members, would be elected by the residents, one for each seven of the thirty-five buildings. Since fourteen buildings were already occupied, two resident directors would be elected as soon as the Riverbay Corporation Board of Directors and the Advisory Council figured out how to hold an election. According to Ostroff, the board's action was part of the UHF's plan to turn the management of Co-op City over to the shareholders. The amendment would have to be approved by the commissioner of housing, but as a spokesman for the Division of Housing said, the change was "a standard procedure." Already adopted in Rochdale Village and Amalgamated Warbasse, it would ensure a "smoother transition" after Co-op City was completed.[2]

Riverbay's actions may have done something to mollify Co-op City's residents, but they did nothing to alleviate its fiscal problems. As these problems went from bad to worse, the board of directors decided to hold an informational meeting for the residents in late March 1971. At the meeting, which was held in the Community Center auditorium and attended by more than 1,200 cooperators, Ostroff spelled out Co-op City's financial predicament. At present, he said, more than 81 percent of the carrying charges were spent on fixed costs, a result in large part of the soaring interest rates on the State Housing Finance Agency's bonds. Operating expenses were also skyrocketing, mainly because of the impact of inflation on the price of oil and electricity. In response to a question submitted by the Advisory Council, he acknowledged that in all likelihood Riverbay would have to raise the carrying charges again, though not before 1973. He could not say by how much, only that "the amount would be dictated by increased costs due to inflation and determined only after meticulous studies." After the informational meeting, the Riverbay board—which by then included the two resident directors, Perry Cohen, a rabbi, and Julius Palmer, a high school teacher—held two regular meetings in May and June at which it reviewed Co-op City's fiscal problems. And on June 23 it held a special meeting at which Ostroff reported that according to the board's Budget and Finance Committee,

Riverbay needed an additional $30 million to finish Co-op City and another $30 million to pay the higher-than-expected finance charges and operating expenses. He therefore recommended that the board ask the State Housing Finance Agency for an additional $60 million and raise the carrying charges by 20 percent on January 1, 1973, and an additional 12.5 percent on July 1, 1974.[3]

Perry Cohen had been "stunned and thoroughly shaken" when Ostroff first raised the possibility of a substantial increase in Co-op City's carrying charges in late May, and he was upset when Ostroff's recommendations came up for a vote on June 23. He was well aware that the increased carrying charges would be a serious hardship for Co-op City's many senior citizens "whose incomes were limited." But he was also aware that Co-op City sorely needed additional capital "to prevent a more costly slow down in construction." Although he knew that most of his constituents would object to an increase in the carrying charges, he felt that he had no choice but to support Ostroff's recommendations. (Cohen also made several proposals to prevent increases in the future, all of which were adopted by the board.) Also "stunned" by Ostroff's recommendations was Arthur Z. Cohen, a hardware company executive who had just been elected as the third resident director and was attending his first board meeting on June 23. He found it "incredible" that Ostroff, president of a corporation worth more than $350 million, did not know until late June that Riverbay would run out of money within one month unless the board voted to increase the carrying charges. Ostroff was either guilty of "gross mismanagement" or outright duplicity. Cohen asked the other members of the board to postpone the vote until he had a chance to look more closely into Co-op City's finances. But they denied his request. Unwilling to vote in favor of "an astonishing increase in carrying charges," even if it was meant to head off the "imminent bankruptcy of the construction account," he abstained.[4]

Julius Palmer was even more troubled by Ostroff's recommendations than the two other resident directors. "I voted against the proposed rent increase," he said, "because I cannot and will not believe that a well run organization could suffer such unimaginable set backs in such a short period of time." Something was wrong at Riverbay, he declared And that something was "mismanagement, waste, [and/or] exploitation." At the June 23 meeting the board was told that unless the carrying charges were increased, "construction would come to a halt and the entire Co-op might collapse." But that possibility had not even been mentioned at previous meetings. Palmer then suggested several things that management could do to generate additional revenue, reduce operating expenses, and thereby alleviate Co-op City's fiscal problem without asking the State Housing Finance Agency for an additional $60 million. He was particularly concerned about the impact of the increase in carrying charges on senior citizens and young couples with children. "What will these people do?" he asked. "How will they pay their rent? Where can they move?" Not least of all, Palmer pointed out that Co-op City's maintenance and security left much to be desired. The lobbies were filthy. And while the porters hid in one room, their supervisors hid in another. "Indeed," he insisted, "even Co-ops located in slums are much cleaner than ours. With the neglect in terms of services and proper maintenance, one would expect a rent decrease, not an increase of 35 per cent." If the three resident directors voted no or abstained, "we could have shown our unity and our commitment to a fair and equitable rent increase—not the exorbitant one [that was proposed by Ostroff]."[5]

But as both Perry Cohen and Julius Palmer acknowledged, it would not have made much difference if the three resident directors voted no or abstained. Most, if not all, of the other Riverbay directors would have voted in favor of Ostroff's recommendation. For Jacob Potofsky, Louis Stulberg, and the other UHF directors, a no vote would have been a vote of no-confidence in Ostroff, whom they had appointed as executive vice president of the UHF and president of the Riverbay Corporation. That the Riverbay board voted in favor of Ostroff's recommendations on June 23 was not surprising. What was surprising was that on June 21, two days before the board's special meeting, Riverbay asked the Division of Housing and Community Renewal to approve an application to the State Housing Finance Agency for an increase in Co-op City's mortgage from $376 million to $436 million. Then on June 24, one day after the board's special meeting, it asked the Division of Housing to approve an increase in Co-op City's carrying charges by 20 percent, effective January 1, 1973, and by 12.5 percent, effective July 1, 1974. Also surprising was that within only a week and a half Commissioner Charles J. Urstadt approved the application for the additional $60 million. Moreover, the *City News* reported, Ostroff had informed Urstadt that Riverbay intended to request a 35 percent increase in Co-op City's carrying charges as early as March 1971—more than two months before the board adopted his recommendations.[6]

OOO

The proposed increase generated a furor in Co-op City. Leading the opposition was the Advisory Council, which held a public meeting at the Community Center auditorium on June 28 that was attended by 2,000 angry residents. Another 1,000 were turned away at the door because there was no room inside. Also attending the meeting were Perry Cohen and Julius Palmer, both of whom told the crowd why they had voted as they did on June 23. Arthur Z. Cohen, who was unable to attend, wrote a statement, which was read for him, explaining why he had abstained. The crowd made its feelings known throughout the meeting. Boos rang out every time Perry Cohen's name was mentioned. One resident shouted, "Throw the Rabbi out!" and another yelled, "Get Cohen out of Co-op City!" At one point two residents charged Cohen, and security guards had to be dispatched to protect him. By contrast, Julius Palmer, the only member of the board who voted against the increase, received a standing ovation after he finished his speech. When he left the stage, one resident kissed him on the cheek and then turned to Cohen, who was standing nearby, and said, "You stink, Rabbi." Before the meeting was over, Cohen was ousted from the Advisory Council's Finance Committee on the grounds that no board member could hold office on the council. Boos also rang out when anyone mentioned Harold Ostroff, who was denounced by Richard Ferguson, vice chairman of the Advisory Council, for breaking his promise to consult with the council before proposing an increase in Co-op City's carrying charges.[7]

The high point of the meeting was Lawrence Sivak's scathing indictment of Ostroff (and, by implication, the Riverbay Corporation and the United Housing Foundation). Ostroff, he pointed out, not only broke his promise to consult with the Advisory Council about future increases but also failed to inform the resident directors in time for them "to question the propriety of the recent increase." He tells them only what he wants them to know "and nothing more." Indeed, he treats both the Advisory Council and the resident directors as "pawns" to be used whenever and wherever he deems necessary. "We are but puppets on a stage with Mr. Harold Ostroff pulling the strings." Sivak also accused Ostroff of luring New Yorkers into Co-op City by setting the carrying charges at an unsustainable level and, once the residents moved in, raising them by 60 percent. The increase was unconscionable, especially for the many senior citizens. How, he asked, would they be able to pay $42.81 per room per month? Sivak also took issue with Ostroff's claim that "this incredible increase" was due solely to inflation. And he found it impossible to believe that Ostroff did not know in March that Riverbay would not be able to pay its bills in July. With friends like Ostroff, Sivak asked, "who needs enemies?" Sivak felt much the same way about Perry Cohen, who, as a member of Riverbay's Budget and Finance Committee, knew about the impending increase well before June 13 but failed to keep the other resident directors informed and thereby betrayed the trust of the residents who elected him to the board.[8]

Besides ousting Perry Cohen from the Finance Committee, the Advisory Council adopted several resolutions, which were meant to serve as guidelines in the upcoming struggle against the increase in carrying charges. One resolution called on the Riverbay Corporation Board of Directors to rescind the increase. Another ordered the council's Finance Committee to devote all its efforts to studying the proposed increase and asked the community's lawyers and accountants to examine Riverbay's financial records. Yet another resolution insisted that Riverbay refrain from even considering another increase until this study was concluded. Under the other resolutions, the intercommunity and legal committees were instructed to explore legislation to reduce Co-op City's carrying charges and turn control of the community over to the residents as soon as possible; the Riverbay board was asked to allow two council members to attend all committee and general meetings; and Harold Ostroff was to be invited to a town hall meeting to answer the community's questions in the near future. Taken together, the meeting and the resolutions were an opening salvo in a long drawn-out fight against the proposed increase in Co-op City's carrying charges. According to the *City News*—which criticized Ostroff for his "callous disregard" of the rights of Co-op City's residents and stressed that a proposed increase of 56 percent without any consultation with the community was evidence of the "Benevolent Despot[ism]" of the United Housing Foundation—they were also evidence that the Advisory Council was fed up with the paternalism of the Riverbay Corporation and determined "to fight the increase to the end."[9]

Ostroff did not attend the June 28 meeting. In a letter to Sivak, which was read to the residents by Michael L. Sicilian, the council's corresponding secretary, he defended Riverbay's decision to raise the carrying charges. Ostroff pointed out that as a result of the inflationary spiral of the past three or four years Co-op City's construction costs had soared, rendering the original estimates "practically meaningless." So had its operating expenses. Faced with a serious cash flow problem, Riverbay had tried to find a temporary solution. But it soon became apparent that it had no choice but to ask the State Housing Finance Agency for additional capital. At the informational meeting in

March, Ostroff said, he had advised the residents of Co-op City's financial problems. But at that time he could not say what would have to be done to solve them. Shortly after, however, the Riverbay board realized that in order to prevent a slowdown in construction, it would have to borrow an additional $60 million and increase the carrying charges accordingly. Ostroff acknowledged that he had promised to consult with the Advisory Council before raising the carrying charges, but there had been no time. "The need to increase the mortgage made it necessary to act sooner than we would otherwise," he stressed. He also pointed out that the increase would not go into effect for a year and a half, which gave the Riverbay board, the Advisory Council, and other organizations time to look for ways to increase Co-op City's nonresidential income, reduce its operating expenses, lobby for legislative aid, and thereby lower the projected increase in carrying charges.[10]

During the late summer and early fall Ostroff made a few more attempts to address the growing concern about the increase. In late July he sent a letter to all the residents, saying that the decision had been the most difficult that he and the other Riverbay directors had ever had to make. But he claimed that there was nothing else the board could have done "to bring Co-op City to completion and maintain its fiscal integrity." He was concerned about the plight of the many senior citizens who were living on a fixed income and the many young couples who were raising children. But he was also troubled by "the extreme and rude forms of criticism" that had been heaped upon some members of the Riverbay board. After describing Co-op City's fiscal problems at length, he expressed the hope that the board and the residents might in time reach a "mutual understanding." Three weeks later Ostroff attended another meeting of the Advisory Council, at which Sivak attacked him for violating "a sacred trust" when he failed to consult with the council before recommending an increase in the carrying charges. Ostroff apologized. He had made a mistake, "a real beaut," and one that he deeply regretted. But he stood by the board's decision. Ostroff's apology notwithstanding, many residents were disappointed. Jerome Glanzrock, a leader of the United Democratic Club of Co-op City, called the meeting "an exercise in futility." The apology changed nothing, added Sol Oratofsky, the leader of one of Co-op City's senior citizens clubs. And Leonard Hanks, the president of the Tenants Council, said that he had not trusted Ostroff before and did not trust him now. "He was sorry after the first rent hike, he said he was sorry now, and he will be sorry after the next one, but he will do it the same way when he has to."[11]

Clinging to the hope that a "mutual understanding" might still be reached, Ostroff accepted the Advisory Council's invitation to attend a town hall meeting in mid-September. According to the *City News*, he "appeared [more] haggard, uneasy and less confident" than he did when he met with the council in mid-August, perhaps because he had just received three phone calls threatening his life if he came to the meeting. For his protection, no fewer than nine security guards, four New York City patrolmen, and at least two NYPD plainclothesmen were dispatched to the Community Center auditorium. From the start Ostroff was put on the defensive. In response to Sivak's opening remarks, he defended the UHF against charges of corruption and mismanagement. And in response to hostile questions from the audience, he denied that he knew that the original carrying charges would double in a few years and that they were set at $25 per room per month in order to lure New Yorkers to move to Co-op City. "Five years ago," he said, "[neither I] nor anybody else could have predicted that we would run into the inflation[ary] spiral that the country is caught up in." He also denied that Riverbay was indifferent to the plight of Co-op City's many senior citizens. Indeed, he told Sol Oratofsky, it was doing its utmost to persuade the state legislature to enact a bill to subsidize seniors—a bill, he added, that was likely to pass at the next session. And to a woman who argued that by increasing the carrying charges Riverbay was driving residents out of Co-op City, forcing them "to go to someplace cheaper even if they don't want to leave," Ostroff replied, "I don't think there is anywhere else to go."[12]

Some residents agreed with Ostroff. In a letter to the *Co-op City Times* one wrote that it was time for residents to "face reality." At a time when no middle-income housing was being built, credit should be given to the UHF, "the only people foolish enough to make the attempt to house 'the poor forgotten middle-income family.'" And Harold Ostroff should be thanked, not abused. "He fought to get Co-op City approved, which was very unwelcome to everyone in the [Baychester] community, who seemed to have preferred a swamp with hot and cold running rats." The increase in Co-op City's carrying charges would not be reduced by abusing the UHF officials, he wrote. "Help must come from the State and Federal Governments." In another letter to the *Co-op City Times*, Eugene M. Kaufman, a member of the Advisory Council, strongly objected to the attacks on Ostroff and Cohen. "[Have] those persons who have attacked Mr. Ostroff come forth with anyone who has Mr. Ostroff's experience in building and operating middle income developments?" he asked. "The answer is 'No.'" And "have those persons who attacked Rabbi Cohen's action at the Board of Directors' meeting come up with an alternative to his vote when all the facts are considered rationally? Again, the answer is 'NO.'" It was time for Co-op City's residents to face the facts. "Neither Mr. Ostroff, the Board of Directors [n]or United Housing are the cause of the economic conditions in the United States that have resulted in the outrageous [increases] that we have all been faced with in our normal everyday life."[13]

But most residents felt otherwise. Calling Ostroff the "enemy," Michael Sicilian wrote, "Behind a facade of benevolence, he has perpetrated a fraud of the cruelest kind." And by doing so he shattered "the dream of lower middle income groups and retirees to live in a clean, comfortable and safe environment [at] a price they could afford." Once the UHF decided to sponsor Co-op City, he pointed out, it attempted "to attract [residents] with the hoax of moderate rentals." After the families moved into the "Promised Land," the UHF assumed that they would have "little choice but to stay and pay once the trap was sprung." If Ostroff, "with all his experience and know-how, couldn't see the handwriting of spiraling inflation in the period of 1964-1971," Sicilian said, "then he is in worse shape than we are." Stephen Kaufman, chairman of the board of the Co-op City Civic Association, agreed with Sicilian. By increasing the carrying charges, the Riverbay Corporation Board of Directors turned middle-income housing into upper-middle-income housing, which not only shattered the dreams of the cooperators but undermined the legislative efforts to alleviate the housing shortage. Kaufman also attacked Commissioner Urstadt, who, he pointed out, had taken the position that if Co-op City's residents asked the Division of Housing to deny Riverbay's application for an increase, the burden of proof would be on them. "He who is charged with the duty to protect the public has abdicated that responsibility to the Board of Directors of Riverbay Corporation."[14]

Although most Co-op City residents supported the Advisory Council, Sivak, Ferguson, and its other leaders knew that it would be very hard to get the increase rescinded or even reduced. Ostroff was steadfast in his defense of the increase. And so long as he was in charge, there was little or no chance that the board of directors would reconsider its decision. In late September Julius Palmer called on Ostroff to resign, charging him with "betrayal of trust; dereliction of duty; irresponsibility; mismanagement; [and] hypocrisy." But Ostroff had no intention of stepping down. Even the *City News*, no friend of Ostroff's, thought that Palmer's call was "unduly harsh and premature." Urstadt, who had the final say, confirmed in early July that he would hold "a full public hearing" in the spring of 1972, to which the *City News* responded, "The time to discuss the issue is now," not next year. But as Urstadt told one resident, Co-op City's costs had gone up sharply, and Riverbay sorely needed additional revenue, which the state, with "severe budgetary limitations" of its own, was unable to provide. Hence "it is my unenviable task to review and all-too-often approve a rent increase for [Co-op City and many of the other] State-aided Mitchell-Lama projects." He wished that there were other alternatives for Co-op City, and he would be willing to listen to proposals to reduce or eliminate the impending increase. But given that Urstadt believed that what was at stake was not only the solvency of Co-op City but also the integrity of the Mitchell-Lama program and the State Housing Finance Agency, it was highly unlikely that he would turn down Riverbay's application for an increase.[15]

These obstacles notwithstanding, the Advisory Council pressed ahead. Besides holding meetings at which the residents vented their anger at Ostroff, Cohen, and Riverbay's other board members and drafting elaborate plans that spelled out the tasks of its finance, legal, and other committees, the council spent a good deal of time attempting to mobilize the community. Its Executive Committee met with representatives of many Co-op City's voluntary associations, all of whom were asked to lend their support to the Advisory Council's campaign. "We need one voice—a united voice," said one of the backers of this approach. But this was easier said than done. Some groups were willing to follow the Advisory Council's lead, but others would only join a coalition in which each group had equal standing. Richard Ferguson opposed this arrangement, arguing that the campaign to stop the increase in carrying charges would be ill served if the groups acted independently "and in their own selfish interests." Julius Palmer agreed with him. "The worst possible thing we can do at this time is to start fighting each other and breaking off into small groups," he said. "We need unity now more than at any time since Co-op City was opened." The Advisory Council and community groups, some of whose leaders argued that the struggle was too much for any one organization, remained at odds for a while. But eventually they reached an agreement to join forces and set up a Steering Committee, which included leaders of both the Advisory Council and the community groups, to lead the fight against the impending increase.[16]

The Advisory Council also spent a good deal of time attempting to raise money. At the outset it was clear that a substantial amount, perhaps as much as $100,000, according to Sivak, would be needed to hire outside experts.

Chief among them were auditors to examine Riverbay's finances, management consultants to study its operations, and, if need be, lawyers to challenge the increase in court. It was far from clear how the money would be collected, who would collect it, and where it would be kept, but over time these issues were resolved. On a Saturday in early October the Advisory Council held its first Fund Raising Day. In the lobby of each apartment house it set up tables that were manned by council members from 9:00 a.m. to 2:00 p.m. and from 3:00 p.m. to 7:00 p.m. Afterwards council members would go to the apartments of residents who had not donated and give them another chance. The Advisory Council hoped that each family would donate at least $2, but as Jack Blacklin, vice chairman of the Finance Committee, conceded, the drive "didn't go as well as we hoped it would." Roughly $14,500 was raised and deposited into a checking account at the Co-op City branch of the Amalgamated Bank. Although it was, said one resident, "a good start," it was "only a drop in the bucket," said another. Some residents held that the Fund Raising Day fell short of its goal because it was held over the Columbus Day weekend, when many residents were out of town. Also out of town were some council members who were supposed to man the tables. Other residents, including Leonard Hanks, refused to participate on the grounds that the Advisory Council had not spelled out how it would spend the money.[17]

By late October, four months after Co-op City's residents learned about the impending increase, it seemed that the Advisory Council was making progress. A good many elected officials—city, state, and federal—had endorsed its campaign to prevent the increase. The Riverbay board's decision to raise the carrying charges without giving the residents an opportunity to voice their opposition was "arbitrary, capricious, and unconscionable," said State Senator John Calandra. And Congressman Mario Biaggi denounced Commissioner Urstadt for being "arrogant [and] dictatorial" and urged Governor Nelson Rockefeller to launch an investigation of the Department of Housing's approval of "the unconscionable increases" at Co-op City. Moreover, Harold Ostroff had issued an apology to the Advisory Council in August, and Perry Cohen had resigned from the Riverbay board in September. Apparently, wrote the *City News*, he felt that "the price of involvement" was too high. The Advisory Council and community groups had resolved their differences, and the Steering Committee was up and running. After a second Fund Raising Day, which was held on October 31, it had about $25,000 in the bank. But many of the Steering Committee's leaders believed that something more had to be done to jump-start their campaign. And for that they needed outside help. Hence in mid-October the Advisory Council voted to retain legal counsel. To that end Paul Gurevich, a representative of the Building 22 Association, submitted a list of sixteen New York law firms, and the Steering Committee formed a committee to recommend one.[18]

OOO

The committee's initial efforts were disappointing. Some of the law firms were not interested, and others were too expensive. Solomon Ploss, a member of the Steering Committee, then suggested that it add to the list Phillips, Nizer, Benjamin, Krim & Ballon, a prominent New York firm that had been founded by Louis Phillips and Louis Nizer in 1928, and try to arrange a meeting with Nizer, a man, said Milton Forman, another member of the Steering Committee, "whom we immediately recognized as one of the most famous attorneys of our time." Born in England in 1902, Nizer moved to New York as a child and went to Columbia College and Columbia Law School, from which he graduated in 1924. Over a career that spanned more than forty years, he emerged as one of the country's most celebrated (and highly paid) lawyers. Although perhaps best known for representing Quentin Reynolds, a foreign correspondent who sued right-wing columnist Westbrook Pegler for libel and was awarded $175,000, the largest such award at the time, Nizer had many other well-known clients, among them Charlie Chaplin, Salvador Dali, Mae West, Julius Erving, and Spyros Skouros, onetime chairman of the board of 20th Century Fox, general counsel to the Motion Picture Association of America, and executive secretary of the New York Film Board of Trade. As well as a brilliant litigator, Nizer was a prolific author whose best-known book was *My Life in Court*, a colorful account of several of his most memorable cases that was published in 1961 and had a long run on the *New York Times* best-seller list.[19]

Most members of the Steering Committee thought that Ploss was "either joking or dreaming," wrote the *City News*. As Forman recalled, they "chuckled at the idea that a man so important in his field would want to trouble himself with our problems." But Ploss pressed ahead and made an appointment with Nizer (and two of his associates). "We were hoping," said Forman, "that he could somehow give us advice that would afford this community some hope, never really believing that he himself would become personally involved." But things went better than expected. After meeting with a delegation from the Steering Committee led by chairman Larry Dolnick, Nizer, who seemed well aware of Co-op City's problems, said that he was willing to represent the Advisory Council and for $5,000 would make a preliminary investigation. Depending on what the investigation found, he might even be prepared to file suit to block the impending increase in carrying charges, The Advisory Council promptly held a special meeting at which it voted overwhelming in favor of retaining Nizer's firm. "We got exactly what we really need," said Lawrence Sivak, "an attorney able to conduct a thorough preliminary investigation into the situation so that we can determine the best alternatives, legal or otherwise, in terms of combating the increase or reducing the amount of the increase." The Advisory Council also set up a committee to act as a liaison between Nizer and the community. Chaired by Forman, it included members of the Steering Committee and the council's finance, legal, and executive committees. As the *City News* wrote, many residents thought that the Steering Committee had "hit the 'jackpot.'"[20]

To conduct the preliminary investigation, Nizer turned to Jay F. Gordon, one of the two associates who had met with the Steering Committee delegation. In an effort to find out why so many families had moved into Co-op City, he spoke with residents and reviewed the 1965 and 1967 information bulletins (as well as Ostroff's October 1968 letter). In an attempt to figure out why the carrying charges had skyrocketed, he examined Riverbay's financial records, chief among them the many contract modifications. Gordon also interviewed Henry Nussbaum, director of the Division of Housing's Bureau of Finance. He wanted to know not only why the division had gone along with Abraham E. Kazan's practice of deliberately underestimating the construction costs of UHF projects, but also why it had waived its "liquid asset pre-qualification rule." Under what Gordon called the Division of Housing's "own prudent rule," Community Services, Inc., should have had about $13 million in liquid assets before it was approved as Co-op City's general contractor. But the records showed that it had "less than 1% ... of the amount required!" In effect, Gordon later said, the Division of Housing gave CSI "a blank check drawn on the accounts of the future owners of Co-op City." The *City News* reported that Gordon would not say anything about his findings, only that the preliminary investigation was nearing an end and that before long Nizer would meet with the Liaison Committee and, in all likelihood, offer to continue to represent the Advisory Council in its fight against the impending increase.[21]

At the meeting, which was held on March 27, 1972, Nizer told the Liaison Committee that the preliminary investigation showed a "reasonable possibility of success" and that as a result Phillips, Nizer was willing to continue to represent the Advisory Council. Given that a huge amount of money was at stake and that one or more state agencies were involved, he warned that the fight would be "a long and hard one." To wage it Phillips, Nizer would need an additional $45,000 right away and possibly as much as $150,000 later on. According to the *City News*, Nizer also said that a certain degree of secrecy would be required because he "did not want to tip his hand to any future legal opponents." "At this point in the investigation," he went on, "you will just simply have to trust us to do what is in the best interests of your community." One day later the Advisory Council held a special session, at which Forman told its members that after meeting with Nizer and his associates he was convinced "that we are on our way to victory." The council then voted unanimously in favor of Jack Blacklin's motion that it continue to retain Phillips, Nizer, raise $45,000 as soon as possible, and continue its fund-raising effort until it reached $150,000, which, Forman acknowledged, was a great deal of money (and $127,000 more than the Steering Committee had collected thus far). But it came to only $10 per family. And given that the proposed increase in carrying charges would cost each family from $40 to $70 per month, the $10 would be money well spent.[22]

A week later the Advisory Council held a much-anticipated town hall meeting, the purpose of which was to give Nizer an opportunity to bring the community up to date. After Sivak welcomed the more than 1,300 residents who filled the Community Center auditorium and spilled into the second-floor lobby, he turned the floor over to Forman, the chairman of the Liaison Committee. Before introducing Nizer, Forman reminded the residents that most of them had moved into Co-op City with the assurance that it was and would remain a middle-income community in which they could afford to live comfortably for the rest of their lives. Many had even given up rent-controlled apartments. Then suddenly they were told that they would have to pay from $40 to $80 more per month in carrying charges, "with no promise that more would not be asked of us in the future." In what Forman called these "dark and terrible days," many men thought about taking second or third jobs, and many women, even those with children, thought about going to work. Many families also considered moving out of Co-op City. Feeling anxious and helpless, many residents wondered, "How will we be able to survive?" But from this despair, said Forman, had arisen a group of "community minded people" who would not "give in but would stand up and fight for survival." The Advisory Council then "moved into action." And so did the Steering Committee, which found in Louis Nizer "an attorney who has done things in his field that other attorneys can only dream about, a defender of the underdog [and] a humanitarian of the highest caliber." With Nizer on their side, Forman declared, "we are on the threshold of a new beginning."[23]

Accompanied by Jay Gordon and George Berger, the other associate who met with the Steering Committee delegation, Nizer began a long and eloquent speech by telling the residents, "You're supposed to be a landlord and you're suffering worse than a tenant." Then after briefly mentioning the Mitchell-Lama act and the United Housing Foundation, he pointed out that the original estimate for building Co-op City had been $250 million. But the construction contract was modified five times, which brought the final cost up to $422 million, an increase of almost 70 percent. According to the information bulletin, any increase was supposed to be borne by CSI, the general contractor, not passed on to the residents, and certainly not in the form of higher carrying charges, which had already been raised from $23.02 per room per month to $40.49. Nizer then asked, "Is there any of you in this room tonight who was consulted before [any] of these increases went into effect?" "Is there any one of you in this room who was so much as notified that the guaranteed price construction contract was going to be changed five times?" "Is there anyone in this room tonight who was told that this financial obligation was going to be increased by 75%?" In each case, the audience responded with a resounding "No!" And yet, Nizer pointed out, the commissioner of housing and community renewal had approved all of the increases without even holding a public hearing. Now he says that he will hold a hearing on the pending increase. But he also says, "The burden of proof will be on the tenants to show that these increases shouldn't go through," even though "by virtue of conscience, of law, of equity, of justice, [and] of morality," it should be on the commissioner.[24]

Nizer also said that his firm was looking into charges that Riverbay had leased Co-op City's commercial property at unreasonably low rates, a scam from which some officers had made a substantial profit. Even worse, he went on, when the residents bought stock in Riverbay, it was supposed to be given to them. "That's the indicia of your ownership. That's what you get for your money." But the Division of Housing had not yet issued a Certificate of Acceptability, and the residents had not yet received their stock. And "until you get that stock," Nizer said, "you are owners without ownership, owners without all the prerogatives of ownership," including the power to run their community. He then went on to say, "Where there is great injustice, there will be found a remedy." He could not believe that the governor would "sit by." Nor could he believe that the legislature would "sit by." And if need be, "we're going to fight in the courts." Nizer concluded by saying that "there's no reason why you should have these increases, there's no reason why you shouldn't get recompense for those you've paid, there's no reason why this shouldn't stop and stop quickly. And if you will place faith in us, as I do in you, we will see it done." When he finished, the crowd gave him a one-minute standing ovation. Jack Blacklin then urged everyone to contribute to the war chest. So did Larry Dolnick, who also said that he and the other four resident directors of the Riverbay board would give "their total and complete support to Mr. Nizer and the community."[25]

George Schechter, a resident of a Co-op City townhouse and vice president of the Riverbay Corporation, was skeptical about the Advisory Council's decision to retain Nizer. Although he acknowledged that the residents had the right to hire a lawyer in their attempt to stop the proposed increase, he believed that they were "reaching for pie in the sky." "No legal gimmick is going to overcome four years of serious inflation," he declared. But most residents were more optimistic, especially after Nizer agreed to continue to represent them. Nizer "wouldn't risk his reputation unless he feels he will win," said Eva Trungold. "I think Nizer has something up his sleeve," remarked Jackie Kozarsky, "or else he wouldn't go ahead." "I have complete confidence in the man," he added. Richard Ferguson pointed out that "there are no guarantees, but if anything can be done, [Nizer is] the person to do it." He is "one of the cheapest investments we can make." Borough President Robert Abrams agreed, saying that he had long thought that legal help would be needed "to look into the validity of the increase." And he "support[ed] and applaud[ed]" the decision to retain Nizer. Many residents were extremely optimistic after the town hall meeting. As Nizer walked down the stairs of the Community Center, Rubin Messing came up to him, shook his hand, praised his speech, and then said, "I have full confidence that you will not let us down." Nizer smiled, promised to do his utmost, and told Messing, "We have a very, very good chance of winning the case."[26]

At one point during his town hall speech Nizer remarked that he was going to attend the Division of Housing's public hearing on the proposed increase, a remark for which he was given a long round of applause. Commissioner Urstadt had said in July 1971 that he would hold a hearing in the spring of 1972. In March 1972, after much discussion of logistics, the division announced that it would be held in the Community Center auditorium on the afternoon and evening of April 18 and the morning and afternoon of

April 19. The first meeting was presided over by Fred Hecht, assistant commissioner of the Division of Housing, and attended by several members of his staff. The first speaker was Louis Nizer, who was outraged that the burden of proof was on the residents and was offended that the commissioner was not at the hearing. Nizer declared that the proposed increase (and, for that matter, the previous increases, which were approved without a public hearing) was illegal. Calling the hearing "inappropriate" and "improper," he declared that he did not intend to participate in a proceeding "to give some kind of imprimat[ur] to an action which was in violation of an expressed contract." Whereupon he walked out of the auditorium. All but one of the more than 400 residents who were at the hearing followed him, as did several elected officials, Riverbay resident directors, and community group representatives. Given that the handful of Division of Housing officials and Riverbay Corporation officers were left "virtually alone in the auditorium," wrote the *Co-op City Times*, Hecht adjourned the hearing.[27]

Within hours the walkout turned into a boycott. That evening more than 250 residents assembled outside the Community Center and urged other residents to skip the second session and, as one put it, "let those five characters [the State Division of Housing officials] just sit there." When it was clear that none of the residents would attend, the hearing was adjourned. Hecht reconvened the hearing on Wednesday, but no one spoke except Harold Ostroff, who thanked the commissioner for holding the hearing at Co-op City. Since there were no other speakers on the list and so few people in the audience, Hecht adjourned the hearing again. According to the *City News*, most residents were exhilarated by this turn of events. "Walking out is the best thing that could have happened," said one. "Go back? What for? There's nothing to go back for." "They are playing around with us and we are not standing for it," added another. "We would give respect to them if they are sincere and honest, but they are not." Commenting on the walkout, Richard Ferguson said, "I think that Nizer's stance was a correct one, and it really underscores the injustice which we see was done by approving a rent increase without public hearings prior to its approval." In an editorial the *City News* wrote, "We are proud of the residents who followed Mr. Nizer by boycotting the hearing." And it hoped that Commissioner Urstadt would see their "refusal to participate" for what it was—"a gesture of protest," a sign of "frustration," and a "cry [for help]" of 16,000 families."[28]

Nizer's town hall speech did more than just lift the spirits of many Co-op City residents. It also gave a boost to the Advisory Council's fund-raising efforts. "Had it been anyone but Louis Nizer, I wouldn't give a cent to this war chest," said Jerry Goldberg. Most residents gave $10. Some donated $15. And Congressman James Scheuer, whose district included Co-op City, contributed $170. The Independent Democratic Club and several other community groups also made contributions, as did the Citywide Co-op City Aid Committee, whose leaders were R. Peter Straus, president of radio station WMCA, Congressman Jonathan Bingham, and former US attorney Robert Morgenthau. By mid-April the war chest had reached $90,000, and by mid-May $100,000. To raise the rest of the money, Arthur Z. Cohen, one of Riverbay's resident directors, proposed that the board of directors allocate up to $150,000 in corporate funds for the war chest. In defense of the proposal, he and the other resident directors stressed that Nizer had no intention of suing Riverbay. The resident directors also argued that the non-resident directors who sat on the board of the UHF, against which Nizer was likely to file suit, had a conflict of interest and should not be allowed to vote on Cohen's motion. But Ostroff ruled against them. He also refused to permit Lawrence Sivak to vote because his recent election to the board was being challenged. After Morton Schwartz, the state's representative on the Riverbay board, said that the Division of Housing would not approve such an expenditure on the grounds that it was an improper use of corporate funds, all eight of the non-resident directors who attended the meeting voted against Cohen's motion.[29]

Harold Ostroff strongly defended the board's decision. Cohen's proposal, he said, was "a politically-motivated move" whose primary purpose was to perpetuate "the myth that the members of [the] Riverbay board are either callous or indifferent to the effects of rent increases." Pointing out that the non-resident directors had long been in the forefront of the movement to provide the best possible housing at the lowest possible cost, he insisted that "nothing can be further from the truth." But the resident directors were livid, outraged less by the board's decision than by how they reached it. The non-resident directors did not say a word about his motion, said Cohen. In what he called the "most revolting experience of my life," there was "no response. No debate. No nothing. Total insensitivity to the community." Larry Dolnick agreed. He pointed out that there was "not a word, not a murmur, not even a snicker. Just absolute silence," adding that "it is quite inconceivable, almost unbelievable, that such an august body of men of such great stature could not and would not open their mouths even to give a dissenting opinion on such an important issue." Reflecting the growing rift between the resident- and non-resident directors, Arthur Oshins remarked that the non-resident directors, whom he called the UHF's "imperial representatives," just "sat there like faces carved in a Mt. Rushmore of the damned." By a vote of eight to four they won "a Pyrrhic victory," one that "they will live to regret."[30]

OOO

Early in June Nizer met with Hecht and Ostroff as well as several officers of the Riverbay Corporation and the Division of Housing (and their lawyers) at the division's Midtown Manhattan office. The purpose of the meeting, Nizer said, was to find out whether the conflict between Riverbay and the residents could be resolved "without the time and expense of a lawsuit." Nothing came of the meeting. As Nizer told the residents, "We had no alternative but to complete our preparations and file a suit on your behalf." As Milton Forman pointed out, Nizer then went "full speed ahead with the legal proceedings." Since it was not feasible to sue on behalf of Co-op City, he began to compile a list of residents, all of whom were shareholders of Riverbay. He hoped to prevail on some of them to serve as plaintiffs. In the end Milton Forman and fifty-six other residents were willing to do so. Hence in mid-September Nizer moved to block the pending increase in carrying charges by filing a $110 million suit in the US District Court for the Southern District of New York. Named as defendants in what was known as *Forman v. Community Services, Inc.* were the United Housing Foundation, the Riverbay Corporation, Community Services, Inc., the State of New York, the State Housing Finance Agency, and Harold Ostroff, George Schechter, and six other officers of the UHF and/or CSI. Nizer alleged that all the defendants except Riverbay had engaged in stock fraud, a violation of the federal securities acts of 1933 and 1934, by issuing (or in the case of New York State and the State Housing Finance Agency, by approving) a false and deceptive prospectus to lure New Yorkers to buy apartments in Co-op City.[31]

Ostroff was dismayed by Nizer's lawsuit, which, he said, was a declaration of "war" on the UHF, an organization that had done more than any other to solve New York City's housing problem. Pointing out that most residents were "satisfied and pleased with [Co-op City]," he blamed a small group for failing to realize that the increase in carrying charges was due to the nation's rampant inflation. He also took the group to task for raising "false hopes" among the residents who contributed to the $150,000 war chest. No one would win when cooperators sued themselves and their community,

Ostroff insisted. "At a time when we should be making every effort to obtain greater support for reasonably priced housing, we should not squander our resources fighting among ourselves." Schechter was also dismayed. After saying, half in jest, that "very few individuals ever become defendants in a $110,000,000 lawsuit," he pointed out that New Yorkers moved into Co-op City because the UHF was known for building the best possible housing at the lowest possible cost. Despite the increase in carrying charges, it was still the best buy in the city. The lawsuit would not reduce the carrying charges, he insisted. But it would discourage other nonprofit groups from building low- and middle-income housing, which would be unfortunate for the 8,000 families on Co-op City's waiting list and a great many other New Yorkers. Schechter also said that the money that had been raised to pay Nizer and his associates could be better spent on lobbying for government assistance, hiring additional security guards, buying another ambulance for the Co-op City Ambulance Corps, and building ball fields for the Co-op City Little League.[32]

Although Ostroff and Schechter felt that the lawsuit was misguided, they knew that the UHF had to take it seriously. Indeed, said Jacob S. Potofsky, it had no choice but "to defend itself," not to mention its subsidiary and officers. To do so, the UHF had to find a lawyer who could hold his own against Nizer. Hence in early October the foundation retained Simon H. Rifkind, a partner in Paul, Weiss, Rifkind, Wharton & Garrison, one of the largest and most prominent law firms in New York City and one with close ties to the Democratic Party establishment. Born in Russia in 1901, Rifkind came to the United States as a child and lived with his family on New York's Lower East Side. After graduating from City College of New York and Columbia Law School, he worked as a legislative secretary to Senator Robert F. Wagner and then as a member of Wagner's law firm. In 1941 President Franklin D. Roosevelt appointed him to the federal district court in New York, on which he sat until 1950, when he joined Paul, Weiss. Among his many clients were not only General Motors and a host of other blue-chip companies but also Jacqueline Kennedy Onassis and US Supreme Court justice William O. Douglas, who sat on the high court from 1939 to 1975. After Douglas retired, he said that Rifkind was "the most outstanding advocate" of all the lawyers who ever appeared before him. Also involved in the UHF's defense, though in a much less important way, were Attorney General Louis J. Lefkowitz, who represented New York State and the State Housing Finance Agency, and David Peck, a former presiding justice of the First Department of the

New York State Supreme Court's Appellate Division and now a partner at Sullivan & Cromwell, another eminent law firm, who represented the Riverbay Corporation.[33]

Forman v. Community Services, Inc. was heard in the US courthouse in Foley Square, which was located in Lower Manhattan, a stone's throw from the New York City Hall and Municipal Building (and about twenty miles from Co-op City). The case was assigned to Judge Lawrence W. Pierce. One of the few African Americans on the federal bench, Pierce had a varied and highly impressive career. Born in Philadelphia in 1924, the son of a research assistant and a piano teacher, he enrolled in St. Joseph's College in 1942, only to leave a year later and enlist in the US Army, in which he served as an infantryman in Italy. After the war he returned to St. Joseph's, graduated in 1948, and then went to Fordham Law School, where he was associate editor of the *Fordham Law Review.* After graduating in 1951, he spent a decade as a staff attorney for the Legal Aid Society and as an assistant district attorney of Kings County. Subsequently, he worked as deputy commissioner of the New York City Police Department, director of the New York State Division for Youth, and chairman of the New York State Narcotics Addiction Control Commission. After spending a year as a visiting professor at the Graduate School of Criminal Justice of the State University of New York at Albany, he was appointed by President Richard M. Nixon to the US District Court for the Southern District of New York in 1971, a position he held until 1981, when President Ronald Reagan appointed him to the US Court of Appeals for the Second Circuit.[34]

In his complaint to the district court, which was amended in late October, Nizer charged that all the defendants except Riverbay had issued or approved two information bulletins that had induced New Yorkers to move to Co-op City by deliberately underestimating construction costs and carrying charges and omitting and misrepresenting other material facts. Nizer also accused CSI and some of the other defendants of breaching their fiduciary responsibilities by building a $27.2 million power plant that was never used to generate electricity and leasing retail space at less than fair market value, which deprived Riverbay of $500,000 a year. The complaint further charged that New York State and the State Housing Finance Agency had violated the federal Civil Rights Act of 1871 and thereby deprived Co-op City's shareholders of due process of law. In view of what he called "a gross fraud," committed "with wanton indifference to legal obligations" and involving "a high degree of moral culpability," Nizer asked the court to reduce

Co-op City's mortgage so that it covered only a sum "properly and lawfully charged" to Riverbay. Until the case was adjudicated, he also urged the court to enjoin Riverbay from collecting carrying charges that were attributable to the amortization, interest, and service fees of any portion of the mortgage above that sum. Moreover, Nizer argued, the court should award damages to the plaintiffs to compensate them for the payment of carrying charges in excess of the amounts spelled out in the information bulletins, for the cost of the $27.2 million spent on the idle power plant, and for the $500,000 a year in lost commercial rental income. The court should also award the plaintiffs punitive damages "in an amount to be determined" and other relief as "may seem just and proper," Nizer added.[35]

A few weeks later Attorney General Lefkowitz filed an answer to the amended complaint on behalf of New York State and the State Housing Finance Agency. Besides denying most of Nizer's charges, he argued that under the Eleventh Amendment to the US Constitution the state and its housing agency were immune from suit in the federal courts. He also insisted that they were not "persons" under the Civil Rights Act of 1871. Among his other affirmative defenses, he pointed out that neither New York State nor the Housing Finance Agency had even issued securities within the meaning of the securities acts of 1933 and 1934. A month and a half later Simon Rifkind asked Judge Pierce to dismiss the amended complaint against the UHF, CSI, and the eight individual defendants on the grounds that shares in the Riverbay Corporation were not stock within the meaning of the federal securities law and therefore that the US District Court had no jurisdiction in the case at hand. He argued that "the thousands of families residing in Co-op City have not made a business investment. Rather these families have purchased a right to reside in the development, to settle in a low-priced apartment free from the deteriorating housing, crime, bad schools and other unfortunate aspects of life in depressed urban neighborhoods." Rifkind also pointed out that shares in a housing cooperative had little in common with stock in a commercial enterprise, stressing that they would never appreciate in value and also that when residents moved out of Co-op City and sold their shares to Riverbay, which they were required to do, they would only receive what they had paid for them.[36]

Two months later Nizer submitted a memorandum in opposition to the defendants' motion to dismiss the amended complaint. Although he did not deny that the State Housing Finance Agency had not issued any stock, he pointed out that it had underwritten the project. "Without the Agency there would never be a Co-op City and there would never be a Riverbay," he wrote. Since its action facilitated the distribution of Riverbay stock, it was liable for damages. Moreover, as a "separate legal entity," the SHFA had no immunity under the Eleventh Amendment, and the State of New York had waived its immunity under the Mitchell-Lama act. Citing "the all-pervasive supervisory role of the Commissioner of Housing and Community Renewal," Nizer argued that New York State was liable for damages as well. Moreover, he pointed out, the Securities and Exchange Commission regarded shares in a cooperative enterprise as securities. And cooperative enterprises were no more exempt from the anti-fraud provisions of the federal securities laws than commercial enterprises. Nizer also claimed that securities should be given "an expansive rather than a restrictive interpretation." And if a profit motive was an essential feature of a security, Riverbay's shares "would more than qualify." The shareholders obtained a very good apartment at a very low price and, if they moved out of Co-op City, could sell their stock for more than the purchase price. Indeed, Nizer said, the shares were not incidental to the occupancy of an apartment. Rather they represented "a style of living different in kind and quality from the ordinary landlord-tenant apartment relationship, which stems from the resident's ownership of his own dwelling."[37]

Although Nizer's memorandum was very powerful, it did not sway Judge Pierce, who handed down his decision in early September 1973. Based on the amended complaint, he acknowledged that "if ever there was a group of people who need and deserve full and careful disclosure in connection with proposals for the use of their funds," it was the plaintiffs, most of whom had limited financial resources and no lawyers or accountants to advise them. But, he went on, "the question before this Court is not whether the plaintiffs *should* be protected," but rather, "whether or not they *are* protected by the federal securities laws." Based on his understanding of the legislative intent of Congress and the rulings of the Supreme Court, he held that they were not. Congress, he wrote, passed the securities acts of 1933 and 1934 to protect investors from the abuses of the financial marketplace, "both for their own well-being and the health of the nation's commercial enterprises." It "did not intend to sweep into the ambit of federal securities laws, state-encouraged, nonprofit transactions made pursuant to a state emergency housing law." A central feature of a security was the expectation of profit, Pierce stressed. But none of the documents involved in the sale of Riverbay stock—not the information bulletins, the subscription agreement, the apartment application, or the occupancy agreement—"ever, once use material, tangible profits as an inducement." Hence Pierce found that Riverbay's shares were not securities within the meaning of the federal securities law. He therefore dismissed Nizer's complaint for lack of jurisdiction—and not, he stressed, on the merits of the plaintiff's case, "which may well deserve to be fully aired [in the New York State courts]."[38]

No sooner had Pierce handed down his decision than Nizer announced that he intended to file an appeal with the US Court of Appeals for the Second Circuit. Early in January 1974 he fired the opening salvo in what a *New York Daily News* reporter wrote was "shaping up as the most publicized court battle with an off-beat theme since Clarence Darrow and William Jennings Bryan clashed in the Scopes 'monkey' trial." In a brief of nearly fifty pages, which was accompanied by hundreds of pages of documents and exhibits, Nizer urged the appellate court to overturn Pierce's ruling that Riverbay shares were not securities under federal law. If Pierce's decision was allowed to stand, he argued, those who speculate for profit are protected while those who have invested their entire savings in the most important purchase of their lives "are left exposed." "To deny these people the protection of the federal securities laws is to fly in the face of justice and of all the authorities." Citing the legislative history of the securities laws and the Supreme Court decisions about them, Nizer called on the appellate court to adopt an "expansive" rather than a "restrictive" view of securities. Taking issue with Pierce, he insisted that the purchasers of Riverbay stock were parties to an "investment contract" from which they had an expectation of profit. Pointing out that the shareholders saved a lot of money by moving into Co-op City, Nizer argued that "in a very real economic sense" the saving of money was profit. So was the residents' ability to deduct a portion of the carrying charges from their income taxes and the opportunity to benefit from the leasing of commercial space for shops and professional offices. Nizer did not deny that residents who moved out of Co-op City were required to sell their shares to Riverbay at the original price. But he contended that this did not mean that they were not securities. And since this restriction was "unenforceable" under the Uniform Commercial Code, the shares could be sold on the open market—and at a substantial profit.[39]

In late February Rifkind submitted a long brief of his own in which he urged the Court of Appeals to uphold the trial court's decision. Echoing Pierce's words, he argued that "the non-profit nature of Riverbay's shares, the non-commercial nature of the development and the rigid statutory controls over the enterprise compel the conclusion that the shares are not 'securities' under federal law." The securities acts of 1933 and 1934, he said, were intended to regulate conduct "in the commercial market," especially stocks traded for "speculation or investment," not shares in housing cooperatives. He pointed out that the plaintiffs not only "ignored the plain language of the statute[s]," but also "substantially misinterpreted the words of the Supreme Court" according to which profit "is an indispensable ingredient of all securities." Rifkind took exception to Nizer's claim that Riverbay shareholders profited from low carrying charges and the rental of commercial and professional space. He also disputed Nizer's argument that the residents of Co-op City could sell their shares on the open market if Riverbay declined to exercise its option to buy them. With 7,000 prospective purchasers on the waiting list and an extremely low turnover rate at Co-op City, it was inconceivable that Riverbay would be unable to find new purchasers for its apartments. Moreover, the corporation had a reserve fund of $1 million to "guard against the remote possibility" that it had trouble finding buyers. In any case, Rifkind pointed out, the Mitchell-Lama act barred the residents of Co-op City (and other housing cooperatives) from reselling their shares at a profit.[40]

On April 4, 1974, more than eighteen months after Nizer filed suit on behalf of Milton Forman and the fifty-six other residents of Co-op City, a panel of three justices, James L. Oakes, Albert S. Christensen, and, as presiding judge, Paul R. Hays, heard oral arguments in the US courthouse in Lower Manhattan. As the appellant, Nizer spoke first. After Judge Oakes reminded him that the issue before the court was whether Riverbay shares were securities under federal law and not whether the defendants had engaged in fraud, Nizer urged the panel to reverse the trial court's decision. Arguing that Pierce's ruling had "fatal errors," he summarized the by-then-familiar arguments that Riverbay shares were securities within the meaning of the 1933 and 1934 acts. Rifkind, who spoke next, called on the panel to uphold Judge Pierce's ruling. Despite repeated questioning from justices Oakes and Christensen, he stuck to his position that Co-op City's residents had purchased their apartments without any expectation of profit and that the UHF's purposes were strictly "eleemosynary." Hence, he concluded, the trial court was correct in holding that shares in Riverbay were not securities and that the federal court did not have jurisdiction in the case at hand. Rounding out the hearing was Daniel Cohen, an assistant attorney general, who urged the court to remove the State of New York and the State Housing

Finance Agency from the suit on much the same grounds that Attorney General Lefkowitz spelled out in his answer to the amended complaint.[41]

In a unanimous decision, which was issued on June 12, the appellate court overruled the trial court. Writing for the panel, Justice Oakes said that the ruling was based on the "literal approach" to securities, according to which "'stock' certificates in a 'stock' corporation is sufficient in itself to bring transactions in the 'stock' within the literal definition of the [federal securities acts]." Following the Supreme Court's landmark decision in *Securities and Exchange Commission v. Howey*, Oakes pointed out that whether shares were securities depended on whether an "investment contract of some sort exists," and especially whether the purchasers had an expectation of profit when they bought the shares. In the case of Co-op City, he held, they did. They shared in the income from the leasing of retail, professional, and parking space. They derived certain tax benefits, notably the right to deduct a pro rata share of the mortgage interest payments from their federal income taxes. And they obtained housing "at an amount substantially below the going rate"—a savings, said Oakes, that was "money in one's pocket." Given that Riverbay's shares were securities, the federal courts had jurisdiction, Oakes held. He also dismissed Cohen's motion to sever the State of New York and the State Housing Finance Agency from the suit. The state had waived sovereign immunity by enacting the Mitchell-Lama act and by "voluntarily entering into a field under federal regulation." The agency, which was not an "alter ego" of the state, had no immunity either. And agencies such as the SHFA have always been deemed "persons" under the Civil Rights Act of 1871. Without expressing an opinion about the merits of the appellants' claims, the circuit court remanded the case to the district court.[42]

ooo

The Court of Appeals decision was "a major victory" for Nizer and the residents of Co-op City, wrote the *City News*, a victory that showed the wisdom of Nizer's decision to fight the increase in carrying charges by filing suit in federal court. It did not mean that these charges would be reduced, or even that the UHF, the State of New York, and the other defendants would be found "guilty of wrongdoing." What it meant, said the *City News*, was that Co-op City's residents would have their "DAY IN COURT," where the merits of their case would at long last be adjudicated. This feeling of optimism was premature. By late July it was evident that the UHF, New York State, and the other defendants were going to file an appeal with the US Supreme

Court. In early August—at the request of Simon Rifkind and over the objections of George Berger, one of Nizer's associates—the Court of Appeals
granted a stay of its order remanding the case to the district court. Since the
high court would not convene until September—and would probably need a
few months to decide whether to take the appeal—the stay would probably
remain in effect until early 1975 or even longer if the high court decided to
hear the case. Shortly after the Court of Appeals denied a motion asking the
full court to review the decision of the three-judge panel, Rifkind petitioned
the Supreme Court for a writ of certiorari. In a separate brief—and on different grounds—so did Daniel Cohen. And George Berger filed a brief in opposition to both petitions.[43]

Given that the Supreme Court granted certiorari in only about one out
of twenty-five cases for which it received petitions, Rifkind and Cohen had
their work cut out for them. They had to persuade at least four of the nine
justices not only that the Court of Appeals decision might well be erroneous,
but also that it would have dire consequences, legal and otherwise. Hence in
addition to arguing that shares in Riverbay were not securities under federal law, Rifkind insisted that if allowed to stand the Court of Appeals decision would undermine the effort to build state-subsidized and -regulated
nonprofit cooperative housing, which would exacerbate the nation's housing
problem. It would stifle the construction of other cooperatives and condo-
miniums too. Rifkind also claimed that the "literal" approach to securities
adopted by the Court of Appeals was at odds with the intent of Congress
and in conflict with the rulings of other appellate courts. Lastly, its decision undermined "the long-established definition of 'investment contract'"
and ignored the guidelines of the Securities and Exchange Commission. For
his part Cohen seconded Rifkind's position. He also argued that if the justices held that the state's regulation of the development and financing of
Co-op City was "the subject of litigation" in federal court, the calendars of
the district court judges would be clogged for years. If the states could be
sued in cases of alleged stock fraud, they would be faced "with huge contingent liabilities or the option of abandoning securities regulation." "Neither result," Cohen argued, "was intended by the Congress or the Eleventh
Amendment."[44]

In his brief Berger urged the Supreme Court to deny certiorari on the
grounds that the case was "not yet ripe for review." Pointing out that the
Court of Appeals had merely upheld the jurisdiction of the federal courts,
expressed no opinion on the merits of the complaint, and remanded the

case to the district court "for further proceedings," he argued that the decision was not "final" but "interlocutory" (or, in lay terms, provisional) and
that it was highly unusual for the high court to review an "interlocutory"
decision. In response to Rifkind's petition, he added that there was no conflict among the circuit courts that required the Supreme Court to take such
an extraordinary step. Berger also said that the Court of Appeals decision
was in accord with prior high court decisions about how the securities laws
should be construed, how stock (or shares) should be interpreted, and how
an "investment contract" should be defined. It was also consistent with the
rules and regulations of the SEC. The decision, he concluded, informed real
estate developers and state agencies that they should make "complete and
truthful disclosures" to prospective purchasers. If that has a profound impact on the real estate industry, "it is long overdue." In response to Cohen's
petition, Berger argued that the New York State Housing Finance Agency
had no claim to immunity on the basis of the Eleventh Amendment. "To the
extent that the defense may be applicable to the State, it has been waived,"
he added. Finally, the legislative history of the 1934 federal securities act
revealed that Congress considered the state a "person" under the statute.[45]

Over Berger's objections, the Supreme Court granted certiorari on January 20, 1975, probably, in the words of Justice Lewis F. Powell Jr., because
of "the importance of the issues." It was expected that the court would hear
arguments in the spring and issue a ruling by midsummer. The decision to
grant certiorari set off a flurry of activity in March and April. Rifkind submitted a brief and a reply brief. So did Lefkowitz. Nizer filed a brief of his
own. Two amicus curiae briefs were submitted as well, one from the State
of Ohio, in which Attorney General William J. Brown urged the high court
to reverse the Court of Appeals decision, and another from the Securities
and Exchange Commission, in which Solicitor General Robert H. Bork asked
the high court to affirm the appellate court's ruling. Once the briefs were
filed, the court heard oral arguments on April 22. Appearing for the petitioners were Rifkind and Cohen. Appearing for the respondents was Nizer,
whose position was supported by Paul Gonson, associate general counsel of
the SEC. Although the arguments were compelling, they added little to the
briefs, which were long, learned, and full of historical references and legal
citations. When all was said and done, the only issue before the high court
was the same one on which the district court had ruled one way and the appellate court another. As Powell put it, it was "whether shares of stock enti-
tling a purchaser to lease an apartment in Co-op City, a state subsidized and

supervised housing cooperative[,] are 'securities' within the purview of the Securities Act of 1933 and the Securities Exchange Act of 1934."[46]

By a vote of six to three the Supreme Court held that they were not. And on June 16 it overruled the Court of Appeals. Writing for the majority, Justice Powell rejected the notion that Riverbay shares were securities because they were called stock. After saying that the federal securities laws were enacted "to eliminate abuses in a largely unregulated securities market," he held that Riverbay's shares have none of the characteristics that "in our commercial world fall within the ordinary concept of a security." They do not pay dividends. They are not negotiable. They cannot be pledged or hypothecated. And among other things, they cannot appreciate in value. "In the present case," Powell claimed, "there can be no doubt that investors were attracted solely by the prospect of acquiring a place to live, and not by financial returns on their investment." Despite the Court of Appeals ruling, he contended that the residents' ability to deduct part of their carrying charges from their income taxes was not a form of profit. Nor was it a form of profit that the residents obtained an apartment at well below the going rate. And the residents were not attracted to Co-op City by the prospect of sharing in the proceeds from the rental of commercial, professional, and parking space. "What distinguishes a security transaction—and what is absent here—" Powell went on, "is an investment where one parts with his money in the hope of receiving profits from the efforts of others, and not where he purchases a commodity for personal consumption or living quarters for personal use." Much like Judge Pierce, who, he said, "properly dismissed" the complaint, Powell stressed that the decision was based solely on the question of federal jurisdiction, not on the merits of the respondents' allegations.[47]

A little over a month after the Supreme Court handed down its decision, Nizer addressed a large crowd at the Community Center auditorium. He came to Co-op City, he said, because he was afraid that the residents might be demoralized, which was understandable. He acknowledged that he too was disappointed, not only by the court's decision, but also by how long it took to reach it. "It's a tragedy that we've lost these two years or more." But he was also optimistic. The Supreme Court, he pointed out, had not ruled on the merits of the case, only on the issue of jurisdiction. In addition to filing an application for a rehearing, which was very much a long shot, he was also going to file suit in state court. "If we cannot get relief in the Federal Court," he declared, "we will get it in the State Court." Did the other side lose heart when the Court of Appeals reversed Judge Pierce's decision? he asked. "They did not, and don't you lose heart now." Pointing out that he had tried cases in forty states, where he faced "all kinds of difficult situations," he insisted that when you know you are right, "no matter what the technicalities are," you will win. All it took was "persistence and determination." Pledging the full support and resources of his law firm, Nizer concluded by saying that "we feel that you have been done a great wrong" and that "we are going to continue [the struggle in] another jurisdiction." And "if you will just stand firm, we will stand firm, and we will have a celebration together."[48]

CHAPTER 9

"NO WAY, WE WON'T PAY"

From the outset most residents of Co-op City had great faith in Nizer. By March 1974, less than two and a half years after the Advisory Council retained him, they had raised $149,000 to cover the estimated $150,000 in legal expenses. But even after the Court of Appeals reversed Judge Pierce, many residents began to lose confidence that the increases in carrying charges could be stopped by litigation. In an attempt to persuade the state legislature to subsidize Co-op City's interest payments and take other steps to reduce the project's expenses, many residents wrote letters, signed petitions, and participated in rallies and demonstrations, both in Albany and New York City. The results were disappointing. By May 1974, when it seemed likely that the Riverbay Corporation intended to raise the carrying charges again after the 12.5 percent increase went into effect in July, the *City News* reported that there was "an undercurrent of pessimism and militancy on the part of some community leaders." At a meeting of the Building 29 Association, which was attended by 200 residents, chairman Larry Stovall said that they should consider going on a "rent strike" rather than pay any additional carrying charges. Al Abrams, chairman of the Advisory Council and a guest at the meeting, agreed. The council was exploring "the possibility of taking some drastic measures to dramatize the fiscal plight of Co-op City," he told the crowd. One was to install a chain on the New England Thruway. Another was to refuse to pay any increased carrying charges. "Maybe the time has come to open up our mouths and ... yell we're not going to pay."[1] A year later, more than a month before the Supreme Court overruled the Court of Appeals, the longest and largest rent strike in US history got underway at Co-op City.

Rent strikes had a long history in New York City, an even longer history than nonprofit cooperative housing. Starting in 1904 and continuing on and off until 1907, hundreds of tenants on the Lower East Side and in Browns- ville and other working-class immigrant neighborhoods went on strike to force the landlords to rescind rent hikes of 20 to 30 percent. Another and much more widespread round of rent strikes involving thousands of tenants and hundreds of buildings in Manhattan, Brooklyn, and the Bronx broke out shortly after World War I, when many landlords took advantage of the standstill in residential construction and the sharp decline in vacancy rates and raised rents as often as a few times a year. Thanks to the passage of the Emergency Rent Laws of 1920, by which the state legislature imposed rent control in New York and other big cities, there were very few rent strikes in the 1920s. But during the 1930s a good many tenants went on strike in Harlem and other working-class neighborhoods, not because their landlords were raising the rents, but because as a result of the Great Depression they could not pay even reasonable rents. Rent strikes were few and far between after World War II broke out and rent control, which had expired in New York City in 1929, was reimposed as a wartime measure. But during the early and mid-1960s many residents in Harlem and other African-American neighborhoods withheld their rent to protest the egregious conditions in their apartments and the landlords' refusal to do anything about them. Some middle-class tenants also withheld their rent in the 1960s and 1970s in an effort to force their landlords to make repairs.[2]

There is no evidence that many (or indeed any) residents of Co-op City had participated in a rent strike before moving there. But there is scattered evidence that as early as the late 1960s and early 1970s some residents were prepared to consider withholding their monthly carrying charges for one reason or another. In June 1969, as I mentioned earlier, Harriet Colodney threatened to organize a rent strike if Riverbay, which had turned off the air- conditioning during a heat wave, did not turn it back on. A year and a half later Leonard Hanks, who had succeeded Colodney as head of the Tenants Council and later filed a suit against Charles J. Urstadt to annul the 15.1 per- cent increase in carrying charges, urged all residents to withhold their pay- ments until Judge Jacob B. Grumet issued his ruling—and, if he did not issue it shortly, to pay the carrying charges without the 15.1 percent increase. And in January 1972 Milton Forman, the lead plaintiff in Louis Nizer's suit against the United Housing Foundation and the State Division of Housing, declared, "Should justice fail us, we can always have a rent strike." As I also pointed out earlier, Irwin and Dana Wolfe began to withhold their carrying charges in November 1971 in an effort to force Riverbay to repair the cracked walls in their apartment, which, they claimed, was virtually uninhabitable. They continued to withhold their monthly payments even after Riverbay instituted foreclosure proceedings.[3]

Other than the Wolfes, few if any residents of Co-op City withheld their carrying charges in the late 1960s and early 1970s. And nothing came of the occasional threats of a rent strike. To understand why, it is helpful to keep in mind that the residents of Co-op City were not typical tenants. Indeed, they were not tenants at all. They did not lease their apartments. They owned them. Hence a strike against Co-op City would be a "strike against your-self," said George Schecter, a resident of Co-op City and vice president of the Riverbay Corporation. Nor was the UHF a typical landlord. Rather it was a quasi-philanthropic nonprofit organization whose objective was to build the best possible working-class housing at the lowest possible cost. A rent strike was also very daunting for the residents of Co-op City—much more daunting than it had been for the New Yorkers who took part in previous rent strikes, which pitted tenants against landlords (and the city marshals and schlep-pers who carried out the evictions). As Jack Newfield and Paul Du Brul, two astute observers of New York City politics, wrote, a rent strike at Co-op City would pit "an unlikely group of revolutionaries," most of whom were ordinary working-class New Yorkers, against a formidable group of institutions: the UHF (and, in the words of journalist Richard Karp, "the assembled sachems of New York's labor unions"); the State of New York, which held Co-op City's mortgage; the City of New York, which levied its property taxes; the judicial system, which handled foreclosure proceedings; the financial institutions that served as trustees for the bondholders; and "a generally hostile media."[4]

Moreover, a rent strike was much more risky for the residents of Co-op City than it was for the New Yorkers who took part in previous rent strikes. In those strikes it was customary for the landlords to bring summary pro-ceedings against the tenants. If the courts authorized the marshals to oust the striking tenants, they would lose their homes and, until they found an-other apartment, move in with neighbors or live on the streets. (Unless the schleppers exercised due care, their belongings would often be severely damaged too.) But in the case of Co-op City (and other nonprofit housing cooperatives), a spokesman for the State Division of Housing pointed out, "Should the cooperators['] refusal to pay increased rentals mean that [the Riverbay Corporation] will not have sufficient funds to meet its debt service

obligations, the state will have no choice but to institute foreclosure proceedings." (Indeed, if Riverbay did not have the funds to pay its property
taxes, the city might also start foreclosure proceedings, which is what it
did when some residents in the Big Six Towers and thirteen other nonprofit
housing cooperatives withheld their carrying charges in 1968.) Unless the
tenants called off the strike, the court would appoint a receiver to manage
Co-op City or the state would take it over. In either case, the striking tenants would lose not only their homes but also their equity, the $450 a room
they had paid for their apartments, which for many was their most valuable
asset. And as Harold Ostroff warned, Co-op City would become a rental, not
a co-op, and its residents would become tenants, not owners.[5]

To understand how hard it would be to carry out a successful rent strike
in a nonprofit housing cooperative, the residents of Co-op City had only to
look at the recent history of Rochdale Village, the UHF project that had been
completed in 1965. Much like Co-op City, Rochdale Village developed a severe fiscal crisis, one that "grows worse with each passing day," said its board
of directors in June 1971. Although the residents had ousted the UHF directors and elected a board of their own, Rochdale Village's carrying charges
soared in the late 1960s and early 1970s. When they were raised in June
1974 from $31.46 to $37.41 a room as of July 1, 1974, and to $41.47 a room
effective January 1, 1975, the United Shareholders of Rochdale Village, an
offshoot of the Rochdale Village Tenants Council, launched a rent-increase
strike. About 10 percent of the cooperators took part. Declaring "rent yes;
increase no," the striking tenants withheld the additional carrying charges
from their monthly checks. The UHF brought summary proceedings against
the striking tenants. And Maurice Harbater, a Queens housing court judge,
issued a final order against them. In an attempt to block the increase in
carrying charges and stop the eviction of hundreds of residents, the United
Shareholders filed suit in the state supreme court, a suit that dragged on for
several months. Judge Daniel F. Fitzpatrick issued a temporary stay of Harbater's order, but Judge James F. Crisona lifted it. Judge Alfred Lerner then
ruled in favor of the United Shareholders on the grounds that the residents
had been denied due process. But in early December the Appellate Division
overruled him. Even before the Court of Appeals upheld the Appellate Division six months later, the Rochdale Village rent strike fizzled out, a result in
large part of the residents' fear of eviction.[6]

000

In January 1974, about six months before the Rochdale Village rent strike got underway, the *City News* reported that Co-op City was also in dire financial straits. According to Larry Dolnick, a member of the Riverbay Corporation Board of Directors and the chairman of its Operations, Budget, and Management Committee (OBMC), which was responsible for preparing the budget for the fiscal year that started on April 1, Co-op City was facing a deficit of more than $5 million (or about $325 per household). The deficit, Dolnick explained, was largely a result of the cost of oil, which had doubled; of electricity, which had skyrocketed (and would increase an additional $1 million a year if the Public Service Commission approved Con Edison's proposed rate hike); and of labor, which had gone up $300,000 a year because of the new contract with Local 32-E of the Service Employees International Union. During the next month and a half things went from bad to worse. Based on new projections of the cost of utilities, the OBMC informed the Riverbay board that it now estimated that the deficit would be roughly $10 million. As if that was not bad enough, the State Division of Housing, which had the final say over Co-op City's budget, advised Riverbay that the OBMC's projection of the cost of utilities, which were based on the estimates of General Manager Edward Aronov and came to $7.1 million, was too low. A "more realistic figure," in the words of the *City News*, would be $12 million. Indeed, Co-op City's electric bill alone would come to $6.5 million and not, as Aronov estimated, $3.25 million. Although it turned out that Riverbay had overpaid New York City $2 million in property taxes and that another $2 million was available from surplus construction funds, the final budget, which was approved by the board in late May, still included a projected deficit of just over $10 million.[7]

The news about Co-op City's budgetary problems took most residents by surprise. Only a year earlier—or a couple of months after the carrying charges had been raised 20 percent—the OBMC, which was then chaired by Arthur Oshins, had informed the Riverbay Board of Directors that Co-op City was in sound financial condition. Management, it said, had submitted what it regarded as a very tight budget for fiscal 1974. And by virtue of cutbacks in administrative expenses and insurance costs, the OBMC had reduced the proposed budget by 10 percent. Given that more than five-sixths of Co-op City's $41.7 million budget was earmarked for interest payments, property taxes, and other expenses beyond the control of the Riverbay board, this was no mean feat, the OBMC pointed out. Despite these savings, it conceded that there would be a budgetary deficit in fiscal 1974, though it did not say how large the deficit would be. The OBMC assured the board that thanks to the substantial reductions in operating expenses and the projected 12.5 percent increase in carrying charges, which was scheduled to go into effect on July 1, 1974, it would be possible for management to cover the deficit in fiscal 1974—and indeed even in fiscal 1975 and at least part of fiscal 1976—without imposing additional increases in carrying charges or making severe reductions in basic services. To keep Co-op City in sound financial shape in the years to come, the OBMC acknowledged it would be necessary to find ways to increase revenues, keep operating expenses under strict control, and prevail on the state legislature to take steps to reduce its mortgage payments and property taxes. But for the time being the residents had little to worry about.[8]

As well as a surprise, the news about Co-op City's budgetary problems came as a shock to most residents, who were concerned that the deficit would lead to yet another increase in carrying charges. As Dolnick remarked in January, the Riverbay board had forestalled an increase in 1973 by tapping into certain escrow and reserve funds that were mandated by the state. But these funds would not be available in 1974, he warned. In March Lawrence Sivak, another member of the OBMC, pointed out that the then-projected deficit might be reduced by $3 million to $5 million if Riverbay could dip into capital funds that were thought to have been depleted and by millions more if the state legislature enacted laws that eliminated Co-op City's sales and franchise taxes. But that would still leave a sizable deficit. Riverbay's directors estimated that for each $1 million deficit the carrying charges would have to be raised $1.14 per room per month. After the 12.5 percent increase went into effect on July 1, the carrying charges would go up from $37.11 to $41.81. If the deficit was $5 million, they would increase to $48.51, which was 78 percent higher than in 1969. Writing in late March, the *City News* insisted that it was time for the residents of Co-op City to "recognize the inevitable." In addition to the impending 12.5 percent increase, the carrying charges would soon go up anywhere from 10 to 30 percent. The state legislature might provide relief, especially if the community let Albany know "how badly we need help," but, the *City News* went on, "nobody should lull residents into a false sense that nothing is going to happen. It will, and rents will go up."[9]

As the *City News* reported, the prospect of another increase in carrying charges was expected to spur a legislative drive that was already underway. Sponsored by the Joint Legislative Steering Committee—also known as Steering Committee II, which consisted of representatives of the Advisory Council, Co-op City's political clubs, many of its voluntary associations, and some of Riverbay's board members—the drive was designed to persuade the state legislature (and Governor Malcolm Wilson) to provide financial relief to Co-op City and other Mitchell-Lama projects. As I mentioned earlier, the drive culminated in April 1974, when 2,500 residents of Co-op City and more than 4,000 residents of other Mitchell-Lama projects took part in a massive bus caravan to Albany to lobby for what they called a nine-point program to save middle-income housing in New York City. Before it adjourned in late May, the legislature enacted six laws that would reduce Co-op City's deficit by $1 million. But it shelved the mortgage-interest subsidy bill—the one bill, wrote the *City News*, that "could have wiped out Co-op City's entire deficit." As a result the Riverbay board was left with little choice but to increase the carrying charges by about $7 per room per month. Frustrated by the legislature's inaction, some residents started talking about refusing to pay the increase by, in effect, going on a partial rent strike. But in late May Riverbay's five resident directors—Dolnick, Sivak, Arthur Taub, Richard Ferguson, and Arthur Cohen—urged Co-op City's residents to hold off while they tried to find a way to head off an increase in carrying charges that would be supported by the community, if not necessarily by the ten non-resident members of the board.[10]

Two weeks later the resident directors told a group of community leaders that they had found a way to head off an increase. It was spelled out in a six-page proposal that they would submit to the full Riverbay board at its regularly scheduled quarterly meeting in mid-June. Under the proposal, Riverbay would withhold up to $16.3 million of the $52.6 million it owed the State Housing Finance Agency for the interest and amortization of its mortgage over the next two years—$4.7 million in equal monthly installments in fiscal 1975 and $11.6 million, also in equal monthly installments, in fiscal 1976. In defense of this proposal, the resident directors pointed out that in order to pay its bills and remain solvent until March 1976, Riverbay would have to raise carrying charges on July 1, 1974, by $10.62 per room per month, in addition to the $4.75 per room that had already been approved, an increase of 40.4 percent. This "unconscionable" increase would force many families to spend more than one-quarter of their income on housing, said Lawrence Sivak. (If Riverbay raised the charges on October 1, 1974, the increase would be 45.1 percent.) Although the proposal was radical, the repercussions would not be too drastic, Arthur Taub claimed. The city-sponsored Mitchell-Lama projects were $18 million in arrears, and though their boards of directors had refused to comply with the Housing and Development Administration's orders to raise carrying charges, "so far nothing has happened." The resident directors stressed that their proposal was a "holding" action, one that would enable Riverbay to pay its bills until the state legislature took steps to solve Co-op City's financial problems. It would therefore put the burden for solving these problems "where it should be, with the State of New York."[11]

Harold Ostroff lost no time in attacking the resident directors and their proposal. Writing in the *Co-op City Times*, he took them to task for failing to consult with Co-op City's manager, seek advice from its lawyers, and consult with Riverbay's non-resident directors and New York State's housing officials. This failure led them to exaggerate the size of the deficit and the increase in carrying charges needed to cover it. Even worse, Ostroff pointed out, the resident directors refused "to face the hard decisions that must be made from time to time to protect Co-op City." They misled the residents into thinking that "somehow someone else will produce a miracle and inflation will go away" and that "if the Board does not vote an increase, an increase can be avoided," which was "simply not true." The proposal would also do "irreparable harm" to Co-op City and its residents, and not only because it would alienate the elected officials on whom Co-op City and other Mitchell-Lama cooperatives were counting for financial aid. Under the law the State Division of Housing was required to safeguard the millions of dollars invested by thousands of bondholders "who, in good faith, lent the money to make the development possible." If Riverbay withheld all or even part of its mortgage payments, the state would have no choice but to take over Co-op City, a step that would probably turn it into a rental, increase the residents' costs, and wipe out their equity. A state agency would also manage the project with less "compassion and understanding" than the Riverbay Corporation. "It would be easy to pass the buck to the State," Ostroff concluded, "but it will be the Co-op City resident who will pay the bill."[12]

In an attempt to generate support for their proposal, the resident directors urged Co-op City's residents to write, phone, or send telegrams to the ten non-resident directors, all but one of whom was appointed by the UHF. (As I pointed out earlier, the tenth was selected by the State Division of Housing.) The newly formed Co-op City Coalition, a coalition of building associations and civic groups, went even further. In "An Open Public Statement to the Board of Directors of Co-op City," it warned that if Riverbay refused to adopt the resident directors' proposal, it would lead a boycott of several organizations that were closely affiliated with the UHF. It would call on residents to withdraw their savings from the two Co-op City branches of the Amalgamated Bank, of which Jacob S. Potofsky, a member of the Riverbay board, was chairman; urge residents to cancel, surrender, or return all unused portions of premiums from the Urban Insurance Company, an "arm," wrote the *City News*, of the UHF; and withdraw their shares from the Riverbay Consumers Cooperative Society, a step that would affect the UHF-sponsored Federation of Cooperatives, which acted as manager and purchaser for Co-op City's three supermarkets. Ben Cirlin, chairman of the Building 19 Association and one of the leaders of the proposed boycott, said that the Riverbay board "hasn't seen anything yet." But other community leaders felt that the coalition had gone too far. If the residents withdrew their shares from the Riverbay Consumers Cooperative Society, they believed, Co-op City's three supermarkets might have to declare bankruptcy, a move that would have an adverse impact on Co-op City's financial stability.[13]

The showdown took place on June 19 at the UHF's headquarters on Grand Street in the Lower East Side. In what the *City News* called "an orderly but spirited" rally in favor of the resident directors' proposal that was organized by the Co-op City Coalition, 400 Co-op City residents chanted, "No way, we won't pay." Thousands of other residents signed petitions urging the Riverbay board to adopt the proposal. But Ostroff was not swayed by the rally or the petitions. In his presidential report—and without prior notification to the resident directors—he made a proposal of his own. Rather than adopt the resident directors' proposal or increase the monthly carrying charges, he called on the board to set up a special finance committee whose five members would review Co-op City's fiscal condition, meet with state housing officials, study all possible alternatives, and report back in early September. The resident directors moved that Ostroff's proposal be tabled on the grounds that it had not been included in the agenda. But the non-resident directors voted down their motion. The resident directors then argued against Ostroff's proposal, which they decried as "no more than a plan to circumvent the intent of our [proposal]," and in favor of their own proposal, which they insisted was aimed at the State of New York, not the UHF. But the non-resident directors countered that the board had not yet explored all the options and that until it did they could not support the resident directors' proposal. The meeting dragged on for three hours. In the end the board voted ten to five to adopt Ostroff's proposal and, without taking a vote, to refer the resident directors' proposal to the special finance committee.[14]

On the day before the Riverbay board tabled the resident directors' proposal, the Advisory Council, which had supported the resident directors' proposal but opposed the Co-op City Coalition's proposed boycott, announced that if need be it would support a rent increase strike. In a resolution, which was passed unanimously, the council declared that it had "reached the end of the road." In an attempt to solve Co-op City's financial problems, it had "tried all legal means." It had appealed to the state legislature. It had also filed suit in state and federal court. But thus far, the resolution went on, "all our efforts have met with limited success." The Advisory Council therefore had no alternative but to inform Riverbay and the state that "any further increase beyond the projected [12.5] percent due to start July 1, 1974 will not be paid by this community." Left unsaid in the resolution was who (or what) would lead the fight against any further increase. Besides the Advisory Council, Co-op City had a great many political, civic, fraternal, and other voluntary associations, but none of them was devoted exclusively to Co-op City's financial problems. Hence on July 9 a group of community leaders formed a committee, which would be known as Steering Committee III, whose sole purpose was to lead the fight against any increase in carrying charges. The committee consisted of twelve members—three resident directors and three representatives each from the Advisory Council, senior citizens clubs, and Co-op City Coalition. Al Abrams, head of the Advisory Council, was the committee's chairman, and Larry Dolnick, one of the resident directors, was its vice chairman.[15]

Any hopes that the Steering Committee, the Riverbay Corporation, and the State of New York would reach a consensus about Co-op City's financial problems were soon dashed. At a meeting held in mid-August at the State Division of Housing's offices in Manhattan—which, said one observer, was "a lesson in futility"—Ostroff recommended that Riverbay meet its deficit by putting off paying some of its bills and withdrawing $800,000 from funds that had been set aside for reserves and contingencies. But this recommendation was opposed by Sivak and Dolnick, two members of the Steering Committee, on the grounds that it would bring Co-op City to the "brink" of financial disaster, a view that was shared by the *City News*. Also opposed to Ostroff's proposal was Commissioner Lee B. Goodwin, the former assistant director of the State Housing Finance Agency, who had been appointed to replace Charles J. Urstadt when he resigned in March 1973 to join a group of investors who had recently acquired a majority interest in Douglas Elliman, a major New York real estate firm. Ostroff's proposal would stretch Co-op City finances too thin, she argued. Goodwin also opposed the proposal to with-hold part of Co-op City's mortgage payments, a proposal that was supported by Steering Committee III. The state had an obligation to the bondholders, she insisted; no matter how much she sympathized with the plight of Co-op City' residents, she would not shirk her responsibility. If Riverbay withheld its mortgage payments, she warned, the trustees for the bondholders would bring foreclosure proceedings and the Division of Housing would take over Co-op City. Riverbay had no choice but to raise the carrying charges before the end of the year (and, if possible, at its quarterly meeting in September) and to raise them enough not only to cover Co-op City's current deficit but also to ensure its long-term solvency.[16]

In the face of Ostroff's and Goodwin's opposition to the resident direc-tors' proposal to withhold part of Co-op City's mortgage payments, Steering Committee III focused its efforts on what it called a "rent collection drive." Planning for the drive—an idea that was first broached at a meeting of the Building 9 Association and referred to the Steering Committee by Lawrence Sivak—got underway in late July (and before long was backed by Assembly-man Alan Hochberg, City Councilman Stephen Kaufman, and many other elected officials). Under the plan the residents would make out checks for their carrying charges to the Riverbay Corporation, which was what they normally did, but instead of giving (or mailing) them to management, they would hand them over to other residents, who, under the supervision of area marshals and building captains, would man rent collection stations in the lobby of each apartment house. The stations would be open from 7:00 p.m. to 9:00 p.m. from September 3 to September 9. The residents, all of whom were volunteers, would then turn the checks over to the Steering Commit-tee, which would deliver them to management on September 10, in time to avoid a late fee. As Al Abrams stressed, the rent collection drive was not a rent strike, which would have been premature. Rather it was a way "to stifle all attempts to increase carrying charges." In defense of the drive, Gil Nar-rins, president of the Co-op City Coalition and a member of Steering Com-mittee III, declared, "We have played by the rules—we went to Albany, we met with management, we were gentlemen and ladies—and still we face in-creased rents. Management has got to understand that we are not fooling around."[17]

At the outset Steering Committee III's members expected that at least 9,223 (or more than 60 percent) of Co-op City's 15,372 families would partici-pate in the rent collection drive. But once the drive got underway they became even more optimistic. In the end the turnout far exceeded expectations: 12,947 (or almost 85 percent) of the cooperators handed their checks over to the Steering Committee's representatives. (Given that some apartments were vacant, some residents had paid their September carrying charges in advance, and some residents were too old or too infirm to participate in the rent collection drive, the Steering Committee claimed that the turnout was more like 95 percent.) On September 10, which Larry Dolnick called "a day to remember," a group of Co-op City residents, watched by reporters and cameramen from the *Times*, *Post*, and *Daily News*, wheeled ten shopping carts filled with plastic bags that contained envelopes with close to $3 million in checks into Edward Aronov's office. Aronov said that he "was pleased to accept them," though he might have been taken aback when Abrams told him, "I am not sure if you will ever see this kind of money again if the deficit goes higher and our rents go up." Calling the drive "a major success," the *City News* wrote, "The people of Co-op City have sent a message loud and clear—to the state Government in Albany, the Housing Commissioner's office at 2 World Trade Center, and United Housing Foundation's headquarters at 465 Grand Street—that they are prepared to fight any future rent increases with the unity and strength that can be ignored only at their peril."[18]

ooo

As Al Abrams pointed out, the September rent collection drive was "just the beginning of a very long struggle," one that would pit Co-op City's residents against the UHF and the State of New York. But before long he found out that Co-op City's residents were also in a struggle with one another. The origins of this struggle went back to early December, when the United Democratic Club of Co-op City (UDC)—which represented the community's regular Democrats, as opposed to its reform Democrats, who belonged to the Independent Democrats of Co-op City—asked for a vote on Steering Committee III. The committee turned down the request on the grounds that it was a nonpolitical and nonpartisan body. It was willing to invite Co-op City's two Democratic clubs, two Republican clubs, a conservative club, and a liberal club to participate in Steering Committee affairs, but only as nonvoting members. This slight offended Marc Goodman, a member of both the UDC Executive Committee and the Advisory Council, which was the cornerstone of the Steering Committee. At an emergency meeting of the Advisory Council that was held in late January 1975, attended by 65 of its 113 members, and closed to the public, he moved that the council sever ties with the Steering

Committee. With most of the members present sharing his belief that the Advisory Council should assume "its rightful role" as the only duly elected body that represented all of Co-op City's residents and therefore that the council and not the Steering Committee should "lead the community in its efforts to seek an equitable solution to Co-op City's financial plight," Goodman's motion was adopted by a margin of three to one.[19]

The Advisory Council's decision infuriated the Steering Committee, whose leaders denounced the UDC and what it called "the UHF pawns," the "frightened little people" who voted in favor of Goodman's attempt to undermine the unity of the residents, which, said Lawrence Sivak, was absolutely essential "at a time when Co-op City is literally running out of dough." The Steering Committee insisted that it was in no way usurping the function of the Advisory Council. And though it acknowledged that the Advisory Council's decision would hamper its efforts to prevent an increase in carrying charges, it vowed to "fight alone" if need be. The Advisory Council's decision also troubled many of its members. At the urging of Assemblyman Alan Hochberg and the *City News*, which called on the council to reconsider the decision, one-third of them signed a petition asking the council's Executive Committee to hold another meeting. At this meeting, which was attended by 1,000 residents, Goodman introduced a resolution to rescind his previous resolution. Another council member, Al Afterman, introduced a resolution that called on the Advisory Council and the Steering Committee to work together in the interest of "rent stabilization." Both resolutions were adopted by a near-unanimous vote. An amendment to Goodman's resolution that would have required that all Steering Committee decisions be approved by the Advisory Council was ruled out of order. To the dismay of a few Advisory Council members like Morris Schweiger, who declared that the council's action was "a complete sellout" to "a group of self-appointed leaders who are unanswerable to anyone but themselves," the controversy left Steering Committee III stronger than ever.[20]

The controversy also led to a change in the leadership of the Steering Committee. Two weeks before the Advisory Council voted to sever its ties with the committee, Al Abrams, chairman of the council, resigned as chairman of the committee. He explained that when he took the job he was aware that there would be difficulties, but he had hoped that they could be overcome. But as time passed the conflict between the Advisory Council and the Steering Committee got worse. What started as a dream ended up as a nightmare, and he found it untenable to lead both organizations. Since he felt he owed "any leadership role in this community" to the Advisory Council, he had no choice but to resign as chairman of the Steering Committee, a move, he hoped, that would "help to heal the wounds that have festered for many months." After canvassing the members of the Steering Committee, the Executive Committee, which consisted of Larry Dolnick, Charles Parness, and two others, selected Charles Rosen, who it turned out was much more militant than Al Abrams, as the new chairman. As I pointed out earlier, Rosen and his wife had moved to Co-op City from a run-down neighborhood on the Upper West Side not because they had a strong interest in cooperative housing, but because they wanted to live "in a safe, clean[, inexpensive,] and integrated community." And they had no intention of staying for more than a couple of years. But after a while, and almost inadvertently, Rosen got involved in community affairs, first as chairman of the Building 22 Association, then as vice chairman of the Co-op City Coalition, and eventually as a member (though not one of the original members) of the Steering Committee. He was chosen its new chairman not only because most of the other committee members did not want the job, but also, he later recalled, because he was a hard worker who had been very helpful to Al Abrams and because he was not affiliated with any of Co-op City's warring political organizations.[21]

Then in his early thirties, Rosen was a "red-diaper baby." His father, who migrated from Poland and worked in the needle trades, was a former anarchist. His mother, who came from what is now the Ukraine and also worked in the needle trades, was a Socialist and later a Stalinist. Charlie, as he was better known, was a Marxist (and onetime member of the Progressive Labor Party), but as Larry Dolnick remarked, he was not someone who tried to impose his political ideology on others. Although Rosen, a linotype operator for the *New York Post*, was a member of Local 6 of the International Typographical Union, he had nothing but disdain for the leaders of New York's quasi-Socialist labor unions, which were the backbone of the UHF. He also had a deep-seated antipathy for New York City's banks and Co-op City's bondholders. Rosen was outspoken, tireless, charismatic, and, said Eliot Engel, a leader of the United Democratic Club, "very bright." Indeed, observed Ben Cirlin, Rosen was "just in a different league than the rest of us." Rosen had his detractors, one of whom lambasted him for insulting the state legislators on whom Co-op City was counting for financial aid and pointed out that at a recent meeting with them "his rantings and ravings left everyone embarrassed." But his detractors were far outnumbered by his supporters.

Saying that the Steering Committee's members had much in common with the founding fathers, one likened Rosen to Samuel Adams, "an activist in thought and deed," and stressed that "his ability and drive make him invaluable." And wrote another, "I've seen [Alan] Hochberg and [Hugh] Carey in action," but "with all due respect to the assemblyman and governor, I wouldn't take ten of them to one Charlie." Before long, said journalist Joe Klein, most residents of Co-op City "accepted Charlie's leadership without a qualm."[22]

In the aftermath of the September rent collection drive the *City News* reported that Steering Committee III was expected to start making preparations in the near future for a "rent increase strike," which, a spokesman for the State Division of Housing warned, would force the State Housing Finance Agency to take over Co-op City. During the next few months, however, the committee made little progress. The campaign for the three open resident-director spots on the Riverbay board, which went on in October, revealed that the seven candidates were sharply divided about how to prevent an increase in Co-op City's carrying charges. Some, including Lawrence Sivak and Larry Dolnick, favored moving ahead with a rent strike. Others, notably Cy Goldberg and Robert Carrington, the only African-American candidate, called instead for a legislative rally that would be designed to generate support for a mortgage-interest-reduction bill, the most important of the Mitchell-Lama bills to be introduced at the upcoming session of the state legislature. (Sivak saw no point in a legislative rally because Congressman Hugh Carey, the Democratic candidate for governor, had already pledged to support the bill, and Governor Malcolm Wilson, the Republican incumbent, had long opposed it.) The movement for a rent strike gathered some momentum in late November, when the resident directors told the non-resident directors that if the state legislature did not take steps to stabilize rents in Co-op City, most residents were ready to join a rent strike—even if it was against the law.[23] But the movement got bogged down in early 1975 by the rift between the Advisory Council and the Steering Committee.

Harold Ostroff also did his utmost to slow down Steering Committee III's efforts to organize a rent strike by postponing an increase in Co-op City's carrying charges. In September 1974 he took what the *City News* called "the unprecedented step" of pushing back the Riverbay board's quarterly meeting from early September to late October. He rarely convened the special finance committee that was supposed to monitor Co-op City's income and expenses (which was nothing but "window dressing," said Larry Dolnick). In November Ostroff announced that Riverbay would probably be able to put off any increase in carrying charges until March 31, 1975, the end of the fiscal year. After Carey was elected governor, he assured the residents that there was a good chance that the state legislature would enact a mortgage-interest-reduction law. When the resident directors reintroduced a resolution to withhold part of the mortgage payments, the non-resident directors turned it down, but on Ostroff's recommendation, the board did not make its January and February mortgage payments until the very end of February. It also attempted to ease Co-op City's cash flow problems by refusing to put money in the reserve fund and, among other things, asking vendors to wait 120 rather than 90 days for their payments. Again at Ostroff's urging (and with the support of both the resident and non-resident directors), the board adopted a budget in early March that projected a $10 million deficit but did not include an increase in carrying charges to cover it. Apparently Ostroff and the other board members hoped that this step would put the onus for any increase on the State of New York rather than the Riverbay Corporation.[24]

Ostroff regarded these gimmicks as a way to buy time. But with Co-op City's expenses exceeding its revenues by about $800,000 a month, time was running out. When the State Division of Housing refused to accept Riverbay's proposed budget, the Steering Committee realized that it would not be long before the board raised the carrying charges, probably by as much as 25 percent and possibly by even more. Rather than wait for the board to act, the committee narrowly approved a resolution in mid-March that spelled out how it intended to stabilize rents in Co-op City. Stressing that its efforts to obtain financial aid from the state legislature had been unsuccessful, it declared that it was time to take a more militant approach, one inspired by the slogan "No Way, We Won't Pay." Pointing out that this approach would have profound ramifications not only for Co-op City but also for other Mitchell-Lama projects, the Steering Committee resolved that from April 1 to April 15 it would launch a campaign to collect $3 from every household in order to hire lawyers and accountants and cover incidental expenses. From April 15 to April 30 it would retain a lawyer and begin an "educational campaign" to persuade as many residents as possible to support "mass action." From May 1 to May 7 it would conduct a rent collection drive, similar to the September rent collection drive, and on May 8 a delegation of Co-op City residents would make "a pilgrimage" to Albany and deliver the checks to Governor Carey and other state officials. Indicative of its more militant approach, the Steering Committee would announce at the capital that if no legislative relief was forthcoming in the next few months, it would lead Co-op City's 15,372 families on a rent increase strike starting on June 1.[25]

When the State Division of Housing refused to accept Riverbay's proposed budget, Commissioner Goodwin advised Ostroff that in view of Co-op City's huge deficit—which, according to her staff, came to almost $9 million in fiscal 1975 and would come to nearly $10 million in fiscal 1976—it was imperative that the board increase the carrying charges and ask the division to approve the increase "as soon as possible." Hence shortly after Steering Committee III issued its ultimatum, Ostroff proposed at its April meeting that the board raise the carrying charges from $42.77 per room per month to $53.46, an increase of 25 percent. The increase, he stressed, could be modified or perhaps rescinded if the state legislature enacted the mortgage-interest-reduction and other Mitchell-Lama bills before the end of the current session. Over the strong objections of the resident directors, the non-resident directors voted in early April to raise the carrying charges $14.25 per room, an increase that would go into effect on July 1 but would be retroactive to April 1. A day later the resident directors, one of whom castigated Ostroff for failing to recognize that his primary responsibility was to Co-op City's residents, not to its bondholders, resigned from the board. They explained that it would be a conflict of interest for them to stay on the board and at the same time support (and perhaps even lead) the Steering Committee's proposed rent increase strike, which they all intended to do. They added that if the residents who went on strike lost their equity, anyone who backed the strike while serving on the board could be sued for damages.[26]

Believing that Riverbay sorely needed additional income to pay its bills and remain solvent, Ostroff and his associates, chiefly Vice President Schechter and General Manager Aronov, attacked Steering Committee III for its attempt to block the proposed 25 percent increase in carrying charges. Instead of calling on Co-op City's already hard-strapped residents to contribute $3 per household to hire lawyers, Schechter said, the committee should have sought the help of Senator Abraham Bernstein, Assemblyman Alan Hochberg, and Bronx Borough President Robert Abrams, all of whom were attorneys willing to give legal advice free of charge. Ostroff added that if the Steering Committee launched a rent strike and forced management to ask the court to order it to hand over the withheld carrying charges, the residents would have to pay Riverbay's legal bills too. Ostroff and Schechter were also highly critical of the Steering Committee's plan to conduct a May rent collection drive and, in Schechter's words, "'dump' the checks on

Governor Carey's lap." In conjunction with the Coordinating Council of Co-operatives and the Mitchell-Lama Council (and with the support of many of New York's powerful labor leaders), Riverbay had made a determined effort to obtain financial aid from Albany. The prospects for a mortgage-interest-reduction and other Mitchell-Lama bills were now better than ever, said Ostroff. Why, he and Schechter wanted to know, would Steering Committee III propose to take action that would embarrass the governor and alienate the legislators, the very people "whose help is needed if we are to succeed." Or as Schechter put it, "We can't win by making enemies of friends."[27]

Even more objectionable to Ostroff and his associates was that the Steering Committee, which had initially called for a rent increase strike, subsequently decided to hold a rent strike, a strike that would begin even before the State Division of Housing approved Riverbay's proposed increase in carrying charges. A rent strike was problematic, said Aronov. Riverbay had no cash and no reserves. If the residents withheld their carrying charges, management would have no money to pay for essential services. "No money—no oil; no oil, no heat; no hot water, no air conditioning." A rent strike was also immoral, wrote Schechter. The State Housing Finance Agency bonds, which had provided more than 90 percent of the funds to build Co-op City, were purchased by "individual and institutional investors in good faith." And they were entitled to a return on their investment. A rent strike would be illegal too, said Ostroff. If the residents withheld their carrying charges and Riverbay was therefore unable to make its mortgage payments, the state would institute foreclosure proceedings and then take control of Co-op City. Whether it remained a cooperative or ended up a rental, the residents would lose their equity, the $450 per room they were supposed to get back when they moved out of Co-op City and sold their shares. But other New Yorkers would not buy their shares and move into their apartments if, as a result of the rent strike, Co-op City was in default and, wrote Schechter, had no money even "to pay porters and handymen." A rent strike, he insisted, was just "too big a gamble with the $32,000,000 investment of our members, a gamble, I believe, we would lose."[28]

Rosen and other members of the Steering Committee did not let these charges go unanswered. In defense of its fund-raising campaign, the committee said, "If people think we can run buses to Albany, print leaflets and signs, prepare fact sheets for every family and keep lawyers on call to guarantee that whatever happens they are legally protected and that isn't going to cost everybody some money, then they are not serious about fighting a rent increase." Three dollars a family was not much to ask when River-bay was proposing to raise the carrying charges $10 or more per room per month. And in the event that the Steering Committee raised more than it needed, the excess would be returned to the donors on a pro rata basis. In defense of the committee's plan to conduct a May rent collection drive and then deliver the checks to Governor Carey, Rosen wrote, "We are not looking to embarrass or insult anyone," least of all the governor. Under pressure from Co-op City's UDC, one of the largest Democratic clubs in New York State, Carey had made a commitment during his gubernatorial campaign to pro-vide financial aid to Co-op City. But where was the aid? Rosen wanted to know. When Ostroff expressed guarded optimism about a mortgage-interest subsidy, Rosen asked him, "What support for interest subsidy do you see? Coming from where? Proposed by whom? In what amount?" As well as a "responsible and prudent" effort to call attention to Co-op City's fiscal plight, the May rent collection drive was a well-intentioned attempt to persuade the governor to honor his commitment, Rosen insisted. Or, as Dolnick declared, "we have to have something more concrete than promises and vague com-mitments by political leaders."[29]

Charles Parness, another member of Steering Committee III, also dis-agreed with Aronov. A rent strike would not lead to "any disruption of services to anyone in Co-op City," he wrote. Plenty of money would be available—from Co-op City's business enterprises, from non-striking resi-dents' carrying charges, and, if need be, from Steering Committee payments. "If at any time our services are cut," he said, "this community should know that it will be by direct and deliberate orders of Mr. Aronov, and not due to any action by your resident directors or Steering Committee III." In re-sponse to Schechter's charge that a rent strike would deprive Co-op City's bondholders of the return on their investment to which they were entitled, Rosen declared, "I don't give a hoot for the millionaire 'orphans' who own [Co-op City's] bonds; their profits mean nothing to me." Taking issue with Ostroff, Rosen insisted that the striking residents would not be evicted. If Riverbay or New York State brought foreclosure proceedings against the striking residents, the Steering Committee's lawyers would defend them in court. If the court ruled against them, the committee would pay the carry-ing charges, which would stop the foreclosure proceedings. In the unlikely event that the court issued eviction warrants, it was inconceivable that the city would order the marshals to oust more than 50,000 men, women, and children from their homes. What would they do? Rosen asked. Bring in the police, the National Guard or the Green Berets? In no housing cooperative, not even in Rochdale Village, were the striking residents evicted, the Steering Committee pointed out. Nor would the striking residents lose their equity. To the contrary, Parness explained, they would get their investment back only if other New Yorkers purchased their shares and occupied their apartments. "Do you want to guess," he went on, "how few people will want to move into Co-op City when we get a rent increase of $10 per room per month?"[30]

ooo

A rent strike would succeed "only if we [the residents of Co-op City] stand together," said Arthur Taub, a member of Steering Committee III and, before he resigned in May 1975, a resident director of the Riverbay Corporation. But would they "stand together"? Would they support the Steering Committee's militant approach? Would they contribute to its fund-raising campaign? Would they participate in its May rent collection drive? And above all would they withhold their payments to Riverbay and instead hand their checks over to Steering Committee III? Eliot Engel, the leader of Co-op City's United Democratic Club, was confident that they would. Speaking at a meeting of the UDC, he declared that if the State of New York forces them to go on a rent strike, "we will do it. We will stand up and fight together, and shout loud and clear 'Not One Cent More.'" Engel had reason to be confident. Many residents of Co-op City believed that the proposed increase in carrying charges was "unconscionable." Coming after the 20 percent increase that went into effect on January 1, 1973, and the 12.5 percent increase that went into effect on July 1, 1974, the proposed increase would raise the carrying charges 70 percent for residents who had moved to Co-op City three or four years earlier. Residents whose carrying charges had been raised 15.1 percent on July 1, 1970, would have to pay twice as much as they had when they moved in. Many residents could not afford the increased carrying charges, said Marion Groden, the leader of Co-op City's Republican Club. Some would be forced to choose between paying their rent and feeding their family. Others might have to go on welfare, which, said Senator Abraham Bernstein, "should be avoided at all costs."[31]

Riverbay's proposed increase left many residents feeling desperate, wondering, wrote a *New York Post* reporter, how they could manage if over five years their carrying charges rose 100 percent and their wages went up only 40 or 50 percent. The proposed increase also left many residents feeling betrayed. The UHF had assured prospective residents that Co-op City's carrying charges would be $23 (and later $25) per room per month, which was well within the means of most working-class New Yorkers. Trusting in the UHF's assurances, which were reinforced by the State Division of Housing, many New Yorkers moved out of their rent-controlled apartments and into Co-op City. Once there they found out that the carrying charges would not be enough to cover Co-op City's costs. They also came to believe that the UHF had been well aware of the problem from the outset but, in an effort to attract prospective residents, had not disclosed it. Only after the residents moved in did Riverbay start to raise the carrying charges. As Lisa Goodman, whose monthly carrying charges went up from $136 to $236, remarked, "We expected increases at some time, but not astronomical increases in so short a time." Other residents complained that had they known that the carrying charges would be raised so much, they would never have moved into Co-op City. One even said that he would have gone to Florida instead. In no other housing cooperatives had the carrying charges gone up so much as in Co-op City, one resident pointed out. Under rent control, added another, a private landlord could not have raised the rents so much. Lawrence Sivak probably spoke for many of these residents when he said, "All we are demanding was what we were told, no more, no less."[32]

Many residents felt betrayed for another reason. Ostroff called them co-operators. And Schechter insisted that they were owners, not tenants, and that a rent strike would be a strike against themselves. But many residents did not view Co-op City as a genuine cooperative. As Dolnick pointed out, its "day-to-day existence and all future plans" were controlled by the Riverbay Corporation Board of Directors, only a minority of whose members were elected by the residents. And the board, Taub stressed, was "usually left with no alternative but to ratify decisions made by Mr. Ostroff and his associates," the non-resident directors, none of whom lived in Co-op City. Indeed, said Taub, the claim that Co-op City was a cooperative was "absolutely hogwash." As most residents saw it, Co-op City would not be a genuine cooperative until the State Division of Housing issued a Certificate of Acceptability, which would allow them to elect the board of directors. Under the Mitchell-Lama act this certificate was supposed to be issued after all construction was completed and all contracts were reviewed. Co-op City had been finished and occupied for more than three years, but the Division of Housing had not yet issued a Certificate of Acceptability. Indeed, residents were advised that they might have to wait another two years for one. Some state legislators had introduced bills to amend the Mitchell-Lama act in a way that would have required the State Division of Housing to issue a Certificate of Acceptability as soon as the cooperative was occupied and to empower the residents to elect the board of directors within six months after the first residents moved in or three months after 60 percent of the apartments were occupied. But these bills went nowhere.[33]

Although the residents of Co-op City had bought their apartments for $450 a room, said Betsy Brown, a well-known journalist who spent the last few years of a long career writing about real estate for the *New York Times*, "they still felt like tenants." Charles J. Urstadt agreed. Co-op City's residents do not think of themselves as "property owners," he wrote. "To them, they are still tenants who are required to pay a lump sum or 'key money' to obtain the[ir] apartments." According to another well-informed New Yorker, most residents of Mitchell-Lama and other middle-income housing cooperatives felt much the same way. Most Co-op City residents were not what the UHF expected, Brown pointed out. They moved there not because they felt a strong commitment to cooperative housing, but because they wanted a brand-new, reasonably priced, and air-conditioned apartment with large rooms and an eat-in kitchen. They had been tenants for most of their lives, and in their minds they were still tenants. Indeed, when Harriet Colodney and her associates formed an organization to fight the first major increase in carrying charges at Co-op, they called it the Tenants Council. Viewing themselves as tenants, few residents of Co-op City were "imbued with the brotherly spirit the union-sponsored builders hoped would develop in the project," wrote Brown. "They viewed the builders not as brotherly but as paternalistic." Thanks to New York State's rent control laws, many Co-op City residents had hitherto enjoyed stable rents for two and a half decades. Even Schechter acknowledged that the residents "had a rent control mentality." They seemed to think that rents go to the landlord and "services come from God."[34]

Besides seeing themselves as tenants, many residents of Co-op City saw the United Housing Foundation (or its surrogate, the Riverbay Corporation) as their landlord. (Indeed, even before Co-op City was conceived of *Co-op Contact*, a publication of the UHF, complained that many cooperators tended to look upon management as their landlord.) Although few residents were inclined to go as far as Taub, who characterized the UHF as a typical "slumlord," many were highly critical of Ostroff and his associates. They were aware that Co-op City's fiscal problems were in part a result of the nationwide inflationary spiral, and especially the skyrocketing cost of oil, which Ostroff blamed on Saudi Arabia and the other members of OPEC. But as one resident wrote, the UHF was not run by amateurs. "If Mr. Ostroff, with all his experience and knowledge, couldn't see the handwriting of spiraling inflation on the wall in the period of 1964–1971, then he is in worse shape than we are." Other residents wanted to know who if not Riverbay was responsible for Co-op City's soaring costs and growing deficit. Many residents also held Community Services, Inc., Co-op City's general contractor, responsible for the project's structural problems, especially the cracked walls that, as I mentioned earlier, left many apartments on the top floor of the thirty-five high-rise apartment houses virtually uninhabitable. Why, they wondered, did it take so long and cost so much to repair the walls? (It is perhaps worth noting that the residents were not yet aware of some of Co-op City's even worse structural problems.)[35]

Some residents were fed up with Riverbay for different reasons. Among the most outspoken were Bernard Cylich and three other leaders of the Building 7 Association. In July 1974 they wrote a long letter to Lawrence Sivak, one of Riverbay's resident directors, which was printed in the *Co-op City Times*. They complained that their building was rapidly deteriorating for lack of proper maintenance. Conditions were so bad that they were reluctant to invite guests to their homes. They also found it hard to discourage other residents from moving out and to encourage prospective residents to move in. They had repeatedly told management about the problem, but all they got was a "run around." Management responded, if at all, in a "syrupy" way, "sweet and slow." Its lackadaisical approach was shortening the life of the building, endangering the equity of the residents, and undermining the financial well-being of Co-op City. Warning that the problem would soon become a catastrophe, Cylich and his associates threatened to send the letter to the press unless something was done to upgrade the maintenance of their building. Another resident who was fed up with Riverbay was Sheila Silver, who worked in an office in the Garment District. Management, she said in November 1975, "treated us with contempt the moment we moved in here. If anything went wrong, like once the air conditioning went off, and you'd walk into the office, very politely, to ask when is the air conditioning going back on, they'd say, 'Whatsamatta? In the old neighborhood you had air conditioning? Here you can't live even one day without air conditioning?'... What kind of way is that to treat a cooperator?" she asked.[36]

Another reason the residents of Co-op City might well stand together was that they shared a deep sense of frustration with both the state legislature and the state and federal courts. In their attempt to block the increases in carrying charges, they wrote to elected officials. They stood on picket lines outside the UHF headquarters on the Lower East Side. They held rallies outside the Manhattan offices of Governor Nelson A. Rockefeller and the State Division of Housing. And they traveled in "caravans" to Albany, where they met with state legislators and other officials. As Charlie Rosen later recalled, "everybody was lovely." But nothing came of these meetings. At a previous legislative session bills were introduced to reduce mortgage interest rates at Co-op City and other Mitchell-Lama projects. But none of them passed—and even if they had passed, they would probably have been vetoed by Governor Malcolm Wilson. Nor was there reason to think that things would be different in the current session, which was scheduled to adjourn at the end of May 1975. Especially infuriating to many residents of Co-op City was that the State of New York had bailed out Con Edison, the Urban Development Corporation (UDC), and other private (or quasi-public) corporations in severe fiscal trouble. "If the state can find $80-million for the UDC, which has no people," Rosen asked, "why can't it find $10-million for Co-op City?," which has over 50,000. Referring to the federal government, Al Abrams said, "We want the same government that finds loot for mismanaged corporations [like Lockheed Airlines] to cough up some money for us."[37]

As I pointed out earlier, the residents of Co-op City also asked the courts to block the increase in carrying charges. On behalf of the Tenants Council, Gerald P. Halpern filed suit against Charles J. Urstadt in the New York State Supreme Court. But Judge Jacob B. Grumet ruled against him, and the Appellate Division upheld his decision. On behalf of the Advisory Council, Louis Nizer filed suit against the UHF and the State Division of Housing in US District Court. Judge Lawrence W. Pierce dismissed his complaint, but the Court of Appeals overruled Pierce. So as of June 1, 1975, the date on which Steering Committee III intended to begin the rent strike, the case was pending in the US Supreme Court. As Richard Karp, a reporter for *Barron's National Business and Financial Weekly*, pointed out, Rosen and his associates "were fairly sure that it [the Supreme Court decision] would go against them." If it did, the only option for the residents would be to file suit in state court, where the case would be argued on its merits and "could drag on for years," Karp noted. Rosen knew that "without federal securities law as a legal weapon, he stood no chance in court."[38] In June the high court reversed the Court of Appeals. (A month later Nizer told a huge crowd at Co-op City that he was prepared to file suit in state court, a suit in which he expected to prevail. About the rent strike, which was then in its second month, he had nothing to say except that neither he nor his firm was involved in it in any way.) Nor would things have been much better for the residents of Co-op City if the Supreme Court had upheld the Court of Appeals. If it had, the case would have been remanded to the district court, which would have been obliged to rule on the merits of Nizer's claims, which would have dragged on for at least a year—and then, if one side or the other appealed, for another two or three years.

Riverbay's leaders argued that Steering Committee III had no authority to collect the carrying charges and that Riverbay management had no authority to accept anything less than the full payment. But most residents believed that management would not be so insensitive to the well-being of the community that it would curtail, much less eliminate, essential services if the Steering Committee was willing to provide the necessary funds. Given that the rent strike was supposed to start at the beginning of the summer, it would have been extremely unpleasant if the air-conditioning was turned off. And it would have been downright dangerous if the garbage was left to rot in the basements or on the streets. Most residents also believed that it was highly unlikely that Riverbay or the state would bring foreclosure proceedings against them, which was what happened at Rochdale Village. But as Larry Dolnick pointed out, Co-op City was not Rochdale Village, where only 10 percent of the residents took part in the rent strike. Given that the Steering Committee was supported by the Advisory Council, most voluntary associations, and Riverbay's resident directors, it was likely that a great majority of the residents would withhold their carrying charges. According to Yavner, Gallet, Freedman & Brett, the Manhattan law firm that had been retained by Steering Committee III to defend the striking residents, if the state brought foreclosure proceedings against all the striking residents, it would take the courts six years to handle all the cases even if they worked eight hours a day, six days a week.[39]

There was a good chance that some judges would issue eviction warrants against the striking residents. There was also a good chance that some residents would resist if the marshals and schleppers attempted to oust their families from their homes. As Sol Oratofsky, president of the Senior

Citizens Club of Co-op City, said, "We remember picket lines; we've had our head[s] broken, and we're willing to do it again." But it was far from clear that Mayor Abraham D. Beame, a Democrat who succeeded John V. Lindsay in 1974, would send the New York City police into a Democratic stronghold like Co-op City to reinforce the marshals and schleppers. It was also far from clear that Governor Hugh Carey, a Democrat who replaced Malcolm Wilson in 1975, would mobilize the National Guard, a move that would probably have angered Borough President Robert Abrams and a host of other federal, state, and local officials, many of whom were Democrats and strong supporters of Steering Committee III. "Half of New York City has a relative in Co-op City, or knows somebody here," remarked Charlie Rosen. "How would a lot of broken heads make the [state] administration look?"[40] Also, despite dire warnings by Ostroff and Schechter, few residents believed that they would lose their equity if they took part in a rent strike. As Rosen and others pointed out, in no housing cooperative, not even in Rochdale Village, had striking residents lost their equity. If their investment was in jeopardy, most residents of Co-op City held, it was because of the "astronomical" increase in carrying charges, not the impending rent strike.

Steering Committee III had its detractors, perhaps the most outspoken of whom was Sidney Weinberger. A lawyer, former resident of Rochdale Village, and onetime vice president of its board of directors, Weinberger moved to Co-op City in the early 1970s and lived in a townhouse with his wife and two children. Shortly after moving in, he became involved in community affairs as a member of the Advisory Council and an unsuccessful candidate for the Riverbay board. Weinberger was also a member of the UHF board of directors and vice chairman of the Coordinating Council of Cooperatives. In an effort to heal the growing breach between Co-op City's residents and the UHF, he and about forty others had organized the Cooperators for Co-op City in late 1972. Its principal objective was to improve the image of Co-op City. Although troubled by the increase in carrying charges, Weinberger blamed Co-op City's fiscal problem not on the UHF or Riverbay, but on the nationwide inflationary spiral. And he believed that government aid was the only solution. As vice chairman of the Coordinating Council of Cooperatives, he charged that Steering Committee III's leaders were demagogues who, "overwhelmed by their sense of importance," were directing their ire at the wrong place when they attacked the UHF. Charlie Rosen responded that Weinberger and his associates were determined to destroy the Steering Committee and any other organization that they could not control. Referring to the

Steering Committee's leaders, Weinberger shot back, "If they weren't such a bunch of hypocrites, they would voice their protest by urging residents to withhold federal, state and city income taxes."[41]

Some residents of Co-op City had strong reservations not so much about Steering Committee III per se as about its militant approach, and especially its proposed rent strike. Indeed, the talk of a rent strike, which became widespread in 1974 and 1975, left a few residents extremely anxious. They feared that if most or even many residents withheld their carrying charges, Riverbay would have no option but to cut back on essential services, among them gas, electricity, hot water, heat in winter, and air-conditioning in summer. If management had to lay off porters and handymen, who would clean the lobbies, halls, garages, and grounds, put out the garbage, and fix the appliances? And how could management pay Westinghouse to repair the elevators, which were indispensable in the high-rise buildings? Some residents were also afraid that if Riverbay could not meet its mortgage payments, the State of New York would take over Co-op City and begin foreclosure proceedings. If so, the residents would be evicted and their equity lost. As one resident pointed out, there had been no foreclosures in some New York City Mitchell-Lama housing cooperatives that were in arrears. But in these cases the city held the mortgages and the elected officials had not brought foreclosure proceedings for political reasons. The Co-op City mortgage was held by private investors who were highly unlikely to feel so constrained. Another resident stressed that the state would not provide the funds that Co-op City so desperately needed even if its residents went on a rent strike. Speaking of Governor Carey, he asked, "Where is he going to get the money from?"[42]

ooo

By early May, if not earlier, it was evident that Steering Committee III had far more supporters than detractors. Although Charlie Rosen said in early April, "I can't tell you [Co-op City's residents] we will win. I am not a soothsayer," the committee's campaign got off to a promising start. Many residents agreed with Edwin Scharfenberg, who praised the committee's proposal that every cooperator contribute $3 to enable the committee to hire lawyers and accountants and cover its incidental expenses. "When weighed against a rent increase of $12 per room per month," he pointed out, "$3 is a very small price to pay." In early April Steering Committee III established what became known as the Co-op City Rent Stabilization War Chest, which was coordinated by Joel Dannenberg. From the very start, said Charles Parness, it did well. By mid-April, at which time the fund-raising drive was underway in only some of the buildings, 35 percent of the families had made contributions. Although neither the *City News* nor the *Co-op City Times* revealed how much money was contributed to the Rent Stabilization War Chest, it was a substantial amount. Indeed, it was enough for Steering Committee III to cover incidental expenses and even to hire Yavner, Gallet, Freedman & Brett, which was given a $5,000 retainer and potentially a fee of as much as $25,000 to defend the striking residents in court and, if need be, to prevent Riverbay from curtailing essential services.[43]

In accord with the Steering Committee's timetable, the May rent collection drive began a month after the April fund-raising campaign started. In a leaflet that was distributed throughout Co-op City, the committee explained that the drive—which was supported by Congressman Jonathan B. Bingham and other elected officials, but opposed by Harold Ostroff and other UHF leaders—was designed to demonstrate the community's deep-seated objections to the proposed increase in carrying charges. It worked as follows. From Wednesday, May 1, through Tuesday, May 7, volunteers manned tables in the lobby of every high-rise building from 7:00 p.m. to 9:00 p.m. (The tables were also manned for a few hours in the mornings and afternoons in buildings that had a sufficient number of volunteers.) The volunteers provided the residents with an unsealed envelope, into which they put their checks or money orders and their carrying charge computer cards. The volunteers gave the residents a receipt and sealed the envelopes, which were handed over to the building captains, who did a nightly tally under the supervision of the area marshals and then handed the envelopes over to the Steering Committee. Based on the results of the September rent collection drive, the committee's leaders expected to collect at least $3 million in checks and money orders. In the end the May drive fell short of the September drive, but not by much. Of the 15,372 families in Co-op City, 12,233 (or about 80 percent) gave checks and money orders worth nearly $3 million to the Steering Committee.[44]

After tallying the checks and money orders and storing them in a safe place, Steering Committee III took the next step in its effort to stabilize rents in Co-op City. Rather than hand the money over to Edward Aronov, as it did after the September rent collection drive, the committee packed the envelopes into five large black bags, which were then loaded into three automobiles. A delegation, which included Charlie Rosen and ten other members of the Steering Committee, then drove to Albany on Wednesday, May 8. At noon they met with Governor Carey and brought more than 2,000 checks and money orders to his office. In a letter to Carey written two days earlier, Rosen said that the Steering Committee was delivering the checks to him as chief executive of New York State, "the only avenue where we can seek economic relief." Rosen also pointed out that Congressman Bingham, Senator Bernstein, Assemblyman Hochberg, and a host of other elected officials—as well as all the district leaders of Co-op City's political clubs—had hailed the Steering Committee's decision to hold the May rent collection drive and deliver the checks to Albany as "a responsible and prudent effort on Co-op City's behalf." The *City News* was favorably impressed too. "The symbolic gesture of dumping over $2 million in rent checks at Gov. Hugh Carey's office door," it wrote, "is a way of saying that middle income families cannot afford [to pay] $300 to $400 a month in carrying charges." The delegation returned to Co-op City the same day. And on Friday, May 10, the Steering Committee handed the checks and money orders over to Aronov.[45]

By all accounts the Steering Committee's meeting with Carey—which was arranged by Senator Bernstein and attended by Bernstein, Assemblyman Hochberg, and Judah Gribetz, the governor's counsel—was quite cordial. Carey told Rosen and his associates that he was well aware that the increased carrying charges were having a baneful impact on middle-income families. He also acknowledged that New York State had an obligation to honor its commitment to Co-op City and pledged that he would talk with Commissioner Goodwin about ways to alleviate its financial problem. Based on the remarks by the governor and Senator Bernstein—who said that Goodwin was in no rush to approve the proposed increase in Co-op City's carrying charges—some members of the Steering Committee were willing to consider postponing the rent strike and giving the governor more time to come up with a solution. But many others were not inclined to trust the politicians. They were also worried that a postponement would slow down the Steering Committee's momentum. After a four-hour meeting on May 18, the Steering Committee voted unanimously to proceed as planned and start the rent strike on June 1. As Rosen put it, "This is the battle that has to be fought. We either permit the continuously imposed rent increases to bleed this community to death, or we make it clear to the state that we are prepared to fight for our homes and the survival of Co-op City and other Mitchell-Lama developments." If any members of the Steering Committee still had hopes that the state would help Co-op City, they were dashed a week later when Robert Mortgate, the governor's deputy secretary, and

Stephen Berger, head of his Housing Task Force, said that in view of the state's budgetary problems, there was little chance that the Mitchell-Lama bills would be enacted before the legislature adjourned.[46]

Knowing that it could not stop Steering Committee III from launching a rent strike on June 1, the Riverbay Corporation made a last-ditch attempt to blunt its impact. In a long article published in the *Co-op City Times* on May 31, Riverbay implored residents to pay their June carrying charges "in the usual way"—and thereby ensure the solvency of Co-op City. The Steering Committee's proposed rent strike was untimely. The State Division of Housing had not yet held hearings on the increase in carrying charges, much less approved it. Indeed, the proposed rent strike was not so much a rent strike as a "takeover of the financial management of Co-op City!" It was "in essence a 'coup d'etat.'" The Steering Committee had no authority to "intercept" Riverbay's revenue and then decide which expenses would be paid and which obligations would be honored. This authority was vested in the board of directors, which had no legal right to delegate it "to an ad hoc group, regardless of its purported support." A payment to Steering Committee III was not the same as a payment to Riverbay Corporation. Any resident who made such a payment would be delinquent. Riverbay would provide essential services as long as it had sufficient funds, but if the residents went on a rent strike, it would soon run out of money. And it could not take money from the Steering Committee to pay for these services. By withholding their carrying charges, Riverbay warned, residents would run the risk of eviction. And if as a result of a default they were unable to sell their apartments, they would lose their equity. Instead of going on a rent strike, the residents of Co-op City would be much better off putting pressure on Governor Carey and other state officials to provide much-needed financial assistance.[47]

Most residents were not swayed by Riverbay's appeal. They believed that by refusing to provide Co-op City with financial aid the state had left them no choice but to go on strike. Or as Rosen put it, we went on strike "because we were forced out the door, not because we went out the door." Based on the Steering Committee's assurances that it would give Riverbay the necessary funds, most residents were confident that management would be able to maintain essential services even if they withheld their carrying charges. They were also inclined to trust Rosen when he declared that even if the state brought foreclosure proceedings against the striking residents, no one would be evicted—and no one would lose his or her equity. Thus, starting on May 30, hundreds and then thousands of residents put their computer cards and their checks and money orders, which were made out to the Steering Committee, not the Riverbay Corporation, into envelopes that they handed over to the volunteers who manned the tables in the lobbies of all the high-rise buildings (and at designated places in the townhouse clusters). The envelopes were then given to the Steering Committee, which deposited the money in Manufacturers Hanover Trust, a major New York City bank. Within three days more than half the families were on rent strike—a sign, wrote the *Co-op City Times*, that the Steering Committee had "the overwhelming support of the community." And by May 15, when the rent collection drive came to an end, about 90 percent of Co-op City's 15,372 households had withheld their carrying charges, sending a message to the state, said Larry Dolnick, that "a rent increase of $14.25 per room per month is not only unthinkable, but unacceptable."[48]

CHAPTER 10

THE GREAT RENT STRIKE

As Charlie Rosen pointed out, the strike was not aimed at the United Housing Foundation, much less at the Riverbay Corporation or at Co-op City. Rather it was aimed at the State of New York, which had refused to provide the much-needed financial aid for Co-op City and other Mitchell-Lama developments. (Indeed, shortly after the strike got underway, Rosen said, not entirely facetiously, that Governor Carey is "our landlord," Commissioner Goodwin is "the super[intendent]," and General Manager Aronov is "the groundskeeper.") Although the UHF was strongly opposed to the strike, it was more than willing to let the state deal with it. Hence on June 2 Harold Ostroff and the other eight non-resident directors resigned from the Riverbay board, an action that was hailed by Rosen but denounced by the *City News*, which accused Ostroff and his associates of "taking the easy way out of a tough situation." In their letter of resignation, which was hand-delivered to all the residents, the non-resident directors stressed that they had done their best to keep Co-op City solvent and hold down the carrying charges. But "we do not believe," they wrote, "that we can legally agree to turn the fiscal management [of Co-op City] over to others; nor can we permit any group without legal authority to decide which bills will or will not be paid." They were not willing to take the residents to court either, even if that was the only way to get the money to run Co-op City. "Our position has, therefore, become impossible," the non-resident directors concluded.[1]

Given that the State Housing Finance Agency had underwritten Co-op City's $436 million mortgage, Commissioner Goodwin believed that the Division of Housing had no choice but to take over the project. She promptly accepted the resignation of the nine Riverbay board members. She did so, she said, "with deep regret," not only because Ostroff and his associates had served Co-op City "so selflessly," but also because, as leaders of the UHF they had "pioneered in the development of middle-income cooperative housing in New York State." Pursuant to the Mitchell-Lama act, Goodwin then appointed six officers of the State Division of Housing directors of the Riverbay Corporation. Under the leadership of Robert A. Infantino, who replaced Ostroff as president, and with the help of Edward Aronov, who stayed on as general manager, the new board would henceforth oversee the day-to-day operations of Co-op City. It started out by affirming Riverbay's existing contracts with its employees and vendors. It also asked the Division of Housing's lawyers whether it could accept the Steering Committee's offer to provide funds to maintain essential services. It then tried to figure out what to do about the rent strike. In view of Goodwin's deep-seated opposition to the strike—which she lambasted as an attempt "to coerce the state into granting financial relief by threatening the continued viability of the largest middle-income cooperative in the nation"—there was no doubt that the board would take a hard line.[2]

The new board could have withdrawn the old board's application for a 25 percent increase in carrying charges. But after Commissioner Goodwin announced that the state did not have the money or authority to maintain essential services in Co-op City if the residents withheld their carrying charges, it pressed ahead. As planned, the Division of Housing held a public hearing in Co-op City on June 5 and June 6 to give the residents an opportunity to voice their objections to the proposed increase. The principal witness was Herbert Freedman, one of the Steering Committee's lawyers, who called the hearing "a sham" and the increase "outlandish and unconscionable." When Fred Hecht, the assistant state housing commissioner, denied Freedman's request to terminate the hearing and deny the application, most of the residents walked out. Two weeks later Goodwin approved the application. Soon after the public hearing, the Riverbay board sent out late notices to about 14,000 residents, most of whom had taken part in the strike. As a result of a technical glitch, the notices were not valid. The board resent them a week later. Given that the late fee was only $5—small change when the carrying charges were already more than $40 per room per month and would soon be raised to more than $50—the late notices were largely symbolic. At about the same time management threatened to lay off 137 maintenance men, security officers, and office personnel, a move that would have reduced Co-op City's workforce by 25 percent. But under pressure from the Division of Housing, it rescinded the layoffs.[3]

These measures did not have much of an impact on the rent strike. The great majority of residents turned their checks and money orders over to the Steering Committee rather than the Riverbay Corporation. And a host of elected officials, federal, state, and local, supported the strike. Chief among them was New York Congresswoman Bella Abzug, who told 200 members of the Independent Democratic Club of Co-op City that the rent strike was a microcosm of the nationwide struggle by working people to wrest control of the country from big corporations and other special interest groups. The Independent Democratic Club also supported the strike and even gave the Steering Committee several large banners and 3,000 balloons, all of which were inscribed with the slogan "No Way, We Won't Pay." Not to be outdone, the Co-op City Republican Club urged all residents to join the strike. "We must end these raises once and for all," said Helen Presser, one of the club's leaders. The Mitchell-Lama Council, which represented dozens of housing cooperatives, also supported the rent strike—the first time the council had ever endorsed a rent strike, said its chairman, Murray Raphael. Also in favor of the strike was the Metropolitan Council on Housing, a citywide tenants' organization. By late June, a few weeks after Rosen raised the possibility that Steering Committee III might organize a blockade of the New England Thruway and the Hutchinson River Parkway, the Steering Committee announced at a rally on the Co-op City Greenway that it intended to extend the strike into July.[4]

Before long Infantino and the other board members realized that more drastic measures would be needed to break the strike. Hence on June 11 Riverbay filed suit in the state supreme court not only against Steering Committee III, but also against Rosen, twenty-one other community leaders, and the Manufacturers Hanover Trust Company, which held much of the money that had been collected by the Steering Committee. At the hearing, which took place in a packed Bronx courtroom two days later, Riverbay's lawyers, Golenbock & Barell, asked Judge Joseph A. Brust to enjoin the Steering Committee from soliciting, collecting, and withholding Co-op City's monthly carrying charges. In a written brief, which was supplemented by Infantino's affidavit, Riverbay argued that the Steering Committee had used "unlawful and ill-conceived tactics" to induce Co-op City's residents to withhold their June carrying charges, which was a violation of the occupancy agreement. It had also sent representatives to the apartments of the non-striking residents "in an obvious attempt to pressure them into submission." By so doing, Riverbay contended, the Steering Committee had jeopardized "the health, safety and well-being of thousands of residents" who would soon be deprived of such essential services as sanitation, maintenance, and security. Taking exception to the Steering Committee's claims, Riverbay stressed that if Co-op City was unable to make its mortgage payments because of the strike, the State Housing Finance Agency would begin foreclosure proceedings, and the residents would face eviction and the loss of their equity.[5]

The Steering Committee, which was represented by attorneys Herbert Freedman and Jeffrey Gallet as well as Senator Abraham Bernstein, strongly opposed Riverbay's request for a temporary injunction. In a written brief supplemented by Rosen's affidavit, the committee pointed out that it had offered to release funds to Riverbay to ensure the continued provision of essential services and that the possibility of foreclosure was so "remote" that the residents were in no risk of being evicted or losing their equity. The committee also submitted statements from Bronx Borough President Robert Abrams and other elected officials who supported the strike and an affidavit from 6,000 residents saying that they had withheld their carrying charges voluntarily. Above all, the committee argued that if granted the injunction would deprive Co-op City's residents of their constitutional rights of free speech and due process. Brust was not swayed by the Steering Committee's defense. Four days later he ruled that "Riverbay's right to free and unfettered collection and use of the monthly carrying charges ... is patently clear and the [Steering] Committee has no claim or color of right thereto." He also agreed with Riverbay that the carrying charges were necessary to cover Co-op City's operating expenses, mortgage payments, and property taxes. Indeed, he found the committee's offer to release a portion of the funds evidence of "the immediacy of Riverbay's plight." Brust therefore granted Riverbay's request for a temporary injunction, forbidding the Steering Committee and its leaders to urge or otherwise encourage Co-op City's residents to withhold all or part of their carrying charges and ordering Manufacturers Hanover Trust to turn the money in Steering Committee III's escrow account over to the Riverbay Corporation.[6]

000

Brust's ruling infuriated the Steering Committee's leaders and their support-ers. Charlie Rosen denounced it as "reprehensible" and "un-American." "No injunction is going to stop the struggle for rent stabilization," he claimed, es-pecially not an injunction by a "political hack" whom he referred to as "yo-yo Brust." Rosen said that the committee would file an appeal. In the meantime he vowed to defy the injunction, even if he might be found in contempt and sent to jail. In what the *City News* called "a show of solidarity," Al Abrams, a member of the Steering Committee, declared, "Rosen will never go to jail alone. He's done too much for this community to stand by himself." Esther Smith, the chair of the Advisory Council and the only African American on the Steering Committee, said that if need be she too was prepared to go to jail. And Murray Lerner, chairman of the Coordination Council of Senior Cit-izens and one of many Jewish members of the Steering Committee, quipped, "If we have to go to Riker's [Island]," the site of New York's largest and most notorious jail, "I want them [the prison officials] to know I must have ko-sher food." Eliot Engel, president of the Independent Democratic Club, de-nounced Brust's ruling as "unconscionable and unbelievable." It smacks, he said, of "the means employed by totalitarian countries to silence their citi-zens." His political rival, Jerome Glanzrock, leader of the United Democratic Club, agreed. Under Brust's decision, he pointed out, "If we attempt even to discuss the withholding of carrying charges with a neighbor or a husband or wife, we could be held in contempt of court and be subject to fine and impris-onment." Borough President Abrams, Senator Bernstein, and other elected officials also decried Brust's ruling on the grounds that it deprived Co-op City's residents of their rights to free speech and due process under the First, Fifth, and Fourteenth amendments of the Constitution.[7]

For Rosen and his associates things went from bad to worse in the im-mediate aftermath of Judge Brust's ruling. The Steering Committee's law-yers promptly filed an appeal with the First Department of the Appellate Division. The case was assigned to Justice Louis A. Capozzoli, a former as-semblyman, congressman, and municipal court judge who was elected to the state supreme court in 1957 on a Democratic-Liberal ticket and appointed to the Appellate Division by Governor Nelson A. Rockefeller nine years later. After reviewing the written briefs, Capozzoli ruled on June 23 that in light of the importance of the issues the case should be adjudicated not by a single judge but by a five-judge panel. He was, however, willing to grant a limited stay that would affect only the money that had been collected by the Steer-ing Committee in June. He ordered the committee to turn the money over to the court, which would hold it until the Appellate Division issued a ruling. The next day the Steering Committee gave the court about $740,000 that was held by Manufacturers Hanover Trust and, wrote the *Co-op City Times*, $2 million to $2.1 million of "undeposited checks that were kept in an undisclosed location, known only to certain members of the Steering Committee." On June 25 the Appellate Division vacated Justice Capozzoli's limited stay and ordered that roughly $2.8 million be released to the Riverbay Corporation. A week later Supreme Court Justice Wallace R. Cotton issued a supplemental order that allowed Riverbay to deposit the money into its account.[8]

These legal setbacks did not deter the Steering Committee. At a rally held on the Greenway on June 26 and attended by about 5,000 residents, its leaders announced that despite Judge Brust's injunction, they intended to continue the rent strike in July. "We won't pay the increase," Rosen told the crowd, "we won't let [anyone] intimidate us." Following the by-then-familiar procedure, the residents were asked to put their checks—without the 25 percent increase that had been approved by Commissioner Goodwin—into sealed envelopes and give them to the volunteers who would man tables in the lobbies of the apartment houses. (Shortly afterwards the committee decided that it would take the checks to the Midtown Manhattan office of Governor Carey on July 10.) Nathalia Lange, another member of the Steering Committee, pointed out that the Advisory Council had recently voted unanimously to support the Steering Committee and its rent strike even after Rosen warned its members that they would be violating Brust's injunction by endorsing the strike. "We're gonna have 100 percent in July," Lange declared. And Assemblyman Alan Hochberg said that he had come from Albany to show his support for the Steering Committee. Councilman Stephen Kaufman, another strong supporter of the Steering Committee, told the crowd, "Whatever you decide, I support it 100 percent." (Three and a half months later the *City News* reported that Kaufman, who lived in Co-op City, had been paying his monthly carrying charges, with the 25 percent increase, to the Riverbay Corporation, which raised doubts about just how much he supported the rent strike.)[9]

Besides holding large rallies on the Greenway and small ones in the buildings, the Steering Committee took several other steps to ensure the success of the rent strike. To cover its operating expenses it asked each family to contribute an additional $5. It set up four service centers where residents could go for advice about late fees and other problems. And it assured residents that they would not be ousted from their homes for withholding their

carrying charges. The committee also organized a boycott of the Amalgamated Bank, whose chairman was Jacob S. Potofsky, a leader of the UHF and a
former director of the Riverbay Corporation as well as the head of the Amalgamated Clothing Workers of America. The result was that more than a few
residents moved their accounts from the Amalgamated Bank to the Marine
Midland Bank. The committee also urged residents, many of whom were
members of New York City labor unions, to write, phone or send telegrams to
their union leaders demanding that they support "the current struggle of the
people of Co-op City to save their homes." The committee sought the support of the Mitchell-Lama Council and the Metropolitan Council on Housing, whose chairwoman called the Co-op City rent strike "electrifying" and
praised the striking residents for letting the state know that "you pushed
us this far and you're not going to push us any further." Not least of all, the
Steering Committee set up two subcommittees, the Rent Strike Subcommittee, whose members would manage the strike in violation of Brust's injunction, and the Rent Stabilization Subcommittee, whose members would focus
their efforts on political, legislative, and other matters that were not banned
by the injunction. In the event that the members of the Rent Strike Subcommittee were found in contempt of court and sent to prison, the members of
the Rent Stabilization Subcommittee would take their place.[10]

As the rent strike dragged on into a second month—and with no end in
sight—Governor Carey came under intense pressure from members of his
party to resolve the conflict. At the tail end of the legislative session, Senator Bernstein, Assemblyman Hochberg, and more than a score of other
Democratic legislators met with Commissioner Goodwin and Richard Ravitch, chairman of the HRH Construction Corporation and head of the state's
Housing Development Administration, and came up with a plan to bail out
the hard-strapped Mitchell-Lama projects. Included in the plan, which was
endorsed by Carey, was a proposal to allocate $10 million in loans to these
projects, $2.5 million of which was earmarked for Co-op City, whose repre-
sentatives had asked for $4 million. Hochberg relayed the proposal to Rosen,
who promptly rejected it. Calling it "a band-aid," he said that the offer was
"totally inadequate." As he and other Steering Committee members pointed
out, a $2.5 million loan would not do much to alleviate Co-op City's fiscal
plight. Indeed, it would reduce the recently approved increase in carrying
charges only from 25 percent to 18 percent. Even more objectionable to the
committee was that the offer "was contingent upon our agreement to stop
immediately our rent strike." Upon learning of the committee's reaction,

Carey withdrew the offer and proposed instead to allocate $10 million to aid Mitchell-Lama families who were spending more than 25 percent of their income on housing. The proposal, which would have benefited fewer than 1,000 of Co-op City's more than 15,000 families, was passed in the Assembly but shelved in the Senate.[11]

Few New Yorkers were as troubled by the rent strike and the state's response to it as Senator Bernstein, who, along with a few other legislators, Republicans as well as Democrats, had urged Governor Carey to remove Commissioner Goodwin from office. (Also fed up with Goodwin was the *City News*, which described the "State Housing Czar" as "callous, insensitive, and condescending.") Shortly before the legislature adjourned, Bernstein made a last-ditch attempt to end the crisis by proposing an amendment to the supplemental budget by which the state would appropriate $20 million for Mitchell-Lama housing. The amendment, he stressed, was not a subsidy, but a loan that would have to be repaid after ten years in installments spread over twenty-five years at an interest rate of only 4.5 percent. Although the amendment applied to all Mitchell-Lama projects, Bernstein pointed out, it would bring "immediate relief to Co-op City." It would eliminate the need for an increase in carrying charges and wipe out most of Co-op City's deficit. Above all, it would bring about the end of the rent strike and restore "normalcy" to Co-op City's 15,000 families. Claiming that both the Division of Housing and the Carey administration had failed Co-op City, Bernstein insisted that the legislature was its "last hope" and warned that if it adjourned without passing the amendment, "Co-op City may very well become the 'Ghost Town' of the East." Despite Bernstein's impassioned plea, the amendment was voted down, largely, wrote the *City News*, because of "the State's tight budget crunch."[12]

Fully 82 percent of Co-op City's residents went on strike in July. And late that month Rosen announced at another large rally on the Greenway that the Steering Committee intended to continue the strike in August and, if need be, in the fall and winter months. A week or so later a spokesman for the Division of Housing said that state officials had started to talk about bringing foreclosure proceedings on Co-op City's $436 million mortgage, a prospect that Rosen and the other Steering Committee members had long discounted. On August 4 the State Housing Finance Agency filed suit in state court against the Riverbay Corporation, which, as a result of the strike, owed about $8.5 million in mortgage payments, $5 million in state mortgage escrow payments, more than $1 million in city property taxes, and $500,000 in state supervisory fees. Also named in the suit were 11,500 striking residents as well as a handful of public institutions and private companies that would otherwise have been entitled to file a claim against Riverbay for unpaid bills. What Paul Bellica, executive director of the SHFA, called "the largest single residential foreclosure in [American] history" was filed with regret. But he said that the agency had no choice. The Co-op City rent strike had jeopardized its ability to pay off its bonds and notes. And only by bringing foreclosure proceedings against Riverbay could the SHFA safeguard the interests of Co-op City's bondholders and ensure that the agency could sell its bonds and notes for middle-income housing and other state projects.[13]

Rosen dismissed the lawsuit, saying that it was nothing but a ploy by the state to intimidate the striking residents, that it would be a long time before the court reached a decision, and that it was as likely that 50,000 people would be evicted from Co-op City as it was that "flowers would bloom [in New York City] in the winter." But if the suit was a threat, it was not a hollow one. During litigation the court would probably appoint a receiver, who would collect Co-op City's carrying charges and oversee its operating expenses. If the court eventually ruled in favor of the State Housing Finance Agency, the consequence would be dire for both Co-op City and its residents. Upon foreclosure, the agency would take Co-op City from Riverbay and, in order to pay off the mortgage, would then sell it in whole or in part to a private firm. As a result, Co-op City would lose its status as a cooperative and be stripped of its tax abatement, without which its property taxes would soar. If the receiver or new owner elected to rent the apartments and if at some point more than 20 percent of the apartments were occupied by tenants, the residents who owned their units would lose the right to deduct their share of Co-op City's interest payments and property taxes from their federal income taxes. In the end all the residents, even the residents who had paid their carrying charges in full to Riverbay, would lose the $450 per room that they had paid for their apartments.[14]

Shortly after the SHFA filed suit, events took an unexpected turn. Although 11,000 to 12,000 residents supported the rent strike, another 3,000 or so paid their full carrying charges to the Riverbay Corporation. Many of these residents felt that the strike was aggravating Co-op City's fiscal plight and alienating its friends in the state legislature. They also claimed that Co-op City's reputation was being tarnished by the many unsightly banners and flags that hung from the terraces, doors, and windows saying NO WAY, WE WON'T PAY and CO-OP CITY ON STRIKE. It was time for a change, these residents believed. On August 7 twenty-five of them formed an organization that was called Common Sense and chaired by Suzie Cantor and Norman Kriegel. Its objective was to challenge the leadership of Rosen and Steering Committee III and its hope, said Cantor, was that "once people have a reasonable alternative, they won't have to go on with the strike." In an attempt to find "a reasonable alternative," Common Sense met with Commissioner Goodwin on August 11. At the meeting, which George Schechter helped arrange, they discussed a plan to form a board of distinguished outsiders to help resolve the conflict. Perhaps in an attempt to bolster Common Sense's credibility, Goodwin later pledged to allow Co-op City's residents to elect the Riverbay board within a year after the State Housing Finance Agency and the Division of Housing reached an agreement with Co-op City's residents about how to solve the project's financial problems and ensure its long-term solvency.[15]

On August 14 Common Sense held a public meeting at the Co-op City Community Center that was attended by 200 to 300 residents, most of whom wanted to learn about the organization's plans and its recent meeting with Commissioner Goodwin. No sooner did the meeting get underway than a group of twenty-five to fifty striking residents attempted to disrupt it. Gathered outside the Community Center, they called the entering residents "scabs" and at one point tried to block the entrance, which was cleared by Co-op City security officers. Inside the auditorium they jeered each time Goodwin's name was mentioned, bringing the meeting to a halt on several occasions. When Ed Kelly, one of the leaders of Common Sense, mentioned the commissioner's pledge to allow Co-op City's residents to elect the Riverbay board, they shouted, "It's a lie! It's a lie!" After the meeting was over someone splashed red paint on the door to Norman Kriegel's apartment, and someone threw rocks through a window in the townhouse occupied by Kelly. Speaking for Common Sense, Larry Cantor, Suzie Cantor's husband, blamed the disruption and the vandalism on members of the Steering Committee, which, he said, had "tacitly condoned this violence by not actually opposing it." Common Sense was neither for nor against the rent strike, he stressed. It was "simply trying to act as a catalyst to get the two sides together and thereby arrive at some reasonable solution to the financial problems of Co-op City residents that would meet with the approval of the State Housing [Division]."[16]

As things went from bad to worse in Co-op City, Senator Bernstein renewed his effort to resolve the conflict. In mid-August he wrote a letter to

Justice Alfred J. Callahan, who had the unenviable task of presiding over not only the SHFA's suit against the Riverbay Corporation but also the River-bay Corporation's suit against the Steering Committee and twenty-two of its members. In this suit, which was filed on August 6, Riverbay asked the court to issue a permanent injunction against the rent strike, to hold the commit-tee and its members in contempt for disobeying Judge Brust's order, and to fine them $60,000 apiece and send them to prison for up to six months. The son of Joseph Callahan, who had been the minority leader of the State Assembly and an appellate court judge, Alfred Callahan was born in the Bronx and, after graduating from Harvard Law School, practiced law in New York and also served as an aide to Senator Robert F. Wagner and Governor W. Averell Harriman. Described by two journalists as "a minion of the Bronx County Democratic machine," he was elected a city civil court judge in 1964 and a state supreme court judge in 1973. In his letter to Callahan, which fo-cused on Riverbay's suit but also applied to the SHFA suit, Bernstein pointed out that the trial would drag on for a long time. And regardless of the out-come, the result "will not in the slightest solve the 'gut' problems of Co-op City." Indeed, it might well "engender greater antagonisms and polarize the parties." He therefore asked Callahan "to initiate settlement discussions and negotiations by arranging a conference of all the parties involved," including Commissioner Goodwin, members of her staff, and representatives of the governor's office and the State Housing Finance Agency.[17]

Acceding to what Bernstein acknowledged was "an unusual request," Callahan invited the parties and their lawyers to meet in his chambers on August 18, the day on which Riverbay's suit against Steering Committee III and its twenty-two members was scheduled to start. While hundreds of spectators jammed the Bronx courthouse on the Grand Concourse, the par-ties and their lawyers met for two hours, during which time the judge advised them that they had reached "an impasse" and that the only way out was to negotiate. Rosen and a few other members of the Steering Committee then met with Goodwin for another two hours in the office of Borough President Robert Abrams, who was deeply concerned about the plight of Co-op City's residents, severely troubled by the recent acts of violence against Common Sense, and therefore willing to act as a mediator. Also present at the meeting were the parties' lawyers, Senator Bernstein, and a representative for Sen-ate Minority Leader Manfred Ohrenstein. The next day the negotiators met, again in Abrams's office, for seven hours. By August 20 they had reached an agreement that was acceptable to Callahan. Under the agreement, which the

parties regarded as a first step in the effort to settle the dispute by negotiation, Riverbay's request for a contempt citation and a permanent injunction
would be put on hold for thirty days, and the SHFA's foreclosure proceedings
would be postponed indefinitely. The state would not initiate the eviction
of residents who had withheld their carrying charges, and Riverbay would
not subject them to late fees. Although the Steering Committee would not
stop the rent strike, it would turn the money it had already collected over to
Riverbay. All things considered, Abrams said, it was "a good day" for the residents of Co-op City.[18]

OOO

The *City News* praised Justice Callahan for prodding the Steering Committee and the Division of Housing "to sit down and finally try to negotiate a
settlement of the Co-op City rent strike." The upcoming negotiations represented "a breakthrough," it wrote. Assemblyman Alan Hochberg agreed. Reflecting the view of many residents, he said that he was confident that the
negotiations would be conducted in "good faith" and that "progress will be
made." But Larry Dolnick, a member of the Steering Committee negotiating
team, which was headed by Charlie Rosen and also included Esther Smith
and Charles Parness, cautioned that "the struggle isn't over." Even with the
participation of Borough President Abrams, Senator Bernstein, and a representative of Senator Ohrenstein, Rosen was skeptical that a settlement
could be reached by September 30, the date to which the contempt hearings had been postponed. He had good reason to be skeptical. The Steering
Committee had long been at loggerheads with Commissioner Goodwin, who
led the Division of Housing's negotiating team, which included representatives of the State Housing Finance Agency and lawyers for both the division
and the agency. Moreover, both sides were still at odds on many issues. To
give just one example, early on Rosen complained that Riverbay's financial
records had never been made available to the residents or to the resident directors. A spokesman for the Division of Housing responded that the Steering Committee had been given an opportunity to inspect Riverbay's books
at the public hearing about the application for a 25 percent increase in carrying charges, but "chose to walk out of the meeting."[19]

Despite the many differences between the Steering Committee and the
Division of Housing, the negotiations got off to a smooth start. In the first
couple of meetings the parties reached an agreement about how the money
that had been collected by the Steering Committee would be turned over to

the Riverbay Corporation. And the Division of Housing agreed to give the Steering Committee Riverbay's books, which, said a state assistant attorney general, "could fill two moving vans." But negotiations soon got bogged down. The Steering Committee team made a handful of proposals to alleviate Co-op City's financial problems. But the state negotiating team rejected them on the grounds that some were "impossible and unthinkable," others were "impracticable," and still others were a "violation" of the covenant with the bondholders. The state negotiators also made several proposals that it thought would resolve the conflict. Among them were that Riverbay cut its operating expenses by reducing the number of security guards and shortening the air-conditioning season; that a Co-op City Self-Help Committee be formed to encourage residents to lend money to Riverbay at 8.5 percent interest; that Riverbay appeal to the federal government for aid under the national housing program; and that Co-op City's carrying charges be raised by an indeterminate amount, but less than 25 percent. With the exception of a recommendation that the residents increase their investment in Co-op City by a maximum of $50 per room, the Steering Committee rejected the state's proposals.[20]

The issue came to a head on September 10, when the Steering Committee submitted a twenty-two-point proposal to wipe out Co-op City's deficit, eliminate the need for a 25 percent increase in carrying charges, and thereby end the rent strike. In the proposal, which was published in its entirety in the *City News* and the *Co-op City Times* and summarized in the *New York Times* and the *Bronx Press-Review*, Rosen and his associates lambasted the state, saying that with all its resources, which included the $1 million that Riverbay was forced to pay each year in supervisory fees to the Division of Housing and the State Housing Finance Agency, its only response to the fiscal crisis was "to place an overwhelming burden on the pocketbooks of the residents." Now, the committee boasted, a group of "ordinary citizens" who had no "training and experience" and used "only figures supplied by the State and Riverbay Corporation" had figured out how "to wipe out the entire 1975–76 budgetary deficit of $9,750,000"—and to do so "with a mere 43 cents a room monthly increase [in carrying charges]." After thanking Senator Bernstein, Borough President Abrams, and Yavner, Gallet, Freedman & Brett for their advice, the Steering Committee stressed that what was happening to Co-op City's residents "was going ... to happen to all low-income people in similar housing circumstances." Unless the state accepted the twenty-two-point proposal, the rent strike would continue, which would

lead to the collapse not only of the SHFA but also of all publicly funded housing in the country. And given that the Ford administration was bent on "dis-
mantling" the federal government's low-income housing programs, no help
could be expected from Washington.[21]

To wipe out most if not all of Riverbay's nearly $10 million deficit the
Steering Committee proposed that Riverbay sell or lease the Co-op City
power plant, which would save $4.6 million a year; that the state relieve
Riverbay of paying the interest and amortization on a $26.8 million es-
crow account that was held for the bondholders by the SHFA, which came
to $2.6 million a year; that the state waive the supervisory fees of the Divi-
sion of Housing and SHFA, which would save more than $1 million a year;
and, among other things, that the authorities exempt Riverbay from state
and city sales taxes. The Steering Committee's proposal also estimated that
Riverbay could generate an additional $4 million to $5 million in revenue
from rebates on property taxes, fees from insurance and litigation claims,
and other sources. To end the rent strike the Steering Committee also insisted that the Division of Housing revoke the 25 percent increase in carrying charges, retroactive to April 1, 1975; that the SHFA and Riverbay rescind
all legal actions against the committee and its leaders; that the Division of
Housing reimburse the committee for legal fees incurred in fighting the injunction, contempt charges, and foreclosure proceedings; and that the Division of Housing issue a Certificate of Acceptability to Co-op City and transfer
the voting stock to its residents. Once that was done, the Steering Committee would serve as an interim board of directors for ninety days, after which
the newly empowered shareholders would for the first time elect a permanent board, all of whose members would have to be residents of Co-op City.[22]

The response to the twenty-two-point proposal was extremely favorable
in Co-op City. Although the *Co-op City Times* had reservations about some
of the proposals, the *City News* praised the Steering Committee negotiators, a "group of honest, caring men" who, with "near bashful innocence," approached Riverbay's problems "as though they were their problems—which
they are—and looked at the huge cooperative as though it was their money
that was being spent." These men "have acted responsibly, creatively and
thoughtfully," relying not on "gimmickry" but on "common sense." And their
proposal, which applied "sound financial reasoning" to reduce expenses
and increase revenue, showed the Division of Housing "for what it is. A top-
heavy bureaucracy with no concern for the people or the development which
it supervises: a slothful, money-eating slug." At a rally on the Greenway on

September 17, at which Rosen explained the twenty-two-point proposal to 13,000 residents (and took the opportunity to disparage Goodwin and her group of "flunkies"), Senator Bernstein praised the Steering Committee leaders and their proposal. Referring to Rosen, Smith, Dolnick, and Parness, he said, "I would hire them as my negotiating team any time." Assemblyman Hochberg also hailed the Steering Committee leaders "for their efforts to stabilize rents in Co-op City" (and blasted Goodwin for refusing to consult with him and Bernstein). Borough President Abrams said that he too was proud to have taken part in the negotiations. After pledging to support the continuation of the rent strike, he told the crowd, "I am with you."[23]

By contrast, the Division of Housing was highly critical of the twenty-two-point proposal. In a written response it conceded that some of the measures were reasonable. Among them were the proposals to impose a moratorium on all new contracts that affected the structure of the Riverbay Corporation and the lifestyle of Co-op City's residents; to drop the lawsuits against the Steering Committee and its members; to issue a Certificate of Acceptability to Co-op City and transfer the voting stock to the residents; and to hold an election in which the shareholders would pick the Riverbay Corporation Board of Directors. But the Division of Housing insisted that, in the words of the *City News*, "the bulk of the Steering Committee's proposal to erase Co-op City's budget deficit would either have little immediate effect on the existing situation or be unrealistic, unfeasible or illegal if implemented." To give a few examples, the division said that it had no objection to the sale or lease of Co-op City's power plant, provided that the Riverbay board deemed it practical. But it stressed that this measure "cannot be counted on to generate immediate revenue." The division also held that it could not waive its supervisory fee without an appropriation to replace the funds, and it insisted that it had neither the authority nor the funds to reimburse the Steering Committee for its legal expenses. Perhaps most important, the division pointed out that much of the savings projected in the twenty-two-point proposal were contingent upon action by the state legislature, which was anything but a sure thing.[24]

Shortly after the Division of Housing rejected most of the Steering Committee's proposals, it came up with a proposal of its own, one that stunned Steering Committee III and most Co-op City residents. Under this proposal, which was transmitted to Rosen by Fred Hecht, assistant commissioner of housing, Co-op City's carrying charges would be raised 82 percent over the next five years. The 25 percent increase that was approved in June would be rescinded, and in its place a series of annual increases would be imposed—to wit 15 percent, 15 percent, 22 percent, 5 percent, and 7.5 percent. These increases would enable Riverbay to refinance a portion of its mortgage, which would make an additional $28 million available to management. As a result, Co-op City's deficit would rise to $14.3 million in June 1974, fall to $188,000 in June 1979, and turn into a $158,000 surplus in June 1980. But at the same time its carrying charges would soar from $42.77 to $77.90 per room per month. Rosen considered the state's proposal "totally unacceptable," as did Smith, Dolnick, and Parness. The state's proposal notwithstanding, Rosen was optimistic that the negotiators could resolve Co-op City's financial problems without increasing the carrying charges. And he was convinced that the Steering Committee's twenty-two-point proposal was "workable." Senator Bernstein was more pessimistic. He was convinced that the talks were not "moving forward to any appreciable degree" and beginning to wonder whether the state was negotiating in "good faith."[25]

It turned out that Bernstein was right. On September 26 negotiations broke down, with each side accusing the other of refusing to bargain in good faith. The Division of Housing charged that the Steering Committee team had failed to show up at the September 22 and September 25 meetings and had turned over only $2.5 million of the $7.5 million in carrying charges that the committee had collected in July, August, and September, which was a violation of the agreement on which the negotiations were based. Aware that Riverbay needed the money to provide essential services, the committee was using the $5 million as a bargaining chip. Rosen and his associates denied these charges, pointing out that the committee had asked the division to postpone the two meetings so that it could meet with elected officials from Washington. They also stressed that the processing of the checks was very time-consuming (and had been delayed by the observance of the Jewish Holy Days). For its part, the Steering Committee charged that the Division of Housing—which, said Rosen, had "acted in bad faith from Day 1 of the negotiations" and shown nothing but "contempt for the community's leadership"—had rejected its twenty-two-point proposal out of hand, a charge that a spokesman for the division denied. Nathalia Lange, chair of the Steering Committee's Publicity Department, accused the Division of Housing of playing "dirty pool," charging that it had dragged out the negotiations in an attempt to leave the committee's lawyers less time to prepare for the suits against the Steering Committee and its supporters, both of which had been postponed again to October 7.[26]

Following the breakdown of negotiations, the Steering Committee decided to hold on to the $5 million it had already collected until the Division of Housing was prepared to bargain in good faith. It also resolved to continue the rent strike in October. From October 3 to October 15, volunteers would collect the carrying charges without the 25 percent increase and give the checks and money orders to the Steering Committee, which would hold on to them rather than turn them over to Riverbay. A spokesman for the Division of Housing took strong exception to the Steering Committee's decisions, insisting that without the revenue from the carrying charges Riverbay would eventually have to curtail heat, hot water, and other essential services. Pointing out that the committee "seems to think that Riverbay Corp[oration] runs on thin air," he warned, "at some point we're going to be forced to cut back because vendors are not going to wait for [their] money indefinitely." Senator Bernstein disagreed. In view of the Division of Housing's intransigence, "a full-fledged strike is justified," he declared. And in a telegram sent to Governor Hugh L. Carey, he blamed the impasse on Commissioner Goodwin, who was "guilty of bad faith, divisive tactics and ineptness." By virtue of her "arrogance and duplicity," she had deeply alienated Co-op City's residents and severely undermined New York State's credibility. Once again he urged the governor to remove Goodwin from office, to replace her with someone more sensitive to the needs of the community, and, above all, to "personally take control and reopen negotiations."[27]

Carey was not swayed by Bernstein's appeal. Shortly after the negotiations broke down, Peter Goldmark, director of the state's Bureau of the Budget, told Assemblyman Andrew Stein, a Manhattan Democrat who had been asked to arrange a meeting between the Steering Committee and the governor or his top aides, that neither Carey nor his aides would do anything that would "undercut Goodwin." Stein said that Carey was "doing Co-op City a terrible disservice by passing the buck." He insisted that the governor's refusal to intervene would be a disaster not only for Co-op City and its bondholders but also for the State Housing Finance Agency, whose financial situation was growing more precarious every day. $69 million of the agency's short-term notes, $38 million of which had been issued for Co-op City, was coming due on October 15. And as a result of the Co-op City rent strike, the end of which was nowhere in sight, it was far from clear that the SHFA would have the money. The situation was so grim that on September 26 Moody's, a leading rating service, withdrew its rating for three issues of the SHFA (and for one issue of a state agency that underwrote the construction of hospitals). It was the first time a rating had been withdrawn on a New York State issue. Moreover, the banks and other financial institutions were growing concerned that the SHFA might default and be having second thoughts about the moral obligation bonds that had been issued for Co-op City and other large-scale state projects. On October 1 the agency was informed that the capital markets were closed to it "for the foreseeable future."[28]

A week after the negotiations broke down, Riverbay filed another lawsuit against twenty-two members of the Steering Committee, asking the court to hold them in contempt for refusing to turn the $5 million over to management. In a supporting affidavit Commissioner Goodwin stressed that the Division of Housing had agreed to negotiate on the condition that the committee would hand over all the money it had collected in July, August, and September. She also pointed out that, without the $5 million, Riverbay would not be able to maintain essential services and "the health, safety and well-being of thousands of residents," especially the elderly, would be seriously "imperiled." The lawsuit got underway on October 7, the same day that the Steering Committee and its leaders went on trial for violating Judge Brust's temporary injunction. Herbert Freedman, a partner at Yavner, Gallet, Freedman & Brett and counsel for all the defendants except Al Abrams, who was represented by Senator Bernstein, urged Justice Callahan to focus the hearing exclusively on the suit in which Riverbay asked the court to hold the Steering Committee and its members in contempt for violating Judge Brust's temporary injunction and to issue a permanent injunction against the committee and its supporters. But Callahan ruled against Freedman, stressing that he was not persuaded by counsel's argument that what was done with the July, August, and September checks had nothing to do with Judge Brust's injunction.[29]

Shortly afterwards, Governor Carey reached an agreement with Mayor Abraham Beame and other members of the Board of Estimate whereby the city would bail out the State Housing Finance Agency if the state would resume negotiations with the Steering Committee. At Carey's behest, Goodwin agreed to meet with Rosen and his associates at the Division of Housing's office at the World Trade Center on October 26. The meeting ended almost as soon as it started. Afraid that Steering Committee III would stash most of the money it had already collected some place beyond the jurisdiction of the state supreme court, Goodwin insisted that it would have to turn the $5 million over to Riverbay before the negotiations began. Another prerequisite of the negotiations, she said, was that the Steering Committee agree that Co-op City's residents would pay the increased carrying charges retroactive to April 1. It was "the price of admission," remarked the committee's vice chairman, Larry Dolnick, who stressed that "nothing will be gained or lost if Charles Rosen, myself or anyone else goes to jail. If necessary, other people will continue our struggle." Goodwin even refused to consider the committee's offer to turn over the money if the state agreed to postpone the trial for two weeks, an offer, Rosen explained, that was made because "there is no point to negotiate if there is a trial, and there is no point to have a trial if there are negotiations." The Steering Committee, he stressed, was led to believe that the Carey administration was ready to bargain in "good faith." Instead the state officials and their lawyers treated the committee's negotiators "with utter contempt." Indeed, said the Steering Committee, when asked what the state had "brought to the bargaining table," Goodwin replied, "Nothing."[30]

ooo

As soon as the second round of talks broke down the state resumed its efforts to break the strike in the Bronx County Courthouse, where Riverbay was asking Justice Callahan to hold the Steering Committee members in contempt for violating Judge Brust's temporary injunction, to issue a permanent injunction against the Steering Committee's rent strike, and to order the Steering Committee members to show cause why they should not be held in contempt for refusing to turn the $5 million in carrying charges over to management. The trial, which started on Tuesday, October 7, was eagerly anticipated. Several thousand Co-op City residents gathered outside the courthouse, carrying placards that read CO-OP CITY ON STRIKE and DON'T SEND MY DADDY BEN CIRLIN TO JAIL, chanting, "No way, we won't pay, we'll remember election day," and hanging Governor Carey in effigy for failing to keep his campaign promise to rescue Co-op City. Several hundred other residents jammed the corridors and the courtroom. Riverbay was represented by Arthur Handler and Michael Silberberg, the Steering Committee by Herbert Freedman and his partner Errol Brett (and Al Abrams by Senator Bernstein). On Wednesday, October 8, Callahan denied a motion by the Steering Committee's lawyers to dismiss Riverbay's suits and quash Brust's injunction. He also urged both sides to continue to negotiate when court was not in session. After the lawyers engaged in a host of procedural skirmishes and the justice laid down a handful of ground rules, the trial got underway.[31]

In his opening statement Handler told the court that he intended to prove that the twenty-two Steering Committee members had "openly, publicly and notoriously" defied Judge Brust's order to stop the rent strike. To substantiate his claim, he called to the stand his principal witness, Edward Aronov, Co-op City's general manager. Aronov testified that over the past four months the Steering Committee had violated the injunction by preventing Riverbay from collecting Co-op City's monthly carrying charges. He also said that from the balcony of his apartment on the twenty-sixth floor of Building 20A he had heard Rosen, Dolnick, and Parness speak at a rally on the Greenway in mid-July at which they urged all residents to withhold their carrying charges. And he had observed the Steering Committee's volunteers set up tables in the lobbies and collect checks and money orders from the residents. He denied that management had authorized the Steering Committee to collect the monthly carrying charges or advised the residents that they could disregard the 25 percent increase. Not least of all, Aronov testified that the rent strike had done "irreparable harm" to Co-op City. By virtue of the strike, Riverbay had received less than $1 million of its normal monthly rent roll of $3.9 million and was now way behind in its payments to vendors, among them Consolidated Edison, which had charged Co-op City $15,000 for failing to pay its bill on time. It was also $15 million in arrears in mortgage payments, $2 million in arrears in property taxes, and $700,000 in arrears in supervisory fees.[32]

In his daylong cross-examination of Aronov, Brett made several salient points. When Aronov reluctantly admitted that he had given Rosen computer printouts that contained confidential information about Co-op City's residents, Brett argued that he not only violated "the norms of confidentiality and common decency" but also "encouraged, aided and abetted the rent strike." (This argument intrigued Callahan, who observed that it would be improper for Riverbay to bring a legal action against the Steering Committee if it had done anything to facilitate the rent strike.) In response to Aronov's statement that he had overheard Rosen, Dolnick, and Parness urge Co-op City's residents to withhold their carrying charges at the rally in mid-July, Brett introduced evidence that Aronov lived too far from the Greenway to have heard anything that was said at the rally. Turning to the charge that the rent strike had done "irreparable harm" to Co-op City, Brett forced Aronov to acknowledge that the Steering Committee had offered to give management a portion of the June carrying charges to help maintain essential services, an offer that Riverbay rejected. Under questioning by Brett,

Aronov even conceded that as early as February, four months before the rent strike got underway, Riverbay had been very hard pressed to make its mortgage payments and meet its operating expenses. He also admitted that several months before the strike he had recommended that the Riverbay board could alleviate Co-op City's growing financial problems by raising garage and laundry fees and cutting back on heat, hot water, electricity, and air-conditioning.[33]

Riverbay's lawyers called several Steering Committee leaders to the stand. Questioned by Handler, Rosen admitted that on a few occasions he had said that he was prepared to continue the rent strike in defiance of Judge Brust's order—which, he said, was "undemocratic," a violation of his constitutional rights as an American citizen—and that if need be he and other members of the committee were ready to go to jail. He also acknowledged that he had been reimbursed $3,000 to $4,000 for time lost from his job at the *New York Post* (as well as for some out-of-pocket expenses). But he denied that the Steering Committee had coerced residents into taking part in the rent strike, and he added that the committee had forbidden its supporters to pay visits to the non-striking residents and put pressure on them to join the strike. Handler also asked Rosen to tell the court where the money the Steering Committee had collected, which was now about $8 million, was being kept. But Rosen, who was probably the only member of the committee who knew, refused to answer. Citing the Fifth Amendment, he claimed that the answer might tend to incriminate him. For the same reason Rosen also refused to answer when Handler asked, "Are you prepared today to defy Judge Brust's order?" By the time he stepped down from the witness box, he had pled the Fifth Amendment fifteen times. Handler argued that his questions did not tend to incriminate Rosen and therefore did not fall within the purview of the Fifth Amendment. After initially indicating that he tended to agree with Handler, Callahan decided that he would accept briefs from both sides before issuing a ruling. His ruling, wrote the *City News*, would have "a pivotal and possibly decisive impact on the way the rent strike case is finally decided."[34]

Other Steering Committee members, most of whom were questioned by Michael Silberberg, were more forthcoming than Rosen. Larry Dolnick testified that he had backed the committee's efforts to persuade Co-op City's residents to continue the strike in defiance of Judge Brust's order and also that he had solicited support for the strike from other Mitchell-Lama developments. As a member of the committee's negotiating team, he had taken part in the discussions to retain custody of the $8 million, though he pointed out that "Rosen wouldn't tell me where the checks are." Charles Parness, the committee's treasurer, said that he had written the checks for the committee's operating expenses, paid the bills for the ubiquitous flyers, and helped tabulate the June checks, a process that was supervised by Joel Dannenberg, who was also called to the stand. When asked if he was prepared to obey Judge Brust's order, Dannenberg replied, "So far as it doesn't violate my constitutional rights." Among the other Steering Committee members who testified was its secretary, Sam Steinberg, who at one point told the court that many elected officials were supporting the committee, a remark that prompted Callahan to say that he was not interested in knowing which officials supported the rent strike. The politicians were only after the tenants' votes, he remarked. Al Abrams was also called to the stand, but the Steering Committee's lawyers told the court that he was ill. Whereupon Handler requested that Abrams bring in a doctor's note saying when he would be able to appear in court.[35]

Early in November, by which time the rent strike was entering its sixth month, a few proposals were made to settle the lawsuit. At the urging of Callahan, Riverbay offered to drop the charges, provided that the Steering Committee ended the strike and turned over the money and that the residents allowed the SHFA to foreclose on Co-op City and take over the development and dropped the lawsuit that Louis Nizer had filed in state court in early November, a suit in which he accused the UHF and the State of New York of fraud and asked for substantial but unspecified damages. The Steering Committee rejected this proposal out of hand. The lawyers for both sides also agreed to drop charges against a dozen defendants, all of whom were members of the Rent Stabilization Subcommittee, which had not done anything to violate Brust's injunction. Although Callahan had recently ruled that Rosen had the right to plead the Fifth Amendment, he and nine others were still at risk. To put pressure on them to settle, Callahan threatened on November 10 that if Rosen, Dolnick, Parness, and Smith did not turn over an estimated $10 million to Riverbay by November 14, he might sentence them to up to six months in jail. The threat did not faze the Steering Committee's leaders. Their imprisonment would only solidify the community's support for the rent strike, said Rosen, who added that "Riker's Island [the site of the city's main and most notorious jail] is not a good setting for negotiations." When it was clear that the Steering Committee was not going to turn over the money, Callahan held the ten remaining defendants in contempt.[36]

Early in the trial, which ended on November 20, more than six weeks after it started, Justice Callahan, who was fed up with the Steering Committee's lawyer's frequent objections, said, "I'll give you 10 to 1 odds that this case will be appealed no matter how I finally rule." And so it was—by both sides. The Steering Committee filed an appeal with the First Department of the Appellate Division in late November and asked Justice Myles J. Lane to issue an interim stay of Callahan's ruling until the full court could review the case. Lane refused and referred the request to the full court, which also refused to grant a stay. Riverbay's lawyers were also disappointed by Callahan's ruling. Although he had held Rosen and the other nine Steering Committee leaders in contempt, he had declined to fine or imprison them. According to Rosen, Callahan believed that the purpose of a contempt citation was not to punish the offenders but to force them to comply with the court's orders and therefore that he was inclined to leave the decision about punishment up to one of his fellow judges. On Callahan's advice, Riverbay's lawyers then filed another suit in the Bronx Supreme Court. The case was assigned to Justice Isidore Dollinger, a former Bronx district attorney and, it was widely believed, a close confidant of Bronx Democratic Party leader Patrick Cunningham. Early in December the two parties gathered in Dollinger's courtroom, where Riverbay's lawyers attempted to persuade him to fine and perhaps even imprison the Steering Committee's leaders for defying Judge Callahan's order to hand the money that had been collected over to Riverbay.[37]

After a relatively short trial, Dollinger ruled in Riverbay's favor on December 22, pointing out that the Steering Committee and its leaders had already been held in contempt by Judge Callahan and could only "purge themselves" by handing over an estimated $17 million within five days. If they refused, he would fine the committee $250,000 and each of its leaders $5,000. For each day the defendants ignored his order, Dollinger would increase the fine by $5,000 for the committee and $1,000 for its leaders. The fines were "preposterous," said Rosen, who added that "if we had that kind of money we wouldn't have gone on a [rent] strike." Rosen also told a crowd of about 2,000 residents that the Steering Committee would not "pay a dime" to the state-controlled Riverbay board until it agreed "to sit down and negotiate with us." In the meantime, he added, "let them [the fines] pile up." When the Appellate Division denied the committee's request for a stay of Dollinger's ruling a week and a half later, pile up they did. Making matters worse for the committee, Judge Callahan had a change of heart. On December 30, he fined the committee an additional $50,000 and each of its leaders an additional $5,000. Less than two weeks later he issued a permanent injunction against the Steering Committee and its members, barring them from carrying on a rent strike or in any way encouraging the residents of Co-op City to withhold their monthly carrying charges. Despite these legal setbacks—and the possibility, said Herbert Freedman, that if the defendants did not pay their fines, the court might attach their bank accounts, repossess their cars, garnish their wages, and perhaps even send them to jail for up to six months—the Steering Committee carried on. And in January 1976 the rent strike entered its eighth month.[38]

During the next few months several other lawsuits were filed that were in one way or another a product of the rent strike. Acting on behalf of the area marshals and building captains, who had been barred from doing anything to facilitate the strike, the Steering Committee challenged Dollinger's injunction on constitutional grounds in federal court. In separate cases Judges Inzer B. Wyatt and Milton Pollack ruled against the committee. Pollack even went so far as to say that Errol Brett, the committee's lawyer, was wasting the court's time. In another case Charlie Rosen's parents, David and Eva Rosen, who had moved into Co-op City in November 1974 and paid their carrying charges with the 25 percent increase, sued Riverbay for cutting back on essential services, which, they argued, breached Co-op City's occupancy agreement and jeopardized its residents' life, health, and safety. The suit was dismissed on the grounds that there was no emergency at Co-op City. In yet another case the Steering Committee asked the court to order Riverbay to accept $650,000 in checks that a citywide tenant organization, which was acting as an intermediary for the committee, had offered the Division of Housing in February on the condition that the money was used to purchase fuel and rehire laid off Co-op City workers. The division rejected the offer on the grounds that it would not be proper to allow the Steering Committee to dictate "which bills for which services should be paid, and for what amounts." But while the case was still pending, Riverbay agreed to take the money. The court later ruled that it had to accept the checks if the Steering Committee did not place any conditions on the use of the money.[39]

Of all the cases that were heard in the first half of 1976, by far the most important was filed in August 1975, when the State Housing Finance Agency instituted foreclosure proceedings against the Riverbay Corporation and the 11,500 striking residents. Early in November, a month or so after the first round of negotiations broke down, Frank Ioppolo—a member of Donovan,

Leisure, Newton & Irvine, a "white-shoe" Manhattan law firm founded in 1929 by William J. Donovan, who is best known today as the head of the Office of Strategic Services during World War II—said that the SHFA was preparing to move ahead with the suit. Pointing out that Riverbay had failed to make its mortgage payments since March and thus was in violation of its mortgage agreement, Ioppolo claimed that the issue was clear-cut—indeed so clear-cut that that there was no reason to hold a trial. Hence he was inclined to ask the court for summary judgment. Stressing that "foreclosure totally short-circuits the normal eviction process," he also contended that Rosen and other Steering Committee members were misleading Co-op City's residents by claiming that it was inconceivable that the state would oust 60,000 people from their homes. In December Justice Dollinger denied the Steering Committee's motion to dismiss the SHFA's lawsuit. And after a couple of months of legal skirmishing, the trial was set for March 23. It would be heard by Judge Nathaniel T. Helman, a former state senator who had been appointed a city court judge in 1960 and elected to the state supreme court a year later.[40]

Representing the 11,500 striking residents was Herbert Freedman, the Steering Committee's lawyer, who urged Justice Helman to deny the SHFA's request for summary judgment on the grounds that the UHF had engaged in fraud and other irregularities in the building of Co-op City. Based on an affidavit by Rosen—as well as evidence from Nizer's federal and state lawsuits—the defense alleged that the UHF had deliberately understated the cost of construction. Along with CSI, it had hired subcontractors not because they were the lowest bidder or the most qualified, but because they were well connected politically. Some subcontractors even submitted fraudulent bids in order to get the job, and one stole material from Co-op City to build a house outside New York City. The subcontractors also took advantage of the inflationary spiral to increase their profits and funneled some of these profits to the UHF and CSI. The defense also alleged that the UHF knew that the original carrying charges were too low to cover Co-op City's fixed costs and operating expenses and that the Division of Housing was well aware of these efforts to defraud Co-op City's shareholders. All these allegations would be proved at trial, said the defense. Lastly, the defense drew upon a report by State Comptroller Arthur Levitt that showed that forty-four of the state's seventy-one Mitchell-Lama projects were not meeting their mortgage payments or reserve fund obligations. And yet Co-op City was the only one against which the state had brought foreclosure proceedings, leading the

Steering Committee to contend that "the foreclosure is designed to crush tenant opposition to increased housing costs."[41]

Judge Helman handed down his ruling on May 10, by which time the rent strike was entering its twelfth month, Riverbay Corporation was $14.8 million behind in mortgage payments and $3.2 million behind in property taxes and the Steering Committee was holding more than $26 million in carrying charges. In a seventeen-page decision, he issued a summary judgment granting the SHFA the right to proceed with the foreclosure and, if it saw fit, to sell all or part of Riverbay's assets. He dismissed the defense's allegations because, even if true, none of them applied to the SHFA. Indeed, he pointed out, the only bar to the foreclosure would have been evidence that there had been fraud in the drafting of the mortgage or in the mortgage itself, an issue that the defense had not addressed. And since Riverbay was long overdue in its mortgage payments, Helman believed that he had no choice but to rule in the SHFA's favor. Expressing concern about the well-being of the thousands of residents whose property rights might be affected "by what is undoubtedly the largest foreclosure in history," he concluded by saying that he hoped the SHFA would not rush to evict the residents. After Helman handed down his ruling, Paul Belica, executive-director of the SHFA, announced that the agency would ask the court to appoint a receiver, who would have the authority to arrange for the sale of Co-op City. At the same time the Steering Committee decided to continue the struggle. "We're not cowed by the threat of foreclosure," Rosen declared. And though he said that Helman had made a terrible decision, he stressed that the committee was in no rush to file an appeal.[42]

ooo

The Steering Committee was in no rush to file an appeal because by the time Helman handed down his decision, Rosen and his associates believed that they were close to an agreement with the Carey administration by which the foreclosure proceedings would be halted, the Riverbay Corporation would be bailed out, and the rent strike would be called off. To understand how this agreement was reached, it is necessary to bear in mind that by January 1976 Co-op City was in dire straits. Despite its legal setbacks in December 1975, the Steering Committee had no intention of stopping the rent strike, much less of turning over an estimated 95,000 checks to management and paying the heavy fines imposed by Judges Dollinger and Callahan. For by then the rent strike was "a way of life in Co-op City," wrote Vivian Gornick, a *Village Voice* reporter. As a result of "the solidarity of the cooperators" and "the organizing abilities of Steering Committee III," she said, "virtually everyone in the housing complex is behind the strike, and nearly 2,000 people are actively involved in its administration." The strike had galvanized the residents, turning them into a community "as nothing else could ever have done" and generating "an enormous camaraderie" among thousands of people "who never knew each other before." With the great majority of Co-op City's residents withholding their carrying charges in early 1976, Riverbay was hard pressed to pay its operating expenses, not to mention its fixed costs, which it had been unable to pay for nearly a year.[43]

Thus starting in early January, Riverbay tried to reduce its operating expenses. On the advice of Tom Woodstock, the assistant general manager (and former controller), who warned that within thirty days "we will be totally broke," management laid off roughly 200 (or almost 45 percent) of Riverbay's 460 employees, a move that was expected to save $58,000 a week. Among the many who received pink slips were janitors, porters, gardeners, groundskeepers, maintenance workers, security guards, and garage attendants. Given that it was the middle of winter, heat and hot water would not be reduced, at least not for the time being. But routine maintenance would be curtailed, and appliances would not be repaired or replaced. Emergency repairs would still be made, and rubbish would still be removed. Halls would still be lit, though not as brightly. And garages would remain open, though the attendants, who used to be on call twenty-four hours a day, would be available only from 4:30 p.m. to 12:30 a.m. Charlie Rosen charged that the layoffs and cutbacks, which he called "a premeditated attempt to crush the [rent] strike," were "endangering the lives of 55,000 residents." And the Steering Committee offered to provide management with funds to pay operating expenses, an offer that was declined. As I mentioned earlier, the cutback in services spurred some residents to file suit against Riverbay for breach of Co-op City's occupancy agreement. The layoffs also prompted many Riverbay employees, most of whom were members of Local 32-E of the Service Employees International Union, to call in sick on January 20. Two months later most maintenance workers and security guards walked off the job to protest the layoffs.[44]

Riverbay also continued its efforts to break (or at least weaken) the rent strike. It served dozens of area marshals and building captains with certified copies of Judge Brust's injunction, reminding them that by participating in strike activities they were running the same risks as the Steering

Committee leaders. With security guards clearing the way, photographers barged into some of the lobbies where the volunteers were collecting the carrying charges and, without asking permission, snapped pictures of the marshals and captains. It was a "type of legal harassment," wrote the *City News*, a "ruthless attempt" to frighten and intimidate the striking residents, said Rosen. Riverbay also subpoenaed the financial records of ten members of the Steering Committee and their spouses, who were ordered to turn over to Riverbay their bankbooks, loan applications, and even Christmas and Hanukkah club accounts. On the basis of these records, they could be summoned to testify in court. When the committee's members and spouses ignored the subpoenas, Riverbay took them to court, where its lawyers charged that they were hiding their assets in an attempt to avoid paying the fines imposed by Judges Dollinger and Callahan. The Steering Committee's lawyers argued that the subpoenas were illegal because they forced wives to testify against husbands and husbands to testify against wives. In mid-February Judge Helman ruled against them, holding that Riverbay had the right to examine the committee leaders and their spouses in order to find any assets that could be used to pay the fines, a ruling that enabled Riverbay to seize the defendants' bank accounts and seal their safe deposit boxes.[45]

The Steering Committee and its supporters took a few steps to counter Riverbay's effort to reduce its operating expenses and break (or at least weaken) the rent strike. Two of them stand out. As a result of the layoff of eleven out of the thirteen laundry mechanics, many of Co-op City's washers and dryers were out of order, a few for as many as three weeks, forcing some housewives to spend hours waiting for a machine and others to drive to a laundromat outside the community, which was not an option for the many elderly residents who did not own a car. Hence in early February two large groups of Co-op City housewives, incensed about conditions in the laundry rooms, held demonstrations in Edward Aronov's office, where they were told to expect increasing inconveniences because of Riverbay's fiscal crisis. When the situation did not improve, another group of housewives staged a "wash-in" in late March. "Equipped with scrubbing boards and basins filled with water," wrote the *City News*, they washed their dirty laundry in Commissioner Goodwin's offices in the World Trade Center, singing, "This is the way we wash our clothes, wash our clothes, wash our clothes. This is the way we wash our clothes every Monday morning." They then hung the clean laundry in the reception area. After disrupting business for three hours, they threatened that if the 200 Riverbay employees were not rehired and Co-op

City's washers and dryers were not fixed, they would take their dirty laundry to Goodwin's home in Southampton and Carey's house on Shelter Island, both of which were on eastern Long Island, far from Co-op City.[46]

An even more serious problem arose in early January. Consolidated Edison informed Riverbay that it had not paid its November bill of more than $700,000 and its December bill of more than $500,000 and threatened to discontinue service unless the November bill was paid forthwith. But as a result of the rent strike, Riverbay did not have the money. As Tom Woodstock pointed out, "If we were to pay one Con Ed bill we would be out of business." In an attempt to ensure that the residents would not be deprived of gas and electricity, a hardship that might lead some to stop supporting the rent strike, the Steering Committee offered to pay Con Ed's outstanding bills. But Arthur Handler, Riverbay's lawyer, warned Con Ed that if it took money directly from the Steering Committee it would violate Judge Callahan's injunction. Judge Helman agreed with him. With Con Ed threatening to discontinue service on February 9, the Steering Committee came up with an ingenious plan. Assuming that Helman's ruling did not bar the residents from paying Con Ed directly, the committee proposed that they make their February checks out to the utility company rather than the Steering Committee and thereby avert the loss of service. Con Ed had no objections to the committee's plan. When it was over, the Steering Committee put thousands of checks worth about $2.4 million into black plastic bags, brought the bags to Con Ed's office in Lower Manhattan, and turned the checks over to one of the company's vice presidents. The $2.4 million was enough to pay Riverbay's outstanding bills and provide close to $700,000 as partial payment of its February bill.[47]

As the rent strike dragged on—and as the conflict between Steering Committee III and the Riverbay Corporation heated up—Governor Carey came under increasing pressure to do something. But New Yorkers were sharply divided about what that something was. On one side were the Steering Committee, most Co-op City residents, many elected officials, most tenant organizations, and the *City News*. In a barrage of letters, telegrams, and mailgrams (as well as a host of demonstrations), these New Yorkers reminded Carey that in his recent gubernatorial campaign he had promised to help the residents of Co-op City and other Mitchell-Lama developments. "HAVE YOU FORGOTTEN YOUR PROMISES?" one resident asked. Another wrote Carey that he now regretted voting for him. Yet another resident, who said that both he and his wife had voted for Carey, told the governor that

Co-op City's 16,000 families "are caught up in an economic squeeze that they can in no manner absorb." In a letter to the *New York Times*, which had recently criticized the Steering Committee and the rent strike, Yetta Weinstein wrote that the residents of Co-op City wanted nothing more than "to live in a safe community with stabilized rents." But the carrying charges had been raised six times in the past five years and were now twice as high as they were when she moved in. When the residents of Co-op City voiced their concerns, the state lied to them, treated them with contempt, and subjected them to "trials, fines, jail, eviction, foreclosure, loss of equity, or any other harassing tactic they can find to frighten and intimidate us with."[48]

Supporters of the Steering Committee insisted that it was time for Carey to honor his commitment to Co-op City. For too long he had allowed Commissioner Goodwin to deal with the problem as she saw fit. Now it was up to him to take charge. At a press conference held in early January at Carey's Midtown Manhattan office, twelve tenant organizations from all over New York City urged the governor to start negotiating with the Steering Committee. As Jane Benedict of the Metropolitan Council on Housing put it, the threat of fines, imprisonment, and other "strike-breaking tactics" were nothing but "a declaration of war on every tenant in New York City." At another press conference, which was held in late January, Assemblyman Frank J. Barbaro and thirty-seven other state legislators, all of whom were concerned about "the possible termination of heat, hot water, electricity, and other essential services [in Co-op City]," called on Carey to appoint a blue-ribbon panel to find out why the rent strike had not been settled. The legislators offered to work with him to find a solution to "this most difficult problem," which "the passage of time will only serve to exacerbate." They believed that if the governor did not take a more active role in the rent strike, as WMCA, a local radio station, was urging him to do, conditions would only get worse in Co-op City. At stake, the legislators argued, was not only the fate of its hard-strapped residents, many of whom would be forced to move out of their apartments, but also the future of the Mitchell-Lama program, without which many low- and middle-income families would be unable to live in New York.[49]

On the other side were the New York Realty Owners Association, a few real estate economists and public officials, some metropolitan newspapers, and the Concerned Citizens of Co-op City, an offshoot of Common Sense that claimed it represented Co-op City's non-striking residents. (Charlie Rosen, no fan of the Concerned Citizens, later wrote that it had so few members that they could have held a meeting in a telephone booth.) In a flurry of letters and articles, the Steering Committee's opponents urged the governor to turn down the Steering Committee's demands for financial aid. As Roger Starr, head of New York City's Housing and Development Administration, wrote, Co-op City had already been heavily subsidized. The state had provided a huge mortgage at below-market interest rates. And besides giving Co-op City a large tax abatement, the city had built its schools, streets, and other public facilities. Now, Starr said, the Steering Committee was asking not for financial aid for Co-op City's elderly and low-income families, but for "an across-the-board additional subsidy for every resident," which the state could not afford. Along the same line, another New Yorker pointed out that as a result of inflation every Mitchell-Lama project had been forced to raise its rent or carrying charges. Why, he asked, should Co-op City be given special treatment? Also opposed to the Steering Committee's demands was the *New York Times.* "No one likes to pay more for housing," it wrote, "yet, it is indisputable that the Co-op City residents would have to pay at least twice as much for comparable dwellings elsewhere." (At $52 a room, Co-op City is "a fantastic bargain," said Lee Goodwin, to which Charlie Rosen replied, "It's a hell of a good buy, but only if I can afford it.")[50]

Opponents of the Steering Committee insisted that it was time for Carey to stand up to Rosen and his associates. Writing to the governor in February, Norman Kriegel, chairman of the Concerned Citizens of Co-op City, pointed out that the strike leaders were brazenly defying the courts. By letting them get away with it, Commissioner Goodwin and the Division of Housing were sanctioning the strike and thereby paving the way for "the inevitable default and foreclosure [of Co-op City]." The rent strike started in June 1975, which was nine months ago, Kriegel reminded the governor, and "nine months is too long." The state might not want "to rock the boat," Kriegel went on, but "there is no boat here any longer; it is well on the way to the bottom." If the state bailed out Co-op City, Kriegel and others charged, it would be unfair to non-striking residents and the residents of other Mitchell-Lama projects. It would also undermine the state's precarious financial condition. The rent strike was already wreaking havoc on the state's bonding capacity, said Ruben Klein, president of the New York Realty Owners Association. If it went on much longer, "there was little hope for the future of middle-income cooperative housing in New York City." Another critic of the Steering Committee was Frank S. Kristof, the prominent real estate economist. Calling the rent strike "a classic example" of "the rent control syndrome," he wrote that "if New Yorkers of nonpoor status, who already receive substantial public subsidies, insist on being protected from the vicissitudes of operating their modern new apartments, it raises the serious question of whether the public sector should be in the housing business at all."[51]

Under increasing pressure to do something about the quagmire into which Co-op City was sinking, Carey took steps to placate both sides. In late January he asked the state legislature to appropriate $22 million for a rent subsidy program that was designed to help the hard-strapped residents of Co-op City and other Mitchell-Lama projects and to build support for the ongoing effort to bail out the State Housing Finance Agency. Of the $22 million, $12 million would be for seniors who earned less than $6,500 and would otherwise have to spend more than one-third of their income on housing. Another $10 million would go to other residents who, as a result of the increases in rents or carrying charges, would have to pay a "disproportionate" share of their income on housing. The program, said a spokesman for the State Division of Housing, would "allow needy tenants and cooperators to remain in their apartments while maintaining the financial viability of the projects." It would also defuse the "explosive situation at Co-op City," wrote the *Times*. A month and a half later Carey made a more controversial proposal, one that infuriated Charlie Rosen, who claimed that it revealed "the utter contempt state officials have for the people of Co-op City." Under this proposal the state would provide a $10 million loan to replenish the SHFA debt service reserve fund, which had been severely depleted by the rent strike. But as a condition of the loan the agency would have to press ahead with its efforts to foreclose on Co-op City and Riverbay would have to continue its legal efforts to break the strike. Referring to Carey's staff, Senator Bernstein said, "They intended to try to sneak [the proposal] through, but I put the kabash on their plan."[52]

At some point, probably in the early spring, Carey took another and, as it turned out, much more important step. Having lost confidence in Commissioner Goodwin, a Rockefeller and Wilson holdover who, as a member of the Division of Housing's staff noted, had been left "almost completely on her own," Carey asked Secretary of State Mario Cuomo to try to resolve the problem. It was an inspired decision. Born in 1932, Cuomo was a native of Queens. The son of an Italian immigrant who worked first as a laborer and then as a grocer, he attended St. John's University and St. John's Law School. Although Cuomo graduated at the top of his class, no Manhattan law firm offered him a job—in all likelihood, he believed, because he was Italian-American. So he went into practice in Queens, where his resolution of two

extremely nasty disputes earned him a well-deserved reputation as an ex-
ceptionally skillful negotiator and mediator. In one case New York City's
Board of Education proposed to demolish sixty-nine homes in Corona to
make way for an athletic field adjacent to an as-yet-unbuilt high school, a
proposal that infuriated the large Italian-American neighborhood. Cuomo
worked out a deal with Mayor John V. Lindsay's deputy Richard Aurelio
whereby all but thirteen of the homes were saved. In another case New York
City's Housing Authority planned to erect three 24-story apartment houses
in Forest Hills, a plan that aroused a furor in the largely middle-class Jewish neighborhood, many of whose residents feared an influx of low-income
African Americans. Cuomo negotiated a settlement under which the development was cut in half and 40 percent of the apartments were reserved for
the elderly. Cuomo was also active in Democratic Party politics. And after
he failed to win the Democratic nomination for lieutenant governor in 1974,
Carey appointed him secretary of state.[53]

Although very few residents were aware of it until early May, Rosen,
Dolnick, Smith, and Parness soon started meeting with Cuomo. And though
previous talks between the Steering Committee and the Division of Housing had gone nowhere, the chances of an agreement were brighter now than
ever. For one thing, Cuomo was a negotiator par excellence, "the Henry Clay
of Queens," wrote a *New York Times* reporter. He was also no Lee Goodwin,
a graduate of Barnard College and Brown and Columbia Universities who
spent much of her time hobnobbing with the city's financial elite and, said
Rosen, looked down on him and his associates, who, in turn, regarded her
as a surrogate for New York's banks and Co-op City's bondholders. For another thing, the Carey administration was extremely anxious to resolve the
problem. It was embarrassed by the Steering Committee's defiance of the
courts. And it was concerned about Co-op City's precarious financial condition, which was jeopardizing the solvency of the SHFA and the state itself.
Not only had about 11,000 residents been handing their checks over to the
Steering Committee for eleven months, but almost 300 of them had vacated
their apartments and, in violation of the occupancy agreement, stopped paying their carrying charges, which cost Riverbay more than $1 million a year.
For yet another thing, the Steering Committee was also under pressure to
settle. Although it claimed to speak for all the residents, it was sharply criticized by the Concerned Citizens of Co-op City, which claimed that the committee did not represent the non-striking residents. Also at odds with the
Steering Committee was a group of Co-op City clergymen who called on the

committee to turn over to the state the $23 million it was holding, a move that they believed would spur negotiations, avoid foreclosure, and, in the words of Eli Matlin, president of the Co-op City Jewish Community Council, prevent "further deterioration of our community."[54]

OOO

The talks between Cuomo and the Steering Committee team went so well that on May 11, a day after Judge Helman ruled that SHFA could go ahead with the foreclosure proceedings, Rosen announced that the two sides had "agreed in principle to a settlement." Rosen's announcement, which was made at a rally at Co-op City, was designed to reassure the many residents who had been stunned by Helman's ruling, leaving some defiant and others in despair, wrote a *Times* reporter. Although Rosen did not spell out the details of the settlement, he stressed that a compromise was "close enough that it was beginning to be reduced to writing." Cuomo was more circumspect. Although he acknowledged that discussions had been underway when Helman handed down his ruling, he insisted that the talks were still ongoing and that all that had been agreed upon thus far was "a loose formulation that never got reduced to a precise form." Insiders were more forthcoming. They disclosed that under the proposed settlement the Steering Committee would turn over the $22 million to $26 million in carrying charges it was holding, in return for which the state would delay foreclosure proceedings and give full control of Co-op City to the residents for six months. Commissioner Goodwin was opposed to the plan, the *Times* reported, because it did not require the residents to pay the 25 percent increase in carrying charges that had sparked the dispute. But Cuomo stressed that foreclosure would not solve any of Co-op City's problems. "'Who,' he asked," wrote the *Times*, "'will buy the $2 billion development, with some tenants being evicted and others refusing to pay rent?'"[55]

Even before all the details were revealed, Cuomo's plan generated a good deal of opposition. The Concerned Citizens of Co-op City feared that once the striking residents took control they would retaliate against the nonstriking residents. Some of them had already been the subject of "strong verbal and even physical abuse," Norman Kriegel told Carey. The Rochdale Village board of directors protested that it would be unjust to exempt only Co-op City from an increase in carrying charges. Any financial aid provided to Co-op City should also be provided to other Mitchell-Lama cooperatives, all of which were "facing the same financial hardships," said Rochdale's president, William L. Booker. The Citizens Housing and Planning Council, a prominent civic group, wrote Carey that while it supported "individual subsidies" for the needy, it opposed "a blanket subsidy" for all Co-op City residents. Such a subsidy would be "an injustice to other New Yorkers who are paying the higher costs of housing." The Association for Government Assisted Housing, whose members owned and operated $2 billion worth of housing and provided shelter to more than 100,000 people, warned that "a capitulation to the Co-op City rent strikers will have the immediate effect of creating a snowball which will result in rent strikes in every Mitchell-Lama building," the consequences of which would be "horrendous to contemplate." Also opposed to Cuomo's plan was the *Wall Street Journal*. In an editorial entitled "The Co-op City Neurosis," it wrote that any compromise with the striking residents would lead to the collapse of "the shaky foundations of New York's housing finance program." It was time for the state to stop playing "political games" and proceed with foreclosure and evictions. And "it will be more humane to throw people out into the June sunshine than into the December snow," said the *Journal*.[56]

Despite strong opposition from these and other organizations, much of which was mobilized by Commissioner Goodwin, wrote the *City News*, Cuomo and the Steering Committee team continued the talks, reached an agreement, ironed out the details, and in early June submitted a formal proposal to Carey. The governor had serious reservations. Much like Goodwin, he was troubled that under Cuomo's plan the residents of Co-op City would not have to pay the carrying charges with the 25 percent increase for the first six months. Even more important, he was afraid that a compromise with the striking residents would jeopardize his administration's attempt to enlist the support of the Republican-controlled State Senate and the US Department of Housing and Urban Development in the effort to rescue the State Housing Finance Agency. A few days after receiving Cuomo's proposal—and a day or so after meeting with the leaders of the Concerned Citizens of Co-op City—Carey refused to accept Cuomo's plan and instructed him to resume negotiations. Cuomo was prepared to do as instructed. But in an interview he pointed out that the governor had "neither accepted nor rejected" the "general parameters" of his plan and that he would only have to "adjust specific parts" of the compromise. He also insisted that the proposal was "the best I can get." There was no way, he stressed, that he could persuade the Steering Committee and residents of Co-op City to pay the increased carrying charges until they had control of the development and time to satisfy themselves that the increase was necessary.[57]

On June 7, Roger Starr sent Carey a telegram saying that it took courage to stand up to the striking tenants and turn down the Cuomo plan. Before long, however, the governor had second thoughts about his decision. He may have decided that Cuomo had done as well as he could. He may have realized that the state legislature, which had just voted down another mortgage-interest-reduction bill, would not help solve the problem. Or he may have been assured that the Cuomo plan would not jeopardize the effort to save the SHFA. Whatever the reason, Carey changed his mind. In late June he announced that his administration had reached an agreement with the Steering Committee to end the rent strike. Under the agreement— which was based largely on the Cuomo plan and, the governor conceded, would leave some parties dissatisfied—the Steering Committee would hand over $15.1 million to the state immediately and another $5 million within six months. In return, the SHFA would stop, but not drop, the foreclosure proceedings. And the Division of Housing would suspend the 25 percent increase in carrying charges. It would also turn Co-op City over to the residents for six months. At the beginning it would be run by an interim board of directors, all but one of whose members would be chosen by the Steering Committee. And within sixty days, by which time the Division of Housing would have issued a Certificate of Acceptability, the residents would elect a permanent board. The board would be empowered to set the carrying charges as it saw fit, but the charges would have to be enough to cover not only Co-op City's operating expenses but also the interest and amortization on its mortgage, which came to $2.26 million a month. Also included in the agreement were provisions that Governor Carey would ask Richard Ravitch to monitor the situation in Co-op City and that he would appoint a special task force to look into the problems of the Mitchell-Lama housing program.[58]

Although Charlie Rosen was disappointed that the agreement did not include a program for rent stabilization, a commitment to drop the foreclosure proceedings, and a provision to rescind the 25 percent increase, he was otherwise extremely satisfied with what he referred to as a "truce." Speaking at a celebratory rally that was held on the Greenway on June 29 and attended by 7,000 residents, he shouted, "We beat them [the state, banks, and bondholders], but good." Also extremely satisfied was Herbert Freedman, the Steering Committee's lawyer, who hailed the agreement as a "tremendous victory," one that would work out well not only for Co-op City but for all the Mitchell-Lama projects. (In a conciliatory tone, the Steering Committee leaders told the crowd that there would be no recriminations against Co-op City residents who had paid the increased carrying charges or public officials who had opposed the rent strike.) The *City News* praised the agreement, which it said was a product of Cuomo's "tenacity" and the Steering Committee's "work," "persistence," and "courage." So did several elected officials. Calling the agreement a "great victory," Congressman Jonathan Bingham sent congratulations to the Steering Committee, Governor Carey, and Co-op City's residents. Above all, he lauded Rosen and his associates for achieving "what any reasonable person would have said a year ago was impossible." Hailing the "incredible solidarity" of the residents and the "outstanding talent" of their leaders, Borough President Robert Abrams declared that the agreement was "a major victory not only for the 60,000 residents of Co-op City but for every middle-income resident of New York City."[59]

According to the *City News*, most residents also viewed the agreement as a victory for the Steering Committee. In random interviews conducted shortly after Carey made his announcement, these residents said that they were pleased that they would not have to pay the 25 percent increase and that they would soon be able to elect the Riverbay directors. Co-op City would at last be "a true cooperative," one pointed out. Most residents were relieved that the rent strike was over too. After thirteen months, another observed, "the community began to get run down." Other residents said that they looked forward to the time when the laundry machines would be repaired and Co-op City would otherwise return to normal. Some acknowledged that after the Steering Committee took over Co-op City, it would face many serious problems. But most expressed confidence that it would be up to the task. At the least it would do a better job than the United Housing Foundation and the State Division of Housing. Perhaps no one was more gratified by the agreement than Lorraine Hanks, one of the leaders of the Co-op City Tenants Council and, with her husband, Leonard, the plaintiff in the lawsuit against Commissioner Charles J. Urstadt. In an open letter to Harold Ostroff, which was published in the *Co-op City Times* on July 10, Hanks reminded him of a meeting in July 1970 at which he and his associates had dismissed the Tenants Council's concerns about the increased carrying charges. At the time she had told him, "[You] may get away with your paternalistic let-them-eat-cake attitude for that day, that year, and perhaps for a few years to come, but there would come a day when the people of

this community would discover what was being done to them was intolerable, and they would rise up and be heard, not only loudly but clearly." "Well,
Harold," she gloated, "that day has come."[60]

The agreement had its critics. Chief among them were Commissioner
Goodwin and Senate Majority Leader Warren M. Anderson, a Republican
from Binghamton. Goodwin believed that under the agreement Co-op City
would not be able to pay its annual property taxes of $4.4 million, much less
make its monthly mortgage payments of $2.26 million. Unwilling to endorse
the agreement, which she would have had to help implement, and perhaps
offended by Carey's decision to put the matter in Cuomo's hands, she resigned on July 7. Although Rosen bid Goodwin "Good riddance," Roger Starr
said that her resignation was "a great loss to the state and city." For his part,
Anderson was worried that the agreement might have "sacrificed the long-
range future viability of Co-op City in exchange for an inadequate stop-gap
solution." Concerned that other Mitchell-Lama projects might follow Co-op
City's lead, he favored appointing a Senate committee to look into the compromise. According to Joseph P. Fried, a *Times* reporter, other New Yorkers
saw the agreement as "a futile and foolish endeavor that has accomplished
nothing except set a bad precedent for other government-sponsored projects, while simply deferring the inevitable day when the disputed increase
at Co-op City will have to be put into effect anyway." One of the agreement's
critics, wrote Fried, was the Association for Government Assisted Housing,
which contended that the residents of other Mitchell-Lama projects, whose
rents or carrying charges were higher than Co-op City's, were now asking
themselves why they should pay more for housing "when nonpayment of
rent, done in an organized fashion, carries no consequences."[61]

The critics could rail against the agreement, but they could not undo it.
Within a few weeks its main provisions were put into place. On July 13 the
Steering Committee handed over to the state tens of thousands of dollars of
carrying charges in what the *Co-op City Times* called "a token of good faith."
A day later Joseph P. Goldman, who had been appointed acting commissioner of housing when Lee Goodwin resigned, turned the Riverbay Corporation over to the interim board of directors. The turnover, wrote the *Co-op
City Times*, took place "quietly and without fanfare." The new board consisted of fifteen members of the Steering Committee, ten of whom had been
the original defendants in the recent lawsuits. As required by the Mitchell-
Lama act, Goldman would later appoint a sixteenth member to represent
the Division of Housing. At its first meeting, which was held on July 14, the

board elected Charlie Rosen chairman and his close associates president, vice president, secretary, and treasurer. The board also set up several committees to oversee the management of Co-op City, rescinded the 25 percent increase in carrying charges, and promised to restore normal laundry service "as soon as humanely possible." It also retained Yavner, Gallet, Freedman & Brett, the Steering Committee lawyers, as Riverbay's counsel. And at a subsequent meeting the board started what the *City News* called "Cleaning House" by accepting the resignations of two of Riverbay's long-term employees, Edward Aronov, its general manager, and Ida Vozick, head of its Apartment Allocation Department.[62]

At about the same time Rosen and his associates made a few other weighty decisions. Although the rent strike was over, they decided to continue dispatching volunteers to collect the monthly carrying charges in the building lobbies. This tactic, they believed, would ensure that the state would honor the agreement and that the Steering Committee could resume the strike quickly if need be. In conjunction with the SHFA lawyers, the Steering Committee lawyers asked Judge Helman to put off the foreclosure proceedings for a third time. With no opposition to this request, he extended the proceedings for six months, or until January 10, 1977, which was as long they could be extended. A much more urgent issue for the Steering Committee was that against the wishes of Mario Cuomo the agreement did not require that the contempt charges be dropped against the Steering Committee and the ten individual defendants. Until these charges were dropped, the committee was facing a $3 million fine and each of the defendants a fine of $235,000. Rosen and his associates were adamant that they would not turn over the remainder of the money—the roughly $20 million that the committee was still holding—until the court granted them amnesty. Before long the committee's lawyers reached an understanding with Judges Helman and Callahan that once the checks and money orders were brought to the court, the charges would be dropped and the fines would be lifted.[63]

What followed were some of the most memorable days in the history of Co-op City (and indeed of nonprofit cooperative housing in general). Following Charlie Rosen's directions, the Steering Committee members picked up the checks and money orders from their hiding places in Co-op City and elsewhere. They took $2 million from an apartment in Building 22 owned by Shirley Sharsky, a former gunrunner for Haganah, a paramilitary Israeli organization. Another $6 million was removed from an apartment in Building 24, and $3 million was found in the attic of a private home in Englewood,

New Jersey, where a former Co-op City resident had stored it after he moved. By far the largest haul, a whopping $9 million, came from a private home on Westervelt Avenue in the Bronx. The owner, another former Co-op City resident, had hidden the money in a dresser built into a wall that concealed a storage room. "None of these people know what they had, and none of them asked," said Rosen. "Some of them thought I was breaking up with my wife." On July 26 the Steering Committee put the checks and money orders into sixty-eight cardboard boxes and one Off-Track Betting shopping bag and jammed them into a yellow truck that had been rented from Ryder for $45. Joined by Rosen, Herbert Freedman, Tom Woodstock, Co-op City's acting general manager, and a Co-op City security guard, Ben Cirlin drove the truck to the Grand Concourse side of the Bronx County Courthouse, where some 200 Co-op City residents were gathered. Also on hand were reporters from the *Times* and the *Daily News* and camera crews from ABC, CBS, and NBC. After the boxes and the bag were unloaded, a human chain of twenty-four men and women passed them into the courthouse, where they were put on metal dollies, wheeled onto a freight elevator, and brought into Judge Helman's courtroom on the seventh floor.[64]

Inside the courtroom, which was filled to capacity, Freedman told Judges Helman and Callahan that from June 1975 through June 1976 the Steering Committee had collected more than 153,000 checks and money orders. Nearly 28,000 had been handed over to Riverbay, and almost 12,000 had been given to Consolidated Edison. The rest, about 115,000 checks and money orders worth roughly $21 million, were in the courtroom. Freedman then asked the judges to drop the contempt charges against the Steering Committee leaders and to lift the enormous fines that had been imposed on them. The SHFA's lawyer had no objection. After Senator Bernstein addressed the court, saying that the events of the past year had been "tragic" and, as a result of the state's refusal to negotiate, a waste of hundreds of thousands of dollars in legal fees, Helman and Callahan granted Freedman's request. The crowd was jubilant, wrote the *City News*. "There was relief, happiness, cheers, hugs and kisses all around us," said Freedman. Now that the defendants and their spouses could draw on their bank accounts and other assets, which had been frozen for months, they felt "they could start to live their lives again." Almost forgotten in the excitement was the money. But reminded by Rosen, a group of residents carried the boxes and the bag out of the courthouse and loaded them into the truck, which Cirlin drove to

Co-op City. Shortly afterwards Riverbay began the laborious task of tallying the checks and money orders and depositing them in the bank.[65]

In mid-November, State Comptroller Arthur Levitt sharply criticized the agreement that ended the rent strike. He argued that it did not require Co-op City to meet all its operating expenses and fixed charges and that it set a precedent that would make it very hard to put other publicly financed housing projects on a sound fiscal basis. A week and a half later Mario Cuomo defended the agreement in the *New York Daily News*. After pointing out that the Co-op City rent strike had "paralyzed government, terrorized banks, and threatened an intolerable deterioration in living conditions for 60,000 people," he stressed that the agreement was only "a temporary arrangement" to end the impasse. A long-term solution to the problem would depend on Governor Carey (as well as the monitor, Richard Ravitch, and the special task force) and the state legislature. What Cuomo did not say was that it would also depend on the Riverbay Corporation, which was controlled by Charlie Rosen and his associates. In the months ahead the world's largest housing cooperative, an enterprise worth more than $400 million, would be run by Rosen, a typographer who was currently on leave from his job at the *New York Post*, and a small group that included Joel Dannenberg, a state bank examiner, Murray Lerner, a retired fur worker, Larry Dolnick, a factory production manager, Ben Cirlin, a school bus driver, and Esther Smith, director of an East Harlem day-care center.[66] Only time would tell how they would deal with what the *City News* called "The Challenge Ahead"—and, above all, whether they would be able to run Co-op City without raising the carrying charges.

EPILOGUE

L ess than a year after Steering Committee III and the Carey administration reached the agreement that ended the Co-op City rent strike, a
group of Abraham E. Kazan's disciples decided to celebrate the cooperative
housing movement and in particular the fifty years of the Amalgamated
Houses, the twenty-five years of the United Housing Foundation, and the
twenty years of the Park Reservoir Houses. The capstone of the celebration
was the publication of a 144-page book entitled the *Golden Jubilee Journal
and Kazan Memorial.* It was compiled by the Golden Anniversary Committee, which included the presidents of the Amalgamated Houses, the United
Housing Foundation, and the Park Reservoir Houses and, as chairman, Abe
Bluestein, the business manager of the Amalgamated Houses as well as
Co-op City. It was edited by Herman Liebman, the Amalgamated Houses'
longtime director of education, and dedicated to two former UHF presidents, Robert Szold, founding partner of Szold, Brandwen, Meyers & Altman, the firm that dealt with most of the UHF's legal problems, and Jacob S.
Potofsky, president of the Amalgamated Clothing Workers of America from
1946 to 1972. To defray the cost of publication, a host of labor unions that
represented the electricians, plumbers, steamfitters, bricklayers, and other
craftsmen who worked on the UHF projects bought ads in the *Golden Jubilee Journal.* So did several of Community Services, Inc.'s subcontractors;
some housing cooperatives and community groups; a couple of organizations, like the Federation of Cooperatives, that were affiliated with the UHF;
and a handful of financial institutions, chief among them the Amalgamated
Bank of New York. Although he was eighty-two years old and on the cusp of
retirement, Herman Jessor, who designed Co-op City and many other UHF
housing cooperatives, purchased an ad too.[1]

The first eleven pages of the *Golden Jubilee Journal* were filled with glowing testimonials by eminent national, state, and local figures. Leading off was President Jimmy Carter, who congratulated the Amalgamated Housing Corporation, the Park Reservoir Housing Corporation, and the UHF on their anniversaries. "You provide a shining example of what can be accomplished through enlightened cooperative civic action," he wrote. Vice President Walter F. Mondale also sent congratulations, as did Senators Jacob K. Javits and Daniel P. Moynihan and Congressmen Jonathan B. Bingham and Herman Badillo. Governor Hugh L. Carey praised Kazan and his followers for proving that "low-cost housing could be built for working people in large numbers through the cooperation of a public-spirited organization and an enlightened government housing policy." Former governor Nelson A. Rockefeller hailed the success of cooperative housing in New York State as "a victory in which all can share." Among the other public officials who paid tribute to the Amalgamated Houses, Park Reservoir Houses, and UHF were Assemblyman G. Oliver Koppell, Mayor Abraham D. Beame, City Councilman Stanley Simon, and Bronx Borough President Robert Abrams, who praised the pioneers of cooperative housing for "a record of achievement that is unparalleled in the annals of American housing." Albert Shanker, president of the United Federation of Teachers, also wrote a testimonial, as did Maxwell Brandwen, president of the Amalgamated Bank, and George Meany, president of the AFL-CIO, who praised the Amalgamated Clothing Workers of America for helping to make "the dream of home ownership a reality for many thousands of American workers and their families" and, in so doing, for "greatly strengthen[ing] the fabric of American society."[2]

Following the testimonials were several essays about the Amalgamated Houses and the Park Reservoir Houses. Hyman Bass, president of the Amalgamated Housing Corporation, wrote a brief history of his cooperative from its origins in the late 1920s. Abe Bluestein wrote about how in the mid and late 1960s, a time when many landlords were abandoning their buildings and many tenants were moving to the suburbs, the Amalgamated tore down five of its old walk-ups, which held 263 apartments, and replaced them with two new 20-story, centrally air-conditioned towers that housed 316 families. Harmon Zapakin wrote an even briefer history of Park Reservoir, of which he was the president. Both Bass and Zapakin stressed that their cooperatives did more than just provide high-quality, low-cost housing for working-class families. They also fostered a host of activities that, in Bass's words, created "new roads to community living in a great metropolitan center." Agreeing with him was Murray H. Finley, president of the Amalgamated Clothing and Textile Workers Union, the result of the merger in 1976 of the ACWA and the Textile Workers Union of America. By virtue of the ACWA's pioneering efforts, he wrote, the Amalgamated Houses, the Park Reservoir Houses, and other cooperatives had done more than just produce tens of thousands of homes for moderate-income New Yorkers and clear many of the city's slums. They had also spurred the growth of shopping centers and credit unions as well as a host of social, cultural, and educational institutions, among them nursery schools, day camps, summer camps, dance and drama classes, ceramic and art studios, and all sorts of fraternal and civic organizations, many of which were described in separate articles in the *Golden Jubilee Journal.* "The real meaning and value of cooperative communities is that they constitute a whole new way of life for the families," Finley pointed out.[3]

In a lighter vein, several current and former residents wrote moving accounts of what it was like to live in the Amalgamated and Park Reservoir Houses. Pioneers and newcomers, young and old, they reminisced about growing up and raising families in what one resident described as "a community of good folks living together in a wealth of trees, birds, flowers, and fresh air with all the facilities of city life nearby." And "to top it all, a beautiful apartment!" The "Amalgies," as they called themselves, disagreed on a wide range of political issues, another resident wrote, "But they all cared more than anything that the community would survive and grow." For children, wrote one resident, the Amalgamated was "an extended family." And for adults it was a place to raise children (and, in many cases, to help raise grandchildren), to care for the lawns and flowers, and then, said one resident, to "grow old, retire, play pinochle in the park and, in God's good time, pass on to Miami Beach or Valhalla." Some residents had fond memories of the Workmen's Circle Nursery School and the Twin Pines Day Camp, where they learned to swim, played softball and volleyball, and ran "3-legged races." Other residents spoke highly of the Jewish and English drama clubs, the nearby branch of the New York Public Library, and PS 95, "a school we are all proud of," wrote one. Most residents also remembered the many close friends they made in the Amalgamated and Park Reservoir Houses. Mildred Rothstein Rosenthal, who claimed to be the first baby born in the Amalgamated Houses, recalled "the Mendelson boy," who joined the Lincoln Brigade to fight in the Spanish Civil War, "never to return." Grace Defries, who moved into the Amalgamated Houses in December 1927, spoke for many residents when she wrote, "I and my family enjoyed living here and don't regret one moment of it. There is no place else we would rather live."[4]

Also following the testimonials were several articles about the United Housing Foundation and Abraham E. Kazan, the founder of the UHF and, in the eyes of many Americans, the father of the cooperative housing movement. According to Harold Ostroff, Kazan's successor, the story of the UHF was "one of achievement and leadership, a living example of people working together to translate the ideal of decent housing at reasonable cost into a reality." From the smallest, the Mutual Housing Association, which housed 123 low- and middle-income families, to the largest, Co-op City, which housed 15,372, the UHF's cooperatives "stand out like beacons in a fog surrounding the housing question, proving the efficacy of the cooperative approach to community problems." Indeed, Congressman Bingham pointed out, the foundation's fifteen cooperatives provided housing for 34,000 families. And if Bell Park Gardens, Electchester, Queensview, and roughly a dozen housing cooperatives that were built by groups affiliated with the UHF were taken into account, Robert Moses estimated that the number would be 40,000. Taken together the UHF and its affiliates constitute "the largest private operating sponsors of cooperative middle income housing in the world," he wrote. In addition to its housing cooperatives, other contributors to the *Golden Jubilee Journal* pointed out, the UHF's legacy included the Coordinating Council of Cooperatives, the Federation of Cooperatives, and the New York State Consumer Assembly, each of which supported not only cooperative housing but also cooperative enterprise in general, which, said Ostroff, gave Americans a say in the decisions that affected their lives. "In a society in which there is little opportunity for people to have a meaningful voice in their own affairs," he added, "this may be one of the most significant contributions cooperatives are making to creating a better society."[5]

To commemorate Abraham Kazan's lifelong campaign for cooperative housing, the *Golden Jubilee Journal* reprinted more than a dozen excerpts from the hundreds of articles, reports, and speeches that he wrote or made between 1929 and 1968, three years before his death. And Kazan's obituary, which was published in the *New York Times* on December 22, 1971, was reprinted in the *Golden Jubilee Journal*. Also included were tributes to Kazan from several eminent New Yorkers. Chief among them were Robert F. Wagner Jr., who claimed that cooperative housing "came into its own" during his three terms as mayor of New York City, and Robert Moses, who, as a member of the City Planning Commission and chairman of the Slum Clearance Committee, strongly supported the UHF's Title I housing cooperatives on the Lower East Side. Kazan's accomplishments were "monumental," wrote Wagner, and they changed "much of the face of New York." With "the eye of the banker, the heart of a social worker, and the wisdom of Solomon," Kazan was able "to bring together" a Democratic mayor and a Republican governor, bank presidents and union leaders, local administrators and federal bureaucrats—"men and women of radically different persuasions" who agreed "on only one thing: let Abe do it his way; then it will work." Moses was no less effusive. "It cannot be said too often that every great movement is the lengthened shadow of some one man," he wrote. In the case of the cooperative housing movement, "it was Abraham Kazan." He had "dependable associates and loyal followers," but "without [his] vision, courage and stubbornness," nothing much would have been accomplished. Kazan, Moses went on, was "as nearly a selfless man as I know, at once a servant of the public and leader of the people. The city which has benefited so largely from his forty years of work owes much to his memory."[6]

Ostroff also paid tribute to Kazan as well as to Potofsky, Szold, and the UHF's other leaders. Although he took great pride in what they had accomplished, he acknowledged that there had been disappointments along the way. He regretted that the UHF had been forced to abandon its plans for three housing cooperatives on the Lower East Side—the Robert Owen Houses, which would have housed 1,600 families, and the Seward Park Extension and North Delancey Street development, which would have added 7,000 units to the city's housing stock. Also disappointing to Ostroff was the fate of Twin Pines Village, which was designed to house 6,000 middle-income families in Canarsie. Although Governor Rockefeller was in favor of Twin Pines Village and the State Housing Finance Agency was willing to underwrite it, the project ran into what the UHF regarded as an "unconscionable" delay in obtaining the city's approval. James W. Gaynor, who had just stepped down as the state's commissioner of housing and community renewal, blamed the Lindsay administration. In its defense, Jason R. Nathan, head of the city's Housing and Development Administration, responded that the agency had reservations about the project's "cookie-cutter design" and inadequate planning. It is not clear who was to blame, only that at a time of rampant inflation the longer the delay the higher the cost. And after a while the UHF realized that the cost would be so high that the carrying charges would be out of the reach of most working-class families. Hence in

1972 it shelved the project. Two years later the Starrett Corporation and National Kinney Corporation built Starrett City on the Twin Pines Village site. A rental complex that housed 24,000 people, it was New York's largest housing project since Co-op City.[7] (Although Ostroff did not refer to it in the *Golden Jubilee Journal*, another disappointment was Liberty Harbor, the huge development in Jersey City that never made it off the drawing board.)

Despite these setbacks, Ostroff wrote, "the dream of decent housing at reasonable cost is neither impractical nor unattainable." And with one conspicuous exception, most contributors to the *Golden Jubilee Journal* held that cooperative housing could make the dream a reality for many working-class families in the years ahead. The exception was Roger Starr, former executive director of the Citizens Housing and Planning Council and head of the city's Housing and Development Administration and now a member of the *New York Times* editorial board and Henry Luce Professor of Urban Values at NYU. "It may be a slight exaggeration to say that the cooperative housing movement lies in ruins," he wrote, "but only a blind zealot could possibly describe it as healthy." As evidence, he cited the Co-op City rent strike, in which the residents "made clear to their fellow citiznes [*sic*] that the prospect of successful cooperative ownership of the development they live in is far less important to them than postponement of a rent increase that is ultimately inevitable." He also pointed out that 80 percent of the city-financed Mitchell-Lama cooperatives were in arrears in their mortgage payments. The problem, wrote Starr, was not that Ostroff and his associates were less capable than Kazan. Indeed, they were "men of equal dedication and great intelligence and experience." But the times had changed in a way that made things much harder for them. "We have gone from a period of social democracy, with its idealistic substructure of belief in the value of joint action for the individuals involved, to a period of social anarchy in which the value of an act is to be measured solely by its immediate benefit to its perpetrator. We have gone from a period in which the measured approbation of one's peers supported one's sacrifices, to a period in which one is envied for what he has 'gotten away with' in breaking the terms of a covenant solemnly agreed upon."[8]

Although Starr did not mention it, other changes had taken place that boded ill for the UHF and the cooperative housing movement. After the foundation bought the Jamaica Racetrack and Freedomland sites, it became much harder to find large parcels on the city's periphery that were suitable for housing cooperatives. After Mayor Wagner disbanded the Slum

Clearance Committee, it also became much harder to obtain property for redevelopment on the Lower East Side and in the city's other "blighted areas." And even if the UHF had been able to acquire suitable sites, construction costs and interest rates were now so high, wrote Ostroff, that the new housing was "beyond the reach of all but the most affluent." Especially demoralizing to Ostroff and his associates was the increasing antipathy of the residents of three of the UHF's four largest housing cooperatives. About five years after Rochdale Village was completed, the Rochdale Village Tenants Council gained control of the board of directors. The new board fired Ostroff as Rochdale's president, terminated Community Services, Inc., as its managing agent, and then, charging that it had violated its contractual and financial obligations, filed a $3 million lawsuit against CSI. After several years of conflict between many Amalgamated Warbasse residents and the UHF, a group of dissidents took over the board of directors in 1970. Pointing to construction defects and widespread mismanagement, the new board terminated CSI as its managing agent and also severed its ties with Szold, Brandwen, Meyers & Altman and the Amalgamated Bank. And at Co-op City, which, writes Joshua B. Freeman, was "the Vietnam of the nonprofit cooperative housing movement," the residents denounced the UHF for paternalism and profiteering, lambasted CSI for incompetence and skullduggery, filed a lawsuit against both organizations and their leaders, and launched the rent strike that forced Ostroff and his associates to resign from the Riverbay Corporation Board of Directors.[9]

During the early 1970s the UHF leaders talked about building another large housing cooperative in Brooklyn. Aware that many elderly New Yorkers were moving to Florida, where they were often victimized by unscrupulous speculators, they also talked about developing a retirement community there. But nothing came of these talks. Indeed, after Co-op City, the UHF did not build another housing cooperative in New York or anywhere else. As Peter Eisenstadt writes, "It laid down its shovel and never built another unit of housing." Its leaders, he adds, "were profoundly hurt by the fallout from the Co-op City rent strike and did not want to go through the process again, only to be sued, besmirched, and dragged through the mud by one of their creations." They became "cautious and gun-shy, afraid to engage in the herculean task of planning and building new cooperatives," especially at a time when, as Ostroff pointed out, "Economic conditions [made] it impossible to provide new housing for moderate wage-earners." Once the UHF stopped building, it lost its principal source of revenue, the CSI's building fees, which at their peak in 1972, when Co-op City was under construction, came to $2.2 million a year before taxes. As its revenue dropped and its legal expenses soared, the foundation incurred a large and growing deficit, which exceeded $300,000 in 1974. To avoid insolvency, the board laid off more than two-thirds of its workforce, leaving what Ostroff called "a skeleton staff" to run the organization. (The board also refused to give raises to any employee who earned more than $15,000 a year.) By the late 1970s the UHF was a shell of what it had once been. Ostroff stayed on as head of both the UHF and CSI. But perhaps seeing the writing on the wall, he took a full-time job in 1976 as general manager of the Forward Association, the owner of the *Jewish Daily Forward*, the foremost Yiddish-language newspaper in the United States, and WEVD, a radio station that had been established by the Socialist Party of America in 1927 and named after Eugene V. Debs, the party's longtime leader.[10]

The decline of the UHF left a void that was never filled. As Potofsky warned in 1960, organized labor, long the mainstay of the cooperative housing movement, fell on hard times in the last third of the century. The public-sector unions, which represented policemen, firemen, teachers, and other state and local employees, thrived, but as one well-informed observer wrote in 1991, the private-sector unions "haven't penetrated the growth industries, and the sectors in which they were strongest have all declined." The needle trades unions were especially hard hit when many factories moved from New York to the South and then from the United States to other countries. The Amalgamated Clothing and Textile Workers Union lost so many members that in 1995 it merged with its longtime rival, the ILGWU. For the labor leaders who succeeded Potofsky, David Dubinsky, and Harry Van Arsdale Jr., all of whom were strong supporters of the UHF, cooperative housing was the least of their problems. Even if organized labor had been willing to sponsor new housing cooperatives, it was highly unlikely that New York State and New York City would have helped out. Traumatized by the fiscal crisis of the mid-1970s—and especially the near-collapse of the Housing Finance Agency—the state would have been very reluctant to provide mortgages at below-market interest rates. As Eisenstadt points out, the prevailing view was that "government should, as much as possible[,] get out of the housing [business]." And the city, which had been on the verge of bankruptcy in the mid-1970s, would have been disinclined to offer tax abatements. At a time of fiscal austerity, it was fed up with housing cooperatives like Co-op City, which withheld its property taxes for four years in the late 1970s and owed the city more than $20 million. Indeed, in an effort to force Co-op City to pay back taxes, both Mayor Beame and his successor, Ed Koch, initiated foreclosure proceedings against the development.[11]

The UHF's legacy was mixed. It built tens of thousands of high-quality, low-cost apartments, but not enough of them to solve the housing problem of the working class, which, according to experts, was worse than ever. Indeed, it built only about one-fifth as many apartments as the New York City Housing Authority, which provided public housing for almost 180,000 low-income families. The UHF also cleared seventy-five acres of slums, said Ostroff, mostly on the Lower East Side. At the dedication of Co-op City, Robert Moses had predicted that if the UHF and other like-minded organizations kept up the good work, it would not be long before there were no slums left in New York. But as the years passed the slums remained, the worst of them in Harlem and East Harlem, Bedford-Stuyvesant, and the South Bronx. The UHF's housing cooperatives did spur the creation of a host of other cooperative enterprises, but they did not lay the foundation for Kazan's cooperative commonwealth. An integral part of the UHF's legacy was Co-op City, which celebrated its fiftieth anniversary at the Marina del Rey, a waterfront venue in the northeast Bronx, in December 2018. Although it had gone through "some difficult times," said one of the roughly 600 residents who attended the gala, Co-op City had survived. It was still the world's largest housing cooperative and, as a result of an influx of African Americans and Hispanics, it was the country's largest integrated community. At a time when much of New York was "unaffordable, unapproachable, and even unrecognizable," Co-op City was also "a beacon of opportunity [and] hope" for working-class families, said Letitia James, the first woman and first African American to be elected New York State's attorney general and one of the many dignitaries who took part in the festivities. For thousands of New Yorkers, she went on, it was "a path to home ownership" and a place that fostered "a strong sense of community."[12] But for all that Co-op City was, there was one thing it was not. Despite the hopes of Kazan, Ostroff, and other champions of cooperative housing, it was not the wave of the future, not in New York City and not anywhere else in the United States.

ACKNOWLEDGMENTS

incurred a great many debts while working on *Working-Class Utopias*. Virtually all my expenses were covered by grants from MIT, where I taught for fifty-two years. My thanks to the School of Architecture and Planning, the School of Humanities, Arts, and Social Sciences, the Department of Urban Studies and Planning, and the History Faculty.

MIT's Rotch and Humanities libraries were very helpful, as was the Institute's Interlibrary Borrowing office. Also very helpful were Harvard University's Widener, Loeb, and Law libraries, the New York Public Library, St. John's Law School Library, Tamiment Library, and the New York State Library. Very helpful too were the New York City Municipal Archives, Citizens Housing and Planning Council, Columbia University's Oral History Collection, Rockefeller Center Archives, and Cornell University's Kheel Center for Labor-Management Documentation & Archives.

I am grateful to Michael Munns and Rozaan Boone, who provided me access to the files of the Riverbay Corporation; to Allen Raney, who sent me a copy of the *Hanks v. Urstadt Record on Appeal*; to Charlie Rosen, who loaned me his files about the Co-op City rent strike; and especially to Christopher Hagedorn, who allowed me to borrow more than forty bound volumes of the *City News*, one of Co-op City's two community newspapers.

A few MIT students, among them Tracy Burnett, Ellen Chen, Leif Francel, and Alison Novak, helped with the research. Donald Gonson, David Handlin, and Charlie Rosen read a draft of the book and suggested ways to improve it. Steven Calco, Melissa M. Holland, Lori Reese, Isabelle Y. Liu, Lee Marston, Kenneth Cobb, Jessica M. Shrey, Christopher Hagedorn, Karen Solon, and Jay Gardner helped with the illustrations. Cynthia Buck edited the manuscript. Alexa Selph prepared the index. And Amy Reeve did the proofreading. My thanks to them as well as to Katherine Flynn of the Kneerim, Williams & Bloom Literary Agency, to Michelle Komie, Kenneth Guay, and Mark Bellis of the Princeton University Press, and, as always, to Maria Fuente.

NOTES

PROLOGUE

1. *Cooperator*, December 1968, pp. 1, 10; *Bronx Press-Review*, November 28, 1968; *New York Times*, February 10, March 1, 1965, November 25, 1968.

2. *Cooperator*, December 1968, p. 10; *Bronx Press-Review*, November 28, 1968; *New York Times*, December 26, 1927, September 15 and October 8, 1950, August 6, 1979, February 17, 1986, October 4, 1996.

3. *New York Times*, January 24, May 15, 1966, November 25, 1968, December 22, 1971, March 6, 2006; *Cooperator*, June 1966, p. 5, January 1967, p. 4, December 1968, p. 10; Herman Liebman, ed., *Golden Jubilee Journal and Kazan Memorial* (New York, 1977), p. 24; *Bronx Press-Review*, November 28, 1968.

4. *New York Times*, November 25, 1968, January 28, 1979, January 4, 1984, December 20, 1996; *Cooperator*, December 1968, pp. 10-11; *Bronx Press-Review*, November 28, 1968.

5. *New York Times*, November 25, 1925, February 13, 1991, December 21, 2000, December 3, 2014; *Bronx Press-Review*, November 28, 1968.

6. *New York Times*, June 22, 1969, July 30, 1981; Robert Moses, "The Role of Housing Cooperatives in Urban Development," *Co-op Contact*, November 1956, p. 2; *Cooperator*, December 1968, p. 10; *Bronx Press-Review*, November 28, 1968.

7. *New York Times*, February 24, 1924, April 15, 1958, May 13, 1962; Andrew S. Dolkart, "Homes for People; Non-Profit Cooperatives in New York City, 1916-1929," *Sites*, May 1989, pp. 30-42. See also Peter Eisenstadt, *Rochdale Village: Robert Moses, 6,000 Families, and New York City's Great Experiment in Integrated Housing* (Ithaca, NY, 2010).

8. *Cooperator*, December 1968, p. 1; *New York Times*, May 5, 1939, April 4, 1943, July 1, 1959; Nicholas Farkas, "Co-op City Project, Bronx, NY," *Municipal Engineers Journal*, 1968, pp. 77-78; *Washington Post*, January 9, 1971; Office of the New York State Comptroller, Division of Local Government Services and Economic Development, *Population Trends in New York State's Cities* (2004), p. 7.

9. *Cooperator*, June 1966, pp. 1, 3, 5, and December 1968, pp. 4, 10; Harold Ostroff to Members of the Board of Directors of United Housing Foundation and Community Services, Inc., memo, January 5, 1967, United Housing Foundation Papers, Kheel Center for Labor-Management Documentation & Archives, Cornell University Library; *Bronx Press-Review*, November 28, 1968; *Co-op Contact*, December 1963, pp. 4-5; *Long Island Press*, December 1, 1968; Harold Ostroff, "Labor Co-ops and the Housing Crisis," *AFL-CIO American Federationist*, May 1969, p. 17.

10. *Cooperator*, December 1968, p. 10; *Bronx Press-Review*, November 28,

1968; *New York Times*, November 25, 1968.

11. *Cooperator*, June 1966, p. 1, December 1968, p. 4, February 1969, p. 2; *Co-op Contact*, Winter 1969, pp. 7-8.

12. Jack Newfield and Paul Du Brul, *The Abuse of Power: The Permanent Government and the Fall of New York* (New York, 1977), p. 298; *Bronx Press-Review*, November 28, 1968; Remarks of Robert Moses, City Construction Coordinator and Chairman of the Slum Clearance Committee, at Seward Park, October 11, 1958, United Housing Foundation Papers; *New York Times*, November 25, 1968; *Cooperator*, December 1968, p. 2.

CHAPTER 1. THE ORIGINS OF COOPERATIVE HOUSING

1. 1965 Annual Reports of United Housing Foundation, Inc., and Community Services, Inc., p. 2; *Co-op Contact*, April 1964, p. 11; *Cooperator*, November 1965, pp. 1-2, January 1972, pp. 1-4; *New York Times*, October 25, 1965, December 22, 1971, February 28, 1988; "A Guide to Former Street Names in Manhattan," www.oldstreets.com.

2. *Reminiscences of Abraham E. Kazan* (1968), Columbia University Oral History Collection, pp. 1-18. See also Peter Eisenstadt, *Rochdale Village: Robert Moses, 6,000 Families, and New York City's Great Experiment in Integrated Housing* (Ithaca, NY, 2010), pp. 23-24.

3. *Reminiscences of Abraham E. Kazan*, pp. 18-27; Eisenstadt, *Rochdale Village*, pp. 24-25, 31; *New York Times*, December 22, 1971.

4. *Reminiscences of Abraham E. Kazan*, pp. 27-37; Eisenstadt, *Rochdale Village*, p. 26.

5. *Reminiscences of Abraham E.*

Kazan, pp. 37-40, 54-56; Eisenstadt, *Rochdale Village*, pp. 26-27.

6. *Reminiscences of Abraham E. Kazan*, pp. 68-74; Robert M. Fogelson, *The Great Rent Wars: New York, 1917-1929* (New Haven, CT, 2013), chaps. 1-2.

7. Roy Lubove, *The Progressives and the Slums: Tenement House Reform in New York City, 1890-1917* (Pittsburgh, 1962), chap. 1; Anthony Jackson, *A Place Called Home: A History of Low-Cost Housing in Manhattan* (Cambridge, MA, 1976), chap. 1; Lawrence M. Friedman, *Government and Slum Housing: A Century of Frustration* (Chicago, 1968), p. 28.

8. Lubove, *The Progressives and the Slums*, chaps. 1-5.

9. Ibid.; Fogelson, *The Great Rent Wars*, p. 64.

10. Lubove, *The Progressives and the Slums*, pp. 94, 100. See also Robert M. Fogelson, "The Parsimony of 'the Large-Hearted Rich': An Essay on the Waning of the City and Suburban Homes Company," in Gina Luria Walker & Associates, ed., *The City and Suburban Homes Company's York Avenue Estate: A Social and Architectural History* (New York, 1990), pt. 2, pp. 15-17.

11. Lubove, *The Progressives and the Slums*, pp. 25-26, 91-92, 122-23.

12. Ibid., pp. 12, 19-20, 27; Robert M. Fogelson, *Downtown: Its Rise and Fall, 1880-1950* (New Haven, CT, 2001), p. 322.

13. Fogelson, "The Parsimony of 'the Large-Hearted Rich,'" p. 17; Fogelson, *Downtown*, pp. 320-22; Lubove, *The Progressives and the Slums*, p. 5. See also *New York Times*, June 6, 1880.

14. Fogelson, *Downtown*, p. 323; Fogelson, "The Parsimony of 'the Large-Hearted Rich,'" pp. 19-20.

15. Fogelson, *Downtown*, pp. 323-24;

Lubove, *The Progressives and the Slums*, pp. 6-7, 44-45.

16. Fogelson, *Downtown*, p. 324; Lubove, *The Progressives and the Slums*, pp. 82-84, 133-34; Friedman, *Government and Slum Housing*, p. 4.

17. Lubove, *The Progressives and the Slums*, pp. 44-45, 68-69, 92; Friedman, *Government and Slum Housing*, pp. 4-6.

18. Fogelson, *Downtown*, pp. 324-25; Lubove, *The Progressives and the Slums*, p. 46; Friedman, *Government and Slum Housing*, p. 4.

19. Fogelson, *Downtown*, p. 325; Lubove, *The Progressives and the Slums*, pp. 26-28, 30, 32-33, 125-26, 145-46; Friedman, *Government and Slum Housing*, pp. 26-29, 33-34.

20. Friedman, *Government and Slum Housing*, pp. 33-35; Lubove, *The Progressives and the Slums*, pp. 134-37, 151-56; Jackson, *A Place Called Home*, pp. 122-24. See also *New York Times*, April 13, 1901.

21. Fogelson, *Downtown*, pp. 328-29; Lubove, *The Progressives and the Slums*, pp. 158-63; Friedman, *Government and Slum Housing*, p. 33.

22. Fogelson, *Downtown*, pp. 325-26; Lubove, *The Progressives and the Slums*, pp. 34-35, 100-102, 175. See also Eugenie Ladner Birch and Deborah S. Gardner, "The Seven-Percent Solution: A Review of Philanthropic Housing, 1870-1910," *Journal of Urban History*, August 1981, pp. 403-38.

23. Lubove, *The Progressives and the Slums*, pp. 34-36, 100-102, 109-10; Fogelson, "The Parsimony of 'the Large-Hearted Rich,'" pp. 1-2, 9-16, 33.

24. Fogelson, "The Parsimony of 'the Large-Hearted Rich,'" pp. 3-4, 34-35, 38-53; Friedman, *Government and Slum Housing*, p. 82.

25. Fogelson, *Downtown*, p. 326;

Lubove, *The Progressives and the Slums*, pp. 110-11. See also Joel Arthur Tarr, "From City to Suburb: The 'Moral' Influence of Transportation Technology," in Alexander B. Callow Jr., ed., *American Urban History* (New York, 1973), pp. 202-12.

26. Gordon D. MacDonald, *Apartment Building Construction—Manhattan, 1901-1953* (New York, 1953), p. 18; Joel Schwartz, *The New York Approach: Robert Moses, Urban Liberals, and Redevelopment of the Inner City* (Columbus, OH, 1993), pp. 8-9, 13-14; Fogelson, *Downtown*, pp. 190, 334.

27. Fogelson, *Downtown*, pp. 329-30. See also Robert M. Fogelson, "An Essay on the Ethnic Make-up of the York Avenue Estate," in Walker & Associates, ed., *The City and Suburban Homes Company's York Avenue Estate*, pt. 3, pp. 6-9, 15-18; Sam Levenson, *Everything but Money* (New York, 1966), p. 12.

28. *Report of the Housing Committee of the Reconstruction Commission of the State of New York* (Albany, 1920), p. 4; Fogelson, *The Great Rent Wars*, pp. 139-40.

29. Fogelson, *The Great Rent Wars*, pp. 140-42; Fogelson, "The Parsimony of 'the Large-Hearted Rich,'" pp. 22-23. See also Friedman, *Government and Slum Housing*, pp. 94-95.

30. Fogelson, *The Great Rent Wars*, pp. 142-44, 195.

31. Abraham E. Kazan, "Cooperative Housing in the United States," *Annals of the American Academy of Political and Social Science*, May 1937, pp. 137-43; MacDonald, *Apartment Building Construction*, p. 9; Fogelson, *The Great Rent Wars*, pp. 368-71, 389-90, 396-97; *New York Times*, January 25, 1975.

32. Louis H. Pink, *The New Day in Housing* (New York, 1928), pp. 159-63;

US Bureau of Labor Statistics, *Cooperative Movement in the United States in 1925 (Other than Agricultural)* (Washington, DC, 1925), pp. 1-4, 91-95; Kristin Szylvian Bailey, "The Federal Government and the Cooperative Housing Movement, 1917-1955," PhD diss., Carnegie Mellon University, 1988, pp. 19-20; *New York Times*, February 24 and 27, 1924.

33. US Bureau of Labor Statistics, *Cooperative Movement in the United States*, p. 91; Fogelson, *The Great Rent Wars*, chap. 1; *New York Call*, May 23, 1920, April 18, 1921; Kenneth G. Wray, "Abraham E. Kazan: The Story of the Amalgamated Houses and the United Housing Foundation," master's thesis, Columbia University, 1991, p. 6; *New York Times*, April 22, 1925.

34. Marc A. Weiss, "Own Your Own Home: Housing Policy and the Real Estate Industry," paper presented to the conference "Robert Moses and the Planned Environment," Hofstra University, June 11, 1988, pp. 7-8; Matthew Gordon Lasner, *High Life: Condo Living in the Suburban Century* (New Haven, CT, 2012), chaps. 1-2; Fogelson, *The Great Rent Wars*, pp. 325-27; *Proceedings of the Third National Conference on Housing: 1913*, pp. 113-14.

35. Lasner, *High Life*, pp. 99-102; *New York Times*, April 22, September 19, 1925; Eugene Rachlis and John E. Marqusee, *The Landlords* (New York, 1963), pp. 146-47; Edith Elmer Wood, *Recent Trends in American Housing* (New York, 1931), pp. 260-64.

36. Wood, *Recent Trends in American Housing*, pp. 264-65; *Reminiscences of Abraham E. Kazan*, pp. 79-83; Rachlis and Marqusee, *The Landlords*, pp. 148-49; Fogelson, *The Great Rent Wars*, p. 357; Wray, "Abraham E. Kazan,"

p. 7; *New York Times*, January 14 and 26, March 28, 1927.

37. Andrew S. Dolkart, "United Workers' Cooperative Colony," New York City Landmark Preservation Commission, Designation List 245, June 2, 1992, p. 4; Wray, "Abraham E. Kazan," pp. 7-8; *New York Times*, December 26, 1927; *Cincinnati Post*, May 17, 1928; Wood, *Recent Trends in American Housing*, p. 181.

38. *Reminiscences of Abraham E. Kazan*, pp. 81, 105; *New York Times*, December 26, 1927; Wood, *Recent Trends in American Housing*, pp. 180-82; Rachlis and Marqusee, *The Landlords*, p. 151; Pink, *The New Day in Housing*, pp. 131, 135-36; James Ford, *Slums and Housing* (Cambridge, MA, 1936), vol. 2, p. 832.

39. Eisenstadt, *Rochdale Village*, p. 27; Wood, *Recent Trends in American Housing*, pp. 177-80; Rachlis and Marqusee, *The Landlords*, p. 155. See also *Reminiscences of Abraham E. Kazan*, pp. 128-32.

40. Richard Siegler and Herbert J. Levy, "Brief History of Cooperative Housing," *Cooperative Housing Journal*, 1986, p. 15; *New York Times*, June 2, 1902; *Reminiscences of Abraham E. Kazan*, p. 151.

41. *New York Times*, January 7, October 26, 1930; Rachlis and Marqusee, *The Landlords*, p. 156.

42. *Reminiscences of Abraham E. Kazan*, pp. 147-61; *New York Times*, January 7, October 26, 1930, October 31, 1931; Rachlis and Marqusee, *The Landlords*, pp. 156-57.

43. "Housing Activities of Labor Groups," *Monthly Labor Review*, August 1928, pp. 215-17; *Reminiscences of Abraham E. Kazan*, pp. 132-33; MacDonald, *Apartment Building Construction*, p. 9. See also *New York Times*, June 20, 1926.

44. Herman Liebman, ed., *Golden*

Jubilee Journal and Kazan Memorial (New York, 1977), p. 47; Rachlis and Marqusee, *The Landlords*, pp. 157-59.

45. *Reminiscences of Abraham E. Kazan*, pp. 175-79; Rachlis and Marqusee, *The Landlords*, p. 157-60.

46. *Reminiscences of Abraham E. Kazan*, pp. 171-72; Rachlis and Marqusee, *The Landlords*, p. 158; Andrew S. Dolkart, "Homes for People; Non-Profit Cooperatives in New York City 1916-1929," *Sites*, May 1989, pp. 34-36; Dolkart, "United Workers' Cooperative Colony," p. 6.

47. Kazan, "Cooperative Housing in the United States," p. 139; *Reminiscences of Abraham E. Kazan*, pp. 128-32, 140; Rachlis and Marqusee, *The Landlords*, p. 157; Ford, *Slums and Housing*, vol. 2, p. 831; Liebman, *Golden Jubilee Journal and Kazan Memorial*, p. 45.

48. Kazan, "Cooperative Housing in the United States," pp. 137-41.

CHAPTER 2. COOPERATIVE HOUSING AFTER WORLD WAR II

1. "The Great Housing Shortage," *Life*, December 17, 1945, pp. 27, 30-31, 33; Joshua B. Freeman, *Working-Class New York: Life and Labor since World War II* (New York, 2000), p. 105; Roberta Gold, *When Tenants Claimed the City: The Struggle for Citizenship in New York City Housing* (Urbana, IL, 2014), p. 10; *New York Times*, March 12, 1952.

2. Gordon D. MacDonald, *Apartment Building Construction—Manhattan, 1901-1953* (New York, 1953), pp. 9, 18-19.

3. *New York Times*, January 31, February 1, 1949, February 23, 1950, May 11, 1952. See also Mark I. Gelfand, *A Nation of Cities: The Federal Government and Urban America, 1933-1965* (New York, 1975), pp. 59-65, 216-17.

4. *New York Times*, May 11 and 12, 1952; Freeman, *Working-Class New York*, p. 107; New York State Task Force on Middle-Income Housing, *Second and Final Report* (1959), p. 9.

5. *New York Times*, June 22, September 21, 1947, November 12, 1948, November 29, 1949, February 23, 1950, May 11, 1952, April 2, 1953.

6. *New York Times*, June 22, September 21, 1947, February 3, 1950; Kristin Szylvian Bailey, "The Federal Government and the Cooperative Housing Movement, 1917-1955," PhD diss., Carnegie Mellon University, 1988, pp. 26-27; Matthew Gordon Lasner, *High Life: Condo Living in the Suburban Century* (New Haven, CT, 2012), pp. 115-19; US Senate, *Slums and Low-Rent Public Housing: Hearings before the Committee on Education and Labor, S. 2192*, 74th Cong., 1st sess. (Washington, DC, 1935), p. 84; Herbert U. Nelson, "Urban Housing and Land Use," *Law and Contemporary Problems*, March 1914, pp. 158-67; Peter Dreier, "Labor's Love Lost? Rebuilding Unions' Involvement in Federal Housing Policy," *Housing Policy Debate*, 2000, p. 339.

7. *New York Times*, January 5, 1950; Alexander von Hoffman, "A Study in Contradictions: The Origins and Legacy of the Housing Act of 1949," *Housing Policy Debate*, 2000, pp. 309-10; Charles Abrams, "Another String to the Bow," *Survey*, October 1949, pp. 543-46.

8. US Senate, *Housing Amendments of 1949: Hearings before a Subcommittee of the Committee on Banking and Currency, S. 2246*, 81st Cong., 1st sess. (Washington, DC, 1949), pp. 17-23; US House of Representatives, *Housing Amendments of 1949: Hearings before the Committee on Banking and Currency, H.R. 5631*, 81st Cong., 1st sess.

(Washington, DC, 1949), pp. 17-23. See also US Senate, *Housing Amendments of 1949: Senate Report No. 892*, 81st Cong., 1st sess. (Washington, DC, 1949), pp. 46-50.

9. US Senate, *Housing Amendments of 1949*, pp. 250-52 and passim; US House of Representatives, *Housing Amendments of 1949*, pp. 144-45 and passim; US Senate, *Housing Amendments of 1949: Senate Report No. 892*, p. 46; *Wall Street Journal*, August 9, 1949; R. M. Boeckel, *Records of the 81st Congress (First Session): Editorial Research Reports 1949*, vol. 2 (Washington, DC, 1949).

10. *Wall Street Journal*, January 7, 1950; Bailey, "The Federal Government and the Cooperative Housing Movement," pp. 89-91; US Senate, *Middle-Income Housing: Hearings before a Subcommittee of the Committee on Banking and Currency on Amendments to S. 2246*, 81st Cong., 2nd sess. (Washington, DC, 1950), pp. 10-99.

11. US House of Representatives, *Cooperative Housing: Hearings before the Committee on Banking and Currency on H.R. 6818 and H.R. 6742 (Superseded by H.R. 7402)*, 81st Cong., 2nd sess. (Washington, DC, 1950), pp. 139-65, 339-43, 401-15 and passim; US Senate, *Middle-Income Housing*, pp. 175-78, 344-47 and passim.

12. US Senate, *Middle-Income Housing*, pp. 112-37, 194-214, 254-73 and passim; US House of Representatives, *Cooperative Housing*, pp. 201-19, 241-307 and passim.

13. US Senate, *Middle-Income Housing*, pp. 101-37, 194-214 and passim; US House of Representatives, *Cooperative Housing*, pp. 201-19, 241-96 and passim. See also *Chicago Tribune*, February 25, 1950.

14. US Senate, *Middle-Income Housing*, pp. 175-78, 237-53 and passim; US House of Representatives, *Cooperative Housing*, pp. 139-65, 422-32 and passim.

15. *Washington Post*, February 8, 10, and 24, 1950; *New York Times*, February 17, March 11 and 15, 1950; *Chicago Tribune*, February 24, March 11 and 15, 1950; *Los Angeles Times*, February 27, 1950; *Boston Globe*, March 16, 1950. See also Richard O. Davies, *Housing Reform during the Truman Administration* (Columbus, MO, 1966), pp. 119-21.

16. *Chicago Tribune*, February 22, March 9, 1950; *New York Times*, February 22, March 21, 1950; *Washington Post*, March 21, 1950; *Wall Street Journal*, March 23, 1950; *Boston Globe*, March 23, 1950. See also Bailey, "The Federal Government and the Cooperative Housing Movement," pp. 93-94.

17. *New York Times*, February 12, April 6, 10, and 21, 1950; *Wall Street Journal*, April 7, 1950; *Los Angeles Times*, April 4, 1950; US House of Representatives, *Cooperative Housing*, pp. 450-52; *Chicago Tribune*, February 24, 1950. See also Bailey, "The Federal Government and the Cooperative Housing Movement," pp. 94-98.

18. *New York Times*, April 12, July 2, 1950; Bailey, "The Federal Government and the Cooperative Housing Movement," pp. 97-98; Jean A. Flexner, "Cooperative Housing in the United States," *Construction Review*, June 1958, pp. 5-6; *Proceedings of the First National Conference on Cooperative Housing: 1958*, pp. 29.

19. Stephen G. Thompson, "Co-op Housing: NYC versus USA," *Architectural Forum*, July 1959, pp. 132-33, 158; Evelyn Seeley, "*The House*: A Success Story," *Survey Graphic*, February 1948, pp. 70-74, 85; Margaret Hickey,

"'*HOMES*, NOT JUST HOUSING,'" *Ladies' Home Journal*, December 1958, pp. 27, 30, 32.

20. Freeman, *Working-Class New York*, pp. 40-43; David Dubinsky and A. H. Raskin, *David Dubinsky: A Life with Labor* (New York, 1977), pp. 8-9.

21. See chap. 1, notes 35 and 41.

22. Robert M. Fogelson, *The Great Rent Wars: New York, 1917-1929* (New Haven, CT, 2013), pp. 195, 357-59.

23. *New York Herald*, January 8, 1922; *New York Evening Post*, November 17, 1923; *[New York] Real Estate Record and Builders Guide*, April 4, 1923, pp. 359, 372; *New York Times*, April 23, 1922, April 7 and 18, May 12, 1923; International Labour Office, *The Housing Situation in the United States* (Geneva, 1925), pp. 40-43; Fogelson, *The Great Rent Wars*, p. 385.

24. *New York Times*, February 23 and 28, April 9, 1926, May 11, June 12 and 23, 1927; Lasner, *High Life*, p. 97; *Wall Street Journal*, December 15, 1927. See also the remarks of Robert Moses at the opening of North Queensview Houses, Monday afternoon, January 20, 1958, Robert Moses Papers, Manuscripts and Archives Division, New York Public Library.

25. "Legislative Housing Relief in New York: The State Housing Law and the Extension of the Emergency Rent Laws," *Columbia Law Review*, December 1926, pp. 1,015-23. See also *New York Times*, January 8, February 26 and 28, March 13, 1926.

26. Nathan Straus, *The Seven Myths of Housing* (New York, 1944), p. 179; Joel Schwartz, *The New York Approach: Robert Moses, Urban Liberals, and Redevelopment of the Inner City* (Columbus, OH, 1993), pp. 90-93; Samuel Zipp, *Manhattan Projects: The Rise and Fall of Urban Renewal in Cold War New York* (New York, 2010), pp. 77-83; Freeman, *Working-Class New York*, p. 112.

27. Schwartz, *The New York Approach*, pp. 128-33; Robert M. Fogelson, *Downtown: Its Rise and Fall, 1880-1950* (New Haven, CT, 2001), chap. 7; Marc A. Weiss, "The Origins and Legacy of Urban Renewal," in J. Paul Mitchell, ed., *Federal Housing Policy and Programs* (New Brunswick, NJ, 1985), pp. 253-76; Freeman, *Working-Class New York*, p. 114.

28. *New York Times*, February 26, March 13, 1926, August 4, December 19, 1955; Fogelson, *The Great Rent Wars*, pp. 401-2; Hilary Botein, "New York State Housing Policy in Postwar New York City: The Enduring Rockefeller Legacy," *Journal of Urban History*, September 2009, pp. 838-39.

29. Botein, "New York State Housing Policy," pp. 839-41; *New York Times*, January 26, March 18, June 5, 1959, January 7, March 25, April 21, 1960.

30. Botein, "New York State Housing Policy," pp. 840-43; *New York Times*, March 25, April 10, 1960.

31. *New York Times*, June 22, 1947; *Reminiscences of Abraham E. Kazan* (1968), Columbia University Oral History Collection, pp. 232-34, 288-94; Freeman, *Working-Class New York*, pp. 111-12.

32. *Reminiscences of Abraham E. Kazan*, p. 300; *New York Times*, August 15, 1945, March 27, October 23, 1946, November 16, 1947; Schwartz, *The New York Approach*, pp. 134-35; Kenneth G. Wray, "Abraham E. Kazan: The Story of the Amalgamated Houses and the United Housing Foundation," master's thesis, Columbia University, 1991, p. 17.

33. *New York Times*, March 27, August 1, 1947, June 27, 1948, March 11, November 25, 1951; Wray, "Abraham E. Kazan," pp. 18-19.

34. Hilary Botein, "Visions of Community: Post-war Housing Projects of Local 3, International Brotherhood of Electrical Workers, and Local 1199, Hospital Workers Union," *Planning Perspectives*, April 2009, pp. 175–96; *New York Times*, May 13, 1949, October 8, 1950.

35. Botein, "Visions of Community," pp. 175–96; *New York Times*, November 7, 1949, May 27, September 1 and 15, October 8, December 2 and 19, 1950, December 2, 1951, March 11, 1954, September 27, 1966; Freeman, *Working-Class New York*, pp. 112–13.

36. *New York Times*, April 14, 1958; *Wall Street Journal*, April 14, 1958.

37. *New York Times*, February 3, May 29, September 16, 1959, January 9, 1960, August 13, 1963. See also Remarks of Mayor Robert F. Wagner at Groundbreaking of Big Six Towers, December 17, 1960, Mayor Robert F. Wagner Papers, New York City Municipal Archives.

38. *New York Times*, November 20, 1949, May 27, 1950, July 24, 1951, May 16, 1957.

39. *New York Times*, October 27, 1960, March 13, June 17, December 2, 1962, October 20, 1963, July 9, 1967.

40. *New York Times*, January 24, 1957, August 16, 1959, February 25, 1964, April 9, 1967; Botein, "Visions of Community," pp. 187–91.

41. *New York Times*, August 18, 1961, October 8 and 18, 1962, November 21, 1963.

42. *New York Times*, June 21, November 21, 1963, January 21, 1966.

43. *New York Times*, September 3, November 11 and 12, 1948, August 29, October 9 and 12, 1949, March 30, 1950. See also Lasner, *High Life*, pp. 130–31.

44. *New York Times*, December 3, 1948, January 26, May 31, September 14, 1949, February 19, July 15, November 15,

1950, November 20, 1952, April 16, May 3, 1953, November 29, 1955, October 26, 1956, October 20, 1957, January 21, 1958. See also Lasner, *High Life*, p. 133.

45. Schwartz, *The New York Approach*, pp. 185–89, 196–97; *New York Times*, March 21, 1952, September 16 and 17, 1955, May 29, June 21, 1957.

46. *New York Times*, January 3, October 15, 1956, January 10, May 30, December 2, 1958, September 20, 22, and 29, 1959, February 28, 1960, February 15, 1961, March 11 and 20, 1962, June 19, 1963, May 15, 1966.

47. *New York Times*, April 17, October 12, 1961, March 16 and 25, July 29, September 23, 1962, April 9, 1963, June 14, 1964, June 2, 1965, February 10, September 18, October 23, 1966, September 24, 1993.

48. *New York Times*, September 22, 1955, October 12, 1958, January 15 and 24, April 30, June 12, 1960, September 26, November 12, 1961; Jerry Voorhis, "Homes and Neighborhoods," in Jerome Liblit, ed., *Housing: The Cooperative Way* (New York, 1964), p. 84.

CHAPTER 3. THE UNITED HOUSING FOUNDATION

1. *Reminiscences of Jacob Samuel Potofsky* (1965), Columbia University Oral History Collection, p. 188. See also Kenneth G. Wray, "Abraham E. Kazan: The Story of the Amalgamated Houses and the United Housing Foundation," master's thesis, Columbia University, 1991, p. 37.

2. Emma Jacobs, "Amalgamated Housing to First Houses: Re-defining Home in America," senior thesis, Columbia University, 2009, p. 45; *Reminiscences of Jacob Samuel Potofsky*, pp. 187, 189, 199.

3. Wray, "Abraham E. Kazan," pp. 22–24; see also *Reminiscences of Abraham E. Kazan* (1968), Columbia University Oral History Collection, pp. 449–50.

4. Wray, "Abraham E. Kazan," pp. 24–26; Matthew Gordon Lasner, *High Life: Condo Living in the Suburban Century* (New Haven, CT, 2012), pp. 146–47.

5. Wray, "Abraham E. Kazan," pp. 26–27. For a list of UHF members, see an undated United Housing Foundation pamphlet, probably from 1960 or 1961, in the Loeb Library, Harvard University Graduate School of Design.

6. Joshua B. Freeman, *Working-Class New York: Life and Labor since World War II* (New York, 2000), p. 116. See also Minutes of the Annual Meeting of Members of the United Housing Foundation, February 16, 1963, United Housing Foundation Papers, Kheel Center for Labor-Management Documentation & Archives, Cornell University Library.

7. *New York Times*, October 26, 1953, January 17, 1954; *A Story of the Accomplishments of People*, undated pamphlet, Loeb Library, p. 4.

8. *New York Times*, October 28, 1956, August 25, 1957; *Reminiscences of Abraham E. Kazan*, pp. 552–53; *A Story of the Accomplishments of People*, p. 10.

9. *New York Times*, January 23, 1950, March 8, 1951, January 12, 1956; Freeman, *Working-Class New York*, p. 114.

10. Freeman, *Working-Class New York*, pp. 114, 118; Peter Eisenstadt, *Rochdale Village: Robert Moses, 6,000 Families, and New York City's Great Experiment in Integrated Housing* (Ithaca, NY, 2010), pp. 36–37, 43; *New York Times*, January 25, 1959.

11. Freeman, *Working-Class New York*, pp. 118–19; *Reminiscences of Abraham E. Kazan*, pp. 312–13, 319–25, 329; Wray, "Abraham E. Kazan," pp. 31–32.

12. *Reminiscences of Abraham E. Kazan*, pp. 321–25; Roger D. Parmet, *The Master of Seventh Avenue: David Dubinsky and the American Labor Movement* (New York, 2005), pp. 263–65; *New York Times*, October 5, 1955, May 28, 1962; Doris K. Lewis, "Union-Sponsored Middle-Income Housing: 1927–65," *Monthly Labor Review*, June 1965, p. 635.

13. *New York Times*, April 3, 1951, February 21, May 23, 1952.

14. *New York Times*, January 15, November 23, 1953. See also the history of the East River Houses at Cooperative Village, http://coopvillage.coop/.

15. *New York Times*, March 10, 1953, October 22 and 24, 1955; *Reminiscences of Abraham E. Kazan*, p. 341; *A Story of the Accomplishments of People*, p. 8.

16. Wray, "Abraham E. Kazan," pp. 39–44; *New York Times*, June 21, 1955, November 30, 1957; Lewis, "Union-Sponsored Middle-Income Housing," p. 635.

17. Wray, "Abraham E. Kazan," pp. 39–44; *New York Times*, May 19, July 27, August 24 and 31, 1956, January 18, July 18, August 15 and 23, 1957; *Reminiscences of Abraham E. Kazan*, pp. 357–59.

18. Remarks of Robert Moses, City Construction Coordinator and Chairman of the Slum Clearance Committee, at Seward Park, October 11, 1958, Robert Moses Papers, Manuscripts and Archives Division, New York Public Library; *New York Times*, January 27, April 13, June 17, 1957, September 22, October 12, 1958; *Reminiscences of Abraham E. Kazan*, pp. 361, 369–74; *A Story of the Accomplishments of People*, p. 12; Wray, "Abraham E. Kazan," p. 44.

19. *Reminiscences of Abraham E. Kazan*, pp. 404–7; Wray, "Abraham E.

Kazan," pp. 45-46; *New York Times*, June 2 and 30, July 27, 1956.

20. United Housing Foundation, *The Story of the ILGWU Cooperative Houses* (New York, 1966), pp. 5, 18, 26; *New York Times*, August 19, 1957, February 20 and 25, July 16, 1958, November 22, 1962.

21. *New York Times*, March 2, December 8, 1958, June 22 and 30, July 1, August 20 and 25, September 3, December 9, 1959, October 9, 1960. See also Abraham E. Kazan to Robert F. Wagner, January 27, 1959, New York City Municipal Archives; Wray, "Abraham E. Kazan," pp. 45-46.

22. Wray, "Abraham E. Kazan," pp. 45-46; *New York Times*, November 18, 1958, August 20, 21, 24, 25, and 28, September 3, October 14, 1959. See also Robert Moses to His Eminence Francis Cardinal Spellman, memo, September 23, 1959, Moses Papers.

23. *New York Times*, October 14, December 3, 1959, January 10 and 24, February 18, October 9, 1960, July 6 and 29, 1961, May 19, 1962. See also Lasner, *High Life*, pp. 172-73.

24. *Co-op Contact*, June/July 1962, pp. 1-5.

25. *Reminiscences of Abraham E. Kazan*, p. 493; Eisenstadt, *Rochdale Village*, pp. 6, 25, 52-55, 61-62; Freeman, *Working-Class New York*, p. 119. See also Samuel Zipp, *Manhattan Projects: The Rise and Fall of Urban Renewal in Cold War New York* (New York, 2010), chap. 5.

26. *Reminiscences of Abraham E. Kazan*, pp. 493-94; *New York Times*, October 5, 1956; Eisenstadt, *Rochdale Village*, pp. 44-51, 64.

27. *Reminiscences of Abraham E. Kazan*, pp. 494-98; Robert Moses to John J. McCloy, April 30, 1959, Moses Papers; Eisenstadt, *Rochdale Village*, pp. 62-63.

28. *Reminiscences of Abraham E.*

Kazan, pp. 498-503; Eisenstadt, *Rochdale Village*, pp. 65-66; *New York Times*, February 17, 1960. See also Abraham E. Kazan to Nelson A. Rockefeller, March 6, 1963, Nelson A. Rockefeller Papers, Rockefeller Archive Center, Sleepy Hollow, NY.

29. *New York Times*, April 12, 14, and 29, 1960; Eisenstadt, *Rochdale Village*, pp. 66-67.

30. *New York Times*, September 24, 1960, August 26, 1962, July 31, August 31, October 6, December 11, 1963; *Washington Post*, July 24, 1963; *Reminiscences of Abraham E. Kazan*, p. 504. See also Eisenstadt, *Rochdale Village*, chap. 3.

31. *Reminiscences of Abraham E. Kazan*, pp. 525-27; Abraham E. Kazan to Robert Moses, January 7, 1959, Moses Papers; *New York Times*, October 2 and 20, December 10, 1958, January 7, 1959.

32. *Reminiscences of Abraham E. Kazan*, pp. 527-30; *New York Times*, November 22, 1962.

33. *Reminiscences of Abraham E. Kazan*, pp. 528-31; *New York Times*, April 21, May 3, June 5, August 21, 1960; untitled statement, June 7, 1962, United Housing Foundation Papers, Kheel Center for Labor-Management Documentation & Archives, Cornell University Library; Abraham E. Kazan, "A New Trend in Slum Clearance," *Co-op Contact*, April 1963, p. 2.

34. *Reminiscences of Abraham E. Kazan*, pp. 519-22; Ella Howard, *Homeless: Poverty and Place in Urban America* (Philadelphia, 2013), pp. 125-26; *New York Times*, April 11, 1957, October 27, 1959.

35. Howard, *Homeless*, pp. 126-28; *Reminiscences of Abraham E. Kazan*, pp. 522-23; *New York Times*, June 3, October 27, 1959.

36. Howard, *Homeless*, pp. 129-30;

Robert A. Caro, *The Power Broker: Robert Moses and the Fall of New York* (New York, 1975), chap. 45; *Co-op Contact*, January 1960; *New York Times*, December 11, 1960; *Reminiscences of Abraham E. Kazan*, pp. 524-25.

37. *Reminiscences of Abraham E. Kazan*, pp. 474-75; *New York Times*, July 18, 1957, July 23, 1958.

38. *Reminiscences of Abraham E. Kazan*, pp. 475-76; Gwenda Blair, *The Trumps: Three Generations That Built an Empire* (New York, 2010), p. 199; *New York Times*, July 18, August 15, 1957, July 4 and 17, 1958, November 22, 1959.

39. *New York Times*, July 23, September 7, 1958; Blair, *The Trumps*, p. 302.

40. *New York Times*, December 8 and 10, 1958, January 23, February 5, April 13, June 26 and 29, 1959. See also a report by Robert Moses, July 24, 1959, and Abraham E. Kazan to Robert Moses, July 18, 1959, Moses Papers.

41. *New York Times*, August 20 and 21, 1959; *Reminiscences of Abraham E. Kazan*, pp. 476-78; Blair, *The Trumps*, pp. 202-3; Robert Moses to John Cashmore, September 6, 1959, Moses Papers; *Reminiscences of Jacob Samuel Potofsky*, p. 201; *New York World-Telegram and Sun*, undated (probably August 1959), United Housing Foundation Files.

42. *Reminiscences of Abraham E. Kazan*, p. 491; *New York Times*, November 22, December 19, 1959, May 28, 1960, December 2, 1962, September 29, 1963, July 14, 1964; *A Story of the Accomplishments of People*, p. 20.

43. "Report on 23 Housing Cooperatives Affiliated with the United Housing Foundation," *Co-op Contact*, October/November 1964, p. 5.

44. "Report on 23 Housing Cooperatives," p. 5; Robert Moses, "The Role of Housing Cooperatives in Urban Development," *Co-op Contact*, November 1956, p. 7; *Co-op Contact*, June/July 1962, p. 4, December 1963, p. 7, April 1964, pp. 2-3; *Washington Post*, March 5, 1958; Abraham E. Kazan, "Thirty Years of Cooperative Housing—the United Housing Foundation," in Jerome Liblit, ed., *Housing: The Cooperative Way* (New York, 1964), p. 225.

45. *Co-op Contact*, December 1963, pp. 6-7. See also *Reminiscences of Jacob Samuel Potofsky*, p. 198.

46. Kazan, "Thirty Years of Cooperative Housing," p. 224; "Report [of the] President of the United Housing Foundation," *Co-op Contact*, January 1960, p. 4, December 1963, p. 6, April 1964, p. 3.

47. *Co-op Contact*, June/July 1962, p. 4; *Washington Post*, July 5, 1958; *New York Times*, February 5, 1961, April 15, 1962, March 11, 1965; *Reminiscences of Jacob Samuel Potofsky*, pp. 815-19; S. F. Boden, "Has Cooperative Housing Come of Age? The Association for Middle Income Housing," in Liblit, ed., *Housing: The Cooperative Way*, pp. 213-14, 217-19; *Proceedings [of the] Third National Conference on Cooperative Housing: 1960*.

48. *Co-op Contact*, June/July 1962, p. 5, December 1963, p. 4; Minutes of the Annual Meeting of Members of United Housing Foundation, February 16, 1963, United Housing Foundation Files; *New York Times*, July 4, 1959, September 28, 1967; Eisenstadt, *Rochdale Village*, pp. 246-47.

CHAPTER 4. CO-OP CITY

1. *Cooperator*, June 1964, p. 1; Robert Moses, *Public Works: A Dangerous Trade* (New York, 1970), p. 476; *New York Times*, November 25, 1968; *Bronx Press-Review*, November 28, 1968; Roberta Brandes Gratz, *The Living City:*

How America's Cities Are Being Revitalized by Thinking Small in a Big Way (New York, 1989), pp. 94-95.

2. William Zeckendorf, *The Autobiography of William Zeckendorf* (New York, 1970), front cover, pp. 4-6, 150-51, 291; E. J. Kahn Jr., "Big Operator-I," *The New Yorker*, December 8, 1951, pp. 46-73, and "Big Operator-II," *The New Yorker*, December 15, 1951, pp. 41-62; Eugene Rachlis and John E. Marqusee, *The Landlords* (New York, 1963), pp. 257-95.

3. Zeckendorf, *Autobiography*, pp. 291-92; Paul D. Nash, "Fantasia Bronxiana: Freedomland and Co-op City," *New York History*, Summer 2001, pp. 261-70; *New York Times*, May 1 and 26, July 21, August 27, 1959, June 19, 1960. See also *Los Angeles Times*, May 1, 1960; *Chicago Tribune*, June 12, 1960; *Boston Globe*, July 10, 1960.

4. *New York Times*, June 12, 19, and 20, 1960. See also Michael J. Agovino, *The Bookmaker: A Memoir of Money, Luck, and Family from the Utopian Outskirts of New York City* (New York, 2008), p. 80; *Chicago Tribune*, September 11, 1960.

5. *New York Times*, August 7, 1959, June 19, 25, and 26, September 12, 18, 20, and 30, October 24, November 10, 1960, April 30, May 8, June 11, August 18, 1961, May 17, August 13, 1962; *Wall Street Journal*, September 20, 1960.

6. Zeckendorf, *Autobiography*, pp. 290-93; *New York Times*, August 16, December 22, 1961, May 28, December 9, 1963, July 1, September 16, 1964, October 3, 1971; *Wall Street Journal*, May 25, June 12, July 19, 1962, July 1, 1964, February 10, March 15, 1965; Minutes of Special Meeting of the Board of Directors of United Housing Foundation, June 23, 1964, United Housing Foundation Papers, Kheel Center for Labor-Management Documentation & Archives, Cornell University Library. See also Gilbert Burck, "Man in a $100-Million Jam," *Fortune*, July 1960, pp. 104ff.

7. *Reminiscences of Abraham E. Kazan* (1968), Columbia University Oral History Collection, pp. 546-47; Nicholas Farkas, "Co-op City Housing Project Bronx, NY," *Municipal Engineers Journal*, 1968, pp. 79-82.

8. Operational Planning Unit, memo to R. K. Bernstein, J. C. Smith, and M. Isler, October 19, 1964, pp. 2-3, and Richard K. Bernstein, Freedomland memo, November 13, 1964, pp. 4-5, both from the City Planning Commission's files and housed in the Citizens Housing and Planning Council Files, New York City.

9. Peter Eisenstadt, *Rochdale Village: Robert Moses, 6,000 Families, and New York City's Great Experiment in Integrated Housing* (Ithaca, NY, 2010), pp. 106-10. See also *Reminiscences of Abraham E. Kazan*, pp. 471-72; "Democratic Participation in Large Cooperatives," *Co-op Contact*, April 1963, pp. 3, 12; *Cooperator*, March 1972, p. 2.

10. Farkas, "Co-op City Housing Project," p. 94; Harold Ostroff, "The Impact of Housing Cooperatives in Urban Areas," address to the National Association of Housing Cooperatives, February 19, 1966, United Housing Foundation Papers; Samuel Zipp, *Manhattan Projects: The Rise and Fall of Urban Renewal in Cold War New York* (New York, 2010), p. 113; Eisenstadt, *Rochdale Village*, p. 108; Minutes of the Annual Meeting of Members of the United Housing Foundation, Inc., April 25, 1964, United Housing Foundation Papers.

11. Robert M. Fogelson, *Downtown: Its Rise and Fall, 1880-1950* (New Haven, CT, 2001), p. 190; *Hearings before the New York State Commission of Housing*

and Regional Planning (1925), vol. 5, pp. 702-3, Avery Library, Columbia University; Joel Schwartz, *The New York Approach: Robert Moses, Urban Liberals, and Redevelopment of the Inner City* (Columbus, OH, 1993), pp. 13-14; *New York Times*, August 2, 1926.

12. *New York Times*, November 2 and 25, 1907, August 2, 1926; Fogelson, *Downtown*, p. 331; Thomas Lee Philpott, *The Slum and the Ghetto: Immigrants, Blacks, and Reformers in Chicago, 1880-1930* (Chicago, 1991), pp. 96-97.

13. "Mayor's Committee for Better Housing of the City of New York: Report of Subcommittee 5," pp. 15-16, Mayor Robert F. Wagner Papers, New York City Municipal Archives; J. Anthony Panuch, "Relocation in New York: Special Report to Mayor Robert F. Wagner" (1959), p. 58, Wagner Papers; Public Hearings before the City Planning Commission, September 11, 1957, 11:15, at City Hall, Manhattan, p. 41, Wagner Papers; *New York Times*, November 19, 1961; "Special Report: 'Relocation—New York's #1 Problem,'" p. 4, press release, November 2, 1959, Wagner Papers; Zipp, *Manhattan Projects*, pp. 204-7.

14. "Special Report: 'Relocation—New York's #1 Problem,'" p. 1; "Slum Clearance or People Clearance? Fact Sheet on 'Title I' Urban Redevelopment," pp. 1-3, Wagner Papers; *New York Times*, December 1, 1953, January 25, 1954, November 18, 1960; Public Hearings before the City Planning Commission, September 11, 1957, p. 41; Nathan Straus, "Is Rehousing for People?" transcript of broadcast on WMCA, p. 7, Robert Moses Papers, Manuscripts and Archives Division, New York Public Library.

15. *New York Post*, August 9, 1959; *Reminiscences of Abraham E. Kazan*, pp. 532-41; *New York Times*, February 14, 1965; "The Critics Build Nothing," an address by Robert Moses at a luncheon meeting of the New York Buildings Trades Congress, Hotel Astor, New York, Tuesday, November 10, 1959, p. 2, Moses Papers; Public Hearings before the City Planning Commission, September 11, 1957, p. 130; United Housing Foundation, "Position on Tax Exemption in Housing" (1964), pp. 1-5, United Housing Foundation Files.

16. *New York Times*, February 14, 1965. See also Minutes of Annual Meeting of Members of United Housing Foundation, Inc., April 25, 1964, United Housing Foundation Files.

17. *Reminiscences of Abraham E. Kazan*, pp. 547-48; *Reminiscences of Jacob Samuel Potofsky* (1965), p. 193, Columbia University Oral History Collection; Minutes of Meeting of the Board of Directors of Riverbay Corporation, May 15, 1965, Riverbay Corporation Files, Bronx, NY; Eden Ross Lipson, "Co-op City New York or What Would You Do with 500 Acres of Swamp?" (1969), p. 5, Citizens Housing and Planning Council Files.

18. *Reminiscences of Abraham E. Kazan*, pp. 549-50; Samuel E. Bleeker, *The Politics of Architecture: A Perspective on Nelson A. Rockefeller* (New York, 1981), p. 122.

19. *New York Times*, February 10 and 14, 1965; *New York Herald Tribune*, February 10, 1965; *Wall Street Journal*, February 10, 1965. See also Minutes of Special Meeting of the Board of Directors, United Housing Foundation, June 23, 1964, United Housing Foundation Files.

20. *New York Times*, February 10 and 14, 1964; *New York Herald Tribune*, February 10, 1965. See also *Cooperator*, February 1966, supp., p. 1.

21. *New York Times*, February 12,

1965; *Bronx Press-Review*, February 18, 1965.

22. Committee for Excellence in Urban Architecture to the Governor of New York State, Nelson Rockefeller, and the Mayor of New York City, Robert F. Wagner, undated letter (probably February 19, 1965), Citizens Housing and Planning Council Files; *New York Times*, February 20 and 24, 1965.

23. Operational Planning Unit to R. K. Bernstein, J. C. Smith, and M. Isler, pages 1-4, 6; Operational Planning Unit to Richard K. Bernstein, a memo dated November 24, 1964, no page number, Citizens Housing and Planning Council Files.

24. Operational Planning Unit to R. K. Bernstein, J. C. Smith, and M. Isler, pp. 4-6; Bernstein, Freedomland memo, pp. 2-5; Operational Planning Unit to Richard K. Bernstein, no page number.

25. *Journal of Proceedings of the Board of Estimate of the City of New York*, May 20, 1965, pp. 36-37, Citizens Housing and Planning Council Files.

26. Ibid.

27. Co-op City Site Review, Wednesday, April 21, 1965, pp. 1-2, Citizens Housing and Planning Council Files; *Journal of Proceedings of the Board of Estimate of the City of New York*, pp. 37-38.

28. *Journal of Proceedings of the Board of Estimate of the City of New York*, pp. 38-39. See also Harry J. Byrne to Mrs. Herbert J. Stark, April 27, 1965, Citizens Housing and Planning Council Files.

29. *Bronx Press-Review*, June 17, 1965. See also *New York Times*, February 12, 1965.

30. *New York Times*, July 16, 1965; *Bronx Press-Review*, July 22, 1965; *Cooperator*, August 1965, p. 1; *New York Herald Tribune*, February 10, 1965. See also Minutes of Meeting of Board of

Directors of Riverbay Corporation, May 15, 1965, Riverbay Corporation Files.

31. *Cooperator*, June 1965, p. 6, February 1966, p. 4; *New York Times*, February 14, 1965; *Bronx Press-Review*, July 22, 1965; Minutes of Meeting of Board of Directors of Riverbay Corporation, May 15, 1965, Riverbay Corporation Files.

32. *Cooperator*, May 1966, p. 1; *New York Times*, August 8, 1966; Farkas, "Co-op City Housing Project," pp. 79-80.

33. *New York Times*, August 8, 1966; Farkas, "Co-op City Housing Project," pp. 79-80.

34. Farkas, "Co-op City Housing Project," pp. 81-82, 85-86. See also *New York Times*, March 7, 1970.

35. Minutes of Meeting of Board of Directors of Riverbay Corporation, January 20, 1966, and Minutes of Meeting of Board of Directors of Riverbay Corporation, December 20, 1966, Riverbay Corporation Files; *Cooperator*, February 1967, p. 1; "Co-op City Fact Sheet," pp. 1-2, Citizens Housing and Planning Council Files; Farkas, "Co-op City Housing Project," p. 83; *New York Times*, May 21, 1967, March 3, 1968.

36. Minutes of the Special Meeting of the Board of Directors, United Housing Foundation, May 9, 1966, United Housing Foundation Files; *Cooperator*, April 1966, p. 1, May 1966, June 1966, pp. 1, 5; *New York Times*, May 15, 1966.

37. *Cooperator*, June 1966, pp. 1, 5; *New York Times*, May 15, 1966; 1965 Annual Reports of United Housing Foundation, Inc., and Community Services, Inc., United Housing Foundation Files; Remarks of Robert Moses, Chairman of the Triborough Bridge and Tunnel Authority, at the Groundbreaking of Co-op City, Bronx, NY, Saturday Morning, May 14, 1966, pp. 1-5.

38. *Co-op City Times*, March 7, 1970; Harold Ostroff to Board of Directors of Riverbay Corporation, memo, January 13, 1971, p. 4, and Harold Ostroff to Board of Directors of Riverbay Corporation, memo, June 18, 1971, p. 3, both in Riverbay Corporation Files.

39. Seventeenth Annual Report of United Housing Foundation, Inc., 1968, p. 2; Harold Ostroff to the Board of Directors of Community Services, Inc., memo, June 17, 1968, United Housing Foundation Files; *Cooperator*, December 1968, pp. 1-2, 4; *New York Times*, November 25, 1968.

40. Harold Ostroff to the Board of Directors of Riverbay Corporation, memo, January 13, 1971, pp. 4-5, and Harold Ostroff, "Report of the President, April 29, 1971," Riverbay Corporation Files; *New York Times*, July 25, August 20, 1969; *City News*, July 10, 1969; *Co-op City Times*, August 2, 1969.

41. *New York Times*, September 4 and 26, October 2 and 11, 1969; *City News*, July 17 and 31, August 28, September 25, October 2, 1969; *Co-op City Times*, October 4, 1969.

42. *New York Times*, October 11 and 20, 1969; Harold Ostroff to the Board of Directors of Riverbay Corporation, memo, August 10, 1969, and Harold Ostroff to Board of Directors of Riverbay Corporation, memo, February 24, 1972, Riverbay Corporation Files; *City News*, February 25, 1971, March 23, 1972; *Cooperator*, April 1972, p. 3.

43. *Co-op Contact*, Winter 1969, pp. 7-8; *Cooperator*, December 1968, p. 10, March 1972, p. 2; *New York Times*, November 25, 1969; *Bronx Press-Review*, November 28, 1968; Harold Ostroff, "Labor Cooperatives and the Housing Crisis," *AFL-CIO American Federationist*, May 1969, p. 17; Moses, *Public Works*, p. 477.

44. Jacob S. Potofsky to the Board of Directors of United Housing Foundation, memo, May 11, 1967, pp. 1-2, United Housing Foundation Files; *New York Times*, June 28, 1967.

45. *New York Times*, June 28 and 30, July 13, December 28, 1967; Harold Ostroff to the Board of Directors of United Housing Foundation, September 18, 1867, pp. 1-3, and Harold Ostroff, Report for the Meeting of the Board of Directors of United Housing Foundation, January 11, 1968, pp. 1-2, United Housing Foundation Files.

46. *New York Times*, March 9, 1972.

47. *Cooperator*, September 1972, p. 1, April 1973, p. 4; *New York Times*, March 22, July 26, 1973.

48. "Building Cooperative Communities: New York's United Housing Foundation," *Lawyers Title News*, June 1968, United Housing Foundation Files; *Cooperator*, Winter 1969, pp. 7-8.

CHAPTER 5. A MORE OR LESS AUSPICIOUS START

1. Eden Ross Lipson, "Co-op City New York or What Would You Do with 500 Acres of Swamp?" (1969), Citizens Housing and Planning Council Files, New York City; *New York Times*, July 11, 1967, March 17, September 16, November 30, 1968, December 29, 1994, December 6, 2006; *Washington Post*, January 9, 1971; *City News*, June 12 and 19, 1969; "The Lessons of Co-op City," *Time*, January 24, 1969, p. 44; "Kibbutz in the Bronx," *Newsweek*, October 5, 1970, pp. 92-94; Roberta Brandes Gratz, *The Living City: How America's Cities Are Being Revitalized by Thinking Small in a Big Way* (New York, 1989), pp. 95-96.

2. Peter Blake, "Co-op City: The High Cost of Hideousness," *New York*

Magazine, August 9, 1968, pp. 25–28; Gratz, *The Living City*, p. 95; *New York Times*, September 16, November 25, 1968; "The Lessons of Co-op City," p. 44; "Kibbutz in the Bronx," p. 90.

3. *Washington Post*, January 9, 1971; *New York Times*, April 21, September 16, 1968, October 28, 2009; "The Lessons of Co-op City," p. 44; "Kibbutz in the Bronx," p. 90.

4. *City News*, June 12, 1969; *New York Times*, September 2 and 16, November 25 and 30, 1968; "The Lessons of Co-op City," p. 44.

5. *New York Times*, July 21, 1966, April 30, September 13, 1967, March 17, September 16, November 25, 1968.

6. *New York Times*, November 30, 1969. Battcock's name is misspelled as Batock in his letter to the *New York Times*.

7. *Washington Post*, January 9, 1971; *New York Times*, November 24, 1968; *Progressive Architecture*, February 1970, pp. 72–73; *Cooperator*, April 1973, p. 1.

8. Denise Scott Brown and Robert Venturi, "Co-op City: Learning to Like It," *Progressive Architecture*, February 1970, pp. 64–72.

9. Scott Brown and Venturi, "Co-op City," p. 70; Harold Ostroff, "Labor Co-ops and the Housing Crisis," *American Federationist*, May 1969, p. 17; *New York Times*, September 16, 1968, November 9, 1969; *Cooperator*, December 1971, p. 7.

10. Seventeenth Annual Report of United Housing Foundation, Inc., 1968, pp. 2–3; *Co-op Contact*, Winter 1969, p. 8; *New York Times*, September 16, November 9, 1968.

11. *New York Times*, April 20, July 13, 1967, March 17, September 16, November 25, 1968; *Co-op Contact*, Winter 1969, p. 8; *Cooperator*, February 1973, p. 3.

12. *New York Times*, June 5, 1957, December 14, 1969.

13. "Everyone Knocks Co-op City Except Moderate-Income Buyers," *Apartment Construction News*, undated (probably from the late 1960s), Citizens Housing and Planning Council Files; *Cooperator*, February 1966, April 1966; Harold Ostroff to the Board of Directors of Community Services, Inc., memo, September 28, 1967, United Housing Foundation Files, Kheel Center for Labor-Management Documentation & Archives, Cornell University Library; Seventeenth Annual Report of United Housing Foundation, Inc., 1968, p. 2; *New York Times*, June 4, November 12, 1967, September 16, 1968.

14. *Cooperator*, January 1969; Harold Ostroff to Board of Directors of Riverbay Corporation, memo, August 18, 1970, and memo, January 13, 1971, Riverbay Corporation Files, Bronx, NY; "Kibbutz in the Bronx," pp. 93–94; *City News*, July 22, 1971.

15. *City News*, January 2, 1969, September 24, 1970; Frank S. Kristof to Jason R. Nathan, memo, January 30, 1968, Citizens Housing and Planning Council Files; Michael J. Agovino, *The Bookmaker: A Memoir of Money, Luck, and Family from the Utopian Outskirts of New York City* (New York, 2008), pp. 85–86. The census data come from GeoLytics Inc., Urban Institute, and US Bureau of the Census, *Neighborhood Change Database (NCDB) [Electronic Resource] Tract Data from 1970–2000* (East Brunswick, NJ, 2003), with thanks to Heather McCann; "Kibbutz in the Bronx," p. 94.

16. *Los Angeles Times*, December 8, 1972; Lipson, "Co-op City New York," pp. 9, 12; *City News*, January 2, 1969, January 6, 1973; Office of the New York

State Comptroller, Division of Audits and Accounts, *Audit Report on Co-op City (Report A): Interim Report No. 4 on New York State Mitchell-Lama Program* (Albany, 1976), pp. 32–34.

17. Interview with Charles Rosen by Patricia Lamiell, February 26, 1986, p. 16, with thanks to Sarah Colt; "Kibbutz in the Bronx," p. 93; Sonia Sotomayor, *My Beloved World* (New York, 2013), p. 99; Gratz, *The Living City*, p. 96; *New York Times*, July 21, 1966, October 4 and 20, 1970.

18. "Kibbutz in the Bronx," pp. 93–94; *New York Daily News*, September 21, 1969; *New York Times*, January 23, June 12, 1966, June 4, November 12, 1967, November 9, 1969, April 6, 2008; Lipson, "Co-op City New York," p. 2; Sotomayor, *My Beloved World*, p. 99; *City News*, January 2, 1969; Lamiell interview with Charles Rosen, pp. 15–17; Ian Frazier, "Utopia, the Bronx," *The New Yorker*, June 26, 2006, p. 58.

19. *Co-op City Times*, December 5, 1970, March 20, April 10, December 13, 1971, July 7, 1973; Frazier, "Utopia, the Bronx," p. 58; Nina Wohl, "Co-op City: The Dream and the Reality," master's thesis, Columbia University, 2016, p. 21; *City News*, April 9, 1970; *New York Times*, October 26, 1971. For the use of the word "pioneer," see *City News*, December 12, 1972, and December 13, 1973.

20. Wohl, "Co-op City," pp. 21, 23; *Co-op City Times*, November 21, December 5 and 12, 1970, February 27, 1971; *City News*, March 27, 1969; *Bronx Press-Review*, May 18, 1967; *New York Times*, May 21, 1967, May 17, 1968.

21. *Co-op City Times*, March 20, 1971; *City News*, May 28, 1969, August 6, 1970, April 8, 1971.

22. *Co-op City Times*, May 30, December 5, 1970, January 29, 1972; *City News*, August 6, 1970.

23. *New York Times*, October 26, 1981. See also *Co-op City Times*, December 5, 1970, December 13, 1971, January 29, 1972. According to the August 12, 1971, issue of the *City News* (one of Co-op City's two community newspapers), Section 5, which was separated from Sections 1, 2, 3, and 4 by the Hutchinson River Parkway, looked as bleak in the summer of 1971 as it had in the winter of 1968.

24. *Co-op City Times*, March 7, November 21, December 5 and 19, 1970, January 9, 23, and 30, June 6, 1971, July 7, 1973; *Bronx Press-Review*, May 18, 1967, October 24, 1968; *New York Times*, May 21, 1967, September 11 and 29, 1971, September 10, 1973.

25. *Co-op City Times*, July 4, August 8, December 19, 1970, February 13, March 27, April 3, 1971.

26. *Co-op City Times*, August 8, December 19, 1970, February 13, April 3, 1971.

27. *Co-op City Times*, August 7, December 19, 1970, January 30, February 13, March 6 and 17, April 3, 1971.

28. "Kibbutz in the Bronx," p. 93; *New York Times*, May 21, 1967, September 16, 1968; *City News*, January 30, August 28, 1969.

29. *City News*, January 30, February 27, May 8, August 28, 1969, October 17, 1970, February 11, April 4, November 11, 1971; *Co-op City Times*, June 13, October 17, December 5, 1970, January 23, 1971; *New York Times*, May 21, 1967, September 16, 1978.

30. *Co-op City Times*, November 1, 1969, October 17, December 12, 1970, January 16, February 13, March 17, 1971, August 12 and 26, 1972; *City News*, January 14 and 21, 1971.

31. *Co-op City Times*, March 21, August 1, October 17, 1970, June 5, 1971, July 15, 1972, July 7, 1973; *City News*,

January 8, 1970, June 19, July 29, August 9, September 9 and 16, November 11, 1971, January 22, July 20, November 9, 1972.

32. *Co-op City Times*, October 17 and 31, November 21, December 5, 1970, January 23, 1971, June 17, July 15, 1972, September 15, 1973; *City News*, May 15, 1969, January 22, April 2, 1970, December 20, 1973, January 3, 1974.

33. *City News*, April 2, 1970; *New York Times*, April 7, 1965; Wohl, "Co-op City," pp. 29-30.

34. *Co-op City Times*, April 18, May 2, 16, 20, and 23, June 5, 1970, January 19, 1978.

35. *City News*, July 3, August 21, September 25, October 23, 1969, January 8, 1970, April 21, 1971; *New York Daily News*, September 21, 1969; *Co-op City Times*, April 24, 1971; *New York Times*, September 17, 1973.

36. *New York Times*, September 17, 19, and 20, 1973.

37. *Co-op City Times*, July 10, September 4, 1969, November 7, 1970, January 30, March 27, 1971, September 9, 1972; *City News*, July 24, September 18, 1969, January 14, 1971.

38. *City News*, July 10 and 24, September 18, 1969; *Co-op City Times*, November 7, 1970.

39. *City News*, October 18, 1971, June 15, 1972.

40. *City News*, October 28, 1971, June 15, August 10, 1972, March 8, 1973; *Co-op City Times*, August 12, 1972.

41. *Co-op City Times*, March 14, 1970.

42. *Riverbay Corp. v. Klinghoffer*, 309 N.Y.S.2d 472; *City News*, July 10, 1969.

43. *Co-op City Times*, April 22, 1972.

44. *City News*, May 13, 1971, June 7, 1973; *Cooperator*, February 1973, p. 3.

45. *Co-op City Times*, December 5, 1970, January 23, April 12, May 29, June 5, July 3, 1971, April 22, 1972;

Cooperator, February 1973, p. 3; Wohl, "Co-op City," p. 24; *New York Times*, June 19, 1971.

46. *City News*, March 13, 1971, June 7, 1973; *Co-op City Times*, June 17, July 29, 1972; Wohl, "Co-op City," p. 23; *New York Times*, September 18, 1969; *Cooperator*, February 1973, p. 3.

47. *Co-op City Times*, August 8, 1970, February 13, 1971, January 29, April 22, June 14, 1972, August 4, November 6, 1973. See also *City News*, August 13, 1970.

48. *Co-op City Times*, October 18, 1969, August 8, 1970, July 29, 1972; *City News*, August 21, 1969, August 6, 1970, March 4, 1971.

CHAPTER 6. FISCAL TROUBLES

1. Affidavit of Harold Ostroff, in Answer of Respondent, pp. 115-16, *Hanks v. Urstadt*, New York State Supreme Court Appellate Division, First Department, *Record on Appeal*, New York State Library, Albany; Cynthia Ann Curran, "Administration of Subsidized Housing in New York State: Co-op City: A Case Study of the Largest Subsidized Housing Development in the Nation," PhD diss., New York University, 1978, pp. 95, 106.

2. Affidavit of Jay F. Gordon, Sworn to January 30, 1973, in Opposition to Defendants' Motions and in Support of Cross Motion, pp. 149a-150a, and exhibit 29, schedules A, B, and C, May 1, 1971, Annexed to Affidavit of Jay F. Gordon, p. 355a, *United Housing Foundation, Inc., v. Forman*, US Supreme Court, *Record on Appeal*, Harvard University Law Library; Curran, "Administration of Subsidized Housing in New York State," pp. 7, 58-59.

3. Office of the New York State Comptroller, Division of Audits and Accounts, *Report No. 7 on the New York State*

Mitchell-Lama Program—Supervision of Development Costs of Co-op City by the Division of Housing and Community Renewal (Albany, 1978), pp. 3, 17; Affidavit of Jay F. Gordon, pp. 149a-153a; Curran, "Administration of Subsidized Housing in New York State," pp. 93-94.

4. On organized labor in New York City after World War II, see Joshua B. Freeman, *Working-Class New York: Life and Labor since World War II* (New York, 2000).

5. "One Hundred Years of Price Change: The Consumer Price Index and the American Inflation Experience," *Monthly Labor Review*, April 2014, pp. 1-43; *Historical Statistics of the United States: Colonial Times to 1970* (Washington, DC, 1976), vol. 2, pp. 627-29; Curran, "Administration of Subsidized Housing in New York State," pp. 24-26.

6. Office of the New York State Comptroller, Division of Audits and Accounts, *Audit Report on Co-op City (Report A): Interim Report No. 4 on New York State Mitchell-Lama Program* (Albany, 1976), p. 7.

7. *New York Times*, January 12, 1969; Statement of Charles J. Urstadt, Commissioner of Housing and Community Renewal, Informational Meeting on Carrying Charges' Increase at Co-op City, Bronx County Courthouse, Monday, May 11, 1970, 10:30 a.m., in *Hanks v. Urstadt, Record on Appeal*, pp. 54-55; Harold Ostroff to the Board of Directors of Riverbay Corporation, memo, June 18, 1971, United Housing Foundation Files, Kheel Center for Labor-Management Documentation & Archives, Cornell University Library; Seventeenth Annual Report of United Housing Foundation, Inc., 1968, pp. 2-3; *Co-op City Times*, June 21, 1971; Harold Ostroff to Merril

Eisenbud, November 10, 1969, Mayor John V. Lindsay Papers, New York City Municipal Archives.

8. *New York Times*, February 4, 1967, August 22, 1969; *Boston Globe*, February 5, 1967; *Chicago Tribune*, February 21, 1967; *Baltimore Sun*, March 24, 1967; *Los Angeles Times*, March 24, 1967.

9. *New York Times*, August 2, September 4, October 23, 1969.

10. *New York Times*, September 25, October 2, 3, 20, 21, and 27, 1969.

11. *City News*, July 10, 1969; *New York Times*, July 25 and 31, August 2, 1969. See also Harold Ostroff to Board of Directors of Riverbay Corporation, memo, January 31, 1971, United Housing Foundation Files.

12. *New York Times*, September 26, 1969; Regular Meeting of the Board of Directors of Community Services, Inc., September 18, 1969, and Harold Ostroff to Board of Directors of Riverbay Corporation, memo, June 18, 1971, United Housing Foundation Files; *City News*, July 10 and 31, 1969; *Co-op City Times*, August 2, 1969.

13. *Co-op City Times*, November 29, 1969, June 26, 1971; "Brief on Behalf of Respondent Riverbay Corporation," p. 17, Charles J. Urstadt to Riverbay Corporation, May 28, 1970, pp. 30-33, and "Brief for Respondent Urstadt," p. 46, all in *Hanks v. Urstadt, Record on Appeal*; "Defendants' Notice of Motion to Dismiss Amended Complaint," *United Housing Foundation, Inc., v. Forman, Record on Appeal*, p. 76a; Budget Committee to Board of Directors of Riverbay Corporation, memo, June 22, 1971, United Housing Foundation Files.

14. US Bureau of Labor Statistics, "One Hundred Years of Price Changes: The CPI and the American Inflation Experience," *Monthly Labor Review*, April

15, 2014, pp. 88ff. See also Kimberly Amadeo, "US Inflation Rate by Year: 1929-2020," *The Balance*, January 15, 2018.

15. *Co-op City Times*, June 26, 1971; 1972 United Housing Foundation Annual Report; "Cost Inflation Will Drop from Current Peak," *Engineering News-Record*, September 16, 1971, pp. 88-90; exhibit 29, schedules A, B, and C, May 1971, Annexed to Affidavit of Jay F. Gordon, *United Housing Foundation, Inc., v. Forman, Record on Appeal*, p. 355a; *Cooperator*, October 1971.

16. Harold Ostroff to "Dear Subscriber," October 1968, exhibit D, Annexed to Answering Affidavit of Harold Ostroff, *Hanks v. Urstadt, Record on Appeal*, p. 135; Regular Meeting of Board of Directors of Community Services, Inc., September 18, 1969, and Harold Ostroff to Board of Directors of Community Services, Inc., June 18, 1971; "Cost Inflation Will Drop from Current Peak," pp. 88-90; William F. Meyers to Charles J. Urstadt, memo, May 26, 1970, *Hanks v. Urstadt, Record on Appeal*, pp. 34-41; *Cooperator*, October 1971.

17. *Cooperator*, October 1971, April 1972; "Cost Inflation Will Drop from Current Peak," pp. 88-90; Harold Ostroff to Board of Directors of Riverbay Corporation, memo, January 31, 1971, Riverbay Corporation Files, Bronx, NY; 1972 United Housing Foundation Annual Report; Minutes of the Annual Meeting of the United Housing Foundation, April 24, 1971, United Housing Foundation Files.

18. Harold Ostroff to Board of Directors of United Housing Foundation and Community Services, Inc., memo, September 16, 1968, United Housing Foundation Files; *Co-op City Times*, June 26, 1971; Harold Ostroff to Board

of Directors of Riverbay Corporation, memo, June 18, 1971, Riverbay Corporation Files; Regular Meeting of the Board of Directors of Community Services, Inc., September 18, 1969, United Housing Foundation Files; Division of Audits and Accounts, *Audit Report on Co-op City*, p. 37.

19. *Co-op City Times*, July 26, 1971.

20. Curran, "Administration of Subsidized Housing in New York State," p. 104. See also Affidavit of Harold Ostroff, in *Hanks v. Urstadt, Record on Appeal*, p. 120.

21. Curran, "Administration of Subsidized Housing in New York State," p. 24; *New York Times*, February 27, 1970; Harold Ostroff to Board of Directors of Community Services, Inc., June 17, 1968, United Housing Foundation Files; statement of Charles J. Urstadt in *Hanks v. Urstadt, Record on Appeal*, p. 54.

22. Statement of Charles J. Urstadt in *Hanks v. Urstadt, Record on Appeal*, p. 54; William F. Meyers to Charles J. Urstadt, May 26, 1970, *Hanks v. Urstadt, Record on Appeal*, p. 36; Curran, "Administration of Subsidized Housing in New York State," p. 105; *Co-op City Times*, September 18, 1971.

23. Curran, "Administration of Subsidized Housing in New York State," pp. 104, 106. See also *Co-op City Times*, January 18, 1975.

24. Edward Aronov to Board of Directors of Riverbay Corporation, memo, March 25, 1974, United Housing Foundation Files. See also Office of the New York State Comptroller, Division of Audits and Accounts, *Report No. 7 on the New York State Mitchell-Lama Program*, p. 69.

25. *Co-op City Times*, March 27, 1971, September 22 and 29, 1973; Office of the New York State Comptroller, Division of

Audits and Accounts, *Certain Operating Matters of Co-op City: Interim Report No. 5 on New York State Mitchell-Lama Program* (Albany, 1977), pp. 66ff; *New York Times*, September 17, 1973.

26. *Co-op City Times*, September 22 and 29, October 6, 1973; *New York Times*, September 17-21, 1973; Office of the New York State Comptroller, *Certain Operating Matters of Co-op City*, p. 71; *City News*, September 17, 1973.

27. *New York Times*, July 31, 1967; *City News*, December 20, 1973; *Co-op City Times*, March 17, 1971, November 17, 1973; Harold Ostroff to Board of Directors of Riverbay Corporation, memo, March 19, 1974, United Housing Foundation Files; *Cooperator*, January/February 1974; Office of the New York State Comptroller, Division of Audits and Accounts, *Report No. 77 on the New York State Mitchell-Lama Program*, p. 51.

28. Lawrence Sivak to Board of Directors of Riverbay Corporation, memo, March 25, 1971, United Housing Foundation Files; *Co-op City Times*, March 15 and 27, 1971, November 17, 1973, January 4 and 11, March 15, 1975; Harold Ostroff to Joseph Swindler, January 23, 1974, and Harold Ostroff to Board of Directors of United Housing Foundation, memo, January 14, 1974, United Housing Foundation Files; *Bronx Press-Review*, November 7 and 21, 1974.

29. *Co-op City Times*, March 15, 1975.

30. *Co-op City Times*, January 26, 1974, January 4 and 25, 1975. See also Harold Ostroff to Board of Directors of Riverbay Corporation, memo, October 25, 1974, Riverbay Corporation Files.

31. Harold Ostroff to Board of Directors of Riverbay Corporation, memo, June 19, 1971, Riverbay Corporation Files; *Co-op City Times*, February 3, June 2, 1971, February 3, December 23, 1972, January 20, November 24, 1973, March 2, April 11, 1974, February 15 and 22, 1975; *City News*, April 25, 1974.

32. *Co-op City Times*, April 27, 1974; *New York Times*, April 2, 1967; *Cooperator*, February, March 1967, May 1968; Office of the New York State Comptroller, *Certain Operating Matters of Co-op City*, p. 13.

33. *Cooperator*, May 1969; Szold, Brandwen, Meyers & Altman to Board of Estimate of the City of New York, September 15, 1969, Lindsay Papers; Curran, "Administration of Subsidized Housing in New York State," p. 28; *Co-op City Times*, July 16, September 22, 1973; Office of the New York State Comptroller, *Certain Operating Matters of Co-op City*, pp. 12, 14.

34. Office of the New York State Comptroller, *Certain Operating Matters of Co-op City*, pp. 15-16. See also *Co-op City Times*, January 13, 1972, June 30, 1973, September 1, 1974.

35. *Cooperator*, October, November 1970; *City News*, May 14, 1970; *Co-op City Times*, February 6 and 27, May 8 and 22, June 26, 1971; *New York Times*, January 24, 1972.

36. *Cooperator*, March, June 1972; *Co-op City Times*, March 25, 1972, June 16, August 18, September 12, November 4, 1973, May 25, 1974, January 4, 1975; *City News*, January 2, 1975.

37. *Co-op City Times*, January 13, December 23, 1972, March 9, June 8, July 14, 1973, January 5 and 19, 1974. See also *New York Times*, October 29, 1973.

38. *Co-op City Times*, May 12, 1973, February 23, 1974; *City News*, May 10 and 31, 1973, May 9, 1974.

39. *Co-op City Times*, August 21, 1971, October 19, 1974, January 5, March 25, 1975; *City News*, November 8, 1973, February 20, 1975; Harold Ostroff to Board

of Directors of United Housing Foundation and Community Services, Inc., memo, May 20, 1974, United Housing Foundation Files.

40. *New York Times*, April 16, 1973; *Co-op City Times*, June 6, 1970, August 24, November 4, 1972, June 17, 1973; Harold Ostroff to Board of Directors of Riverbay Corporation, memo, June 1, 1972, Riverbay Corporation Files.

41. *New York Times*, January 24, 1972; *Cooperator*, February 1973; *Co-op City Times*, March 25, August 24, October 29, 1972, November 8, 1973, August 22, 1974, March 22 and 29, 1975; *City News*, January 17, 1974; Harold Ostroff to Board of Directors of Riverbay Corporation, memo, August 24, 1972, and Richard Ferguson to Board of Directors of Riverbay Corporation, memo, June 19, 1974, Riverbay Corporation Files.

42. *City News*, July 29, 1971, August 17, 1972; *Co-op City Times*, August 17, 1972, November 19, December 15, 1973, January 4, February 1, March 15, 1975.

43. Harold Ostroff to Board of Directors of Riverbay Corporation, memo, October 29, 1974, Harold Ostroff to Riverbay's Operations, Budget, and Management Committee, memo, December 27, 1974, and Larry Dolnick to Board of Directors of Riverbay Corporation, February 26, 1975, United Housing Foundation Files; *City News*, May 1, 1970, July 29, 1971, April 27, 1972, December 20, 1973; *New York Times*, November 30, 1997.

44. *Co-op City Times*, July 31, 1971, March 18, July 30, 1972, March 8 and 15, 1975; *City News*, August 26, 1971; Harold Ostroff to Riverbay's Operations, Budget, and Management Committee, memo, December 27, 1974, Riverbay Corporation Files.

45. Harold Ostroff to Board of Directors of Riverbay Corporation, memo, October 21, 1974, Riverbay Corporation Files; *City News*, July 20, August 17, 1972, August 30, 1973; *Co-op City Times*, July 31, 1971, December 7, 1974.

46. *City News*, January 17, 1974; *Co-op City Times*, March 15, 1975.

47. Harold Ostroff to "Dear Subscriber," pp. 134-36.

CHAPTER 7. CARRYING CHARGES

1. Annual Meeting of Members of United Housing Foundation, February 1963, United Housing Foundation Files, Kheel Center for Labor-Management Documentation & Archives, Cornell University Library; *Cooperator*, August 1968, April 1970; exhibit 2, 1965 Information Bulletin, Annexed to Affidavit of Jay F. Gordon, p. 174a, *United Housing Foundation, Inc., v. Forman*, US Supreme Court, *Record on Appeal*, Harvard Law Library.

2. *Cooperator*, December 1966, January 1967, August 1968; Harold Ostroff to Members of Board of Directors of United Housing Foundation and Community Services, Inc., memo, January 4, 1967, and Minutes of Regular Meeting of Board of Directors of Community Services, Inc., June 20, 1968, United Housing Foundation Files.

3. Affidavit of Harold Ostroff, in Answer of Respondent, pp. 114ff, *Hanks v. Urstadt*, New York State Supreme Court, Appellate Division, First Department, *Record on Appeal*, New York State Library, Albany; Riverbay Corporation, Schedule C (Revision), March 13, 1967, in exhibit 26, schedules A, B, and C, March 13, 1967, Annexed to Affidavit of Jay F. Gordon, pp. 1-5, *United Housing Foundation, Inc., v. Forman, Record on Appeal*.

4. Riverbay Corporation, Schedule C (Revision), March 13, 1967, pp. 1–5; exhibit 3, 1967 Revised Information Bulletin, Annexed to Affidavit of Jay F. Gordon, pp. 194a, *United Housing Foundation, Inc., v. Forman, Record on Appeal*.

5. Affidavit of Harold Ostroff, in Answer of Respondent, pp. 114ff; Brief on Behalf of Respondent Urstadt, pp. 5, 7, in *Hanks v. Urstadt, Record on Appeal*; Brief on Behalf of Respondent Riverbay Corporation, p. 6, in *United Housing Foundation, Inc., v. Forman, Record on Appeal*; Cynthia Ann Curran, "Administration of Subsidized Housing in New York State: Co-op City: A Case Study of the Largest Subsidized Housing Development in the Nation," PhD diss., New York University, 1978, p. 109; *City News*, July 10, 1969.

6. Affidavit of William A. Conway Jr., Supplementing Answer of Respondent Charles J. Urstadt, Commissioner of Housing and Community Renewal, p. 161, in *Hanks v. Urstadt, Record on Appeal*; Brief on Behalf of Respondent Riverbay Corporation, p. 7; *City News*, November 13, 1969, February 26, 1970.

7. Affidavit of Harold Ostroff, in Answer of Respondent, pp. 114ff.

8. Charles J. Urstadt to Riverbay Corporation, May 28, 1970, Reply Affirmation by Gerald P. Halpern, pp. 89–90, in *Hanks v. Urstadt, Record on Appeal*; Affidavit of Milton Forman, Sworn to January 30, 1973, pp. 369a–70, in *United Housing Foundation, Inc., v. Forman, Record on Appeal*; *City News*, May 14, July 2, August 13, 1970.

9. *City News*, June 26, 1969.

10. *City News*, January 22 and 29, April 2 and 9, 1970.

11. *City News*, January 29, 1970. On the origins of the Co-op City Advisory Council, see *City News*, January 22 and 29, 1970.

12. Affidavit of Harold Ostroff, in Answer of Respondent, p. 105; *City News*, January 8, March 19, July 23, 1970.

13. *City News*, February 26, March 5, 1970. See also Avrum Hyman to John D. Calandra, February 26, 1970, exhibit C, Annexed to Reply Affirmation of Gerald P. Halpern, pp. 92–93, in *Hanks v. Urstadt, Record on Appeal*.

14. *City News*, March 5 and 12, 1970. See also *New York Times*, January 21, 1986.

15. *City News*, March 19 and 26, April 2, May 7, 1970, August 5, 1971; *New York Times*, January 1, 1971.

16. *City News*, May 7, 1970.

17. *Co-op City Times*, March 7, April 4, 1970.

18. Reply Affirmation of Gerald P. Halpern, p. 69; *City News*, April 16, 1970. See also *Co-op City Times*, April 10, 1971.

19. *City News*, May 14, June 4, 1970; Statement of Charles J. Urstadt, New York State Commissioner of Housing and Community Renewal, Informational Meeting on Carrying Charge Increase at Co-op City, Bronx County Courthouse, Monday, May 11, 1970, 10:30 a.m., in *Hanks v. Urstadt, Record on Appeal*, pp. 53–57.

20. *City News*, May 14 and 21, 1970.

21. *City News*, May 14, 1970.

22. *City News*, May 14 and 21, 1970.

23. *City News*, May 14 and 21, 1970.

24. *City News*, May 14, 1970.

25. Petition of Leonard Hanks and Lorraine Hanks to the Supreme Court of the State of New York, County of the Bronx, p. 18, in *Hanks v. Urstadt, Record on Appeal*; Gerald P. Halpern, "Co-op City: Areas of Possible Modification or Relief," memo, May 15, 1970, pp. 1–6,

Nelson A. Rockefeller Papers, Rockefeller Archive Center, Sleepy Holly, NY.

26. Petition of Leonard Hanks and Lorraine Hanks, pp. 1-6.

27. Robert Abrams to Nelson A. Rockefeller, May 15, 1970, Anthony J. Stella to Nelson A. Rockefeller, May 19, 1970, Rockefeller Papers.

28. Urstadt's letter was published in the *Co-op City Times* on June 6, 1970. So were the reports from Meyers and Conway that were attached to his letter.

29. *City News*, June 4, 1970.

30. Gerald P. Halpern to Charles J. Urstadt, June 1, 1970, and William F. Meyers to Gerald P. Halpern, June 11, 1970, exhibits C and B, Annexed to Petition, pp. 45-49, in *Hanks v. Urstadt, Record on Appeal*. See also *City News*, June 4, 1970.

31. *City News*, June 4, 11, and 25, 1970.

32. *City News*, July 2 and 9, 1970.

33. *City News*, June 25, 1970; *New York Times*, January 3, 1968, June 9, 1987.

34. Petition of Leonard Hanks and Lorraine Hanks, pp. 14-22; Reply Affirmation of Gerald P. Halpern, pp. 63-65.

35. Petition of Leonard Hanks and Lorraine Hanks, pp. 16, 22-25; Reply Affirmation of Gerald P. Halpern, p. 89.

36. Reply Affirmation of Gerald P. Halpern, pp. 69-74, 89-90.

37. Petition of Leonard Hanks and Lorraine Hanks, pp. 14, 24; Reply Affirmation of Gerald P. Halpern, pp. 74, 90-91.

38. Answer of Respondent Charles J. Urstadt, pp. 139, 142-46, in *Hanks v. Urstadt, Record on Appeal*; Affidavit of William A. Conway Jr., Supplementing Answer of Respondent Charles J. Urstadt, pp. 151-52, 162, and Affidavit of Harold Ostroff, in Answer of Respondent, pp. 106-7, 124-27, 131.

39. Affidavit of Harold Ostroff, in Answer of Respondent, pp. 114, 117-19, 121-22, 128-29; Affidavit of William A. Conway Jr., Supplementing Answer of Respondent Charles J. Urstadt, pp. 157-59.

40. Affidavit of Harold Ostroff, in Answer of Respondent, pp. 112-14.

41. Answer of Respondent Charles J. Urstadt, p. 146; Affidavit of William A. Conway Jr., Supplementing Answer of Respondent Charles J. Urstadt, p. 162; Affidavit of Harold Ostroff, in Answer of Respondent, pp. 105-7.

42. *Hanks v. Urstadt*, 345 N.Y.S.2d 254.

43. *Co-op City Times*, October 31, 1970; *City News*, November 5, 1970.

44. *Co-op City Times*, October 31, 1970; *City News*, October 29, 1970.

45. Brief on Behalf of Petitioners-Appellants, pp. 1-25, in *Hanks v. Urstadt, Record on Appeal*.

46. Brief for Respondent Urstadt, pp. 1-29, *Hanks v. Urstadt, Record on Appeal*.

47. Brief on Behalf of Respondent Riverbay Corporation, pp. 1-27, *Hanks v. Urstadt, Record on Appeal*.

48. *Hanks v. Urstadt*, 37 A.D.2d 1044; *City News*, November 18, 1971.

CHAPTER 8. THE "SECOND FRONT"

1. *City News*, August 13, 1970.

2. *City News*, August 27, 1970.

3. *Co-op City Times*, March 27, June 26, 1971; *City News*, July 1, 1971. See also Budget Committee to the Board of Directors of Riverbay Corporation, memo, June 22, 1971, Riverbay Corporation Files, Bronx, NY.

4. *City News*, July 1, 1971.

5. Ibid.

6. *City News*, July 1 and 15, 1971;

Charles J. Urstadt to Joseph H. Murphy, June 30, 1971, Annexed to Affidavit of Jay F. Gordon, p. 362a, *United Housing Foundation, Inc., v. Forman*, US Supreme Court, *Record on Appeal*, Harvard University Law Library.

7. *City News*, July 1, 1971; *Co-op City Times*, July 3, 1971.

8. *Co-op City Times*, July 3, 1971.

9. *City News*, July 1, 1971.

10. *Co-op City Times*, July 3, 1971.

11. *Co-op City Times*, July 31, 1971; *City News*, August 19, 1971.

12. *City News*, September 16, 1971; *Co-op City Times*, September 18, 1971.

13. *Co-op City Times*, August 7, November 4, 1971.

14. *Co-op City Times*, July 17, October 14, 1971.

15. *City News*, July 8, August 19, September 30, 1971.

16. *Co-op City Times*, July 17 and 31, August 14, September 4, 1971; *City News*, July 8, August 12, September 16, November 11, 1971.

17. *Co-op City Times*, July 24, August 14 and 18, September 2 and 9, October 16, 1971; *City News*, August 5 and 12, September 5, October 14, 1971.

18. *City News*, July 1, August 26, October 16, November 4, 1971; *Co-op City Times*, September 30, October 23, 1971.

19. *Co-op City Times*, April 8, 1972; *New York Times*, November 11, 1994.

20. *Co-op City Times*, November 6, 1971, April 8, 1972; *City News*, November 4 and 11, 1971.

21. Affidavit of Jay F. Gordon, Sworn to January 20, 1973, in Opposition to Defendants' Motion and in Support of Cross-Motion, pp. 143a–153a, in *United Housing Foundation, Inc., v. Forman, Record on Appeal*; *City News*, March 16, 1972.

22. *City News*, March 30, 1972; *Co-op City Times*, April 1, 1972.

23. *Co-op City Times*, April 8, 1972.

24. *Co-op City Times*, April 15, 1972.

25. *Co-op City Times*, April 15, 1972; *City News*, April 13, 1972.

26. *City News*, April 6 and 13, 1972.

27. *City News*, February 3, March 2, April 13 and 20, 1972; *Co-op City Times*, March 11, April 22, 1972.

28. *Co-op City Times*, April 22, 1972; *City News*, April 20, 1972.

29. *City News*, April 6 and 11, May 11 and 18, 1972; *Co-op City Times*, May 13, 1972. See also *Bronx Press-Review*, May 18, 1972.

30. *Co-op City Times*, May 13, 1972; *City News*, May 11, 1971.

31. *City News*, June 15, July 6 and 13, September 21, 1972; *Co-op City Times*, September 23, 1972. See also *New York Times*, September 20, 1972.

32. *Co-op City Times*, September 23 and 30, 1972.

33. *City News*, September 21, October 12, 1972; *Co-op City Times*, September 30, October 21, November 11, 1972; *New York Times*, November 15, 1995.

34. *New York Times*, September 9, 1981.

35. For the original complaint, see *City News*, September 21, 1972. For the amended complaint, see Amended Complaint, US District Court, Southern District of New York, pp. 6–37, in *United Housing Foundation, Inc., v. Forman, Record on Appeal*. See also *New York Times*, September 20, 1972; *City News*, October 26, 1972.

36. Answer of the State of New York and New York State Housing Finance Agency, pp. 57a–61a, in *United Housing Foundation, Inc., v. Forman, Record on Appeal*; *City News*, November 23, December 28, 1972.

37. *City News*, February 22, 1973.

38. *Forman v. Community Services, Inc.*, 366 F. Supp. 1117. See also *New York Times*, September 7, 1973; *City News*, September 13, 1973.

39. *City News*, September 13, 1973, January 3 and 24, 1974.

40. *City News*, February 28, 1974.

41. *City News*, March 14, April 11, 1974.

42. *Forman v. Community Services, Inc.*, 500 F.2d 1246. See also *City News*, June 20, 1974.

43. *City News*, June 20, August 8, October 3, 1974; Petition for a Writ of Certiorari to the US Court of Appeals for the Second Circuit (hereafter referred to as Rifkind Petition), Petition for a Writ of Certiorari to the US Court of Appeals for the Second Circuit (hereafter referred to as Cohen Petition), Respondents' Brief to Petition for a Writ of Certiorari (hereafter referred to as Berger Petition 1), and Respondents' Brief in Opposition to Petition for Writ of Certiorari (hereafter referred to as Berger Petition 2), all of which are in *United Housing Foundation, Inc., v. Forman, Record on Appeal.*

44. Rifkind Petition, passim; Cohen Petition, passim; *City News*, October 3, 1974.

45. Berger Petition 1, passim; Berger Petition 2, passim.

46. The briefs are available in *United Housing Foundation, Inc., v. Forman, Record on Appeal*; the oral arguments can be found in the Oyez Project at the University of Illinois, Chicago-Kent College of Law. See also *City News*, April 17 and 24, 1975; *Co-op City Times*, April 26, 1975; *New York Times*, April 23, 1965; and, for Powell's remarks, *United Housing Foundation, Inc., v. Forman*, 421 U.S. 837.

47. *United Housing Foundation, Inc., v. Forman*, 421 U.S. 837. For press coverage of the decision, see *New York Times*, June 17, 1975; *Washington Post*, June 17, 1975; *Los Angeles Times*, June 17, 1975.

48. *City News*, July 31, 1974.

CHAPTER 9. "NO WAY, WE WON'T PAY"

1. *City News*, May 23, 1974. See also *Co-op City Times*, March 16, 1974.

2. For a survey of rent strikes in New York City in the twentieth century, see the essays by Jenna Weissman Joselit, Joseph A. Spencer, Mark Naison, Joel Schwartz, and Ronald Lawson in Ronald Lawson, ed., *The Tenant Movement in New York City, 1904–1984* (New Brunswick, NJ, 1986). See also *New York Times*, July 27, 1975.

3. *City News*, June 26, July 2, 1970, January 23, June 15, 1972.

4. Robert M. Fogelson, *The Great Rent Wars, 1917–1929* (New Haven, CT, 2013), chap. 4; *Co-op City Times*, May 3, 1975; Jack Newfield and Paul Du Brul, *The Abuse of Power: The Permanent Government and the Fall of New York* (New York, 1977), p. 296; Richard Karp, "No Day of Reckoning: At Co-op City Only the Taxpayers Are Still on the Hook," *Barron's Business and Financial Weekly*, July 15, 1977, p. 5.

5. Fogelson, *The Great Rent Wars*, chap. 4; *City News*, September 19, November 28, 1974; *New York Times*, November 20, 1968; *Co-op City Times*, April 19, 1975.

6. Peter Eisenstadt, *Rochdale Village: Robert Moses, 6,000 Families, and New York City's Great Experiment in Integrated Housing* (Ithaca, NY, 2010), pp. 226–27; Manager's Report to the Board of Directors of Rochdale Village, October 1974, United Housing

Foundation Files, Kheel Center for Labor-Management Documentation & Archives, Cornell University Library; *City News*, June 24, August 4, 22, and 29, October 3, November 14, December 5, 1974; *Co-op City Times*, October 31, December 7, 1974; *New York Times*, August 11, September 22, 1974.

7. *City News*, January 17, March 7 and 21, May 23, 1974.

8. *Co-op City Times*, March 3, 1973.

9. *City News*, January 17, March 7 and 21, May 23, 1974.

10. *City News*, April 25, May 23, 1974; *Co-op City Times*, February 23, April 20, 1974.

11. *City News*, June 6, 1974; *Co-op City Times*, June 8, 1974. See also "The Budget Deficit: A Statement from the Five Resident Directors," United Housing Foundation Files; and *New York Times*, June 6, 1974.

12. *Co-op City Times*, June 8 and 15, 1974.

13. *City News*, June 6 and 13, 1974.

14. *City News*, June 27, 1974. See also *Co-op City Times*, June 22, 1974; *New York Times*, June 20, 1974.

15. *Co-op City Times*, June 22, July 13, 1974; *City News*, July 11, 1974. See also Newfield and Du Brul, *Abuse of Power*, p. 303.

16. *Co-op City Times*, August 8 and 22, 1969. See also *New York Times*, March 23, April 20, 1973.

17. *Co-op City Times*, July 20 and 27, August 17 and 31, September 7, 1974; *City News*, July 25, August 29, September 12, 1974.

18. *City News*, September 12, 1974.

19. *City News*, December 12, 1974, February 6, 1975; *Co-op City Times*, September 7, 1974, February 1, 1975.

20. *City News*, February 13, 1975; *Co-op City Times*, February 1, 8, and 15, 1975.

21. *City News*, January 23, 1975; *Co-op City Times*, January 18, February 1, March 29, 1975.

22. *New York Times*, October 1, 2006; Joe Klein, "The Temporary Hero of Co-op City," *Rolling Stone*, October 6, 1977; *City News*, April 4, 1975; *Co-op City Times*, April 19, 1975.

23. *City News*, September 19, October 10, November 28, 1974.

24. *City News*, September 19, November 28, 1974, February 27, March 6, 1975.

25. *City News*, January 25, February 20, March 6 and 20, 1975. See also *Co-op City Times*, March 22 and 29, April 26, 1975.

26. *City News*, March 27, April 3, May 1, 1975; *Co-op City Times*, April 26, May 3, 1975.

27. *Co-op City Times*, March 29, April 5, 19, and 26, May 3, 1975.

28. *Co-op City Times*, April 5, 19, and 26, May 3 and 10, 1975.

29. *Co-op City Times*, March 15, April 19 and 22, May 10, 1975; see also *City News*, April 10, 1975.

30. *Co-op City Times*, March 29, April 19, 1975; *City News*, April 17 and 24, 1975; *New York Times*, October 10, 2006; *Washington Post*, January 18, 1974.

31. *Co-op City Times*, August 24, November 28, 1974, April 19, May 3, 17, and 31, 1975; *City News*, April 25, 1974, May 29, 1975; *Bronx Press-Review*, September 15, 1974; *New York Times*, June 18, 1975, January 25, 1976.

32. *New York Post*, January 31, 1976; *Co-op City Times*, November 23, 1974; *City News*, June 27, 1974. See also Ralph Nader, "A Crisis Nearing Climax," May 19, 1976, in Charles Rosen Papers, Bronx, NY.

33. *Co-op City Times*, November 23, 1974, February 20, 1975; *City News*, April 12, 1973, February 20, May 8, July 31, 1975.

34. Betsy Brown, "Coopting the Dream," *Empire State Report*, March 1977, p. 107; *City News*, December 10, 1970; *New York Times*, January 25, 1976.

35. *City News*, May 8, 1975; *Co-op Contact*, February/March 1963, pp. 14–15; "Co-op City Information Bulletin Number One: A Brief Description of the Construction Defect Problems at Co-op City" (1969), pp. 7–9.

36. *Co-op City Times*, July 6, 1974; *Village Voice*, November 24, 1975.

37. Interview with Charles Rosen, January 23, 2011; *Co-op City Times*, March 15, April 26, 1975; *City News*, March 20, 1975; *New York Times*, June 18, 1975; Statement by Al Abrams, Co-op City Steering Committee Chairman, press release, September 10, 1975, Rosen Papers.

38. Richard Karp, "No Day of Reckoning," *Barron's National Business and Financial Weekly*, July 25, 1977, p. 16.

39. *Co-op City Times*, July 27, 1974; *City News*, May 29, 1975. The press sometimes referred to Yavner, Gallet, Freedman & Brett as Yavner, Gallet, Oziel, Freedman & Brett.

40. *Co-op City Times*, July 24, 1971; *Washington Post*, January 18, 1976.

41. *Co-op City Times*, October 7, November 11, 1972, October 6, 1973; *City News*, October 5, 1972, April 17, 1975.

42. *Co-op City Times*, April 26, May 29, 1975; *City News*, August 3, 1974.

43. *City News*, March 27, April 3 and 10, May 8 and 22, 1975; *Co-op City Times*, April 19, May 3, 1975.

44. *City News*, May 1, 8, and 15, 1975.

45. *City News*, May 8 and 15, 1975.

46. *City News*, May 15 and 22, 1975; *Co-op City Times*, May 24, 1975.

47. *Co-op City Times*, May 31, 1975.

48. *City News*, May 22 and 29, June 12 and 19, 1975; *Co-op City Times*, May 24 and 31, June 7 and 14, 1975.

CHAPTER 10. THE GREAT RENT STRIKE

1. *City News*, June 5, 1975; *Co-op City Times*, June 7, 1975; Regular Meeting of the Board of Directors of the United Housing Foundation, June 12, 1975, United Housing Foundation Files, Kheel Center for Labor-Management Documentation & Archives, Cornell University Library.

2. Regular Meeting of the Board of Directors of the United Housing Foundation, June 12, 1975; *City News*, June 5, 1975; *Co-op City Times*, June 7, 1975; *New York Times*, June 18, 1975; Jack Newfield and Paul Du Brul, *The Abuse of Power: The Permanent Government and the Fall of New York* (New York, 1977), p. 307.

3. *New York Times*, June 4, 1975; *City News*, June 5, 12, 19, and 26, 1975.

4. *City News*, June 5, 12, 19, and 26, 1975; *Co-op City Times*, June 7, 1975.

5. *Co-op City Times*, June 14 and 21, 1975; *City News*, June 19, 1975; *Bronx Press-Review*, June 19, 1975.

6. *Co-op City Times*, June 21 and 28, 1975; *City News*, June 19, 1975; *Bronx Press-Review*, June 19, 1975; Newfield and Du Brul, *Abuse of Power*, p. 305.

7. *City News*, June 19 and 26, 1975; *Co-op City Times*, June 28, 1975; Charlie Rosen to the author, email, January 5, 2022, which is on the author's laptop. See also Newfield and Du Brul, *Abuse of Power*, p. 305.

8. *City News*, June 26, 1975; *Bronx Press-Review*, June 26, July 3, 1975; *New York Times*, June 24 and 26, 1975, October 9, 1982; *Co-op City Times*, June 28, July 12, 1975.

9. *Co-op City Times*, June 26, July 5 and 12, 1975; *Bronx Press-Review*, July 3, 1975; *City News*, August 14, 1975.

10. *City News*, June 19, July 3, 10, and 24, August 7, 1975; *Co-op City Times*, June 21, July 12 and 19, August 2, 1975.

11. *City News*, July 17, 1975; *Co-op City Times*, July 12 and 19, 1975.

12. *Co-op City Times*, July 12, 1975; *City News*, June 3 and 24, 1975.

13. *Co-op City Times*, August 9, 1975; *Bronx Press-Review*, August 7, 1975; *New York Times*, August 5, 1975. On the SHFA's fiscal problems, see *New York Times*, September 13, 1975.

14. *City News*, August 7, 1975; *Co-op City Times*, August 9, 1975; *New York Times*, August 5, 1975.

15. *Co-op City Times*, July 26, August 9 and 16, 1975; *City News*, August 14, 1975; *Bronx Press-Review*, August 21, 1975.

16. *Co-op City Times*, August 23, 1975; *City News*, August 21, November 20, 1975; *New York Times*, August 16, 1975; *Bronx Press-Review*, August 21, 1975.

17. *City News*, August 14, 1975. See also *New York Times*, March 12, 1992; Newfield and Du Brul, *Abuse of Power*, p. 307.

18. *Co-op City Times*, August 16 and 23, 1975; *City News*, August 21, 1975; *New York Times*, August 19 and 20, 1975; *Bronx Press-Review*, August 28, 1975.

19. *City News*, August 21 and 28, September 4, 1975; *Co-op City Times*, August 23, 1975; *Bronx Press-Review*, September 4, 1975.

20. *City News*, August 28, September 11, 1975; *Bronx Press-Review*, August 28, September 4, 1975.

21. *City News*, September 11, 1975; *Co-op City Times*, September 13, 1975; *New York Times*, September 11, 1975; *Bronx Press-Review*, September 18, 1975. See also Rosen's email to the author, January 5, 2022.

22. *City News*, September 11, 1975.

23. *City News*, September 11 and 18, 1975. See also *Co-op City Times*, September 20, 1975.

24. *City News*, September 25, 1975; *Bronx Press-Review*, October 9, 1975.

25. *City News*, September 25, 1975.

26. *New York Times*, September 27, 1975; *City News*, October 2 and 9, 1975; *Co-op City Times*, September 20, October 4, 1975.

27. *City News*, October 2, 1975.

28. *City News*, October 2, 1975; *New York Times*, September 13 and 17, October 1, 2, and 9, 1975. See also Suzanne McAllister to Robert Morgado and Walter Kicinski, memo, September 25, 1975, Hugh L. Carey Papers, St. John's Law School.

29. *City News*, October 16 and 23, 1975.

30. *City News*, October 9, 16, and 23, 1975. On the events leading up to the bailout of the State Housing Finance Agency, see *City News*, October 16, 1975, and *New York Times*, October 14, 1975.

31. *City News*, October 9 and 16, November 6, 1975.

32. *City News*, October 16 and 23, 1975.

33. *City News*, October 23 and 30, 1975.

34. *City News*, October 30, 1975.

35. *City News*, November 6, 1975.

36. *City News*, November 13 and 20, December 4, 1975.

37. *New York Times*, November 21, 1975; *City News*, October 16, November

25, December 4, 1975; *Bronx Press-Review*, November 27, 1975.

38. *New York Times*, December 23, 30, and 31, 1975, January 1, 1976; *City News*, December 30, 1975; *Bronx Press-Review*, January 1, 1976.

39. *Co-op City Times*, February 6, March 6, 1976; *City News*, February 19, March 4, 1976; *New York Times*, February 10, 1976; *Bronx Press-Review*, March 4 and 11, 1976.

40. *New York Times*, September 27, 1975, November 2, 1993; *City News*, November 6, 1975, February 26, 1976; *Bronx Press-Review*, December 25, 1975, March 25, 1976; *Co-op City Times*, March 20, 1975.

41. *City News*, April 29, 1976.

42. *New York Times*, May 11, 1976; *Co-op City Times*, May 15, 1976; *Bronx Press-Review*, May 13, 1976; *City News*, May 13, 1976.

43. *City News*, May 13, 1976; *Washington Post*, January 18, 1976; *Village Voice*, November 24, 1975.

44. *City News*, January 15, March 25, 1976; *New York Post*, January 9 and 10, 1976; *New York Times*, January 9, 1976; *Bronx Press-Review*, January 5 and 11, 1976.

45. *City News*, January 8 and 22, February 19 and 26, 1976. See also Newfield and Du Brul, *Abuse of Power*, p. 308.

46. *City News*, February 5 and 12, April 1, 1976; *Bronx Press-Review*, February 12, 1976; Betsy Brown, "Coopting the Dream," *Empire State Report*, March 1977, p. 108. I'm not sure that Goodwin lived in Southampton in 1976, but a *New York Times* obituary, which was published on December 12, 1986, lists Southampton as her place of residence.

47. *City News*, January 15, 22, and 29, 1976; *New York Times*, January 11 and 24, 1976; *Bronx Press-Review*, January

22, February 5, March 18, 1976. See also Rosen to the author, email, January 5, 2022.

48. David Friedman to Hugh L. Carey, January 10, 1977, Joseph S. Schwab to Hugh L. Carey, January 6, 1976, Abraham Schenck to Hugh L. Carey, February 8, 1976, all in Carey Papers. See also *City News*, January 15, 1976.

49. Frank J. Barbaro to Hugh L. Carey, January 26, 1976, and Mark S. Golub to Hugh L. Carey, January 26, 1976, both in Carey Papers; *New York Post*, January 23, 1976. For the statement of the twelve tenant organizations, see the news release dated January 9, 1976, also found in Carey Papers.

50. *New York Times*, December 31, 1975, January 28, February 3, 1976; *New York Magazine*, December 8, 1975, pp. 19–20; *New York Post*, January 31, 1976; Rosen's email to the author, January 5, 2022.

51. Norman Kriegel to Hugh L. Carey, February 9, 1976, and Frank E. Karelsen and Harry J. Byrne, February 11, 1976, Carey Papers; *Real Estate Weekly*, February 2, 1976, and *City Almanac*, April 1976, Charles Rosen Papers, Bronx, NY.

52. *New York Times*, January 22, 1976; *Co-op City Times*, January 24, 1976; Myron Holtz to Abraham Schenck, February 6, 1976, Carey Papers; *City News*, March 11, 1976.

53. *City News*, May 6, 1976; Jo Introne to Robert Morgado and Walker T. Kicinski, memo, September 30, 1975, Carey Papers; *New York Times*, January 1 and 3, 2015.

54. *City News*, October 2, 1975, February 5, March 11, April 1, May 6, 1976; *New York Times*, December 4, 1986, January 3, 2015.

55. *New York Times*, May 12, and 13, 1976; *City News*, May 13, 1976.

56. Norman Kriegel to Hugh L. Carey, mailgram, May 24, 1976, William L. Booker to Hugh L. Carey, May 27, 1976, Allan R. Talbot to Hugh L. Carey, May 27, 1976, Robert L. Hemmerling to High L. Carey, June 1, 1976, all in Carey Papers. See also *Wall Street Journal*, May 24, 1976.

57. *New York Times*, May 13, June 3, 4, and 7, 1976; *Co-op City Times*, June 5, 1976; *City News*, June 3, 1976.

58. Roger Starr to Hugh L. Carey, telegram, June 7, 1976, and Statement by Governor Hugh L. Carey, press release, June 29, 1976, both in Carey Papers; *City News*, May 27, July 1, 1976; *Bronx-Press Review*, June 10, 1976; *Co-op City Times*, July 3, 1976; *New York Times*, June 30, 1976. See also *Washington Post*, June 26, 1976.

59. *New York Times*, June 30, 1976; *New York Post*, June 30, 1976; *City News*, July 1 and 8, 1976; Jonathan B. Bingham to Charles Rosen, July 1, 1976, Carey Papers; *Co-op City Times*, July 3, 1976.

60. *City News*, July 8, 1976; *Co-op City Times*, July 10, 1976.

61. *New York Times*, July 8, 17, and 20, 1976.

62. *City News*, July 15 and 22, 1976; *Co-op City Times*, July 17 and 24, 1976.

63. *Bronx Press-Review*, July 8 and 15, 1976; *City News*, July 8, 22, and 29, 1976; *Co-op City Times*, July 31, 1976.

64. *New York Times*, July 27, 1976; *City News*, July 29, 1976; *Co-op City Times*, July 31, 1976.

65. *New York Times*, July 27, 1976; *Co-op City Times*, July 31, 1976; *City News*, July 29, 1976.

66. *New York Times*, November 21, 1976; *New York Daily News*, November 30, 1976; *Co-op City Times*, July 17, 1976; Newfield and Du Brul, *Abuse of Power*, pp. 305-6; *City News*, July 1, 1976.

EPILOGUE

1. Herman Liebman, ed., *Golden Jubilee Journal and Kazan Memorial* (New York, 1977), pp. 1-2, 75, 129-44. See also *New York Times*, January 14, 1997.

2. Liebman, *Golden Jubilee Journal*, pp. 4-14.

3. Ibid., pp. 15-16, 33-34, 68-69, 87-104.

4. Ibid., pp. 105-6, 109-15, 117-23.

5. Ibid., pp. 10, 24, 29-31, 43, 46, 79-83. See also *1968 Summary of Data: Report on Twenty-Three Housing Cooperatives Affiliated with the United Housing Foundation*, copy in the Loeb Library, Harvard University Graduate School of Design.

6. Liebman, *Golden Jubilee Journal*, pp. 22-24, 44-50, 52-58.

7. Ibid., pp. 29-31; *New York Times*, January 17, March 23, 1969, July 16, 1972, March 21, 1974. See also *City News*, March 16, 1972.

8. Leibman, *Golden Jubilee Journal*, pp. 31, 39-41.

9. Adam Tanaka, *Co-op City at 50: A City in a City*, documentary film, 2019; Liebman, *Golden Jubilee Journal*, p. 31; *City News*, January 22, July 9, October 29, 1970, October 14, 1971; Joshua B. Freeman, *Working-Class New York: Life and Labor since World War II* (New York, 2000), p. 119.

10. Harold Ostroff to the Board of Directors of the United Housing Foundation and Community Services, Inc., memo, May 20, 1974; Regular Meeting of the Board of Directors of the United Housing Foundation, January 17, 1974; Annual Meeting of the United Housing Foundation, April 7, 1973; Regular Meeting of the Board of Directors of United Housing Foundation, Inc., and Community Services, Inc., September 12, 1974; Regular Meeting of Community

Services, Inc., May 22, 1974; all in United Housing Foundation Files, Kheel Center for Labor-Management Documentation & Archives, Cornell University Library; Peter Eisenstadt, "Rochdale Village: Blueprint for a New Housing Option," History News Network; Peter Eisenstadt, *Rochdale Village: Robert Moses, 6,000 Families, and New York City's Great Experiment in Integrated Housing* (Ithaca, NY, 2010), p. 247; *City News*, May 14, 1973; *New York Times*, April 8, 2000, March 6, 2006; *New York Sun*, March 3, 2006. See also Freeman, *Working-Class New York*, pp. 123-24.

11. *New York Times*, April 4, 1960, December 6, 1979, September 2, 1991; "History of the ILGWU," Cornell School of Industrial and Labor Relations; *Wall Street Journal*, October 24, 1979; Eisenstadt, "Rochdale Village"; Annamarie Sammartino, "After the Rent Strike: Neoliberalism and Co-op City," Gotham Center Blog, April 3, 2018; *City News*, September 22, 1977, February 15, May 3, 1979.

12. *New York Times*, December 19, 1975, January 12, 1980, July 6, 1988, November 20, 1994, July 9, 2000, April 6, 2008, February 28, 2016; Richard Price, "The Rise and Fall of Public Housing in NYC," *Guernica*, October 1, 2014; Liebman, *Golden Jubilee Journal*, p. 31; *Co-op City Times*, December 15, 2018.

INDEX

IMAGE CREDITS

Fig. 1: Edith Elmer Wood, *Recent Trends in American Housing* (New York: Macmillan, 1931)

Fig. 2: James Ford, *Slums and Housing* (Cambridge, MA: Harvard University Press, 1936)

Fig. 3: Kheel Center for Labor-Management Documentation & Archives, Cornell University Library

Fig. 4: Kheel Center for Labor-Management Documentation & Archives, Cornell University Library

Fig. 5: Kheel Center for Labor-Management Documentation & Archives, Cornell University Library

Fig. 6: Kheel Center for Labor-Management Documentation & Archives, Cornell University Library

Fig. 7: *Twenty Years of Accomplishment* (New York: United Housing Foundation, 1971)

Fig. 8: Kheel Center for Labor-Management Documentation & Archives, Cornell University Library

Fig. 9: Patrick A. Burns/*New York Times*, July 9, 2000/Redux

Fig. 10: *Progressive Architecture*, February 1970

Fig. 11: *City News*, July 2, 1970

Fig. 12: *City News*, October 14, 1971

Fig. 13: *City News*, April 20, 1972

Fig. 14: *City News*, April 11, 1974

Fig. 15: *City News*, April 15, 1974

Fig. 16: *City News*, October 14, 1975

Fig. 17: Tyrone Duke/*New York Times*, October 10, 2006/Redux

Fig. 18: *City News*, April 1, 1976

Figs. 19a and 19b: *City News*, July 29, 1976

Figs. 20a and 20b: *City News*, July 29, 1976

Fig. 21a: *City News*, August 29, 1974

Fig. 21b: *City News*, November 21, 1974

Fig. 22a: *City News*, February 26, 1975

Fig. 22b: *City News*, July 10, 1975